W9-ABR-821

SOU
P. O. Box 502
Columbia, Mo. 65201

MAHAYANA BUDDHISM

By

NALINAKSHA DUTT,

M. A. B. L. Ph. D. (Cal). D. Litt. (London)
Premchand Roychand Scholar, Hony. Fellow, Asiatic Society
Retd. Professor of Pāli, Calcutta University.

FIRMA K. L. MUKHOPADHYAY
257B, B. B. Ganguly Street
Calcutta-12 : : 1973

Published and Copyright reserved by the author
39, Ramananda Chatterji Street,
Calcutta-9

BQ
7374
.D87
1973

Printed by :
Sri Bankimbehari Das
Orient Press
123/1, A. P. C. Road,
Calcutta-6.

CANISIUS COLLEGE LIBRARY
BUFFALO

PREFACE

The present work is a revised edition of my earlier publication entitled *Aspects of Hīnayāna and Mahāyāna Buddhism.* In this edition matters relating to Hīnayāna have been retained only where these became necessary for the sake of comparison and contrast with Mahāyāna.

I should thank my old friend Sri Bankim Behari Das, the proprietor of the Orient Press, who came forward to undertake the responsibility to print this work even by procuring types with diacritical marks.

Last but not the least, I must thank my student Dr. Miss Kṣaṇikā Sāhā, Ph. D., Research Associate, Centre of Advanced Studies in Ancient Indian History for the help rendered by her in revising the final proofs and preparing the Index of this book.

CONTENTS

INTRODUCTION

The question that naturally arises in our minds, why the omniscient Bhagavān Buddha preached two religious systems : one lower (Hīnayāna) and the other higher (Mahāyāna) or two Truths, one conventional (*Saṃvṛti-satya*) and the other real (*Paramārtha-satya*). The answer to this question is given in the *Saddhama-puṇḍarīka*[1], one of the nine canonical texts of the Mahāyānists. It is as follows :—

Bhagavān Śākya-siṃha, rising from his deep meditation, regained his normal mental state and then addressed Śāriputra with these words "Very deep and extremely difficult it is for the Śrāvakas and Pratyekabuddhas to comprehend the truth attained by the Tathāgatas, who had struggled for it for several aeons. Equally difficult it is for them to penetrate into the meaning of the terse expressions (*sandhyābhāṣā*) used by the Tathāgatas". Śākyasiṃha also before his attainment of *bodhi* at Gaya busied himself with the acquisition of the āveṇika-*dharmas* (eighteen dharmas leading to Buddhahood)[1] and it was after realising the Truth that he became convinced that it could not be imparted by one to another by means of words. Though aware of the futility of the āveṇika-dharmas[2], he had to instruct the Śrāvakas to acquire them only as an expedient because he realised that these āveṇika-dharmas only could appeal to them. He admitted that by acquiring these dharmas the perfect Śrāvakas and Pratyekabuddhas could become free from impurities and would not have any more rebirth but still they would not be capable of realising the highest Truth visualised by the Tathāgatas. Not to speak of Śrāvakas and Pratyekabuddhas, even Bodhisattvas of the highest rank, i.e. the Avaivarttikas (lit. non-receding from the goal) were far away from the realisation of the Truth. Śāriputra was asked to rely on Bhagavān

---

1. Edited by the present writer and published by the Asiatic Society 1954. In 1934 was published an edition of this text by two Japanese savants, Profs. Wogihara and Tsuchida.

2. See *Mahāvyutpatti*.

Śākyasiṃha's words that the three yānas were mere expedients resorted to by Buddhas for imparting training to beings, who clung to different types of practices for spiritual progress.

Thereupon Śāriputra solicited Buddha to explain why he said that the Truth was too deep and subtle to be comprehended by Śrāvakas and why the terse sayings of Buddhas were also unintelligible to them. At the repeated request of Śāriputra, Buddha agreed to explain the real aim of the Tathāgatas is only to those who had implict faith in him and not to those who were still conceited (abhimānika). He said that the Truth could not be the subject-matter of discussion (atarko 'tarkāvacaraḥ) and could be realised by the Tathāgatas within themselves. The Buddhas appear in the world only to help beings to attain the Tathāgata-knowledge and insight (tathagata-jñānadarśana), which may be equated to omniscience (sarvajñatā) and for this, there is really one yāna called Buddhayāna and not a second or a third, though they take recourse to many forms of exposition to suit the different classes of beings whose mental inclinations and mental developments vary on account of their appearance in the world at a time when there are one or more of the five shortcomings (kaṣāyas) due to the Kalpa (time), sattva (type of beings), kleśa (impurities), dṛṣṭi (wrong views) and āyuṣ (length of life).

The above topic is repeated in further details in the gāthās. Buddha said that for those beings, who believed in the existence of the world and its sufferings, he preached his dharma giving reasons and examples, in nine *aṅgas*, viz., sūtra, gāthā, itivṛttaka, jātaka, adbhūta, nidāna and various geyya replete with similies. He held up before them the *summun bonum* of Nirvāṇa and not Buddhahood. Similarly, he preached the *Vaipulyasūtras* to those who had accumulated merits through several existences and were pure, learned, and well-behaved, and to them he held out the goal of Buddhahood.

There was one yāna and not three and if Buddha had preached only Hīnayāna (p. 35, v. 57) then he would have been charged with miserliness (*mātsarya*), envy (*īrṣyā*) and attachment (*chanda-rāga*). If he had straight away asked everybody to seek *bodhi*, then many would not have taken his advice seriously, and would have suffered for that reason longer in the worlds of existence and got entangled in one or more of the sixty two heretical views.[1]

Buddha assured Buddhahood not only to those, who perfected themselves in the six *pāramitās* but also to those, who worshipped the relics of Buddha or erected thereon stūpas of any material, be it of jewel or sand, or made images (*bimba*) of Buddha with any metal or even clay, or drew sketches of the figure of Buddha on paper, wall, etc. or even offered flowers or played musical instruments or sang songs in adoration of Buddha's images or just uttered the words "*Namo'stu Buddhāya*".

There is only one dharma, which is refulgent by nature (prakṛtiś ca dharmaṇā sadā prabhāsvarā) and which is eternal, unshakeable and has a law of itself (*dharma-niyāmatā*). Realising the eternal *dharma*, Śākyasiṃha stayed at the Bodhimaṇḍa for three weeks and felt pity for the suffering beings. He wanted to enter into *parinirvāṇo* then and there, but at the intervention of Brahmā and also remembering what the previous Buddhas had done, he made up his mind to propagate his dharma in three ways (*yāna*) so that it could be intelligible to the beings at large. He then proceeded to Benares and preached his dharma to the five bhikṣus in a modified form using for the first time the words nirvāṇa, arhanta, dharma and saṅgha. At the same time, he initiated the Bodhisattvas, who approached him, into the highest truth. It is this higher teaching that he was going to impart now to Śāriputra and asked him to have implicit faith in his words and assured him that he as well as many other Arhats would ultimately attain Buddhahood.

After listening to the above mentioned words of Buddha, Śāriputra regretted that he and his fellow-brethren were satisfied with the superficial aspect of the teaching and did not exert to dive deep into its inner meaning, which is pure, subtle and beyond discussion, and thereby missed to attain Buddhahood with all its attributes (see ch. III. vs. 5-6). He felt that

1 Vide *Brahmajāla-sutta* of the *Dīgha Nikāya*.

as he was previously a heretical parivrājaka, he was taught only *nirvṛti* (quietude) by realising the non-existence of any substance (soul) in phenomena but it was not real *nirvṛti* attainable only by Buddhas. He was elated at the hope held out by Buddha Śākyasiṃha that he would also in due course become a Buddha. He had no more doubt about the truth and solemnity of the words of Buddha, and he would never mistake those as the beguiles of Māra. He was reminded by Buddha that he had forgotten the Bodhisattva vow taken by him long long ago and that he had received training from Śākyasiṃha in the Bodhisattva secrets and that he, being forgetful of his long past, felt that he had attained Nirvāṇa. This text, *Saddharmapuṇḍarīka*, was delivered by Śākyasiṃha particularly to revive the memory of the Bodhisattva vows taken by the Śrāvakas.

After countless aeons Śāriputra will become the Buddha Padmaprabha and his Buddhakṣetra will be called Viraja and will be full of Bodhisattvas. This prophecy about Śāriputra was applauded by the assemblage of gods and men, who expressed their appreciation of Buddha's saṃdhābhāṣya (enigmatic sayings) by saying that at Benares the doctrine of origin and decay of skandhas (constituents of a being) was explained while the same teacher was now giving an exposition of a subtle inconceivable dharma.

Though Śāriputra had implicit faith in Buddha's prophecy, still he requested Śākyasiṃha to explain why formerly he imparted at all the teaching of *anātmān* (selflessness) and *nirvāṇa* to his disciples like him.

Buddha removed his doubts by telling him a parable, which is as follows :—

There was a fabulously rich man, who had a very large house, which, however, was very old, full of refuses and was the haunt of birds, dogs, worms, reptiles, pretas, yakṣas and piśācas. It had a tottering roof of straw, and had only one door for exit. The house suddenly caught fire. The owner of the house had a number of children playing within the house. He was very much frightened on account of the fire as also of the venomous man-killing beings existing in the house and thought of carrying the children out by his strong arms but the difficulty was that the boys were unmindful of the fire and were going hither and thither and could not be brought together and would not even listen to their father's warning about the raging fire. The father knew his children's inclinations and so he came out of the house and collected beautiful toy-carts drawn by bull, goat and deer and tempted the boys to take them after coming out of the burning house. The boys struggled among themselves to come out first in order to have the best toy-cart. The father then felt relieved at the safety of his sons. When the boys asked for toys, the father, immensely rich as he was, gave each of them not the cheap types of toy-carts but extremely expensive fast carriages (*mahāyānam*), replete with all conceivable furnishings, and drawn by very sturdy bulls.

Buddha then asked Śāriputra whether he would consider the father guilty of telling a lie. When Śāriputra answered in the negative, Buddha told him that he himself might be likened to the rich father, the house to the world (of five organic sense-desires) and the sons to the men of the world unmindful of the fire burning the world. The wooden cheap toy-carts were the various disciplinary and meditational practices prescribed in Śrāvaka-yāna, Pratyekabuddha-yāna and Bodhisattva-yāna, which were held out as the bait for the men of the world to come out of the three worlds of existence (tridhātu). The bait was the attainment of eternal happiness through perfection in *bala, bodhyaṅga, dhyāna, vimokṣa, samādhi, samāpatti* etc. Some of the men of the world, who relied upon Buddha's words, retired from the worldly lives. Of them again some became interested in attaining salvation (parinirvāṇa) for himself only by listening to the teachings and following the practices relating to the four *āryasatyas*. They were the Śrāvakayānists and they might be compared to the boys seeking toy-carts drawn by deer. There were others, who sought self-control without any guide, but who also wanted their own salvation through the comprehension of the law of causation (*hetupratyaya*). They were the Pratyekabuddhayānists and might be compared to the boys asking for toy-carts drawn by goat (*aja*). There were also those, who aspired for omniscience like that of the Buddha by self-acquired perfect knowledge and wished to help all beings to attain *parinirvāṇa* and exerted to attain the qualities, which made a Buddha. These were the Mahāyānists, seeking exit from the *Tridhātus* and might be compared to the boys seeking carts drawn by bulls.

Though the father tempted the boys by showing to them different toy-carts, he actually gave them not toy-carts but actual vehicles of a very high class and so Buddha gave his disciples *Buddhayāna.* In fact, all the four *yānas* were of one nature and so Buddha could not be said to have told a lie by taking recourse to the expedient of teaching his dharma in three different ways, viz., Śrāvakayāna, Pratyekabuddhayāna and Bodhisattvayāna. Buddha avoided teaching the Sūtra to any unbelieving person lest he should be the victim of dire consequences (detailed in the gāthās 113-136) to which a person was destined for not accepting this Sūtra as Buddhavacana. A person's virtues and acquisitions, which entitled him to learn this sūtra from the Teacher, are given in the gāthās 137-147.

CHAPTER I

POLITICAL AND CULTURAL BACKGROUND OF MAHAYANA BUDDHISM

The obscure period in the history of India commenced after the end of the Maurya period, *i.e.*, about the 2nd century B. C., but the stream of Buddhism, which received its impetus from Emperor Aśoka, flowed quietly without being affected by the political changes. During the Maurya period, the early and historical Buddhism became divided into eighteen or more sects, on account of their different views about the interpretation of Buddha's teachings. One of these, viz., the Mahāsaṅghikas interpreted the teachings in a manner, which led ultimately to the appearance of full-fledged Mahāyāna Buddhism. It should be noted that the traces of Mahāyānism are found even in the Pāli *Sutta Piṭaka*, the earliest literature preserving Buddha's teachings, and this has been indicated in the next chapter.

An attempt is now being made to throw some light on the obscure period, mentioned above.

About the 2nd or 1st century B. C. Mahāyāna Buddhism became a reeognised phase of the religion, and it gradually passed on to Central Asia, China, Korea and Japan. In Tibet, Bhutan, Mongolia and in the Far East border of U. S. S. R. appeared its later phase, viz., the Tāntric Mahāyāna Buddhism[1].

The Bactrians and the Parthians

The last king of the Maurya dynasty was Bṛhadratha, who was assasinated by his military-general Puṣyamitra. With the latter started the reign of the Śuṅgas, who ruled over a large empire, which included Magadha, Ayodhyā, Vidiśā, Jalandhara and Sākala in the Punjab. Puṣyamitra had to face a Bactrian invasion and came into conflict with the Bactrian princes, and he ultimately became victorious and drove them out of Magadha,

1. See *infra*.

perhaps, even beyond the Sindhu.[1] He reigned for 36 years (circa 187-151 B. C.). He was succeeded by his son Agnimitra, who was followed by other descendants, and all of them remained in power from 151-75 B. C. The Śuṅgas revived Brāhmanism and patronised the Bhāgavata cult. A Yavana (Yona) prince Heliodoros erected a Garuḍa Pillar and described himself as a Bhāgavata in the inscription of Bhilsā (Besnagar).[2] Though the Śuṅgas were anti-Buddhistic in spirit, the people of Vidiśā expressed their faith in Buddhism, as is proved by the fine gateway railings around the Sāñci stūpa erected by Emperor Aśoka.[3]

During the reign of Bṛhadratha, the various powers, both Indian and foreign, became independent rulers of the territories, which happened to be under their control.

In the 3rd century B. C. the *Mahāvaṃsa* is particularly important for the history of Buddhism in Kashmir, on account of the fact that Majjhantika was sent to Kashmir to propagate Buddhism there. Later the scene of discussions between King Milinda and the Buddhist monk Nāgasena is placed at a spot, 12 yojanas from Kashmir and 200 yojanas from Alasanda or Kalasigāma.[4] The author of the treatise is familiar with the people of the North as he refers twice to Śaka-Yavana, Cīna-Cilāta (=Kirāta=a tribe who lived by hunting birds and animals, probably of Tokharistan), Alasanda, Nikumba, Kashmir and Gandhāra, *i.e.*, the region round about Kashmir.[5]

As regards King Milinda, the treatise states that, at first he became a lay-devotee, built the Milinda-vihāra and then after sometime he handed over the administration of his dominion to his son and joined the Buddhist Saṅgha as a monk, attaining ultimately *arhathood.*[6]

1. *The Age of Imperial Unity* (*of the Bhāratīya Vidyābhavan*), Bombay, p. 95f.
2. *Ibid.*, p. 98
3. *Ibid.*, p. 99
4. *Milindapañha*, p. 82-3.
5. *Ibid.*, p. 327 : Cilāta=Kirāta (=Tokharistan, a *mleccha* country (see Nāgārjunikoṇḍa inscriptions in *EI.*, XX, 1).
6. *Ibid.*, p. 420

Though only two Kharoṣṭhi inscriptions, inscribed at the instance of the Greek rulers, have been discovered at Swat[1] and Taxila,[2] these show that Mahāyāna Buddhism obtained a firm footing in N. W. India and was welcomed by the foreign rulers.[3]

The Bactrian Greeks, who had come up to some parts of Northern India, shortly after the downfall of Magadhan empire, not only adopted the Indian culture but also made a special contribution to its development in course of two centuries of their rule. They carried the tale of Indian wisdom and prosperity across the Indian frontiers to the hordes of Central Asian Steppes on the one hand and to the Græco-Roman world in the west on the other hand.

In the 2nd century B. C. the Greek rulers, viz., the houses of Euthydemus and Eucratides crossed the Hindukush and took possession of Kabul and North-western India. They were followed by Demetrius and Theodorus, who, it appears, were supporters of Mahāyāna Buddhism as they enshrined Buddha's relics and erected sanctuaries. Two Kharoṣṭhi inscriptions incised at the instance of the Greek chiefs have been discovered at Swat[4] and Taxila.[5] These show that Mahāyāna Buddhism had a firm footing in North-western India and was appreciated by the foreign rulers.[6]

Demetrius (=Dattamitra[7] of the *Mahābhārata* I. 139. 23) wrested from Bṛhadratha a considerable portion of Magadha.

1. *CII.*, II, 1, p. 4: By Theodoros the Meridarkh was established a *stūpa*, enshrining these relics of Bhagavān Śākyamuni for the good of many people.

2. *Ibid.*, p. 5: By ... the Meridarkh together with his wife, the *stūpa* was established in honour of his parents for the presentation of a respectful offering.

3. *Ibid.*, p. 94

4. *CII.*, II, i, p. 4 "By Theodoros the Meridarkh was established the *stūpa*, enshrining the relics of Bhagavān Śākyamuni for the good of many people".

5. *Ibid.*, p. 5 "By ... the Meridarkh together with his wife, the *stūpa* was established in honour of his parents, for the presentation of a respectful offering".

6. *Ibid.*, p. 49

7. Dharmamitra in Tibetan (see Journal Asiatique, 1933, p. 27, n. 1)

Menander (=Milinda) carried on several expeditions into the interior of Northern India and made Sialkot (=Sāgala) his capital.[1]

In the history of Buddhism, during the period intervening between Puṣyamitra and Kaniṣka, the reign of King Menander reveals that the foreigners took interest in Buddhism. The *Milindapañha* offers some information about the state of Buddhism in Northern India. The date of the Sanskrit original of this text may be taken as the 1st century B. C.

THE SAKAS

The first horde, after the Greeks to be attracted to India was, the Śakas or the Scythians, who were settled in the Oxus region, which was previously occupied by the Greeks, who were ousted from that region in the 2nd century B. C. by the nomadic hordes, known as Yueh-chihs, a name given by the ancient Chinese. The Yueh-chihs previously settled near the Chinese frontier but they were ousted by other hordes of people. They migrated to the west and compelled the Śakas to leave the Oxus valley and to go in search of a new land for their settlement. The Śakas went to the south. As the Northern Punjab was then in the hands of the Greeks, they entered India through a different route, took possession of the lower Indus Valley and then spread out to Western India. Like the Greeks they also

1. Patañjali in his *Mahābhāṣya* (III. 2. 111) deplores that the Greeks besieged Sāketa (near Ayodhyā) and Madhyamika (=Nagari) near Chitor in Rajputana.

The *Gārgī Saṃhitā* (pp. 94-116) deplored the advance of the Greeks up to the wall of the Puṣpapura (Pāṭaliputra).........having conquered Sāketa and Pañcāla (Doab) and Mathura, the Yavanas reached Kusumadhvaja (Pāṭaliputra). Then a fierce battle ensued with sword and knock-out blows (*hasta-yuddha*).

At the end of the Yuga there will appear the Anāryas destitute of religion. The Brāhmaṇas, Kṣatriyas, Vaiśyas and Śūdras will become inferior and imitate the foreign style of dress and practices, See Lamotte, *op. cit.*, p. 411-2.

adopted Indian culture and before long they became strong propagators of Indian culture outside India.[1]

Like the Greeks, the Śakas also patronised Buddhism and gave donations to the Buddhist Saṅgha, erected *stūpas* and installed images of Buddha.

Maues, the Śaka ruler (60-50 B. C.) established a principality in the Western Punjab. He was followed by Azes (50-30 B. C.), then Gondopherenes (30-15 B. C.), and Pakores (15-10 B. C.)[2]. The Śakas of Syr Daria fell upon Bactria and then entered into India up to Takṣaśilā and Mathurā in the north, and Malwa and Kathiawad in the west. They established themselves in Sind and the Punjab also. Their representatives were known as Satraps (=Viceroys), e. g., of Saurāṣṭra and Malwa. They are referred to as Daivaputra Shāhi Shāhānushāhi-Śaka Muruṇḍa in the Allahabad Pillar Inscription. The Śakas, however, were in favour of Indian civilization and ideals and also introduced the same in Central Asia and the Far Eastern countries. The Śakas are referred to in the Epics as degraded Kṣatriyas along with the Kambojas and Yavanas. The reigning periods of the Scythians in India extended from the 1st century B. C. to the time of the Imperial Guptas.[3] The Śakas sought the help of the Kushāṇas and thereby paved the way for the advent of the Kushāṇa-rule in India.

The Kushanas

The Kushāṇas, at this time, dominated over Afghanistan, after ousting the Parthian successors of the Greeks. They drove out the Parthians from the Gandhāra region, the Śaka ruler Azes becoming a protégé of the Kushāṇas.

Kujula Kadphises (=Kadphises I) was the first Kushāṇa ruler. During his reign, he extended his dominion up to Kipin (Kashmir City) and the neighbouring lands. Very likely he reigned from 16 to 65 A. D.

1. Sten Konow, *op.cit.*, pp. xxvii, 176.
2. P. C. Bagchi, *India and China* p. 3.
3. J. E. Van Lohuizen de Leeuw, *The Scythian Period* (Leiden), p. 388.

He was succeeded by his son Wima Kadphises (Kadphises II), who extended his dominion over the Punjab region watered by the river Sindhu. He was a Śaiva though his father was a Buddhist.

Following the Śaka-Yavanas, the Kushāṇas also adopted Buddhism as their religion and showered their munificence on the erection of *stūpas*, temples and images of Buddha all over Northern India. The earlier Kushāṇas like Kadphises II, as their coins indicate, were Śiva worshippers, but Kaṇiṣka and his successors, as shown by their monuments and inscriptions, offered gifts to the Buddhist Saṅgha, particularly, to the Sarvāstivādins and occasionally[1] to the Mahāsaṅghikas[2].

Introduction of Buddhism into Kashmir

Before the account of the Fourth Buddhist Synod is taken up, it behoves us to deal with the introduction of Buddhism into Kashmir. The kingdom of Kashmir appears in our ancient records as a part and parcel of Gandhāra. In the list of sixteen *mahājanapadas*, Kashmir-Gandhāra is indicated as one *janapada*, indicating thereby that the two countries formed one political unit in the pre-Aśokan days. That it continued to be so is evident from the Greek records, in which Kaspapyros (=Kāśyapapura=Kashmir) is described as a Gandhāric city[3]. In the *Milindapañha*[4], which was composed about the beginning of the Christian era, the two countries were compounded as Kāshmīra-Gandhāra. The Chinese translators of the Buddhist texts, which were dated in the 3rd or 4th century A.D., used the Chinese term Kipin for Sanskrit Kāśmīra. Kipin, however, included Kapiśa-nagar and Gandhāra in addition to Kashmir. In one of its chapters, the *Mahāvaṃsa*[5] designates the two countries as Kāśmīra-Gandhāra, but in another chapter, which deals with an incident of a much later date, it refers to

1. *CII.*, II, i, pp. 137, 145, 155.
2. *Ibid.*,. Wardak Vase inscription, p. 170.
3. *Rājat.* I, p. 27 ; Watters, *op.cit.*, p. 261 ; *PHAI.*, (1932), p. 103
4. *Milindapañha*, p. 331 : Alasanda Kāśmīra-Gandhāra.
5. *Mahāvaṃsa*, XII. 33.

monks as hailing from Kāśmīra-maṇḍala.[1] Yuan Chwang and Ou-k'ong distinguished Kashmir from Gandhāra while Yuan Chwang deals with the two countries separately. Both the travellers described Kashmir as an extensive valley surrounded by mountains, which could be crossed only through a few passes. Ou-K'ong specifies the passes, which were three in number, one in the east, giving access to T'ou-fan (Tibet), the second in the north, leading to Po-liu (Baltistan) and a third in the west, connecting with K'ien-to-lo (Gandhāra).

The second pass, Tāranātha writes, became fit for communication soon after Madhyāntika's death.[2] It is perhaps represented at present by the Gilgit road, and on this road stood the *stūpa*, which yielded the valued manuscripts. In the Government of India's *Census Report of 1931* (pt. 1, p. 321) the following note appears : "There are two Buddhist *stūpas*, one on the hill-side about three miles east of Gilgit and the other on the road to Nagar between Chalt and Minapin. There is a small Buddha carved on the rocks at the mouth of the Kirgah Nāllāh about three miles west of Gilgit, and small Buddha-images and Buddhist relics have been found in Yasin". This note testifies to the fact that Buddhism lingered in this part of Kashmir up to a very late date, and the geographical information given above shows that the culture and beliefs of the ancient people of Kashmir were not very different from those of Gandhāra, i. e., the present Rawalpindi, Taxila, Peshawar etc. where Buddhism flourished in the early days, and that Buddhism may well be pointed out as one of the factors for linking the peoples of the two countries.

The earliest traditions relating to the introducton of Buddhism into Kashmir are preserved in the Ceylonese chronicle, the *Mahāvaṃsa*[3] and the Tibetan Du-lva[4] (Vinaya

1. See Lévi's remarks in *JA.*, 1896, p. 384. Takakusu in *T'ouug Pao*, V, p. 276n. furnishes us with the following information :

Chinese authority always identify Ki-pin with Kashmir up to the 5th century A. D. Yuan Chwang calls it Ka-shu-mi-la while Song Yun writes Ki-pin.

2. Schiefner, Tāranātha, p. 23.

3. *Mahāvaṃsa*, XII, 25, 33. 4. *Dul-va*, vol. XI, 684-690

Piṭaka of the Sarvāstivādins). The *Mahāvaṃsa* tells us that Moggaliputta Tissa, the religious adviser of Aśoka, sent missionaries to the different parts of India. Majjhantika was deputed to Kāśmīra-Gandhāra. About the time of his arrival there, Aravāḷa[1], king of the Nāgas, was destroying the ripe corns of the country by hail-storm. Majjhantika, by his supernatural power, stood on the surface of the lake unaffected by rain and storm. At this the Nāga king became furious and sent forth storm and lightning, and hurled stones and rocks at him but without any effect. Thus convinced of Majjhantika's great power, the Nāga king with his followers submitted to him and listened to his discourses on the evils of anger and hatred. Paṇḍaka Yakkha and Hāritī Yakkhiṇī with their 500 children became his devotees and offered a jewelled throne. When they were fanning him, the residents of Kashmir-Gandhāra came with offerings for the Nāgas, but they offered the same to Majjhantika, who then delivered to them a discourse on *āsiviṣa* (venom of a serpent) and converted them to Buddhism. From that day up to the time of composition of the *Mahāvaṃsa,* i. e., the fifth century A. D. the author says that Kāsmīra Gandhāra continued to be illumined by yellow robes.

A legend, similar to the above, appears with slight variations in the Tibetan *Dul-va* and the traditions derived from it in the works of Tāranātha and Bu-ston, in *Aśokāvadāna,* and in Yuan Chwang's *Records.* The story runs as follows : Madhyāntika, a disciple of Ānanda, was a teacher of Vārāṇasī. His disciples were so numerous that the lay-devotees of Vārāṇasī found it difficult to maintain them, so Madhyāntika left the town for Mount Uśīra in the north[2], where he stayed for three years. After this period Madhyāntika went to Kashmir and settled down on the bank of a lake inhabited by the Nāgas.[3] His presence was resented by the Nāgas, who, how-

1. Apalāṭa in Chinese rendering. See Watters, *op.cit.*, 1, p. 229

2. Identified with a mountain near Mathura. See Watters, *op.cit.*, I. p. 308 ; B. C. Law, *Geog. of Early Buddhism*, p. 34

3. Kalhaṇa also says that Kashmir was full of lakes inhabited by Nāgas. Yuan Chwang records that "according to the local records, Kashmir was originally a dragon lake". Watters, op. cit I, p. 265

ever, were subdued by his supernatural powers. Tāranātha adds that at this time there were in Kashmir nine cities, many villages of mountain-dwellers, a royal residence, twelve *vihāras* and that Madhyāntika brought with him many monks and lay-devotees. and increased the wealth of the country by introducing the cultivation of saffron[1], for which Kashmir has become famous even today. Madhyāntika resided in Kashmir for twenty years and propagated the religion widely. After his demise, when road communication was established between Kashmir and Tukhāra, Kashmirian monks went to Tukhāra and introduced the religion there during the reign of Minara and Imasya[2].

ASOKAN EDICTS re. BUDDHISM IN NORTHERN AND NORTH-WESTERN COUNTRIES

In the edicts of Aśoka, the northernmost countries mentioned are those inhabited by the Yonas, Kambojas and Gandhāras, which must have included the region round about Shahbazgarhi and Mansehra, where the edicts were discovered. Kashmir, it seems, came within his kingdom in the latter part of his life when he realised his mistake of supporting one section of the Buddhist monks to the exclusion of another. The Pāli tradition speaks of the earlier part of his life when he supported the Theravāda points of view. The probability of such a bias for the Theravādins may be traced to his residence in Avanti during the period of his viceroyalty. As it was one of the principal centres of the Theravādins at this time, he imbibed the Theravāda doctrines. The Sanskrit tradition refers to the later part of his life, when he became inclined to the doctrines of the Sarvāstivādins. It is stated in the Pali chronicles that

1. Cf. Watters, *op.cit.*, I. p. 262 : Madhyāntika carried this valuable plant from Gandhamādana Parvata and introduced it in Kashmir. See *Sarvastivāda Vinaya*, Tsa. shih, ch. 40

2. Schiefner, p. 23 : Tāranātha adds (p. 25) "but how far can this statement be taken at its worth is apparent. Minara, according to Tāranātha (p. 23), was the king of Tukhāra. Imasya, however, cannot be identified.

he convened a Synod under the presidentship of Moggaliputta Tissa, who insisted on recognising the Theravādins as the only orthodox monks, dismissing the rest as unorthodox. It is not known how far Aśoka adhered to his view but it will be apparent from the account given below that the monks other than the Theravadins, particularly, the Sarvāstivādins had to leave Magadha for some distant regions. Yuan Chwang records the above event in another form. He writes that during Aśoka's reign there was in Magadha a distinguished monk called Mahādeva, who was a subtle investigator of *name* and *form* (nāmarūpa *i.e.*, mind and matter=physical body) and expressed his extraordinary thoughts in a treatise, which taught heresy". An attempt was made to drown him in the Ganges. This monk, therefore, along with his followers, saved themselves by leaving the place and going to Kashmir, where they settled down on the hills and in the valleys. On hearing this news, Aśoka became unhappy and requested them to return, and on their declining to comply with his wishes, he built for them 500 monasteries and "gave up all Kashmir for the benefit of the Buddhist Saṅgha."[1] The fact underlying this account is that "the investigators of name and reality"[2] were the Sarvāstivādins, whose principal tenet was that *nāma* and *rūpa* were real but momentary and were divisible into 64 elements, which existed upto the attainment of Nirvāṇa, (*i.e. sarvam asti*), and it is for this doctrine they had the appellation, Sarvāstivāda.[3] Then the statement that they resorted to the hills and valleys of Kashmir corroborates the flight of the Sarvāstivāda monks to the north in Kashmir. They had also a centre at Mathurā.

Yuan Chwang must have fallen in confusion in regard to

1. Watters, *op. cit.*, p. 267

2. 'Reality' as the synonym of *rūpa* is wrong. *Rūpa* means physical body or worldly objects, while *nāma* is the constantly changing consciousness (*vijñāna*), the Buddhists do not accept the Upaniṣadic conception of eternal soul (*ātman*).

3. See the present writer's book *Buddhism in Uttara Pradesh* and *Buddhist Sects in India (1971)*. It should be noted that by reality of all (*sarvam asti*) it means that all objects as also *Vijñāna* are subject to momentary changes. In other words, all exists dynamically and not statically.

the name Mahādeva. There must have been two monks of this name, "one was an influential abbot of Pāṭaliputra[1]" who preached the *Devadūtasūtra*[2] and the other a monk, who introduced the tenets relating to the imperfections of an arhat.[3] Mahādeva, the investigator of *nāma* and *rūpa*, must have been a Sarvāstivādin while the other Mahādeva was a Mahāsaṅghika. Yuan Chwang could not also distinguish the Theravādins from the Mahāsaṅghikas, when he wrote that Aśoka supported the Mahāsaṅghikas as against the Theravādins and that 500 Arhats left Pāṭaliputra and propagated the Sthavira school in Kashmir, while the majority of the inferior brethren at Pāṭaliputra began the Mahāsaṅghika School.[4] The Mahāsaṅghikas, as we know, lived originally at Vesāli and later passed on to the south, making their principal centre in the Andhra country[5] at Dhanakaṭaka (present Guntur District).

The statement that Aśoka became later on repentant and wanted the monks, who had fled to Kashmir to return to Magadha might be regarded as an indirect reference to the fact recorded in the *Divyāvadāna*[6] and *Aśokāvadāna*[7] that Aśoka made an attempt towards the end of his life to reconcile the monks of the different schools of Buddhist thought by convening a Council, to which he particularly invited the monks living at Tamasāvana in Kashmir. The Ceylonese chronicles maintain a discreet silence over this incident, and this is not unusual in view of the sectarian spirit permeating the chronicles.

The Sarvāstivādins also claim Aśoka as their patron. They

1. Watters, *op.cit.*, I. p. 269
2. Majjhima Nikāya, III, p. 179
3. Watters, op. cit., I, p. 268. See the present writer's "Buddhist Sects in India".
4. Watters, op. oct., I, p. 269. By the word Inferior he meant Hīnayāna
5. *Ibid.*
6. *Divyā.*, p. 399 : Vasanti Kāśmīrapure surammye ye cāpi dhīrā Tamasāvane 'asmin, IA. 1895, p. 241f.
7. Prof. Przyluski writes in his *Légende de l'Empereur Aśoka*, pp. 101, 117 that a Council of 30,000 monks was held by Aśoka, the professord sources of information being the *Aśokāvadāna* and Tāranātha (Schiefner, p. 38) but we do not find any such reference in Tāranātha.

ignore the name of Moggliputta Tissa and put in his stead the name of Upagupta. Their Avadāna literature is full of episodes dealing with Aśoka's life and munificence. Tāranātha also speaks of his lavish gifts to the Sarvāstivāda monks of Aparāntaka, Kashmir and Tukhāra.[1] Kalhaṇa[2] writes that Aśoka not only built Śrinagari but also covered Suskaletra and Vitastrā with numerous *stūpas*, one of which was so high that its pinnacle was not visible. Yuan Chwang noticed four Aśokan topes, each of which contained relics of Buddha's body. The Avadāna records that Aśoka's liberarlity to the Buddhist monks was carried to such an excess towards the end of his life that his grandson Sampadi[3], whe was in charge of his treasury, refused to carry out his commands and even reduced his food to a myrobalan, half of which was the last gift made by Aśoka to the Buddhist Saṅgha.

Through the activities of the Sarvāstivādins, Kashmir became a centre of Buddhist philosophical studies and was also, according to Tāranātha, the scene of the activities of Vatsa,[4] the propounder of the *ātmaka* theory (*pudgalavāda*) and the founder of the Vātsiputrīya or Sammitīya school. The monk Vatsa taught that *pudgala* (soul, individuality) persists through the innumerable existences of an individual and ceases only on his attainment of Nirvāṇa.[5]

Buddhism and Nāga beliefs

In spite of all the patronage of Aśoka and the glorious accounts of the popularity of Buddhism in Kashmir, the fact remains that Buddhism had to face a strong opposition in the country from the established beliefs in Nāga-worship. Without adverting to the antiquity of the Nāga-worship, it may safely be stated that Nāga beliefs were quite common in India when Buddhism made its appearance and that is the reason why the legend of Nāgas and their conversion by Buddha occur

1. Schiefner, p. 38. 2. Stein, I, p. 19

3. *Divyā.*, p. 430. Tib. nor. lhas byin. It has been restored by Schiefner as Vāsavadattā, but it migto also be Dhanada or Sampadi.

4. Schiefner, *op. cit.*, p. 44.

5. See the present writer's Buddist Sects in India (1971).

occasionally in the Buddhist texts. In Ceylon, Java, and Indo-China, Nāga-worship was no less in vogue, and Buddhism could not help incorporating into itself some of the local beliefs in order to secure a footing in these distant countries. Kashmir was avowedly a land of Nāga-worship. Its two main chronicles the *Nīlamatapurāṇa* and the *Rājataraṅgiṇī* relate how Kashmir was created out of water and left to the care of the Nāgas, of whom Nīla was the chief. The Buddhist chronicles also speak of Kashmir as a land of lakes under the control of the Nāgas. They are generally associated with watery and mountainous regions, and so it is quite likely that Kashmir should be called a land of Nāga-worshippers[1], and attribute the origin of its rites and rituals to Nīla. Buddhism probably undermined the faith of the people and this was supposed to be possible partly on account of the *abhiññās* (superhuman powers) acquired by tue advanced Buddhist monks. Madhyāntika is said to have succeeded in winning over a large section of the populace by the show of his miraculous powers. Kalhaṇa also states it in the *Rājataraṅgiṇī*, verse I. 178 ;

> Te vādinaḥ parājitya vādena nikhilān budhān /
> kriyāṃ Nīlapurāṇoktācchindan nāgamadviṣaḥ // 178 //

[Translation : The (Buddhist) disputants, the Veda-haters after defeating all wise men in disputations, brought to an end the rites and rituals prescribed in the *Nīlamatapurāṇa*.

The *Nīlamatapurāṇa* also could not ignore its influence and help prescribing as follows :—

> Viṣṇur devo jagan nāthaḥ prāpte Brahmāṇa kalau yuge /
> aṣṭāviṃśatime bhāvī Buddho nāma jagad guru // 684 //
> Puṣyāyukte niśānāthe vaiśākhe māsi Kāśyapa /
> tasmāt kālāt athārabhya kāle bhāvinyataḥ paraṃ // 685 //
> śukle sampūjanaṃ tasya yathā kāryaṃ tathā śṛṇu /
> sarvauṣadhai sarvaratnaiḥ sarvagandhais tathaiva ca // 686//

1. *Rājat*, I, 136, 140-4 ; see Kṣemendra's *Samayamātṛkā*, v. 61 re. Kṛtyāśama-vihāra.
2. Raychauchury, *op. cit.*, p. 239. See also *IHQ.*, 1930, p. 343.
3. Przyluski, *op. cit.*, p. 301-2 ; *Divyā.*, *op. cit.*, p. 434 ; Schiefner, p. 81.

Buddhārcāsnāpanaṃ kāryaṃ Śākyoktaīr vāṇais tathā /
sudhāsitaś ca kartavyāḥ Śākyavāsāḥ prayatnataḥ // 687 //
kvac citrayutāḥ kāvyaś caityā devagṛhās tathā /
utsavaṃ ca tathā kāryaṃ naṭanartaka-saṃkulaṃ // 688 //
Śākyānāṃ pūjanaṃ kāryaṃ cīvarāhāra-pustakaiḥ /
Sarvam etad bhavet kāryaṃ yāvat prāptā bhaven maghā
// 689 //

[Transl. O Brahman, in the 28th Kaliyuga, in the month of Vaiśākha on the full-moon day with the conjunction of Puṣyā-nakṣatra, Viṣṇu, the lord of the world, will appear as Buddha, the teacher of the world. Listen how his worship is to be performed. In the bright fortnight, the image of Buddha is to be bathed with water containing all herbs, jewels and scents and by uttering the words of Śākya. The place is to be carefully besmeared with honey ; the temple and the *stūpa* are to have frescoes, and there should be dancing and amusements. The Śākyan worship is performed with *cīvara* (robes), food and books.]

Buddhism and Śaivism

The Kāshmirian history shows that Aśoka built temples both for Śiva and Buddha and during his reigning period, the two religious Buddhism and Śaivism flourished in Kashmir side by side, and even claimed at times the same persons as their devotees. Both Śaivism and Buddhism existed not only in Kashmir but also in Tibet, Nepal and even Mongolia as well as in Champa, Java and Burma. The two cults existed side by side, and had common adherents. The explanation that can be offered for such amity between the two religions is that while Buddhism catered to the ethical and philosophical needs of the human mind, Śaivism, or for the matter of that Brāhmaṇism catered to the devotional and religious needs. Buddhism made no provision for rites and rituals, which were almost a part and parcel of Hindu's life, and naturally took no objection to those prescribed by Brāhamaṇism. All that Buddhism demanded of its followers was *maitrī*

1. Traces of Nāga-beliefs are still to be found in the names of spots in Kashmir like Verinag, Anantanag, Serhnag, etc.

(amity) and *karuṇā* (compassion), and a moral life with faith in Buddha as the liberator of mankind from *duḥkha.* To the unbiased Hindu mind there was not much of difference between Buddhist and Śaiva doctrines. In both the systems, the highest truth or the ultimate reality was inexplicable. In Buddhism it is Nirvāṇa or Śūnyatā, and in Śaivism, particularly the Pratyabhījñas or the Idealist school of Kashmir, denoting it as Śiva. If Śiva be explained as *śānta,* i. e., undisturbed by birth and death, the Buddists would have no objection to accept it as Śūnyatā or Nirvāṇa. Both the systems look upon the phenomenal universe as subject to origin and decay ; the caused and conditioned theory of Buddhism corresponds to the reproductive and destructive cult of Śaivism, the fundamental difference between the two religions being the denial by Buddhism of any real individual self or an infinite self as opposed to the assertion of the latter by Śaivism or Brāhmaṇism generally. As regards the externals, asceticism and certain morphological and metaphysical ideas may be pointed out as the common features of the two systems. Buddhism favoured asceticism but did not look upon it as the essential means of salvation, while in Śaivism, the ascetic ideal of Śiva is placed as compulsory before every devotee for *sādhanā.* With the appearance of Avalokiteśvara and Tārā in the Buddhist pantheon, many mythological and metaphysical ideas woven around Śiva and Durgā were transferred to them while many of Nepal, Tibet and Mongolia in the worship of the ungainly rites of the Śaivites came to be adopted by the Buddhists of Nepal, Tibet and Mongolia in the worship of gods and goddesses.[1] In Siam and Camboja, the worship of Śiva and Durgā is sometimes described as identical with the worship of Buddha and Prajñā, and there is a number of instances of devotees, worshipping both Buddha and Śiva in Champa, Camboja, Java and Nepal. The Yuehchis took to Śiva worship, and Kadphises II and Vasudeva issued coins with Śiva emblems, but Buddhism was no less popular with them. It cannot be said with precision how far the fusion of the two religions took place within India, but

1. Elliot, *Hinduism and Buddhism,* II, pp. 118-9, 123 ; III, 391-2.

there is no doubt that it did happen in Champa, Cambojs, Java, Siam, Nepal and Tibet. In India no two religions are regarded as incompatible with each other and the worship of images belonging to two or more religions is regarded in each as equally meritorious. No Hindu will hesitate to light a candle at the tomb of a Muslim Fakir or offer flowers to a Jaina or Buddhist image. So Kalhaṇa's statements that kings, queens and ministers of Kashmir from Aśoka and later rulers built temples both for Śiva and Buddha can ce accepted as correct.

KANISHKA

Kaṇiṣka embraced Buddhism according to the epigraphic and numismatic evidences. Al-biruṇi and Hiuen Tsang refer to a grand monastery and a Caitya having been built by Kaṇiṣka in Peshawar. The Kushāṇa period witnessed the rise of Mahāyāna Buddhism as also the making of images of Buddha with sharp features by the Indo-Greek sculptors. Prof. Ray Chaudhuri[1] remarks that the Kushāna age was a period of great missionary and literary activities. Distinguished writers like Nāgārjuna, Āryadeva, Asaṅga, Aśvaghoṣa, Vasubandhu appeared at the time and so did also Pārśva, Vasumitra, Saṅgharakṣita, Caraka and the politician Māṭhara also flourished then. Missionaries carried on the propagation of Buddhism from Gandhāra and Kashmir to countries in the north like Eastern Turkestan and Central Asia, and thence gradully to China and from China to Mongolia, and the far eastern countries of U. S. S. R., Korea and Japan where it is still a living religion. Ngan-shi-kao, a Parthian prince, Kāśyapa Mātaṅga (*circa* 61 to 67 A. D.) and several others introduced the religion into China, making Tun-huang, the westernmost cave of China, as their first rendezvous. There were three routes from India to China. The route lay along the Kabul river and reached Hindukush through Peshawar, Jalalabad, Bamiyan and other places. Beyond the Hindukush lay Balkh (Bāhlika, Bactriana). From this place three routes proceeded to the Tarim Basin. In all the places along the

1. *PHAI*, p. 399-440

routes there were Buddhist establishments, probably small in size[1].

In the *Kalpanāmaṇḍitika* it is stated that Kaṇiṣka came to Peshawar and made it his capital.

It is a fact that Kaṇiṣka patronised the Indian religions, art and scholarship. He supported Buddhism particularly.[1]

He became acquainted also with the Sarvāstivāda school of Buddhism, which preserved its scriptures in Sanskrit language.

In the *Śridharmapiṭaka-nidāna-sūtra* (Chinese translation 742 A. D.) it is stated that Chen-tan Kia-ni-cha (Kaṇiṣka) defeated the king of Pāṭaliputra and demanded a large ransom, but he agreed to accept Aśvaghoṣa, Buddha's alms-bowl and a compassionate cock in its stead. Aśvaghoṣa became associated with Kaṇiṣka on the occasion of his expedition towards the eastern parts of India and strengthened his faith in Buddhism.[1]

Aśvaghoṣa afterwards converted Pārśva to the Buddhist faith. About this time a codification of the Buddhist Canon was effected in Sanskrit, though the language of North-western India was a Prākṛit as is found in the Prākṛit version of the *Dharmapada*[2] in Kharoṣṭhi script. A Prākṛit inscription has also been found on the Kurram casket.

The successors of Kaṇiṣka were Vāsiṣka, the latter being an younger brother of the former. Huviṣka was the last great ruler of the Kushāṇas.

The Turuṣkas, i.e. the Kushāṇas built Maṭhas and Caityas. It is said that Kashmir was in possession of the Buddhists. According to Tāranātha (Ch. XII) the great Kushāṇa ruler Kaṇiṣka invited Buddhist monks from all parts of India and had a collection of the Tripiṭaka prepared by them. It took place either in the Kuvana monastery or Jālandhara. Most scholars, however, agree that 500 Arhats and 500 Bodhisattvas in a Council made the collection. Mahābhadanta Vasumitra was the President of the Council and Aśvaghoṣa its Vice-President.

1. *Age of Imperial Unity*, pp. 636, 638. Vide also *The stupas and Vihāras of Kaniska I* by K. Walton Dobbins (Asiatic Society. 1971).

2. Sten Konow, *op. cti.*, p. xxxvi, later edited by B. M. Barua and S. N. Mitra of the Calcutta University.

In the Council, all differences of opinion were reconciled and the Vinaya texts, after thorough revision, were put into writing. At this time appeared also the Mahāyāna teaching of faith in the non-origin of all worldly objects' (*anutpattika-dharma-kṣānti*), in other words, all worldly objects are evanescent.

Since the demise of Aśoka, Buddhism withstood several repercussions and survived in North India. It is signified by donations given by several lay-devotees and monks to the Buddhist Saṅgha. In the session of the Fourth Buddhist Council, took place composition of the Vibhāṣā śāstras, appearance of distinguished authors, and the propagation of Buddhism outside India. These are some of the factors, which rendered the reign of this king as an outstanding event in the history of Buddhism.[1]

THE KUSHANAS

Following the Śaka-Yavanas, the Kushāṇas also adopted Buddhism as their religion and spent lavishly on the erection of *stūpas*, temples and images of Buddha all over N. India. The earlier Kushāṇas like Kadphises II, as their coins indicate, were Śiva-worshippers, but Kaṇiṣka and his successors, as their inscriptions and monuments reveal, offered their gifts to the Buddhist Saṅgha, particularly to the Sarvāstivādins[2] and occasionally to the Mahāsaṅghikas.[3]

Since the demise of Aśoka, Buddhism continued its existence in N. W. India with the patronage of the Śaka-Yavanas and the Kushāṇas. In the reign of Kaṇiṣka, it once more came to the forefront of Indian religions and recovered its lost popularity. The Buddhist ecclesiastical historians like Tāranātha pass silently over the reign of Aśoka, and resume their accounts with the advent of Kaṇiṣka.[4]

1. *CII.*, II, i, pp. 29 f.
2. *Ibid.*, II, i, pp. 137, 145, 155, 176
3. *Ibid.*, Wardak Vase Inscription, p. 170
4. Tāranātha has referred to the reign of Viśoka, Nanda and Mahāpadma and mentions nothing of importance in connection with the history of Buddhism.

Kaṇiṣka and his successors

The reigning period of Kaṇiṣka is of great importance in the history of Buddhism in N. India. It is marked by donations from several lay-devotees and monks to the Buddhist Saṅgha, evidences of which have been unearthed by the archeological department of the Central Government. The session of the Fourth Council, composition of the *Vibhāṣā-śāstras*, appearance of distinguished authors and the propagation of Buddhism outside India are some of the factors, which rendered his reign so important in the history of Buddhism.

Of the successors of Kaṇiṣka, we come across the names of only Vāsiṣka and Huviṣka in the several inscriptions relating to this period. Kalhaṇa[1] mentions the names of three successors : Huṣka, Juṣka and Kaṇiṣka (II). The Wardak Vase inscription discloses the Buddhistic leaning of Huviṣka but there is no clear evidence about such leaning of Vāsiṣka. Tāranātha, however, tells us that the son of Kaṇiṣka maintained several *arhats* and *bhikṣus* in his Puṣkalāvatī palace for five years. Kalhaṇa informs us that Huṣka, Juṣka and Kaṇiṣka (II) built Huṣkapura (mod. Uskur)[2], Juṣkapura (mod. Zukur)[3] and Kaṇiṣkapura (mod. Kanespur),[4] and that these kings, though belonging to the Turuṣka race, were given to acts of piety. They erected *Maṭhas* and *Caityas* at Suskaletra and other places, and the Buddhists of that time acquired great renown as recluses (*pravrajitsa*), and were predominant in Kashmir, defeating their opponents in disputations.

Though the available account of the Kushan rulers are meagre, there are yet ample evidences that Buddhism enjoyed a prosperous time during this period all over N. India and specially in Gandhāra and Kashmir. Kaṇiṣka built a monastery and a Caitya at Peshawar. The Council held under his auspices in Kashmir and the valuable work done in the Council bear a testimony to its influence and popularity.

1. *Rājat.* I, 68 2. Schiefner, *op. cit.*, ch. XIII
3. It is now a small village near Baramula, see Stein, *op. cit.* i, 168n.
4. It is a large village near Srinagar. *Ibid.*
5. It is between Vitastā and the High Road linking Baramula and Srinagar.

BUDDHISM IN KASHMIR

The Fourth Buddhist Conncil

Tāranātha commenced the story of the Council with the conversion of King Siṃha of Kashmir to Buddhism. It is said that King Siṃha became an arhat and his name after ordination was Sudarśana. He preached the religion in Kashmir. Kaṇiṣka was then the king of Jālandhara. He heard of Sudarśana and came to Kashmir to listen to his discourses.[1]

The Buddhist Saṅgha was then divided into eighteen sects.[2] Venerable Pārśva came to Kashmir from the east, and advised King Kaṇiṣka to collect all the monks at Kuṇḍalavana-vihāra[3] (in Kashmir). 500 Arhats, 500 Bodhisattvas and 500 Paṇḍitas[4] took part in the delīberation of the Council[5]. An attempt was made to reconcile the conflicting opinions of the different sects and settle once more the Vinaya, Sūtra and Abhidharma texts. Bu-ston gives an account similar to the above, adding only that "after recitation of the texts, it was settled that the texts acknowledged by the eighteen sects were all of them the words of Buddha."[6] Yuan Chwang's account is substantially to the same effect. He attributed the session of the Council to the confusion that Kaṇiṣka had while listening to the conflicting interpretations of Buddha's words as given by the adherents of different sects. Pārśva explained to the king the cause of his confusion. Yuan Chwang adds that in this Council several expository commentaries on the *Sūtra, Vinaya* and *Abhidharma* were composed and were called the *Upadeśa-sūtras* and *Vibhāṣā-śāstras*,

1. Schiefner, Chapter XII. There is a Kashmirian king of this name in the *Rājataraṅgiṇī*. It may be that king Siṃha was only a prince. Bu-ston (II, p. 160) preserves a tradition that Sudarśana delivered the teaching (of Vinaya) to an Anāgāmin and the latter to Anivartitabuddhi, who in his turn, imparted it to Guṇaprabha.

2. See the present author's "Buddhist Sects in India."

3. Tib. snā. rgyan. nags. kyi. gi.cun. lag. khaṅ=Chinese: Kien tho lo.

4. Tib. so. so. skye. boḥi. pa.ṇḍita=Pṛthagjana-paṇḍita, i.e. the paṇḍitas who were not srotāpannas. Bu-ston, II, p. 97.

5. Schiefner, p. 60.

6. Bu-ston, II, p. 97.

in which the original texts and their different interpretations were discussed. King Kaṇiṣka, according to Yuan Chwang, had all the treatises inscribed on copper-plates and had them enclosed in stone-boxes and deposited them in a *stūpa* made specially for the purpose.

Paramārtha in his *Life of Vasubandhu*[1] refers to this Council though not expressly. He writes that Kātyāyaṇīputra went to Kipin (Kashmir) and there with the co-operation of 500 Arhats and 500 Bodhisattvas arranged the Sarvāstivāda texts, the main treatise of which was the *Jñānaprasthāna-sūtra* in 8 sections i.e. *Pādas.* Its alternative title is the *Aṣṭa-grantha* as it contained eight topics.

A commentary was written on the Abhidharma texts and was called the Vibhāśā-śāstras. Kātyāyaṇīputra then sent for Aśvaghoṣa, who was then residing at Śrāvastī and requested him to give the *Vibhāṣās* a proper literary shape. After completion of the commentary, Kātyāyaṇīputra declared by an inscription on a stone that any portion of the *Abhidharma* text and its *Vibhāṣā* must not go out of this province, but he could not anticipate that a prodigy like Vasubandhu would commit to memory all the words and take them out. The *Vibhāṣā* is so closely associated with Kashmir that it is called in Chinese *Kashmir-shi.*[2]

The Vibhāṣā Śāstras

By the expression *Vibhāṣā-śāstra*, Paramārtha had only in view the systematic exposition of the Sarvāstivāda Abhidharma texts, while Yuan Chwang meant by the expression 'expository commentaries' not only of *Abhidharma* but also of *Sūtra* and

1. Vasubandhu-nāmnā abhidharma-pratyāsaḥ kṛtaḥ. (Abhidharma-kośavyākhyā, p. 1).

Vasubandhusya *Abhidharmakośa-kārikā* and its *bhāṣya* contain the whole of the Sarvāstivāda Abhidharma condensed and versified in a beautiful manner in the *Kārikās.* Yaśomitra has written a *Vyākhyā* on the *Bhāṣya.* Published in Patnā and Japan.

2. *Toung Pao*, Vol. V, pp. 276–281. See Abhidharmakośavyākhyā (Jap. ed) p. 694 : Kāśmīra-vaibhāṣika-nīti-siddhaḥ......Santi Vaibhāṣikāḥ na Kāśmīrāḥ. Kaśmīrāḥ bahirdeṣakā Vaibhāṣikāḥ.

Vinaya, the commentaries on Sūtras being only distinguished as *Upadeśa-śāstra* and not as *Vibhāṣā Śāstras*. It is a matter for regret that the *Śāstras* exist only in Chinese translation and have not yet been studied adequately. About the merits of the works, Yuan Chwang tells us that in these "there is evidence of great study and research. In them he found an extraordinary insight into the Buddhist lore of various kinds and also into the Brāhmanical learning, and the Vedas with their Aṅgas."[1]

Distinguished ācāryas

The composition of the *Vibhāṣā-śāstras* in Kashmir indicates that Kashmir grew up to an academic centre, attracting distinguished ācāryas from other places[2]. The accounts of the Chinese travellers and of Paramārtha, mention the names of Kātyāyaṇīputra, Aśvaghoṣa, Vasubandhu, Vasumitra, Dharmatrāta, Saṅghabhadra, Viśuddhasiṃha, Jinabandhu, Sugatamitra, Sūryadeva, Jinatrāta. Kanakavatsa[3] and many other distinguished teachers and writers, who lived in Kashmir, from the time of Kaṇiṣka. Tāranātha tells us that during the reign of Kaṇiṣka one wealthy brahmin called Sūtra maintained the Vaibhāṣika teacher Dharmatrāta and the earliest Sautrāntika teacher Mahābhadanta Sthavira along with their disciples. Dharmatrāta is well-known as one of the four renowned ācāryas of the Vaibhāṣika school, the other three being Ghoṣaka of Tukhāra, Vasumitra of Maru, and Buddhadeva of Vārāṇasī.[4] One Dharmatrāta, according to the Chinese tradition, was the uncle of Vasumitra, to whom is attributed the authorship of the *Pañcavastu - vibhāṣā-śāstra*, *Saṃyuktābhidharma-hṛdaya-śāstra*, etc. In the Sui Vihāra copper-plate inscription one Dharmatrāta is mentioned as the disciple of Bhava (Bhavya) and teacher of Nagadata (Nāgadatta). In the present state of our knowledge, it is not possible to state whether the Dharmatrātas

1. Watters, I, p. 278.
2. Bu-ston, II, p. 142 : A number of Pratyeka-buddhas had formerly expressed in their entreaties their desire that, that country should be the place where the Abhidharma was to be exclusively studied.
3. Watters, I, p. 283.
4. Bu-ston, II, p. 122.

were one and the same person or different. Vasumitra was another famous figure of Kashmir, but there were five authors bearing this name.[1] In the *Tattvasaṃgraha*, Kamalaśila discusses the opinions of Dharmatrāta and Vasumitra but we do not know which Dharmatrāta and Vasumitra were in his view. The Sautrāntika teacher, Śrīlābha was an inhabitant of Kashmir.[2] He was a disciple of Kuṇāla. Saṃghabhadra was another Kashmirian ācārya, who was a profound scholar of the Vibhāṣā śāstras of the Sarvāstivāda school."[3]. He wrote a commentary on Vasumitra's *Prakarṇapāda* and was the author of the *Abhidharmāvatāra-śāstra*[4]. One of his distinguished students was Vasubandhu[5], who studied with him the Vibhāṣās, śāstras of the 18 schools, Sūtras and Vinayas, six systems of Indian philosophy and the art of dialectics. He compressed the Abhidharma texts and their Vibhāṣās in his *Abhidharmakośa* and *Bhāṣya*, and sent them to the Kashmir Vaibhāṣikas, who were highly pleased to get them.[6] Vasubandhu later on turned from the Sarvāstivāda point of view to that of the Sautrāntika, as is evidenced in the expression of his opinions in the *Bhāṣya*, and which elicited vehement criticism from Saṅghabhadra, who was a staunch Sarvāstivādin and wrote two treatises to refute Vasubandhu's later views.[7]

Guṇaprabha and Vimalamitra were the two other teachers, whose names occur in the *Records* of Yuan Chwang. Guṇaprabha is mentioned by Tāranātha and Bu-ston as a great authority on the *Vinaya* of the Mūlasarvāstivādins and as the author of several works[8]. Yuan Chwang refers to the monastery at Matipur, where he composed his treatises. As regards Vimalamitra, Yuan Chwang[9] writes that he "was a native of Kashmir and an adherent of the Sarvata (i.e. Sarvāstivāda) school, having made a profound study of canonical and

1. Watters I, p. 241-5 ; Schiefner, p. 297.
2. See Nanjio, p. 375.
3. *CII.*, II, i, p. 141.
4. For details, see *Asia Major*. II, p. 78.
5. Schiefner, pp. 67, 79.
6. Watters, I, p. 325.
7. Watters, II, p. 280.
8. Bu-ston, II, p. 142.
9. Watters, I, p. 210-211 ; Bu-ston, II, p. 143.

heterodox scriptures, and had travelled in India to learn the mysteries of the Tripiṭaka.

Kaṇiṣka, according to the traditional, epigraphic and numismatic evidences, adopted Buddhism as his religion. Al-biruṇi and Hiuen-Tsang speak of the grand monastery erected at the instance of the emperor Kaṇiṣka at Peshawar. It was during the period of his reign, images of Buddha with sharp and delicate features were carved for the first time by the Indo-Greek sculptors. Prof. Ray Chaudhuri[1] remarks that the Kushan age was not only a period of wide and deep literary activities of the Buddhist savants but also of missionary activities beyond the frontiers of India. Among the savants may be mentioned the names of Pārśva, Vasumitra, Saṅgharakṣita, Asaṅga and Vasubandhu, Nāgārjuna, Āryadeva, and Aśvaghoṣa. Besides the Buddhist authors, there appeared at this time the founder of the Āyurvedic system, Caraka, and the politician Māṭhara.[2] From Gandhāra and Kashmir, both Indian and non-Indian monks risked their lives by travelling on foot or mules over the hilly regional and mountainous tracks at the foot of the Himalayas in order to carry the message of Buddha to the semi-civilised races of Central Asia and Eastern Turkestan, from which places again at a later date the religion was carried to China, Korea, Mongolia and ultimately to Japan.

THE ROUTES

The route from Gandhāra proceeded along the Kabul river passed by Hidda and Nagarahāra (Jālālābad) and reached Bamiyan, a valley surrounded on all sides by snowy cliffs of the Hindukush. It was a halting place for the monks going to Central Asia and thence to China. It was also the seat of a Government and attracted pilgrims and traders from all the neighbouring countries. It became an important centre of Buddhism in the early centuries of the Christian era and continued to be so up to the 8th century. A number of grottos

1. *PHAI.*, pp. 399-400 ; *The Age of Imperial Unity*, p. 146-7.

2. There was at a much later date a noted dialectician called Māṭhara.

in the hills around Bamiyan was converted into Buddhist temples of the Ajanta type. Colossal images of Buddha were carved out of the hills. Hiuen Tsang states that at Balkh there was a monastery called Nava-saṅghārāma (Naubahar), the only institution on the north of Hindukush, where resided a number of commentators of the Canon. Towards the end of the 7th century, the monastery was destroyed by the Moslems and its chief priest was converted to Islam. They, according to Al-biruṇi, inaugurated the study of Indian astronomy and mathematics in Baghdad.[1]

Bactriana was the meeting place of two different routes, leading to Central Asia and China. Of these two, the shorter one was preferred by the Buddhist missionaries, travelling to China through Kashgar. There was another shorter route joining Kashgar with the upper valley of the Indus. It passed through Gilgit[2] and the Yasin valley up to Tashgurkhan, where it joined the other route towards Kashgar. By the middle of the 7th century Kashgar and Yarkand abounded in hundreds of Buddhist monasteries"[3]

According to the Buddhist traditions, Khotan was colonised by the Indians from N. W. India. It is said that Kuṇāla's courtiers and followers, infuriated at the inhuman act of a queen of Aśoka of blinding Kuṇāla, left the country with Kuṇāla and set him up as the king of Khotan. There was an intimate relation between N. W. India and Khotan during the Kushan period. Khotan played an important part in the history of Buddhism. The premier monastery in Khotan was Gomati Vihāra, one of the biggest seats of Buddhist learning in Central Asia.

Kucī[4] was another important place in Central Asia and played the same role as that of Khotan in the diffusion of

1. P. C. Bagchi, *India and China* (1944), p. 11-12.

2. A number of manuscripts was found in a stūpa here; for details, see the present writer's *Gilgit Manuscripts*, Vol. I, Intro.

3. P. C. Bagchi, *op. cit.* (1944), p. 11-12.

4. *Ibid.*, p. 13f. for detailed treatment, see Dr. Kshanikā Sāhā's *Central Asian Buddhism* (1970).

Buddhism. The ancient rulers of Kucī bore Indian names, such as Suvarṇapuṣpa, Haradeva, Suvarṇadeva, etc.[1] Fragments of a few manuscripts in Sanskrit and Kuchean-Sanskrit (bilingual) have been discovered from the Kucī region[2].

The next stage on the northern route was Karasahr, the monks of which place rendered a great service in the propagation of Buddhism in China. Turfan was the third centre situated on the northern route farther towards the east.

Two routes, of which one came from the south and the other from the north of the Tarim Basin, met on the Chinese frontier at a place called Yu-men-kuan or the Jade gate. Not far from it was Tun-huang cave, which was, at one time, one of of the largest centres of the Buddhist culture. In the hills near Tun-huang was located a number of grottos converted into monasteries between the 5th and 8th century for the use of Buddhist monks proceeding to China. These grottos were called by the Chinese Ts'ien-fo-tong or the Caves of Thousand Buddhas.[3]

In ancient times there were other overland routes from India to China. One of these passed through Assam, Upper Burma, and Yunan, and the other through Nepal and Tibet. There were also sea-routes from India to South-east Asia, and thence to China.[4]

Missionaries

The Parthians occupied a portion of North-western India and came to be known as the Indo-Parthians. Towards the middle of the 2nd century A. D. a Parthian prince embraced Buddhism and later became a monk. His name was Ngan-she-kao (lit. Parthian *Lokottama*). He translated a number of Buddhist texts into Chinese. He resided in the White Horse Monastery (Po-ma-sse). The ancient Sogdians[5], a branch of the Parthians, settled at

1. P. C. Bagchi, op. cit. (1944) p. 15.
2. Hoernle's *Manuscript Remains in Eastern Turkestan.*
3. P. C. Bagchi, op. cit., p. 17.
4. *Ibid.*, p. 18f.
5. There are a few Sogdian translations of the Budhhist texts, see Hoernle's *Manuscript Remains in Eastern Turkestan.*

Samarkand and Bokhara. They went to Eastern Turkestan and established many Buddhist centres towards the beginning of the Christian era. Senghui was another Sogdian monk, who migrated to Tonkin and propagated the religion in South China.

Kaṇiṣka belonged to the Yueh-chi race. He made Mahāyāna Buddhism a state religion in India. He established a close relation between Kashmir and Kucī. He took personal interest in the propagation of the religion outside India. A few Buddhist missionaries of the Yueh-chi race went to China in the 2nd and 3rd centuries A.D. Among them the most distinguished was Dharmarakṣa (Fa-hu=lit. protector of the law), who went to China in the middle of the 3rd century A.D. He resided at Tun-huang cave on the western frontier of China. He translated a few Buddhist Sanskrit texts into Chinese.

The monks of Kucī (northern part of Central Asia) also took an important part in the propagation of the religion in China. The noted and the most accurate translator of the Buddhist texts into Chinese was Kumārajīva, son of an Indian Kumārāyaṇa, who was a minister of the king of Kucī and a princess Jīvā of the royal family of Kucī. In Kashmir where the Sarvāstivādins predominated, Kumārajīva studied the Buddhist Sanskrit literature and philosophy of the Sarvāstivādins with Bandhudatta. He returned to Kucī, wherefrom he was taken by force to China in 401 A.D. He was in China till his death in 413. His translations revealed remarkable improvement on the works of the earlier writers. Vimalākṣa, a senior monk of Kashmir, worked with him from 406 to 413 A.D.[1]

Many Kashmirian scholars went to China. One of them was Saṅghabhūti. He wrote a commentary on the Sarvāstivāda Vinaya Piṭaka. He was in China from 381 to 384 A.D. Two other Kashmirian scholars, Puṇyatrāta and his pupil Dharmayaśas went to Central Asia where he translated a number of texts of the Sarvāstivādins from 397 to 401 A. D. and later in China from 424 to 453 A.D. Buddhayaśas was another monk of

1. P. C. Bagchi, *op. cit.*, p. 40.

Kashmir, who went to Kashgar, en route, for Kucī. Guṇavarman, a prince of Kashmir first went to Ceylon and thence to Java, wherefrom by the sea-route he reached Nanking (Jetavana monastery) in 431 A.D. Many scholars of countries other than Kashmir also went to China by different routes.

The suzerainty of the Kushāṇas did not uproot the Śakas from India altogether. The Śaka-Satraps or Kshatrapas (Chatrapatis) in the different provinces of western India owned their allegiance to the Kushāṇas. The Śakas, *i.e.*, the Scythians adapted themselves to the Indian customs and religious beliefs. About 15 A.D. Mathura became the head-quarters of the Śaka Satraps, according to the Mathura inscriptions.

The Kushan supremacy declincd after Vāsudeva (145—176 A.D.) and the Śaka Satraps became independent rulers of the large parts of Central and Western India, which were under their control. A flood of light is thrown by an extract from the Jaina treatise *Kālakācārya-kathānaka.* It runs as follows :—

to sūri-pajjuvāsaya-
Sāhiṃ rāyāhirāyaṃ aha kāuṃ
bhumjaṃti rajja-sukkhaṃ
sāmaṃta-paiṭṭhiyyā sesā
Sagakulāo jenaṃ
samāgayā, teṇa re Sagā jāyā ;
evam Saga-rāīṇaṃ
eso vaṃso samuppanno.
... ...
kāl'aṃtareṇa keṇai
uppaḍittā Sagāṇa taṃ vaṃsaṃ
jāo Mālava-rāyā
nāṃeṇaṃ Vikkamāicco
... ...
tassa vi vaṃsaṃ uppā-
ḍiūna jāo puṇo vi Sagarāyā
Ujjeṇi-pura-varīye
paya-paṃkaya-paṇaya-sāmaṃto
paṇa-tise vāsa-sae

Vikkama-savaccharassa volīṇe
parivattuṇa ṭhavio
jeṇaṃ saṃvaccharo niyao.
Saga-kāla-jāṇaṇ'-satthaṃ
eyaṃ pāsaṃgiyaṃ samakkhāyaṃ
mūla-kahā-saṃbaddhaṃ.
pagayaṃ ciya bhannae iṇhiṃ

[*Translation* : Kālakācārya had a sister called Sarasvatī, who joined the convent. King Gardabhilla of Ujjayinī was fascinated by her beauty and ravished her. Kālakācārya, being enraged, went to the west of the Sindhu and lived with a Shāhi (Śaka) chief, over whom he obtained great influence by means of his astrological knowledge. Gradually he came to know that his patron and 95 other chiefs, who lived in the same locality, obeyed a common overlord. Kālakācārya persuaded his patron to invade the kingdom of Gardabhilla with the aid of all of his 95 fellow-chiefs and he himself joined the army that marched along Sind and Gujrat and beseiged Ujjayinī. Ujjayinī fell and the Śakas established their supremacy in Mālava. After 17 years, Vikramāditya, son of Gardabhilla, regained his kingdom by expelling the Śakas. Kālakācārya, after defeating Gardabhilla and releasing his sister, went to the court of Sātavāhana at Pratiṣṭhāna. The Jaina tradition, given above, has a definite historical value.[1]

After the Indo-Greeks, the Scythians ruled over western India, Gujrat, Kathiawaḍ and the Ajmer region of Rajputana till the time of Candragupta II, who annexed their dominions to the Gupta empire. The Scythians ruled at first as Viceroys under the suzerainty of the Kushāṇas. Chasṭana was a viceroy of the Kushāṇas, ruling over the south-western provinces of the Kushan empire. His son Jayadāman died early and so his grandson Rudradāman succeeded him and defeated Śātakarṇi, lord of Dakṣiṇāpatha. The earliest known Kshaharāta was

1. H. Jacobi, *Das Kālakācārya-Kathānakaṃ ZDMG*. 34 ; (1880) ; *Age of Imperial Unity*, p. 155 ; J. E. Van Lohuizen de Leeuw, *The Scythian Period*, p. 385

Bhumaka. He was succeeded by Nahapāna (119-125 A. D.).[1] But the relation of Bhumaka to Nahapāna is not known. Nahapāna's son-in-law Ṛṣabhadatta (Usavadāta) was the viceroy of the southern provinces ruled over by his father-in-law. He was a Hinduised Śaka and ruled over the districts of Govardhana (Nasik) and Mamaṭa (Poona), southern Gujrat and the northern Konkan from Broach to Sopārā and also Malwa, Kathiawaḍ and the Marāṭhā country and a large part of Rajputana. Shortly after 124-5 A.D. the Sātavāhanas of Pratiṣṭhāna, Gautamīputra Śātakarṇi, ousted the Kshaharātas, Śakas, and Yavanas, and became the lord of Surāṣṭra, Kathiawaḍ, Kukura (in the Gujrat, Kathiawad region), Anupa (Maheśvara region on the Narmadā), Aparānta (northern Konkan), Ākara (East Malwa) and Avanti (West Malwa), Ṛiṣika (on the Krishnā), Asmaka (in the Hyderabad state), Mālaka (with Paiṭhan on the Godāvarī) and Vidarbha (Berar). Gautamīputra claimed suzerainty over the whole of the trans-Vindhyan range, Malaya (Travancore hills), Eastern Ghats and other mountain ranges encircling the peninsula of South India (*trisamudra-toya-pīta-vāhana*). He was succeeded by his son Vāsiṣṭhiputra Pulumāyi (106-130 A. D.). Before his death Gautamīputra Sātakarṇi lost most of the districts he had conquered to another dynasty of Scythian rulers known as the Kārdamakas. The Sātavāhana king Gautamīputra Sātakarṇi defeated the Śaka Satraps. The Śakas under Chaṣṭana and his grandson Rudradāman defeated the Sātavāhana kings (106-130 A. D.) and recovered most of the northern districts. In the Junagarh inscription of Rudradāman, he is represented as the ruler of many countries including Ākara, Avanti, Anupa, Aparānta, Surāṣṭra and Ānarta (Dvārakā region in Kathiawaḍ). It is also claimed that Rudradāman defeated the republican tribe Yaudheyas of southern Punjab and the adjoining regions.

Rudradāman was a patron of classical Sanskrit and studied grammar, poetry, music and logic, and composed treatises in Sanskrit prose and verse.

---

1. *The Age of Imperial Unity*, Ch. XIII, pp. 182, 201, detail list of Satraps

Rudradāman was followed by a series of Satraps up to 304-5 A. D.[1]

The Scythian ruler Nahapāna (119-135 A. D.) was in possession of the northern part of Mahārāṣṭra and the Konkan as well as of Malwa, Kathiawaḍ and Rajputana. The immediate predecessor of Gautamīputra Sātakarṇi, who restored the fallen fortunes of the dynasty, continued its precarious existence as the subordinate allies of the foreigners. Gautamīputra Sātakarṇi is said to have conquered the Scythians, the Indo-Greeks and the Indo-Parthians (*śaka-yavana-pallava-nisūdana*) and established the dynasty of the Sātavāhana (*Sātavāhana-kula-yaśaḥ-pratiṣṭhāpana-kara*) about 124 A. D. The dominion of Sātakarṇi, according to the Nāsik Praśasti, included Aparānta, Anūpa, Surāṣṭra, Kukura, Ākara, and Avanti. His dominion also included Ṛṣika (district round Ṛṣika-nagara on the Krishnā), Asmaka (territory about Bodhan) in the Hyderabad State, Mūlaka[2] with Pratiṣṭhāna (modern Paiṭhān on the Godāvarī) and Vidarbha (Berar). The direct rule of this king seems to have extended over the whole territory from the Krishnā in the south, to Malwa and Kathiawād in the north, and from Berar in the east to the Konkan in the west. But Gautamīputra claimed suzerainty over the whole of the trans-Vindhyan region of India.[3]

THE SATAVAHANAS

(30 B. C.—270 A. D.)
approximately

After the Maurya and Śuṅga periods, the Sātavāhanas of the Upper Deccan came into prominence as the lord of Dakṣiṇāpatha. At the time when the Greeks, the Śakas and the Kushāṇas were carrying on their operations of conquest in the northern and western parts of India, the Andhras established

1. *The Age of Imperial Uniiy*, p. 185f.

2. In the *Sutta Nipāta*, Asmaka and Mūlaka are mentioned as Andhra countries.

3. *Age of Imperial Unity*, p. 201

a powerful kingdom in the south. They were also designated as the Andhrabhṛtyas, the word "*bhṛtya*', perhaps signified their allegiance to the Mauryas and Śuṅgas, while the last Śuṅga king Bṛhadratha was ousted by his minister Vasudeva, the founder of the Kāṇva or Kāṇvāyana dynasty. The last Kāṇva ruler was overthrown by Simuka, the founder of the Sātavāhana dynasty. He maintained a large army and conquered several countries. He extended his dominion from the mouth of the river Krishnā to whole of the Deccan plateau. His western capital was at Pratiṣṭhāna (Paiṭhan) and the eastern capital at Dhānyakaṭaka, where the Amarāvatī and Nāgārjunikoṇḍa stūpas were erected. This dynasty ruled over the countries, south of the Vindhyas for 300 years from 30 B.C. By ousting the Kāṇvas, the Sātavāhanas brought the whole of Magadha under their control.[1]

The Vākāṭakas were followed by the Ābhiras, a foreign tribe, which entered into Northern Mahārāṣṭra, the southern and eastern parts of India and gave their own name to their settlements, e.g., Āhraura (Ābhravāṭaka) in Mirzapur district, U. P. The Ābhīras advanced up to the Deccan. According to the *Purāṇas*, the Deccan was held by the Ābhīras after the Andhrabhṛtyas. In the *Viṣṇu Purāṇa* (V. 38) and the *Mahābhārata* (Muṣala Parva, Ch. VII) they are described as *dasyus* and *mlecchas*.

After the Ābhīras, the Vākāṭakas were followed by the Bodhis and Ikṣvākus.

The founder of the Ikṣvāku dynasty was Śāntamūla (Chāntamūla) (2nd quarter of the 3rd century A. D.). The Ikṣvākus were known Śripārvatīya Andhras. King Śāntamūla was succeeded by his son Māṭhariputra Vīrapuruṣadatta (3rd quarter of the 3rd century A. D.). Records of the reign of Vīrapuruṣadatta have been found in the inscriptions of Amarāvatī and Jaggayyapeta and Nāgārjunikuṇḍa.[1] In the inscriptions are mentioned many benefactions of four female donors to the Mahācaitya.

Vīrapuruṣadatta's son was Ehuvula Śāntamūla II.

1. R. C. Majumdar, *Ancient India*, p. 135

Gautamputra Sātakarṇi was a patron of Buddhism next in importance to that of Kaṇiṣka. He was succeeded by Vāśiṣṭiputra Pulumāyi, who ruled for 28 years. During Pulumāyi's reign, the Śakas of Malwa and Kathiawaḍ under Rudradāman fought against the Sātavāhana rulers and regained their power. A later Sātavāhana king Yajñaśrī Sātakarṇi conquered the southern dominion of the Western Satraps and ruled over the the whole of Deccan and the eastern part of the Central Provinces. He was the last of the great rulers of the Sātavāhana dynasty.

Pulumāyi's successor was Śivaśrī Sātakarṇi (*circa* 159-168 A.D.). The next rulers were Śivaskanda Sātakarṇi identified with Vāśiṣṭiputra Sātakarṇi (167-174 A. D.) and Yajñśrī Sātakarṇi (174-203 A.D.). The death of Yajñaśrī (3rd centnry A.D.) led to the dismemberment of the Sātavāhana empire. The Vākāṭakas were the feudatories of the Sātavāhanas. A Vākāṭaka king is mentioned in an early inscription of Amarāvati. He visited the Buddhist establishment at Amarāvati for pilgrimage.

Northern India after the Kushāṇas

After the Kushāṇas, the undermentioned tribal republics wielded great powers.

In Rajputana and the adjoining regions, there were the following tribal states :—

(i) Arjunāyanas of Bharatpur and Alwar states.

(ii) Uddehikas of Bharatpur state.

(iii) Mālavas of Jaipur state, parts of the Punjab and the adjoining tracts of U. P. and Rajputana.

(iv) Sibis (Sibipura, mod, Shorkot in the Jhang district of the Punjab). The Sibis later migrated to Rajputana in the district Nāgari near Chitor.

(v) Rājanyas along with Yaudheyas in North-western Rajputana.

(vi) Uttamabhadras, neighbours of the Mālavas, lived in Pushkara near Ajmer.

Most of these tribes submitted to the Scythians and the Kushāṇas. After the decline of the Kushan empire in the

4th century A. D. they acknowledged the suzerainty of the Guptas. It may be pointed out that in Rajputana and the adjoining regions Buddhism did not reach at all. In the exhaustive account of Hiuen Tsang of the Buddhist establishments in the whole of India from Kashmir to the Andhra province, there are no references to monasteries in Rajputana and the adjoining regions, where, it seems, Jainism found a firm footing.

It should be noted also that the Buddhist religious movement was not affected by the political changes that took place after the Kushāṇas and the Sātavāhanas. The Buddhist monks and scholars carried on their activities in the solitude of their monasteries and practised the ethical and meditational practices as prescribed in the Piṭakas. Mahāyānism appeared about this time. Its followers continued the ethical and meditational practices of the old system but added to it their own outlook about the final emancipation (Buddha-hood) and the consequential fulfilment of the six *pāramitās* in order to become perfect Bodhisattvas. The attainment of Bodhisattvahood was no doubt a long and arduous process but its followers did not fight shy of the same.

After the Kushāṇas, besides the tribal republics mentioned above, the Śakas ruled over Gujrat and a part of Malwa but their power was on the wane. They fought with the Sātavāhanas and were mostly defeated and ousted from the trans-Vindhyan region. After such political disintegration, the Guptas established their empire. Candragupta I, whose queen was Kumāradevī, a Licchavi princess, crushed the rulers of the small kingdoms and annexed them to his empire.

Samudragupta, son of Candragupta I and Kumāradevī, succeeded his father and carried on military campaigns in the various parts of India.[1] He defeated a number of rulers, among whom nine may be mentioned. They are,

(1, 2) Nāgasena and Gaṇapati Nāga of the Nāga family, the serpent-worshippers were rulers of Padmāvatī (Gwalior state), Vidisā (Bhilsa) and Mathurā.

1. The Classical Age, p. 9

(3, 4) Acyuta and Candravarman ruled respectively over Ahicchatra (near Bareilly) and Western Bengal (Bankura district).

(5, 6, 7, 8, 9) Rudradeva[1], Matila, Nāgadatta, Nandin and Balavarman (location not known). These five tributary kings were stationed on the frontiers of Samudragupta's empire. The nine states may be divided into two groups. The first group comprised the Mālavas (Eastern Rajputana), Mewar, Tonk, and Ktah). Arjunāyanas, Yaudheyas (border of the Bahawalpur state), extending up to Yamunā and included Bharatpur. Of the second group, the Sanakānikas near Bhilsa, Ābhīras (Central India—Ahirawara) between Bhilsa and Jhansi. The remaining three states, viz., Prārjunas, Kākas and Kharparakas (north and east of Bhilsa).

SAMUDRAGUPTA
(320—380 A. D.)

Of the Gupta rulers, the most distinguished was King Samudragupta, whose accession to the throne took place about 320 A. D. Samudragupta ruled over the territory extending on the east up to the whole of Bengal, on the north up to the foothills of the Himalayas (excluding Kashmir), West Madrakas (in the Punjab), on the south from Bhilsa to Jubbalpore and thence along the Vindhya range of the hills. He conquered Araṇyarājyas (forest states). He defeated the twelve rulers of the Deccan, viz., Mahendra of Dakṣiṇa Kośala (Drug, Raipur, Bilaspur, and Sambalpur districts), Vyāghra-rājya of Mahākāntāra (Jeypore state, Orissa), Hastivarman of Veṅgi, 7 miles north of Ellore. In short, Samudragupta's empire comprised the whole of Northern India (except Kashmir), Western Punjab, Sind, Gujrat, highlands of Chattisgarh, and Orissa as far south as Chingleput and probably even further.

Samudragupta ruled directly over his empire through his officials. His suzerainty was acknowledged by the Śaka and

1. Rudradeva, according to Prof. D. C. Sircar, may be identified with Rudradāman II or his son Rudrasena III and Nāgadatta, a king of N. Bengal.

Kushan principalities of the west and the north-west. The Pallavas of the south beyond the Kṛishnā were his feudatories. Ceylon and other islands in the south seas maintained friendly relations with him. He was a follower of Brāhmanism. He died about 380 A. D.

CANDRAGUPTA II

(379/380—413/415 A. D.)

Samudragupta had many sons and grandsons but he was succeeded by his son Candragupta II, who used the epithet "Parama Bhāgavata", i.e., he was a staunch Vaiṣṇava. His chief enemy was the Śaka ruler Rudrasiṃha III of Gujrat and Kathiawad. He defeated Rudrasiṃha III and thereby ended the Saka rule in India.[1]

During the reign of Candragupta II, the Chinese pilgrim Fa-hien (399-414 A. D.) visited India and furnished us with an account of the state of Buddhism in India, so his account has been given in the next few pages.

FA-HIEN

(399-414 A.D.)

During the reign of Candragupta II, Fa-hien came to India and stayed here for 14 years. His main object was to find out the original Vinaya texts, as he believed that the monks of China were not strictly observant of the disciplinary rules, prescribed in the Vinaya Piṭaka. The information, which he has given us, about the state of Buddhism at the time of his visit to this country is scanty and is devoted more to legends connected with the events of Buddha's life-time than to the actual state of the religion in India at his time. On his way to India, in Central Asia and Afghanistan, he observed that the quinquennial assemblies of monks[2] were held in those regions and these lasted for a number of days. He reached Udyāna, where he saw many monasteries with inmates, professing

1. *The Classical Age*, p. 18.
2. Confirmed by Hiuen Tsang (see Wrtters, op. cit, p. 63)

Hīnayāna Buddhism (very likely Sarvāstivāda and Dharmagupta). At Rohi in Afghanistan there were 3000 monks of both Hīnayāna and Mahāyāna schools[1]. In Udyāna there were 500 monks with a large number of lay-devotees. In Gandhāra he saw a *stūpa* and a monastery (built very probably by Kaṇiṣka), the monks of which were Hīnayānists. From Gandhāra he took four days to reach Takṣaśilā, where he found four *stūpas* and the faithful scattering flowers and lighting lamps. In Peshawar there was an alms-bowl, believed to have been used by Buddha. The alms-bowl was kept in a *stūpa* built by an Yueh-chih king (very probably Kaṇiṣka), who also constructed by its side a monastery. In Bhida (Pi-ta) on the bank of the river Jhelum, Buddhism was in a flourshing condition and the monks studied both Hīnayāna and Mahāyāna. From Bhida he passed through a number of monasteries where resided many monks and came down to Mathura, where he noticed 20 monasteries and 3,000 monks.

Fa-hien gives us the interesting information that the Vaiśyas (*Seṭṭhis*) built monasteries and endowed them with fields for cultivation, gardens, orchards, along with the tillers of soil, and cattle. These grants were inscribed on metal-plates so that their successors might act according to the directions given in the plates. A share of the crops and yields of the garden had to be given to the monks for their maintenance. He further observed that the regular duties of the monks were to perform acts of piety, to study the scriptures and to practise meditation.

At Mathura he saw 20 monasteries and 3,000 monks. He noticed also the *stūpas* of Śāriputra, Mahāmaudgalyāyana, and Ānanda, representing *Abhidharma*, *Vinaya* and *Sūtras* respectively. This has been described more accurately by Hiuen Tsang[2] thus :

1. Fa-hien gives in round figures and these also by 100s and 1000s. The figures are evidently fantastic and so these should not be taken seriously but these indicate that Buddhism was existing at the places and give an idea of its popularity.

2. Watters, *op. cit.* I, p. 302

The Ābhidharmikas worship Śāriputra, Samādhists Mudgalaputra, Vinayists Upāli, Bhikṣhuṇīs Ānanda, Śrāmaṇeras Rāhula, and the Mahāyānists the various Bodhisattvas, particularly, Mañjuśrī and Avalokiteśvara and the Prajñāpāramitā (i. e. Prajñā-devī). Then he went to Jetavana (Śrāvastī) and referred to the traditions associated with the famous place. Likewise, he referred to the events of Buddha's time associated with Vaiśāli, Pāṭaliputra, Rājagṛha and Vārāṇasī. In a monastery at Patna he found a copy of the Mahāsaṅghika-Vinaya. He stayed there for 3 years to learn Sanskrit and to copy the Vinaya texts. He then went to Saṅkāsya and saw the Aśoka Pillar. He writes that Aśoka erected a square stone-pillar, 50 cubits high with a lion on its top and images of Buddha in the niches on its four sides. There he constructed a monastery by the side of the pillar. Some heretical teachers disputed with the Śramaṇas about their right of residence at that place. The Śramaṇas, being weak, could not stand against their claim. At this place, there were a thousand monks and nuns, who were provided with their food from a common store. They pursued their studies, some in Hīnayāna and some in Mahāyāna. Fifty yojanas from here, a monastery known as Dragon-vihāra was built. Here Fa-hien stayed up to the end of the rainy season retreat (=varṣā-vāsa). From here he travelled south-east for 7 yojanas and reached Kanauj on the bank of the Ganges. Here he saw two monasteries, the inmates of which were Hīnayānists. He crossed the Ganges and came to Sāketa.

At Sāketa there were only heretics, while at Jetavana (Śrāvastī) there were rest-houses for all travellers, including heretical teachers and Buddhist monks. There were a few followers of Devadatta, who made offerings to the three previous Buddhas but not to Śākyamuni. At Kapilavastu only, very recently some monks had gone there but he noticed that a Śrāmaṇera was the head of the monastery.

Fa-hien then reached Pāṭaliputra, where he came across a distinguished Brāhmaṇa called Rādhasvāmī, who was a Buddhist by faith. He had clear discernment and deep knowledge. He taught Mahāyāna doctrines. He was revered by the king of the country. He was instrumental in popularising Buddhism. Śramaṇas from other countries came to him to comprehend the Truth.

By the side of the Aśoka stūpa, there was a Mahāyāna monastery, grand and beautiful ; there was also a Hīnayāna monastery. The two together had about 600 to 700 monks. Here was another teacher known as Mañjuśrī, who was proficient like Rādhasvāmī. To him flocked Mahāyāna students from all countries.

Every year on the 8th day (i.e. aṣṭamī) of the 2nd month (i. e. Jyaiṣṭha), the rich and prosperous made four-wheeled chariots shaped like a *stūpa*. In the chariot were placed images of various gods, a Buddha image with figures of Bodhisattvas as attendants. There might be 20 such chariots. The local Brahmins invited the Buddhists. The Vaiśyas (i. e. Seṭṭhis) distributed gifts and medicines. The ceremony lasted for two days. Fa-hien stayed in Pāṭaliputra for three years to learn Sanskrit and to copy the manuscripts. He copied the Mahāsaṅghika Vinaya as well as the Sarvāstivāda Vinaya, the Saṃyuktābhidharma-śāstra, Vaipulya sūtras, and Mahāsaṅghika Abhidharma.[1]

From Pāṭaliputra he proceeded to Campā (Bhagalpur), where he found Buddhism in a flourishing state. From Campā he proceeded to Tāmralipti, which had a sea-port. In this country there were 20 monasteries, with monks in every one of them. Fa-hien stayed here two years for copying the Sūtras and drawing sketches of the images of Buddha. From here, at the beginning of winter, he embarked on a large merchant-vessel to Ceylon, reaching there in 14 days. In Ceylon, he stayed for two years, copied the Mahīśāsaka Vinaya, Dīrghāgama, Saṃyuktāgama and the Saṃyukta-sañcaya-piṭaka. He embarked therefrom and reached Java (Javadvīpa) where he stayed for 5 months and then sailed again in a large

1. Nanjio, A Catalogue of the Buddhist Chinese Tripiṭaka, Nos. 399, 466.

Fa-hien refers to Rājagṛha (Indra-śāla-guhā), Śūraṅgama-sūtra and the stūpas at Gaya. He could not go to Vārāṇasī.

merchant-vessel to China. He reached China after a perilous voyage and was received there with great honour.

The time of Fa-hien's sojourn in India from 399 to 414 A. D. coincided almost with the reigning period of Candragupta II, and so it may be inferred that the state of Buddhism in India as per Fa-hien's account may be regarded as authentic.

Fa-hien writes that during the reign of Candragupta II, the people were numerous and happy ; they did not have to register their households (perhaps properties) and appear before any magistrate ; the only conditions were that those, who cultivated the royal land, had to give a portion of their gains, i.e., crops to the king. He does not refer to the lawlessnesses, from which Hiuen Tsang suffered at a later date. He speaks of peace and prosperity and contentment prevailing in the empire of Candragupta II.

I-tsing (671-695) mentions one Śrīgupta, who built a rest-house for the Chinese pilgrims and endowed it with 24 villages. It has been inferred from this that Śrīgupta was a small independent ruler of Magadha about 400/500 years before I-tsing, i. e., about 2nd/3rd century A. D. Hence, Śrīgupta may be regarded as the founder of the Gupta dynasty, which rose to prominence under Candragupta II.

BUDHAGUPTA
(477—496 A. D.)

Candragupta II was succeeded by his son Kumāragupta (415-455 A. D.), followed by the latter's son Skandagupta (455/6-467 A. D.), who conquered the Hūṇas. The Gupta empire extended, at his time, from the Bay of Bengal to the Arabian Sea. The official genealogy of the Later Gupta rulers ignores Skandagupta and traced the line from Kumāragupta, through his two sons Budhagupta (477-496 A. D.) and Narasiṃhagupta. He invited Vasubandhu[1], the famous Buddhist teacher, to be the tutor of his son, Narasiṃhagupta Bālāditya. During Budhagupta's reign the Hūṇas under Toramāna and Mihirakula made inroads into his territory

1. Re. Vasubandhus, see infra ; see also p. 23 above.

while the Maitrakas of Kathiawad Peninsula, who were formerly Senāpatis of the Gupta rulers, asserted their independence and adopted the title of Mahārājās. Their example was followed by other such feudatories. Budhagupta was succeeded by his brother Narasiṃhagupta.

NARASIMHAGUPTA, HIS SONS AND GRANDSONS (497-570 A. D.)

Narasiṃhagupta took the title of Bālāditya. He triumphed over Mihirakula, the persecutor of the Buddhists, and became a great patron of Buddhism. After him, there was political disintegration. In the 6th century, the Maitrakas asserted their independence and became Maharājās of Valabhi. Śilāditya I Dharmāditya (606-612 A. D.), according to Hiuen Tsang, built a large Buddhist temple with artistic structure and installed in it images of seven Buddhas and held a religious assembly every year, to which the Buddhist monks of all countries were invited. He offered to every monk three robes and the minor requisites (*parikkhāras*). His pious works were continued by his successive generations.[1]

VASUBANDHUS

It is a baffling problem to solve how many distinguished monk-scholars bore the name of Vasubandhu. In Kaṇiṣka's Council, the date of which cannot be later than the 2nd century A. D., Kātyāyaṇīputra is said to have composed the *Jñānaprasthāna-sūtra* and other scholars its six *Pādas* (supplements) (see above). It is said that Vasubandhu, a noted figure in the Council and a prodigy, summed up the contents of the *Abhidharma-vibhāṣā-śāstra*, in the form of *Kārikās* called the *Abhidharmakośakārikā* and later wrote a *bhāsya* (commentary) on it. In the *Bhāṣya*, he argued that *Ākāśa*, *Pratisaṃkhyā-nirodha* and *Apratisaṃkhyā-nirodha* held by the Sarvāstivādins as real and positive are not correct. It was argued that *ākāśa* (space) meant that in which there was no obstruction ; on its analogy it was contended that the two *nirodhas*

1. Watters, *op. cit.*, II, p. 242

also meant, similarly, absence of all kinds of impurities (*kleśass* and *upakleśas*). The Asaṃskṛtas are not real and positive (vide *Kośa*, II, 64, pp. 282, 284). From this conception, it is not a very wide jump to the Vijñaptimātratā view of the Yogācāra-Vijñānavādins. Hence, on the basis of these arguments, it may be concluded that the earlier Vasubandhu,[1] brother of Asaṅga lived about the 2nd century A. D. Hence, this Vasubandhu was different from the teacher Vasubandhu of Candragupta II and his son Bālāditya, whose reigning period was 500 to the middle of the 6th century A. D. Hiuen Tsang writes that Narasiṃhagupta was the last Gupta ruler, who defeated Mihirakula. He referred to him as a great patron of Buddhism and builder of the grand Saṅghārāma of Nālandā.

One Vasubandhu was born in Peshawar. His father was Kauśika and mother Bilindi. He was the second of the three brothers. Hiuen Tsang saw on the east side of Pārśva's chamber the old house of Vasubandhu, the author of the *Abhidharma-kośa-śāstra*, a book of 600 aphorisms, being the "Disquisitions on the treasure of Buddhist philosophy." It was sent from Ayodhyā to the Kashmir Vaibhāṣikas, who were very pleased with it. In the meantime he became a follower of the Sautrāntika school and in his *Bhāṣya* he criticised the Kashmir Vaibhāṣikas. This book was written in Ayodhyā during the reign of Vikramāditya or his son Bālāditya. It was refuted by Saṅghabhadra, who composed two treatises, in which he refuted those views and defended the Vaibhāṣikas. Vasubandhu dealt with both Mahāyāna and Hīnayāna philosophy. The book was translated into Chinese twice by Paramārtha and Hiuen Tsang. This Vasubandhu, writes Hiuen Tsang, should not be confused with the 21st Patriarch, by which he evidently meant that Vasubandhu, who was associated with the tradition of the Kashmir Council held under the auspices of Kaṇiṣka. He is the author of the *Abhidhārma-prakaraṇa-pāda-śāstra*. A contemporary of Vasubandhu, Ācārya Manoratha composed also a

1. F. Frauwallner, *On the date of the Buddhist Master of Law Vasubandhu*, (Rome) 1951. See also, Winternitz, *History of the Buddhist Literature*, pp. 356-363, 611-614, etc.

Vibhāṣā-śāstra. Hiuen Tsang (I, p. 291) records that in Sākala there was a Buddhist monastery with about 100 monks, all of them were of the Hīnayāna school. In this monastery P'usa Vasubandhu composed the *Paramārtha-satya-śāstra.*

It is also necessary to bring in here the information given by Hiuen Tsang (Watters, I, p. 361) that to the south-east of Ghoṣitārāma in Kauśāmbī (near Allahabad) there was a two-storeyed building with an upper chamber made of old bricks, where lodged Vasubandhu and composed the *Vijñapti-mātratā-siddhi* (Nanjio : Vidyāmātra-siddhi), the first Chinese translation of this book was made by Bodhiruci (520 A. D.), the second by Paramāɹtha (560 A. D.) and the third by Hiuen Tsang (661 A. D.).

Vijñapti-mātratā-siddhi has another title, which in Chinese means "the śāstra refuting the existence of both 'matter and mind'. This book has been compressed into small philosophical poems entitled *Viṃśatikā* and *Triṃśikā*, edited by Prof. Sylvain Lévi. It has an explanatory commentary on the nature of 'mind and matter.' In Ming collection, it is named *Mahāyāna-Laṅkā-sūtra-vidyā-mātra-śāstra.* Asaṅga composed also the *Yogacaryā-bhūmi-śāstra.*

King Narasiṃhagupta's son was Kumāragupta, who defeated the Maukhari king Iśānavarman, and ruled from 550 to 570 A. D. Kumāragupta's son Dāmodaragupta also defeated another Maukhari king, but he died in the battle. Dāmodaragupta's son Mahāsenagupta is described in the *Harṣacarita* as the ruler of the territory from Mālava to Bengal. Mahāsenagupta revived partially the glories of the Guptas but he had to suffer misfortunes. The Maitraka king Śīlāditya I Dharmāditya took possesslon of a considerable portion of Mālava, the Kalacurī king Śaṅkaragaṇa occupied Ujjayinī in 595 A. D. and Śaśāṅka asserted his independedce in Bengal. After such discomfitures, Kumāragupta and Mādhavagupta had to take shelter in the court of Prabhākaravardhana of Thaneswar, whose mother Mahāsenguptā Devī was a sister of Mahāsengupta. The two sons remained with Rājyavardhana, son of Prabhākaravardhana and then with his brother Harṣavardhana.

Post-Gupta Period

After the dissolution of the Gupta empire in the 6th century A. D., a number of states not only asserted their independence but also tried to gain control over other countries. Śaśāṅka of Bengal was a Mahāsāmanta (= feudatory chief) of Mahāsenagupta of the Later Guptas. He freed himself from the yoke of Mahāsenagupta[1], and extended his dominion from Bengal to Mahendragiri mountain in the Ganjam district in the Andhra Province. He killed king Rājyavardhana by alluring him with false promises.

Buddhism during the reign of Śaśāṅka in Bengal

Śaśāṅka the Gauḍ-rāja was no doubt a cruel persecutor of Buddhism and the Buddhist recluses, and it is said, that he did not spare even the sacred images of Buddha of Bodh-Gaya[2] and that he went to the length of uprooting the Bodhi tree of Gaya. It is rather surprising that inspite of evil designs of Śaśāṅka, the people of Bengal including the Brahmins extended due courtesies and respect to the Buddhist recluses as also to the followers of the Jaina and other faiths. The Indians in general by their innate nature were very tolerant and did not hesitate to show due regard to the religieux of non-Brāhmaṇic sects. In Śaśāṅka's days, according to the figures furnished by Hiuen Tsang[3], it is apparent that there were monasteries and religieux all over Bengal. The figures are as follows :—

Areas	Number of monasteries	Number of religieux	Sects
Kajaṅgala (region round Rajmahal)	6/7	300	Sammitīya
Puṇḍravardhana (= North Bengal)	20	3,000	Hīnayāna and Mahāyāna

1. The *Classical Age*, p. 74

2. In Beal's *Records of the Western World*, II, p. 121 appears this information :—Śaśāṅka failed to remove the image of Buddha of Bodh-Gaya, and so he enclosed it with a brick wall. He destroyed the stone, which had a foot-print of Buddha, set up by Aśoka.

3. Watters, *op. cit.*, II, p. 183f

Karṇasuvarṇa (= West Bengal, Murshidabad, etc.)	3	2,000	Sammitīya
Tāmralipti (= Tamluk, Midnapore)	10	1,000	not mentioned
Samataṭa (=Baṃlādeśa)	30	100	Sthavira

It may be stated that the neighbouring province, Assam had neither Buddhist monasteries nor religieux. The poeple of Assam were mostly Śaivas as also its king Bhāskaravarman, who, however, had to attend the religious assemblies held under the auspices of King Harṣavardhana.

Rise of the Maukharis (Assam)

Puṣyavarman[1] was the earliest historical ruler of Kamrup, in the Brahmaputra valley of Assam. There were three other kings of this family, ruling in different places. Yajñavarman, Śārdulavarman and Anantavarman ruled in the neighbourhood of Gaya in the 6th century A. D.[1] The Maukhari king Iśānavarman ruled from 550 to 576 A. D. The Later Guptas challenged the power of the Maukharis, after Iśānavarman, in the 6th century A. D. The genealogy of the Varmans stands thus :—

1. Puṣyavarman (350 A. D.)[2]

   ....

   ....

8. Bhūtivarman = Vijñānadevī

   (founder of the family ; after disintegration of the Guptas, he asserted independence). Kamrup was one of the feudatoıy states of Samudragupta in the 4th/5th century A. D. Kamrup in Bhūtivarman's time extended up to the west of North Bengal.

   ....

   ....

1. *The Classical Age*, p. 89 ; a royal seal found at Nalanda describes Puṣyavarman as the lord of Prāg-jyotiṣa and had the title Mahā:aādhiraāja, *Ibid.*, p. 89

2. *PHAI.*, (5th edition), p. 603

11. Susthitavarman = Śyāmādevī

12. Supratiṣṭhitavarman   13. Bhāskaravarman

Bhāskaravarman was a contemporary of Harṣavardhana and ruled about the 7th century A. D. Bhāskaravarman was defeated by Mahāsenagupta, who was then the king of Gauḍa. The incident (for details, see the *Classical Age* p. 120) in connection with Hiuen Tsang shows that he became ultimately an ally of Harṣavardhana. Though Bhāskaravarman was a Śaiva by faith, he attended the religious assemblies held by Harṣavardhana at Kanauj and Prayāg.

Another Branch of the Maukharis

(*South Bihar & Uttar Pradesh*)

Another branch of the Maukharis ruled in South Bihar and Uttar Pradesh and that they became very powerful is known from their seals and Inscriptions. The genealogy of this family is as follows :—

1. Mahārāja Harivarman = Jayasvāminī
2. ,, Ādityavarman = Harṣaguptā
3. ,, Iśvaravarman = Upaguptā
4. Mahārājādhirāja Iśānavarman = Lakṣmīvatī (554 A. D.) claimed victories over the Andhras, the Gauḍas, and took the title of Mahārājādhirāja
5. ,, Sarvavarman = Indrabhaṭṭārikā
6. ,, Avantivarman
7. ,, Su.......

These Maukhari chiefs ruled since the time of Budhagupta, i. e. after the decline of the Guptas in the early 6th century A. D. They wielded great power till the latter half of the 6th century A. D.

Grahavarman, the eldest son of Avantivarman, married the princess Rājyaśrī, sister of Rājyavardhana and Harṣavardhana in or shortly before 606 A. D.[1] The marriage was regarded as a bond uniting the two dynasties of Maukharis and Puṣpabhūtis. Śaśāṅka made an alliance with Devagupta, king of Mālava, against Grahavarman of Kanauj and imprisoned Rājyaśrī in Kanauj. The Maukharis were ultimately ousted from Kanauj by the Puṣpabhūtis, of which Harṣavardhana was the outstanding ruler.[2]

Puṣpabhūtis

The kingdom of Thanesvar was founded by Puṣpabhūti. In *Harṣacarita*, Bāṇa does not speak of the consecutive successors of Puṣpabhūti and begins his account with king Prabhākaravardhana of this family. He is given the title of Paramabhaṭṭāraka Mahārājādhirāja. Prabhākaravardhana had two sons : Rājyavardhana and Harṣavardhana, and one daughter Rājyaśrī[2], married to Grahvarman, mentioned above. On receipt of the information about the death of Grahavarman and the imprisonment of Rājyaśrī, Rājyavardhana marched against the king of Mālava and routed the Mālava army. He was, however, allured by Śaśāṅka by false promises and was killed by him. On hearing this news, Harṣavardhana took a vow of vengeance against Śaśāṅka. He made an alliance with Bhāskaravarman. Śasāṅka died between 619 and 637 A.D. Jayanāga was the next Gauḍarāja, who was overthrown by Bhāskaravarman.

The Pushpabhutis

(*Kingdom of Thanesvar*)

The earliest historical kings of the Puṣpabhūti dynasty were

Mahārāja Naravardhana
|
„ Rājyavardhana
|
„ Ādityavardhana = Mahāsenaguptā Devī
|
Paramabhaṭṭāraka Mahārājādhirāja Prabhākaravardhana = Yaśomatī Devī
|
Rājyavardhana | Harṣavardhana | Rājyaśrī

1. *The Classical Age*, p. 79
2. *Ibid*, p. 71

The first three kings of this dynasty flourished between 500 and 580 A. D. They were very likely feudatory chiefs of the Hūṇas, the Guptas or of both. According to the *Harṣacarita*[1] (Cowell 101), Prabhākaravardhana was a lion to the Hūṇa deer, a burning fever to the king of Sindhu, a troubler of the sleep of the Gurjaras (Rajputana), a fever to the elephant of Gandhāra, a destroyer of the skill of Lāṭas, an axe to the creeper, which is the goddess of fortune (i.e. sovereignty) of the Mālavas.[2]

Prabhākaravardhana heard the news of the death of Grahavarman by the king of Mālava, making his sister Rājyaśrī a widow. Rājyavaradhana proceeded with his army against the king of Mālava and routed his army. Śaśāṅka, probably an ally of the king of Mālava allured Rājyavardhana with false hopes and then he treacherouslly put him to death (*HC.*, p. 187, Beal, *op cit.* I,210). Harṣavardhana with his ally Bhāskaravaraman continued his march for a few days and met Bhaṇḍi the milirary general and learnt from him that Rājyaśrī, out of despair, had gone to the Vindhya forest along with her retinue. Harṣa met Rājyasrī just at the moment when she was going to mount the funeral pyre. He returned with his sister to the camp on the bank of the Ganges.

Harṣavardhana & *Harṣacarita*

Bāṇa was a contemporary of king Harṣavardhana and hence his date may be placed towards the end of the 6th century and the beginning of the 7th century A. D. Bāṇa's account of the reign of Harṣavardhana is no doubt full of poetic effusions but still some facts may be elicited from them. The account given in his *Harṣacarita* (edited by Mm. P. V. Kane) is given here briefly :—

Prabhākaravardhan *alias* Pratāpaśīla was a descendant of thc

1. Harṣacarita, Ch. IV, 1-2 commentary Hūṇa-hriṇa-keśarī Sindhu-rāja-jvara Gurjara-prajāgaro Gāndhāradhipa-gandha-dvīpakūṭa-pākalo Lāṭa-paṭva-paṭaccaro Mālava-lakṣmi-lata-parśh pratapaśīla iti prathita-pora nāmā Prabhakaravardhana nāmā rajādhirājaḥ.

2. Anthenticity of the claims made in this passage remainis to be verified.

Puṣpabhūti family. He fought against the Hūṇas of the North-west, king of the Gurjaras (of Rajputana), and the lords of Sindhu, Gandhāra, Lāṭa and Mālava. He was a worshipper of the Sun. The first son of this king was Rājyavardhana and the second son Harṣavardhana, and the third was the daughter Rājyaśrī. Prabhākarvardhana married Yaśomatī. Queen Yaśomati's brother Bhaṇḍi handed over his son as a companion of the two princes. King Prabhākaravardhana procured from the king of Western Mālava his two sons named Kumāragupta and Mādhavagupta. They accompanied the two princes as their shadow. When Rājyaśrī came of marriageable age, she was given in marriage to Grahavarman, son of Avantivarman of the Maukhari family of Kanauj and she went to her husband's place. When Rājyavardhana had grown up to a strong youth able to hold arms, Prabhākaravardhana sent him along with his ministers and devoted feudatory chiefs to the north against the Hūṇas. Harṣavardhana accompanied them for some distance, and when they entered the Kailāsa region, he remained behind and disported himself in hunting excursions.

In the meantime, a courier came from the capital with the news that Prabhākaravardhana was seriously ill. Harṣa returned in hot haste, riding day and night, and reached the capital on the third day after the death of his father and his mother's mounting the funeral pyre, and the necessary ceremonies were being performed by various sects.

About a fortnight after this sad event, Rājyavardhana after conquering the Hūṇas, although he was wounded in the fight. He became very much worried and desired to retire from the worldly life. At this moment he received the sad news that his brother-in-law Grahavarman of the Maukhari dynasty of Kanauj was killed by the machinations of the king of Mālava and that his sister Rājyaśrī was put in prison in Kanauj, in the words of Bāṇa, "with fetters on her feet like the wife of a brigand." The Mālava king also planned to attack Thanesvar. Rājyavardhana started immediately with his army accompanied by Bhaṇḍi's thousand cavalry against the king of Mālava and routed his army, but unfortunately he was seduced by the Gauḍa king Śaśāṅka with false temptations and was killed by him treacherously.

Siṃhanāda, the faithful military general of the Vardhana family, incited him to avenge his brother's death, but he could not do anything without assuming the royal power. As there was no other alternative, Harṣavardhana ascended the throne after worshipping the Sun. At this time, he was approached by a courier from Bhāskaravarman of Kamrup, offering to be an ally of him and expressed his desire to join him in his expedition against Śaśāṅka, who was also his enemy. He brought also the news that his boy-friend Kumāragupta, a son of the Mālava king, laid siege on Kanauj and rescued his sister Rājyaśrī from the prison. Rājyaśrī, however, out of despair proceeded to the Vindhya forest. Harṣa asked Bhaṇḍi to march against the Gauḍa king Śaśāṅka and he himself went to the Vindhya forest in search of his sister. After roaming for several days, he met Vyāghraketu, son of the Bhil chieftain Sarahaketu, who introduced him to a young Bhil called Nirghāta, the military general of the Bhils. He informed Harṣa that the recluse Divākaramitra, a convert from Brāhmanism to Buddhism could help him. Harṣa remembered him as a friend of Grahavarman. Harṣa went to the hermitage of Divākaramitra and found him surrounded by many followers and students of various sects. Just then Harṣa was informed by a Buddhist bhikṣu that his sister was going to immolate herself in a funeral pyre. He met her there and learnt from her that when she was released from the prison by Kumāragupta, she heard the news of the death of Rājyavardhana, and so out of grief, she was going to burn herself in a fire. At the intercession of Harṣa, she wanted to join the Buddhist Saṅgha of bhikṣuṇīs. Harṣa requested her to wait a little, as he would also join the Buddhist Saṅgha after destroying the Gauḍa king Śaśāṅka.

The above account of Harṣavardhana, as given by Bāṇa in his *Harṣacarita*, may be supplemented by the statements of Hiuen Tsang whose sojourn in India took place from 629 to 645 A.D. i.e., during the reign of Harṣavardhana (606-642 A.D.).

Hiuen Tsang records that there were in Kanauj 100 monasteries and 10,000 Buddhist monks and nuns. Regarding Harṣavardhana, he writes that the king carried on wars continually for 6 years and enlarged his kingdom as also his army and reigned in peace for about 30 years. He was just in his administration and punctilious in the discharge of his duties. He prohibited the use of animal food, taking of life, under severe penalties. He erected thousands of *stūpas* on the bank of the Ganges and provided rest-houses for travellers. He built monasteries at the sacred Buddhist sites. He regularly held the quinquennial assemblies, which were also attended by Bhāskaravarman, king of Kāmarūp, showing thereby his sympathetic attitude to Buddhism. Harṣavardhana gave away to the religieux everything except the materials of war. Once a year he summoned the Buddhist monks and provided them with food and other requisites for 21 days. He furnished the chapels with the necessary articles and decorated the central halls of the monasteries. He brought the monks together for discussions, giving rewards for merit. The monks, observant of the rules of the Order strictly, and thoroughly proficient in theory and practice, were placed by him on a high platform, and religious discourses delivered by them were appreciated by him. He merely honoured those monks, who were not learned but were observant of the moral and disciplinary rules of the Order. Those, who neglected the observance of the rules of the Order, were removed from his presence as well as from the country. He carried on visits of inspection throughout his dominion. At the royal palace 1,000 monks and 500 Brahmins were provided with food. The king divided his day into three periods, one of which was devoted to the work of administration and the other two to religious works.

The Chinese pilgrim, on his way back to China, paid a visit to Kamrup at the request of king Bhāskaravarman and the advice of Śīlabhadra, the head of the Nalanda Monastery. At this time an assembly was going to be held at Kanauj. Harṣavardhana asked Bhāskaravarman to send back the pilgrim ; he refused to do so and wrote that he could take his head but not

CANISIUS COLLEGE LIBRARY
BUFFALO, NY

the pilgrim. Harṣa got enraged and asked the king to send his head per bearer. Bhāskaravarman became submissive and came to Kanauj along with the pilgrim, and offered his apology. He also attended the assembly held at Kanauj. Harṣa then went to Prayag for the periodical distribution of gifts to the religieux.

Harṣa is said to be the author of three works, viz., Priyadarśikā, Ratnāvalī and Nāgānanda.

Harṣavardhana was not only a distinguished ruler but also an admirer of literary writers. He was a patron of learning and his court was adorned with poets like Bāṇa, Mayūra and Divākara. He himself, according to the testimony of Bāṇa and I-tsing, was the author of the drama *Nāgānanda*, which is a versified and dramatised form of the story of the Bodhisattva Jimūtavāhana. Though its topic is Buddhistic, it attempts to bring about a harmonious relation between Gaurī and Garuḍa. In the colophon of Nāgānanda is mentioned "Nāgānandam iti nāṭakaṃ. Śrī Harṣadevena kṛtaṃ samāptaṃ." (Vide Bibliotheca edition of Prof. Vidhuśekhara Bhattacharya).

The other two books *Ratnāvalī* and *Priyadarśikā* are very similar to each other. These were composed almost on the same lines as of Kālidāsa's *Mālavikāgnimitra*, having nearly the same plot. In his *Kuṭṭaṇimatam*, Dāmodaragupta ascribed the authorship of the *Ratnāvalī* to a royal author. In the colophon of the *Ratnāvalī* also appears "Iti Harṣadevasya kṛtiḥ samāpteyaṃ Ratnāvalī nāma nāṭikā. (Vide edition of M. R. Kale).

Hiuen Tsang gives a detailed account of the various places in India, where he noticed Buddhist monasteries and monks, mentioning the sects, to which the inmates belonged. Prof. Lamotte has collected all the facts and figures in his *Histoire du Bouddhisme indien*, 2 Vols (Louvain, 1958) from the Chinese original of Hiuen Tsang's Records. His references to the Chinese texts have been replaced by references to Watters' Yuan Chwang for the convenience of general readers.[1]

1. See the present author's book on "Buddhist Seets in India" (1970).

HARṢAVARDHANA
(606-643 A. D.)

It was during the reign of king Harṣavardhana that Hiuen Tsang came to India and furnished us with a detailed account of the state of Buddhism all over India. He has given also an account of king Harṣavardhana's interest in Buddhism, and so it behoves us first to make a survey of hismilitary campaigns and the extent of his empire. His reign began at a critical time when the undermentioned kingdoms asserted their independence in the post-Gupta period :—

(1) Gandhāra and Sindh in North-western India and in Western India.

(2) Lāṭa, Mālaya and Gujrat in the south-west ; the king of Mālava put to death Grahavarman and imprisoned his queen Rājyaśrī, sister of Rājyavardhana and Harṣavardhana.

Harṣavardhana carried on his military campaigns against

(1) Śaśāṅka of Bengal for rescuing his sister Rājyaśrī It was only after Śaśāṅka's death, he could conquer some portions of Bengal. Śaśāṅka died soon after cutting the Bodhi-tree of Gaya, a little before 637 A. D.

(2) Valabhi but he could not meet with success ;

(3) Pulakeśin of the Narmadā region but perhaps, Harṣa had a total failure ;

(4) The Lāṭas, Gurjaras and Mālavas ; he was not successful ;

(5) Magadha was conquered only after Saśāṅka's death and carried on his victorious campaigns up to Orissa and Koṅgoda and that also after 641 A. D., i. e., towards the close of his reign.

Basing on the data supplied by Hiuen Tsang, it may be stated that Harṣa's dominion did not substantially extend beyond Uttar Pradesh, Bihar, Bengal and Orissa.[1]

Reverses met by Buddhism in Kashmir
(5th century A.D. and later)

Some time after the Kushan rule, Buddhism fell on evil days.

1. See the Classical Age, p. 112.

Tāranātha[1] reports that a *mleccha* faith called Ardho appeared for the first time in India and secured many followers. The *mleccha* religion was perhaps confined to Makha[2] and did not spread to Kashmir. Tāranātha then refers to the royal families of Saitā and Turuṣka,[3] stating that king Turuṣka ruled in Kashmir for 100 years as a Dharmarāja, but destroyed the vihāras of Magadha and put the monks of Nalanda to flight.[3] Then Mahāsammata, son of a Turuṣka, brought under one rule the kingdom of Kashmir, Tukhāra and Ghazni, and helped the spread of Mahāyāna teaching. The *Mañjuśrīmūlakalpa* refers to one Turuṣka, who ruled over the Uttarāpatha up to the gate of Kashmir.[4] He was a pious Buddhist and during his reign Mahāyānism, particularly the teaching of *Prajñāpāramitā*, spread in the north. After him appeared Mahāturuṣka, who also erected Buddhist temples and monasteries and propagated the *mantra* and worship of Tārādevī.[5] In the *Mañjuśrīmūlakalpa*, the Turuṣka king is referred to as "Gomi"[6] and his successor as Buddhapakṣa, who, according to both Tāranātha and *Mañjuśrīmūlakalpa*, made good the loss suffered by Buddhism on account of the vandalism of his predecessor by re-erecting several temples and monasteries.[7] Tāranātha adds that he erected many *Caityas* in Ghazni[8] and invited to Kashmir Vasubandhu's disciple Saṅghadāsa, who founded the Ratnaguptavihāra in Kashmir and spread the Mahāyāna teaching there for the first time.[9]

---

1. Tāranātha, *op. cti.*,p. 79 ; Tib. p. 64, l. 3 : *dus de tsam. nak. la. klohi. chos daṅ par byaṅ yin te.*

Tib. *Kla. klo* may be *mlecchas* or *Tukhāras*. Cf. *Mmk.*, p. 621-2, Schiefner, pp. 78, 304. They killed cows by uttering *Bismilla.*

2. *Makha* is mentioned by Bu-ston (II, p. 171) as one of the countries where Buddhism spread anh disappeared. It is perhaps Mecca (Schiefner, *op. cit.* p. 80) ; the founder of the religion is Mamathar (=Muhammad) and the teacher is called Paikhama (Paigambar ?).

3. Schiefner, pp. 103 ff.

4. *Mmk.*, p. 623

5. *Ibid.*,

6. Gomimukhya, Gomiṣaṇḍa. Cf. Gollas of Kosmas Indikopleustes and his coin-legends : jayatu vṛṣa, jayatu vṛṣaddhvaja. Stein, I, p. 43 fn.

7. *Mmk.*, pp. 619-620 ; Schiefner, p. 94-5.

8. Schiefner, p. 103.

9, *Ibid.*, p. 135.

The Turuṣka lord[1] was very likely the well-known persecutor of Buddhism, Mihirakula, whose accession to the throne is placed in 515 A. D.[2] The Chinese traditions as also Kalhaṇa's *Rājataraṅgiṇī* speak of his cruel nature, and his vendetta against the king of Siṃhala. Perhaps there was some sort of provocation from the Buddhists,[3] which incited him to pull down the Buddhist temples and monasteries all over Northern India, and to massacre the monks. The inhuman cruelties and depredations perpetrated by the White Huṇa ruler were, according to Yuan Chwang,[4] checked by Bālāditya of Magadha, but there was none in Kashmir to restrain his atrocious acts of destroying *stūpas* and monasteries and exterminating even the lay-adherents of Buddhism, until his complete overthrow by Yaśodharman. Following Tāranātha, Bu-ston and *Mmk.*, and Kalhaṇa tell us that his son Baka(=Mahāsammata of Tāranātha, Buddhapakṣa of *Mmk.* and Bhadanta of Bu-ston), who brought Kashmir, Tukhāra and Ghazni under one ruler, atoned for his predecessor's sins by erecting *caityas* and monasteries for the Buddhists.

It is written by both Kalhaṇa and Tāranātha that Buddhism had a serious set-back in Kashmir after the reign of Kaṇishka II. Kalhaṇa (I. 180-1, 199) relates that after Nāgārjuna, during whose time "the Bauddhas obtained preponderance in the land by defeating in disputation all learned opponents." There were excessive snow-falls, killing the Bauddhas ; and king Nara, on account of the crime of a Buddhist monk, flew into rage and "burnt thousands of Buddhist vihāras" while Tāranātha informs us that after Nāgārjuna left N. India and went to the south, the religion of the Mlecchas prospered.[5]

Though it is difficult to make out a dependable account of these traditions, it may be assumed that after the Kushāṇas, a Turuṣka royal family ruled over Kashmir. It was very likely the family of Turki Sāhis, who held sway over Northern India for

1. Tib (p. 64) Saita daṅ Turuṣkaḥi 'Gyal-poḥi rigs. ri rnams byuṅ ṅo.
2. Schiefner, p. 94 ; Bu-ston II, p. 119.
3. Kalhaṇa, I, p. 294 ; Bu-ston, II, p. 137.
4. Watters, I, pp. 288-289.
5. Schiefner, pp. 94-5

about a century from the 3rd century A. D. The Turki Sāhis were supporters of Buddhism, and so the religion must have prospered under their rule. It must have been sometime after the disappearance of this royal family that Mihirakula came to the throne of Kashmir and massacred the Buddhists. Towards the end of his life, Mihirakula became a worshipper of Śiva and "established pious observances in the lands occupied by the impure Daradas, Bhauṭṭas and Mlecchas" (I. 312-6). Mihirakula's son recompensed his father's cruel acts by restoring some of the ruined temples and monasteries.

Narendrāditya Khiṅkhila and Pratāpāditya

A few generations later Narendrāditya Khiṅkhila came into power (I, 347). There are a few coins bearing the legends Deva Sahi Khiṅgila, Śrī Narendra, establishing the historicity of this king. Narendrāditya was a worshipper of Śiva and made endowments for the Brāhmaṇas. He was succeeded by his son Yudhiṣṭhira I. The people of Kashmir deposed him and brought Pratāpāditya, a relative of Vikramāditya, from outside and placed him on the throne (II. 5). This new line of rulers worshipped Śiva, the last king of the dynasty being Tunjina.

Jayendra and Saṃdhimat

Tunjina was succeeded by Vijaya, belonging to a different family. Vijaya's son Jayendra had a long and glorious reign, excepting that it was stained by the attempt to kill his very popular minister Saṃdhimat, who ultimately ascended the throne of Kashmir. Saṃdhimat ruled for a long time, built Śiva temples and practised Śaiva-sādhanās. His end was also unhappy, as he was compelled by the people to retire.

Meghavāhana

Meghavāhana, a descendant of Yudhiṣṭhira I, was brought by the people from Gandhāra and placed on the throne (III. 2). He had a soft corner for Buddhism, hailing, as he did, from Gandhāra, a predominantly Buddhistic country. His queen Amṛtaprabhā of Prāgjyotiṣa is said to have built for the use of

Buddhist monks a lofty vihāra called Amṛtabhavana (III. 9), to which a reference is made by Ou K'ong. Her *guru* was a Tibetan, a native of Leh (i.e. Ladakh). His other queens also built monasteries and stūpas, of which the one built by Khādanā is located at Khādanīya about 4 miles below Varāhamūla on the right bank of the Vitastā."[1]

Meghavāhana cherished also some Aśokan ideas inasmuch as he himself was not only keen about observing the *dharma* but compelled his neighbouring kings to abstain from killing living beings (III. 27). With him are associated some *Avadānas*, which extol his extreme sacrifices for the sake of others. His services to Buddhism were so great that the people attributed to his pious deeds an atonement for the sins of his predecessor Mihirakula (III. 57). The long rule of this line of kings was only once interrupted by the reign of the poet Mātrigupta for four years as a viceroy of Vikramāditya of Ujjayinī. The kings were mostly worshippers of Śiva and supporters of Brāhmanism, but during the reign of Pravarasena II, the king's maternal uncle, Jayendra, built the Jayendra-vihāra[2] and placed in it a colossal image of Buddha, known as Bṛhadbuddha. In this vihāra, Yuan Chwang stayed and received instructions in the various śāstras.[3]

During the reign of Yudhiṣṭhira II, his ministers constructed vihāras and caityas (III. 380-1), one of which was Skandabhavana-vihāra, built by Skandagupta.[4] During the reign of Raṇāditya, one of his queens called Amṛtaprabhā placed a fine statue of Buddha in the vihāra built by a queen of Meghavāhana (III. 464). Raṇāditya was succeeded by his son Vikramāditya, who was a devotee of Śiva. His minister Galuṇa had a vihāra built in the name of his wife, Ratnāvalī (III. 476). The last king of this line was Bālāditya.

1. Stein, Intro, I, . 74n.
2. It offered shelter to king Pārtha and his queens (V. 428), but destroyed later by Kṣemagupta.
3. Stein, I, p. 103n.
4. It is located by Stein at Khandabavana, in Srinagar (Stien, I p. 105n.

Lalitāditya Muktāpīḍa
(middle of the 8th century A.D.)

Bālāditya was succeeded by his son-in-law, Durlabhavardhana, whose queen set up the Anaṅgabhavana-vihāra (IV. 3), referred to by Ou K'ong as Ānanda or Ānaṅga vihāra.[1]. The king himself as also his successors were mostly Viṣṇu-worshippers. The noted king of this line was Lalitāditya-Muktāpīḍa, who successfully fought against Yaśovarman (IV. 134). It was after this war that he created, for the better management of his vast dominion, a few high offices, which were filled up mostly by the Sāhis and other princes (IV. 143). He brought under his control a large portion of Northern India as also his neighbouring tribes, the Tukhāras, Bhauṭṭas and Daradas (IV. 165 f. ; cf. 1. 312). The king showed his highest veneration to Viṣṇu and then to Śiva and lastly to Buddha. He built Viṣṇu and Śiva temples and also Buddhist vihāras and stūpas (IV. 188, 201-3). He erected the "ever-rich Rājavihāra with a Catuḥśālā (refectory), a large Caitya and placed in it a large image of Buddha[2] (IV. 200). In one of these vihāras lived Bhikṣu Sarvajñamitra, author of the *Sragdharāstotra.* The king was a nephew of the king of Kashmir. His chief minister was Caṅkuna, who put up two vihāras, one of which was very lofty and contained golden images of Buddha (IV. 211, 215). His son-in-law Iśānacandra, a physician, built also a vihāra (IV. 216). Caṅkuna was known as a Tantrik Buddhist for the acquisition of some magical powers, by which he charmed the king. At the king's request, he imparted the charms to him and took in return the image of Buddha, which had been brought by Lalitāditya from Magadha. Both Kalhaṇa and Ou K'ong testify to its existence.[1]

Jayāpīḍa

One of the notable kings of this line was Jayāpīḍa. Kalhaṇa records that he owed the throne to a Caṇḍāla called Śrīdeva,

1. *Rajat. IV.* 262 ; Stein I, p. 144n.
2. Stein (II, pp. 302-3) has traced some remains of this vihāra at Paraspur. The image was spared by king Harsa. See *infra.*

who killed the usurper Jajjā (IV. 475) and remained always guarded by the fierce Caṇḍālas (IV. 516), specially at night. He bore an antipathy to the Brāhmaṇas, whom he treated very harshly (IV. 640 ff.). He loved learning and assembled learned men in his Court (IV. 848-9). He worshipped both Viṣṇu and and Buddha, and set up Viṣṇu temples, Buddha images and a large vihāra (IV. 484, 507-8) in his capital Jayapura. Very probably it was during his reign that Śāntiprabha lived in Kashmir along with his disciples Puṇyakīrti, Dānaśīla, Viśeṣāmitra, Prajñāvarman and Ācārya Śūra.[1]

Avantivarman (855 A. D.)

Jayāpīḍa was followed by Avantivarman, who along with his ministers showed veneration to Viṣṇu and Śiva. Like Jayāpīḍa, he patronised learning, and prohibited the killing of living beings (V. 64). During his reign Bhaṭṭa Kallaṭa and other Siddhas appeared in the country (V. 66). This seems to indicate that about this time Tantric Buddhism made some headway in Kashmir. The king was a devotee of Viṣṇu, a fact disclosed to his minister Śūra only at the time of his death (IV. 124-5).

Śaṅkaravarman and Pārtha

Avantivarman's son, Śaṅkaravarman, was a Śiva-worshipper. He was miserly and exacted too many taxes from the people. He was uncharitable to the learned and used to speak Apabhraṃśa and not Sanskrit. His queen Sugandhā, who ruled for two years, was a devotee of Viṣṇu but had to spend her last days in a Buddhist convent called Niṣpālaka-vihāra (V. 262). Another king of this line called Pārtha was dethroned through ministerial intrigues and took shelter in the Jayendra-vihāra, where the inmates of the monastery supplied him and his queens with food (V. 428). It was about this time that the Brāhmaṇas regained their ascendancy and were able to place on the throne a king of their own choice, viz., Yaśaskara, who was, however, not of royal descent.

1. Schiefner, p. 204; Bu-ston II, p. 161.

Yaśasakara (939-948) and Kṣemagupta (950-8)

Yaśasakara's rule war marked by an effective administration of justice and equal treatment to the high and low without any discrimination of caste and creed.

Kṣemagupta, one of his successors, burnt down the Jayendra-vihāra (see above) and took the brass of the images of Buddha, and utilised the stores of the Vihāra for erecting a Śiva temple. He appropriated also the 32 villages, which belonged to the vihāra (VI. 172-3, 175).

Saṃgrāmarāja (1003-1028) and his successors

By the marriage of Kṣemagupta to Diddā, the Sāhi's granddaughter, the Sāhi princess, since the reign of Lalitāditya Muktāpīḍa, became more influential in the Kashmir court.

Towards the end of her life, Diddā was able to place her nephew Saṃgrāmarāja on the throne of Kashmir. Saṃgrāmarāja sent a large army to help Sāhi Trilocanapāla (VII. 47-8) but to no effect, as the Sāhis were completely routed by the Turuṣkas under Hammira. From now on the Sāhi princes took shelter in the Kashmir court and acquired great influence during the reign of Ananta, the grandson of Saṃgrāmarāja (VII. 146 f.). One of the Sāhi refugees was Rudrapāla, who became the right-hand man of king Ananta. He fought against the Daradas and defeated them (VII. 175, 375). At this time an epidemic carried away Rudrapāla and many of the Sāhi princes (VII. 178). After Ananta, his son Kalasa came to the throne. He also had four princes of the Sāhi family as his best companions[1] (VII. 274), of whom Vijja was the most trusted and favoured. Towards the end of his life, he destroyed the copper-image of Sūrya and appropriated without fear the brass images of the viharas (VII. 696).

Harṣa (1089-1101)

Kalasa's son was Utkarṣa, who was followed by his son Harṣa, a highly gifted prince and a master of all branches of learning (VII. 610). He is called by Kalhaṇa a Turuṣka and is said to have supported the Turuṣka merceneries (VII. 1095,

1. Vijja described himself as a Rājaputra, (VII. 325, 836.)

1149). Being a Turuṣka he was a *mleccha*[1] by faith, as otherwise he could not have destroyed the Hindu and Buddhist temples. Kalhaṇa writes that "divine images of gold, silver and other materials rolled about even on the street, which were covered with night-soil" (VII. 1093). He spared from spoliation only the temple of Raṇasvāmin and Mārtaṇḍa and spared the two colossal statues of Buddha, one of which was at Parihāsapura built by king Lalītāditya and the other at Srinagar, known as the Bṛhad-buddha at the request of his favourite singer, Kaṇaka and the śramaṇa Kuśalaśrī (VII. 1095-8). Tāranātha records that duiing his reign three distinguished teachers of Buddhism, viz., Śākyamati, Śīlabhadra and Yaśomitra lived in Kashmir. Yaśomitra was a king's son and is well-known by his *ṭikā*[3] on Vasubandhu's *Abhidharmakośabhāṣya.* The Kashmirian Harṣa was a debauch and a cruel and greedy king, and his reign, as Kalhaṇa reports, was marked by unjust exactions, and attempts at conquest of the neighbouring tribes. Vijayamalla, his chief adviser, rebelled against him and joined the Daradas, who were then ruled by Vidyādhara Sāhi, but his attempts to humiliate Harṣa were of no avail (VII. 911).

Jayasiṃha (1128-49)

King Harṣa was succeeded by Uccala, a descendant of Kāṃtirāja, another brother of Diddā, the Sāhi princess. Jayamatī, queen of Uccala, built two monasteries, one of which was in honour of her sister Sullā (VIII. 247-8). This, it is said, was completed by king Jayasiṃha (VIII. 3318), the illustrious ruler, who succeeded Uccala. King Jayasiṃha patronised literary men and there was once more a revival of learning in Kashmir. He looked after the Maṭhas and Vihāras, the first of which that attracted his attention was the one built by his queen Ratnādevī (VIII. 2402, 2433). His chief minister Rilhaṇa was also very pious. He showed his veneration to

1. See Stien, I, p. 353 n. Tāranātha (p. 128) speaks of one Śrīharṣadeva, as having propagated *mleccha* faith but he was of an earlier date, being a contemporary of Dignāga.

2. Schiefner, *po. cit.*. p. 205.

3. Edited by Prof. Wogihara of Japan.

both Śiva and Buddha, and erected a monastery in memory of his deceased wife Sussalā (VIII. 2410-1). Sussalā must have been a great devotee of Buddha, as she erected, on the site of the famous Caṅkuna-Vihāra, which had been destroyed. It had a magnificent establishment for the Buddhist monks (VIII. 2427). Cintā, wife of Jayasiṃha's commander Udaya, adorned the bank of the Vitastā by a monastery consisting of five buildings (VII. 3352-3), and Dhanya, one of the ministers, commenced the construction of a vihāra in honour of his late wife (VIII. 3343-4). Evidently, therefore, the reigning period of Jayasiṃha marked a revival of the Buddhist faith in Kashmir.

THE SAHIS OF KASHMIR

One of the Gilgit manuscripts[1] mentions in the colophon the name of *Śrīdeva Sāhi Surendra Vikramāditya Nanda,* and the spot of this ms. find is in the Dard country, where the Sāhis later on found their asylum. Dr. H. C. Ray has dealt exhaustively with the history of the Sāhis of Afghanistan and the Punjab,[2] and has furnished us with a list of coins, bearing the names of the rulers. It will be observed that "Śrīdeva" formed a part of all these names. It seems that the title "Vikramāditya" occuring in the manuscript got currency in Kashmir since the reign of Pratāpāditya, who was a nephew of Vikramāditya.

Prof. Sylvain Lévi[3] thinks that "the Turk dynasty of Kipin is identical with Al-birūṇī's Shahiyas of Kabul and Kalhaṇa's Sāhi dymasty. The Sāhi princes, according to the testimony of Al-birūṇī, were Turks of Tibetan origin and were zealous followers of Buddhism. The Buddhist dynasty of Sāhis continued without interruption up to the ninth century, when they were replaced by a Brāhmanic dynasty, bearing the same title, and which dynasty existed up to the 11th century."[4]

Kalhaṇa furnishes us with the following account of the career of the Sāhis in Kashmir :—

1. See *Bhaiṣajyagurusūtra,* edited by the present author, p. 32.
2. *Dynastic His. of N. India,* Vol. I, ch. ii. See above.
3. *JA.*, 1895, p. 381.
4. See Al-birūṇi (Sachau), II, pp. 10 ff.

During the reign of Śaṅkaravarman, took place the appearance of Lalliya Sāhi, who ruled over the region between the Daradas and the Turuṣkas, and located his capital at Udabhāṇḍapura (IV. 152-5). During the reign of Śaṅkaravarman's son Gopālavarman, the minister Prabhākaradeva, proficient in the *Kākhorda*[1] witchcraft, carried on expeditions against the Sāhis of Udabhāṇḍapura but later on he bestowed the same on Lalliya's son Toramāna (V. 233). The Tantrin soldiers and Dombas came into prominence about this time (936-7 A.D.). The Sāhi's grand-daughter, Diddā, was married to king Kṣemagupta. She became afterwards the queen regent, and during her regime, her commander-in-chief Yaśodhara led an expedition against the Sāhi ruler Ṭhakkana and captured him (VI. 230-1). Towards the end of her life Diddā made some pious foundations, one of which was a Vihāra with a large Catuḥśālā meant for use by the Kashmirians and the Daiśikas. She was succeeded by her brother's son Saṅgrāmarāja on the throne of Kashmir (1003-1028 A.D.). Kalhaṇa tells us that it was during the reign of Saṅgrāmarāja that the Sāhi kingdom of Trilocanapāla was destroyed by the Turuṣkas under Hammira (VII. 669), and it was brought to an end during the reign of the following king Ananta (1028-63). During the reign of Harṣa, one of his ministers incited Vidyādhara Sāhi, the ruler of Dards, to fight against Harṣa.

The Sāhis had their first seat on the west and south of the Dard country, and then with the disappearance of their independence they were scattered, some Sāhi princes taking to service under the kings in the Kashmir court and some preferring to lead independent lives in the mountainous regions of north Kashmir. The entry of the Sāhi princes into Kashmir court commenced in the reign of Lalitāditya Muktāpīḍa, who for the first time brought under his rule the Tukhāras, Daradas and Bhauṭṭas (see above). Thenceforward, the Sāhi princes, by marriage alliances or otherwise, became closely connected with the Kashmir royalties. Diddā, the Sāhi princess managed

1. See *Bhaiṣajyagurusūtra*, (Gilgint Mss.) pp. 13, 20.

to place on the throne of Kashmir her brother Saṅgrāmarāja, who was followed by his sons and grandsons. Some of the kings of this line had Sāhi princes as their ministers, who wielded great influence over the king and the country. Stein[1] infers from the Lahore Ms. of the *Rājataraṅgiṇī* that 'Sāhi' was the title of the Dard rulers, and these account for the name, Vidyādhara Sāhi, the ruler of the Dards, during the reign of Harṣa. From the above account of the Sāhis, it is apparent that the Sāhi princes lost their independent rulership over the region round about Udabhāṇḍapura but wielded a great influence on the administration of the Kashmir State. About the 10th or 11th century, some Sāhi princes managed to create small independent States for themselves in the mountainous regions of Citral, Yasin, Gilgit, etc., generally known as the country of the Dards.

Testimony of the Chinese Pilgrims

Some of the Buddhist edifices mentioned by Kalhaṇa were noticed by Yuan Chwang and Ou K'ong.[2] Yuan Chwang on his way to Kashmir passed through Hushkara-Vihāra (mod. Uskur, near Baramula) and stayed for one night at the Jayendra-vihāra, built during the reign of Pravarasena.[3] He noticed four Aśokan topes, each containing relics of Buddha's body. He saw 100 monasteries, but the religion followed in these, he remarks, was mixed, hinting thereby that the people worshipped both Buddha and Śiva. He remained for two years in the king's palace, where scores of clerks were engaged by the king to copy for him the Buddhist scriptures under the supervision of Yaśa.[1] Very likely these are the copies, which formed the basis of the Chinese Tripiṭaka of the 6th or 7th century.

The next Chinese traveller of some importance to visit Kashmir was Ou K'ong, who was also known as Dharmadhātu. He came to Kipin in 759 A. D. through the Kabul valley and

1. See his note in p. 339.
2. *L' itinarane d' Ou K'ong* (751-790) translated and edited by Lévi and E. Chavannes in *Journal Asiatique*, 1895, pp. 341-384.
3. See above.

Gandhāra. He lived in Kashmir for four years and studied Sanskrit, as well as the Vinaya texts in seven sections from three teachers. In the convent of Moung-ti or Muṇḍi-Vihāra, he learnt the Śīlas and studied the Vinaya Piṭaka of the Mūlasarvāstivādins. He refers to the following seven other Buddhist establishments besides the Moung-ti-vihāra :[1]

(1) Amitābhavana (2) Anaṅga or Ānandabhavana (3) Ki-tcho (4) Nao-ye-le (5) Je-je (6) Ye-li-t'e-le (7) K'o-toen

He noticed more than 300 monasteries in the kingdom and a large number of stūpas and images. After four years' stay, he went to Gandhāra and resided in the monastery of Jou-lo-li —a monastery carrying the name of the king, its founder, belonging to the line of Kaṇishka.

ARCHÆOLOGICAL SURVEY AND EXPLORATIONS

In 1908 Sten Konow was deputed by the Government of India to search for inscriptions and objects of archaeological interest in Kashmir. In course of his survey, he noticed at the village Uskur (Hushkapura) the ruins of a stūpa about 400 yards to the west of the village and took it to be the one referred to by Ou K'ong as Moung-ti Vihāra.[2] He expected that the other two places, Zukur and Kanespur, if excavated, would bring to light similar ruins. He noticed at Khādaniyār the ruins of the monastery built by queen Khādanā (see above) and discovered a stone inscription in a Brahmin's house at Āṅgom (Hāḍigrāma). It is written in Śāradā characters in Sanskrit and its translation runs thus :—

"Salutation to the exalted noble Avalokiteśvara. Salutation to thee, the Lord of the world, who has become a light to the three worlds, who putest an end to transmigration, who art a moon of delight to the world."

"Formerly a Vaidya Ulhaṇadeva by name made a spotless

1. Watters, I, p. 258-9.

2. See his Notes on a Tour in Kashmir, 1908, p. 2 ; *ASR.*, 1915-16, p. 50. In the beginning of the 8th century a stūpa and a vihāra were built here by Lalitāditya Muktāpīḍa (Kallhaṇa, iv, 180).

shrine of wood, an abode for the lord of the world in the vicinity of the Gaṅgeśvara temple. After these had been burnt by king Siṃha through the will of fate, Rāmadeva, son of Kulladeva, who was devoted to him (i.e., Avalokiteśvara) made yonder shrine excellent with burnt bricks. Anno 73, the 5th day of the bright half of Mārgaśīrṣa."

In this inscription Prof. Sten Konow traced the reference made by Kalhaṇa to the burning of Hāḍigrāma in the region of Jayasiṃha (VIII. 1586). He read the date as 4273 corresponding to the 16th November 1197. Before his survey Paṇḍit Kasi Ram also had traced some ruins of temples in this village (Stein, I, p. 50 n.).

In the *Archaeological Survey Reports of 1915-16*, Rai Bahadur Daya Ram Sahni published an account of the explorations carried on by him. He discovered Buddhist monuments at Parihāsapura, Purāṇādhiṣṭhāna (mod. Pandrethan) and Hushkapura, while Prof. Vogel found remains of a Buddhist stūpa near a village called Malangpura, three miles south-west of Avantipura.

Paṇḍit R. C. Kak, while in charge of the archaeological department of Kashmir, collected several images of Buddha, Bodhisattvas, Buddhist gods and goddesses, fragments of stūpas and railings, and several earthen jars and pots, some of the large sized jars bearing inscriptions in early Gupta characters. But his greatest discovery was the ruins at Harwan (Shaḍhrad-vana), said to have been once the seat of Nāgārjuna. In Paṇḍit Kak's work, the *Ancient Monuments of Kashmir*, he furnished us with an account of the sculptures, architectural style, artistic values of the finds, of which the following were Buddhistic :—

(i) the temple at Pandrethan, the old capital founded by Aśoka and referred to by Kalhaṇa as Śrīnagarī (pp. 114-6) ;

(ii) the stūpa of the mediaeval period at Malangpura, first noticed by Prof. Vogel, on which the remnants of sculptured reliefs depicted 'a furious monster pursuing a man who is flying precipitately before it" (p. 125) ;

(iii) the stūpa, monastery and caitya at Parihāsapura, the erection of which is attributed to Lalitāditya and his ministers Caṅkuna. From the coins discovered in the monastery, it is apparent that it existed up to the time of the king Vinayāditya, Vigraha and Durlabha (pp. 145-8) ;

(iv) the stūpa at Uskur, the erection of which is attributed to Huvishka (2nd century A. D.), on the ruins of which, a second stūpa was built by Lalitāditya in the middle of the 8th century A. D. (pp. 152-4) ; and

(v) the monastery and stūpa at Shaḍhradavana (mod. Harwan). Here Paṇḍit R. C. Kak discoverd a stūpa, bases of chapels and a fiight of steps connecting the stūpa and the chapels, and a large number of brick-tiles. The remarkable feature of the tiles is that they are prepared with a view to present Jātaka scenes or certain scenes from Buddha's life, the other motifs being designs of flowers, aquatic plants, flying geese, girls, musicians, etc. The tiles are numbered in Kharoṣṭhi figures, the use of the Kharoṣṭhi script showed that the buildings were erected before the 5th century A. D. when the Kharoṣṭhi characters ceased to be in use (pp. 109 ff.).

The latest and epoch-making archaeological discovery in Kashmir is the find of several manuscripts deposited in a stūpa at Gilgit, the country of the Dards and the seat of the later Sāhi rulers, the name of the ruler being very likely Śrīdeva Sāhi Surendra Vikramāditya Nanda, whose queens were Śamidevī Trailokyadevī and Vihali. One of the mss. was the gift of this king while there were several others given away by the local devotees like Śulkhina, Śulivarja, Maṃtoṭi, Maṅgalaśūra, Ārya Devendrabhūta. The scribe of the king's ms. was Arya Sthirabuddhi and the collaborator Narendra Datta.

The discovery of the mss. was first announced by Sir Aurel Stein in the *Statesman* on the 24th July 1931. He reported that some "boys watching flocks above Naupur village, about two miles west of Gilgit Cantonment, are said to have cleared a piece of timber sticking out on the top of a small stone-covered mound. Further digging laid bare a circular chamber within the ruins of a Buddhist stūpa filled with hundreds of small votive stūpas and relief plaques common in Central Asia and Tibet."

"In course of the excavation, a great mass of ancient manuscripts came to light closely packed in what appeared to have been a wooden box." "The palaeographic indications of some of the mss. suggest that they might date back to the sixth century A.D."

M. Hackin also paid a visit to the spot and furnished us with the following information (*Journal Asiatique*, 1932, pp. 14-15):

"The place of discovery is situated about 3 miles to the north of Gilgit in the mountainous region. There are four stūpas with square basements placed side by side.

The hemispherical domes of the stūpas A and B are well preserved and it is the third stūpa C which has yielded the mss. This stūpa C has double basements, the lower of which measures 6 metres 60 cm. on each side and the next receding to about 60 cm. on all the four sides. The height of this stūpa is 12 to 15 metres. The diameter of the chamber containing the mss. is 2 metres 40 cm. In the centre of the chamber there were the five wooden boxes, the fifth containing the other four, in which were kept all the mss."

In 1938, Paṇḍit Madhusadan Kaul was deputed by the Kashmir Government to carry on further excavations at the site but he could not discover anything of importance in stūpa A, B, and D but he found 3 or 4 more mss. in stūpa C.

The script used in the mss. is mostly Upright Gupta of a date little later than those used in the manuscript-remains found in Eastern Turkestan[1] and similar to the script found in the Bower mss.[2] The script of the Bower mss. is assigned to the 6th century A. D., and so the Gilgit mss. may also be dated in the 6th or at the latest tn the 7th century A.D. This

1. Edited by A. F. R. Hoernle.
2. See Hoernle's Intro. to the Bower Ms., chap. III.

date takes us to the reign of kings preceding Lalitāditya, who ruled about the middle of the 8th century. The Sāhis were then ruling over the region round about Udabhāṇḍapura up to Gilgit and were occasionally coming into conflict with the Kashmir kings, ultimately succumbing to Lalitāditya in the middle of the eighth century. One would be tempted to identify the king mentioned in our ms. with a son of Vikramāditya, son of Raṇāditya. According to Kalhaṇa, Vikramāditya was succeeded by his brother, Bālāditya ; so it may be suggested that 'Vikramāditya Nanda' of the ms. was related to Vikramāditya and his name was 'Surendra' and his title 'Śrīdeva Sāhi'. This prince probably ruled over the Dard country during the reign of king Bālāditya in Kashmir.

It will be observed that the kings, queens and ministers of Kashmir commencing from Meghavāhana patronised Buddhism more than any other faith, and a large number of Vihāras was built at this time. After a short period, the Chinese travellers visited the country. The mss. copied for Yuan Chwang were, therefore, of the same time as our mss., and it is noteworthy that the Gupta scripts[1] preserved by the Chinese for transcribing the Sanskrit *mantras* in their Chinese translation[1] are similar to those found in the Gilgit mss.

Résumé

In the survey of the traditonal history of Buddhism in Kashmir as given above, there may be chronological errors, or exaggerations of exploits, but the fact remains that from the time of Aśoka, the Buddhist monks penetrated into the valleys of Kashmir and found there a place where they could carry on their missionary activities successfully. It will be observed that the evangelical spirit of the Buddhist monks was a vital factor in the spread of Buddhism. They generally selected, as their fields of activities, those places where cultured religious beliefs had not yet secured a firm footing. Kashmir, therefore, along with its neighbouring regions, offered in those early days a

1. Vide the scripts (block prints) in the Taisho edition of the Chinese Tripiṭaka.

fruitful field to the Buddhist missionaries backed, as they were, by Emperor Aśoka. The original inhabitants of Kashmir were designated by the term 'Nāgas', who were mainly believers in serpent worship—a belief popular in those days almost all over India, including Ceylon. Trade and colonization by the Indian population must have followed the footsteps of the hardy and self-sacrificing monks. This is indicated in the story that many lay-devotees went to Kashmir from Benares, and that the wealth of the country was increased by the cultivation of saffron at the instance of Madhyāntika.

Kashmir offered good opportunities for study and culture and consequently for the growth of Buddhist monasteries as centres of learning. The Sūtra and Vinaya Piṭakas did no doubt take shape in Magadha in pre-Aśokan days, but the development of the Abhidharma Piṭaka must be delegated to a post-Aśokan date and to regions outside Magadha. Kashmir appears to have been the earliest centre where this supplement to the Sūtra Piṭaka emerged ; it is for this reason that the Kashmirian Buddhist monks were referred to mostly as Ābhidharmikas. The Vibhāṣā-śāstras might have been expository commentaries in a general form, but it must be admitted that these texts dealt more with Abhidharma topics than with comments on the Sūtras. The Abhidharma texts of the Sarvāstivādins, a gist of which has come down to us in the masterly treatise of Vasubandhu, the *Abhidharmakośa* and *Bhāṣya* and its *ṭīkā* written by a Kashmirian prince, Yaśomitra, reveal what a large amount of contributions of a subtle character had been made to the Indian stock of knowledge relating to the analysis of mental states of a Yogin, The appearance of the Ātmaka theorists, the Vātsiputrīyas, is also associated with Kashmir, showing thereby the large amount of latitude allowed by the country for philosophical discussions and expressions of new thoughts. Still more remarkable is the harmonious existence of Buddhism and Śivaism side by side without acrimonies and persecution. These existed together in many outlands, and their existence in Kashmir is another such instance. The kings themselves showed their veneration to Śiva, Buddha and even Viṣṇu altogether by erecting temples dedicated to the three deities, and even allowing their queens and ministers perfect freedom in the expression of their veneration to any one of the three deities. One king might have had more than one queen or minister, belonging to different nationalities, professing different faiths ; and it was not unoften the case that the king acceded to the wishes of their queens and ministers of different religious leanings by endowing temples for all the three prevailing faiths. It is evident from the traditional history sketched above that from the time of Aśoka up till the 12th century, Buddhism existed side by side with Śivaism and Viṣṇuism and enjoyed glorious periods at intervals. The credit of Kashmir lies not only in its being a cultural centre for Buddhistic studies but also in being a centre for the dissemination of Buddhist and Hindu cultures in countries abroad. In ancient days Gandhāra and Kashmir were treated as one country and so it cannot be said how far one or the other country was responsible for the spread of Indian culture. But in the post-Kushān period, Kashmir had a direct communication with Tukhāra, Khotan and Tibet, and therefore, much of the Indian culture and religion propagated in those contries was due to the paṇḍitas of Kashmir.

The Kushān rule was followed by an ouslaught on thc Buddhists by Mihirakula, which was partially recompensed by his son Baka. The career of Buddhism in Kashmir was not very happy till the reign of Meghavāhana. From his time it enjoyed a glorious period till the time of Jayāpīḍa. In Avanti-varman's time (855 A.D.) the Brāhmanic faith became ascendant, putting into shade the Buddhist religion up to the reign of Kṣemagupta, who burnt Buddhist vihāras and utilised the brass of the Buddha-images for other purposes. From now on till the 11th century, the Buddhists fell on evil days and all the kings were anti-Buddhistic in spirit. The last of them was Harṣa (1089 A.D.), who cherished the '*mleccha*' faith, and destroyed the Hindu and Buddhist temples. In the reign of Jayasiṃha, there was a revival of Buddhism under the patronage of Jayamatī, queen of Uccala. The Turki Sāhis, according to Al-biruṇī, professed the Buddhist faith and were in power up to the 9th century. Their successors, the Brahmanic Sāhis supported Śivaism and had little regard for Buddhism.

Thus, it is apparent that Buddhism passed through good and evil days from the reign of Aśoka up to the 12th century. It did enjoy glorious periods at intervals, when several stūpas and vihāras were erected for them. To the existence of these monuments the Chinese travellers bear eloquent testimony. The archaeological explorations unfortunately have not yet been carried on extensively, but it may safely be surmised that such explorations, if carried on, will reveal the ruins of many a stūpa and vihāra referred to by Kalhaṇa.

CHAPTER II

MAHAYANIC TRACES IN THE NIKAYAS

Though Mahāyāna Buddhism appeared as a new phase of the religion about the 2nd or 1st century B. C., along with a vast literature on the subject, it may be stated that in the Nikāyas, dated about 487 B. C. and compiled from Buddha's discourses in the First Buddhist Council. There are, however, definite traces that Bhagavān Buddha had at the back of his mind the philosophical outlook of Mahāyāna Buddhism. Prof. Keith[1] and later Prof. Venkataraman[2] and Bhikkhu Jñānānanda[3] have drawn our attention to this fact. Let us take into consideration a few of such sayings :—

In the *Mūlapariyāya-sutta*[4] (i. e. the basic discourse on Buddhism) it is stated that a person regards earth as earth and establishes a relation with it, e. g., in earth, from earth, my earth etc. In the same way, he does with the other four elements (*mahābhūtas*)[5], the various gods as gods, the different kinds of meditation as meditation and establishes a relation with them as indicated above. Even an Arhat regards Nibbāna as Nibbāna and thinks that he has attained Nibbāna. Bhagavān Buddha or the Tathāgata, however, knows earth etc. but does not establish a relation with them (paṭhaviṃ paṭthaviṃ na maññati, etc.) because the Tathāgata is free from all ideas or conceptions while an Arhat is not, hence, this is the difference that exists between an Arahat and a Tathāgata. In other words, earth, water, meditation etc. are merely worldly phenomena

1. *Buddhist Philosophy* (1930)
2. *The Central Philosophy of Buddhism* (1954)
3. *Concept and reality* (1971).
4. *Majjhima Nikāya* 1, Sutta 1 ; *Kathāvatthu*, ix. 2. Cf. *Aṣṭasāhasrikā Prajñāpāramitā* (ASB) p. 9
5. Scientifically earth, water, fire and air can never be separated, earth has watery element and heat ; likewise water has earthy element and heat and so on. At the present state of science, an element is a conglomeration of atoms or ions, hence it is also a composite. Bhagavan Buddha, being omniscient, realised this fact.

with a fleeting existence and do not exist in unchangeable reality.

In the *Alagaddupamā-sutta* (=Water-snake simile)[1] Buddha taught that all *dhammas* (=religious practices), the various *śāstras* (*navāṅgaṃ satthusāsanaṃ*), even all meditational practices of a bhikkhu are mere aids like a raft with the help of which as well as by physical exertion, a person crosses the stream and after reaching the other shore, throws away the raft. Likewise, a bhikkhu, by means of several ethical and meditational practices, becomes a sotāpanna, etc. and after reaching those stages[3] throws away the various practices and strives to attain the highest knowledge, i. e., becomes *sambodhiparāyaṇa*, i. e. he gets rid of his notions, good or bad, and then become destined to attain *sambodhi*, which is beyond all conceptions (*kalpanābahirbhūta*).

In the *Aggi-vacchagotta sutta*[2] Bhagavān Buddha does not give answer to Vacchagotta paribbājaka's questions : sassata loka or asassata loka, i. e. the world is eternal or non-eternal ; antavān or ananta loka (limited or limitless world) and so forth. Buddha then explained it by a simile : Take, for instance, a fire burning off a faggot, when the faggot is exhausted and the fire is extinguished, where does the fire go. Likewise, the Tathāgata is composed of *saṃkhāras* (constituents of an worldly being) and when the *saṃkhāras* are eschewed by him, he disappears in the unknown, unknowable, unfathomable (*ananuvejjo*), i. e. infinity.

Prof. Keith[4] writes that all the world of appearance is summed up by Buddha in the term *pañca upādānakkhandhā* or in one word *saṃkhāras* = ideas and presentations, to which Buddha attached only physical value.

In the *Kevaddha sutta* (*Dīgha Nikāya*, i. 222f.) it is stated that all the elements (*mahābhūtas*), and mind or name and form (*nāmarūpa*) are comprehended by an Arahat with the help of

1. M. N. i. Sutta No. 22
2. M. N. i. „ No. 72
3. M. N. i. p. 488.
4. Buddhist philosophy, p. 47

the law of causation (*paṭicca-samuppāda*) that they are substanceless, unreal (*sabbe dhammā anattā*)[1] as this is essential for attaining Nibbāna. The highest meditation (samāpatti) named Akiñcāññāyatana[2], which means the complete absence of kiñcaṇas (impurities), which are counted as three, viz., attachment, hatred and delusion (rāga, dosa, moha) ; when counted as seven the additional four are I-ness or Mine-ness (māna), wrong views (diṭṭhi), mental and physical impurities (kilesas); and misconduct (duccarita). An Arhat is khīṇāsavo, khīṇa-saṃsāro (free from impurities and free from repeated existences).

In the *Majjhima Nikāya* (i. 141-2) it appears that those, who are in the first stage of sanctification (*sotāpannā*) have no chance of retrogression from that stage and they are destined to attain the highest emancipation (sambodhi)[3]. Further, those wno are faithful followers of the Dhamma are also destined to attain sambodhi.

In the *Majjhima Nikāya* (i. 235) it is stated that those who have attained mental freedom (*vimuttacittā*) and the excellent object (*sadattho*) and perfect knowledge (*samma-d-aññā-vimutto*) may by the highest exertion of insight (*anuttariya-dassanena*) and highest path (*anuttariyenapaṭipadā*) and devote themselves to the worship of the Tathāgata and develop belief in Him as the Teacher of the highest truth are also destined to attain *sambodhi.*

In the *Majjhima Nikāya* (i. 140), it is stated that all the gods (devā), viz., Indra, Brahmā, Prajāpati etc. will not be able to trace the mind (*viññāṇa*) of the Tathāgata as it is unknowable (*ananuvejjo*), unfathomable.

In the *Saṃyutta Nikāya* (III. p. 142) there are also many other passages referring to the Tathāgata. Now let us take up the other Mahāyānic terms, *suññatā* (voidnes, devoid of all attributes), *animitta* (devoid of characteristics) and *appaṇihita* (absence of desire for worldly objects), which are also non-

1. M. N. I p. 299
2. Cf. Dhammapada 421 : Suttanipāta 643 : akiñcanam anādānaṃ tam ahaṃ brūmi Brāhmaṇam.
5. Sabbe te sotāpannā avinipātadhammā niyatā sambodhiparāyaṇā.

existent. These terms occur in the *Dīgha Nikāya* (III. 219 ; cf. *Majjhima Nikāya*, III. 104, 109—Suññatāsutta).

In the *Saṃyutta* (II. 267) and *Aṅguttara* (I. 112) *Nikāyas* occur the statement that the Suttantas delivered by the Tathāgata are deep, supramundane and closely connected with *suññata.*[1]

In the *Saṃyutta Nikāya* (III, pp. 140-2) while giving a discourse on the nature of the unconstituted (*asaṃkhata*), Bhagavā gave the following illustrations :—

(*i*) The Ganges, a large river, carries on the surface of its water mass of foam, which is useless and insubstantial.

(*ii*) Likewise the bubbles seen on earth during the autumnal rains are equally useless and insubstantial.

Like the foam and bubbles are the material constituents, viz, matter (rūpa), feeling (vedanā), perception (saññā), impressions (saṃkhārā) and consciousness (viññāṇa).

A wise person, after eradicating from his mind clinging, hatred and delusion (*rāga, dosa, moha*), then by practising the lower and higher meditations (*jhānas, samāpāttis*) of voidness (*suññatā*), signlessness (*animitta*) and unaspiration (*apaṇihita*), in short, all that is needed, he can realise the unconstituted.

The closing stanza of this section runs thus :—

Dasabala-sela-pabhavā nibbāna-mahāsamudda-pariyantā/
Aṭṭhaṅga-magga-salilā Jinavacana-nadī ciraṃ vahati//

(Transl. Issuing out of the mountain of ten powers (Buddha), water of eightfold path flows for ever upto the Nibbāna-ocean.)

In another passage of the same Nikāya (III, p. 120) appear the following words :—

Dhammaṃ hi passato maṃ passati. Maṃ passato dhammaṃ passati. (Transl. He who realises my teaching visualizes me, and he who visualizes me realises my teaching.)

These instances distinctly show that there were Mahāyānic traces in the *Nikāyas*.

In the *Saṃyutta Nikāya* (II, p. 17 ; MKV., p. 269) : Kaccāyanagottasutta, Bhagavā said to Kaccāyana, in reply to

1. Ye suttantā Tathāgata-bhāsitā gambhīrā lokottarā suññatāpaṭi-saṃyuttā.

his enquiry "What is sammādiṭṭhī = right view, that there are two extreme views, of which one considering from the standpoint of the origin of the world (*loka-samudayaṃ*) upholds the view that the world exists (*atthitā*), and the second, considering from the standpoint of the decay of the world (*loka-nirodhaṃ*) upholds the view that the world does not exist (*natthitā*). The Tathāgata teaches that the two extreme views should be eschewed and the middle view should be accepted (majjhime Tathāgato deseti) i.e., neither *atthitā* nor *natthitā*.

In the *Milinda-pañha* (p. 420) it is admitted that King Menander became a Hīnayāna monk and even attained *arhathood*. He discussed with Nāgasena certain topics relating to Mahāyāna. The topics discussed are

(*i*) the conception of Buddha and Bodhisatta.

(*ii*) the fourfold problem about the existence of the Tathāgata after death and its inexplicability.

(*iii*) Does Buddha accept worship (*pūjā*) ? Is the offering made in the name of the Tathāgata, does he accept the offerings ?

Nāgasena replied,

(*i*) Take for instance the earth produces corn, the earth does not enjoy it while it is consumed by the people. Likewise, by worshipping Buddha, one gets rid of his attachment, hatred and delusion (*rāga*, *dveṣa*, *moha*) and attains *sotāpatti* stage of sanctification and subsequently all the *maggas* and *phalas*, i.e. the four stages of sanctification and their fruits. Ultimately he becomes an Arhat, even a Paccekabuddha, and it is not improbable that he will become Bodhisatta like Maitteya and in due course, attain even Buddhahood.

Apart from the scattered instances, as collected above, there is one sutta in the Majjhima Nikāya called the Ariya-pariyesaṇā sutta (26), which has almost verbatim similarity with the Ājñāta-kauṇḍiṇya Jātaka of the *Mahāvastu*, an avowed text of the Lokottaravādins, an offshoot of the Mahāsaṅghikas, the precursors of Mahāyānism. By way of illustration, a few common stanzas are presented here :—

In the Ariyapariyesaṇā sutta, Brahmā, lord of the Sahā world (Sahampati) addressed to Bhagavā in these words :—

Prāturahosi Magadhesụ pubbe
dhammo asuddho samalehi cintito
apāpur' etam amatassa dvāraṃ
sunantu dhammaṃ Vimalenānubuddhaṃ.

(Formerly. in Magadha appeared wrong teachings thought out by impure persons ; open the door to immortality realised by the Pure, and let the people listen to it).

While in the Mahāvastu the corrsponding stanza is as follows :—

Prādurahosi samalehi cintito
dharmo aśuddho Magadheṣu pūrve
apāvṛtaṃ te amatasya dvāraṃ
śṛṇantu dharmaṃ Vimalenānubuddhaṃ

Brahmā said further

Uṭṭhehi Vijitasaṅgāmo
satthavāha anaṇa vicara loke
desassu Bhagavā dhammaṃ
aññātāro bhavissant ī ti.

(Rise, O Conqueror of the war of miseries, leader of men, free from all impurities, wander forth in this world, O Bhagavā, preach your teaching, there will be persons, who will comprehend it).

In the Mahāvastu the corresponding stanza is,—

Utthehi Vijitasasaṃgrāma
tvaṃ anṛṇaṃ vicara loke
deśehi Sugata dharme
ājñātāro bhavissanti.

Bhagavān Buddha was not close-fisted, i.e., he had no *ācariya-muṭṭhi*. He said that he had preached his *dhamma* absolutely, i.e., without any reserve and without bringing in any extraneous matter (*anantaram abāhiraṃ*). (M. P. S. in D. N. II, p. 100). He laid bare the highest truth (*paramattha-sacca*) as he had realised but his listeners, i.e., the Śrāvakas comprehended his exposition from their own angle of vision. The Theravādins understood it primarily as ethical practices, and secondarily as meditational processes. Nibbāna was the end of all impurities, and it was their goal.

The Mahāsaṅghikas, however, conceived of Bhagavān Buddha quite differently. They expressed their conception by this stanza :—

Sabbābhibhū sabbavidū 'ham asmi /
sabbesu dhammesu anupalitto //
Ahaṃ hi arahā loke, ahaṃ satthā anuttaro //
eko'mhi Sammā Sambuddho' sītibhūto 'smi nibbuto //
(Ariyapariyesaṇā Sutta in MN. I, p. 171.)

(Transl. I am the all conqueror. I am omniscient. I am untouched by all worldly objects. I am the Perfect in this world. I am a teacher incomparabl· ; I am the only enlightened, tranquilized and have extinguished everything (see the present author's *Buddhist Sects in India*, p. 76.)

Re Suññata

Suñño loko, suñño loko ti, bhante, vuccati
Yasmā ca kho, Ānanda, suññam attena vā attanīyena.
(Saṃ. Nik., IV, 34).

(Trnsl. Void is the world, void is the world, people say, O Lord, how does this saying goes ? Because the world is void of the self, Ānanda, of what belongs to the self, i.e., unreal.

Suññaṃ Iokam avekhhasu......Mogharāja Maccurāja
Sutta-nipāta 1119

(Transl. Regard the world as void and ever. The king Death, the false king)

In the *Dhammapada* (vs. 279), there is the general saying :—

Sabbe dhammā dukkhā, aniccā ca anattā.

(=all worldly beings and objects are associated with suffering, impermanence and non-self (i.e. unreal, phenomenal),

Hence, sabbe dhammā anattā ti/yadā paññāya passati //
atha nibbindati dukkhe/esa maggo visuddhiyā //

(Transl When one realises this fact by knowledge, then only his suffering ceases ; this is the way for attaining purity (i. e., perfection).

It should also be noted that Mahāyāna Buddhism was divided into two philosophical schools, viz. Śūnyatāvāda of Nāgārjnna and Vijñānavāda of Asaṅga, and it was later developed into *Vijñaptimātratā-vāda*=absolute pure consciousncss by Vasubandhu. As śūnyatāvāda has already been dealt with in the previous pages, the following stanza deal with Vijñānavāda (idealism).

In the *Dīgha Nikāya*, (I, p. 223) appears the following stanzas :—

Kattha āpo ca paṭhavī tejo vāyo na gādhati ?
Kattha dīghañ ca rassañ ca aṇuṃ thūlaṃ subhāsubhaṃ
Kattha nāmañ ca rūpañ ca asesam uparujjhatīti ?
Tatra veyyākaraṇaṃ bhavati :
Viññāṇam anidassanaṃ anantaṃ sabbato pabhaṃ,
Ettha āpo ca paṭhavī tejo vāyo na gādhati
Ettha dīghañ ca rassañ ca aṇuṃ thūlaṃ subhāsubhaṃ,
Ettha nāmañ ca rūpañ ca asesam uparujjhati.

Idam avoca Bhagavā. Attamano Kevaddho gahapati-putto bhāsitam abhinandīti.

[Transl. Where does the water or earth, or fire or air not find a place ?

Where does the long or short, minute or coarse, good or evil ?

Where do the name and form (i.e., mind and matter) cease totally ?

(Trans. Where does water or earth or fire or air not find a place ? Where does long or short, minute or coarse, good or evil find no place ?

Where does the name or form (nāma-rūpa), i.e., mind and matter cease totally ?

The exposition of the above is as follows :—

"Pure consciousness, i.e., Idealism is signless, infinite and shining like a bright jewel.

In this (pure consciousness) water or earth or fire or air does not exist. Here long or short, minute or coarse, good or evil or name and form cease absolutely (lit. without any remnant).

This was said by Bhagavā and Kevaddha the houeholder's son felt satisfied with the answer.

CHAPTER III

THREE MAIN PHASES OF BUDDHISM

Buddhism may broadly be divided into three Yānas (systems), viz., Hīnayāna or Śrāvaka-yāna, Mahāyāna or Buddhayāna, of which, Tantrayāna is a later phase.[1]

Hīnayāna is ethical and historical, as it commenced from Buddha's *mahāparinirvāṇa* and its scriptures were written in Pāli and later in Sanskrit while the scriptures of Mahāyāna were always in Sanskrit.

The central theme of Hīnayāna is the twelve-linked chain of causation (*Pratītya-samutpādo*=*Paṭiccasamuppāda*), perpetual flux (*santāna*) of mind and matter (nāma-rūpa, consisting of the five elements, *viz.*, *rūpa* (matter), *vedanā* (feeling), *saṃjñā* (perception) and *vijñāna* (consciousness). The adherents of this branch of Buddhism seek individual enlightenment, i. e., *arhathood* and, at the end of the span of life, *Nirvāṇa*, i.e., quietude, eternal peace and bliss (santaṃ sukhaṃ).[2] The aim of Hīnayāna is the realisation of the non-existence of soul, i.e. *pudgalanairātmya* by eradicating mental impurities (kleśāvaraṇaṃ), i.e. mental and physical impurities, while Mahāyāna in contrast seeks both *Pudgala-nairātmya* as well as *Dharma-nairātmtya*, by which they mean that the five elements (*skandhas*) which is the basis for the conception of Pudgala (soul) do not exist, in other words, all the elements, which compose the worldly objects and beings (i.e. Dharmas) do not exist. For attaining this goal, Mahāyāna prescribes the realisation of both *Pudgala-nairātmya* and *Dharma-nairātmya*.

About a century after Buddha's *mahāparinirvāṇa*, Hīnayāna

1. S. B. Das Gupta, *Introduction to Tantric Buddhism*. This branch of the religion was first sub-divided into *Pāramitā-naya* and *Mantra-naya* and then into *Vajrayāna*, *Kālacakrayāna* and *Sahajiyāyāna*.

2. *Dhammapada*, 203-4 ; Nibbānaṃ paramaṃ sukhaṃ ; vs. 23 : Nibbānaṃ yogakkhemaṃ.

became split up into eighteen or more sects[1]. Each sect had its particular doctrinal views. Of the eighteen sects, eleven held orthodox views with certain differences. The remaining seven headed by the Mahāsaṅghikas held semi-Mahāyānic views, paving the way for the advent of Mahāyānism. They conceived of Buddha as superhuman and even super-divine. Their Buddha's *Kāya* conceptions were vague and was in a nascent form. The Sautrāntikas and Harivarman's *Satyasiddhi-śāstra* held views midway between Hīnayāna and Mahāyāna.

Mahāyāna was again sub-divided into two schools of philosophy known as Śūnyatāvāda, i.e., of the Mādhyamika, of which Nāgārjuna was the main exponent and Vijñānavāda of the Yogācāra, the main exponent of which was Asaṅga, who, it is said, was inspired by Maitreyanātha, a Bodhisattva. The Vijñanavāda was further developed to Vijñaptimātratāvāda by Vasubandhu, younger brother of Asaṅga.

The Mahāyānists contend that Buddha realised the highest truth (*paramārtha-satya*) at the foot of the Bodhi-tree. In many of his discourses embodied in the *Nikāyas*, he referred to the highest truth but he also realised that it was not possible for all of his disciples, being of different intellectual levels, would comprehend his deepest teaching. He indicated this by a nice simile in the *Ariyapariyesanā-sutta* of the *Majjhima Nikāya* : In a tank there are many lotus flowers, some of which have risen much above the water-level, some reached just the level of the water while there are many lotuses, which remain within water. By this simile he meant that the Bodhisattvas were like the flowers much above the water-level while the Śrāvakas or Hīnayānists were like the lotuses just on the level of water, and the rest which were within water were the common people (*puthujjanas* or *pṛthagjanas*).

Hīnayāna (Hy.) and Mahāyāna (My.) may briefly be compared thus :—

(*i*) Hy. is ethical and historical, while My. is religious and and metaphysical, being a later phase of Buddhism (2nd or 1st century B. C.).

1. For detail, see the present author's "*Bnddhist Sects in India*".

(*ii*) The Hy. scriptures are recorded in Pāli and later in mixed Sanskrit, while those of Mahāyāna are in pure Sanskrit.

(*iii*) In Hy. the conception of non-ego (*anātman*) is that the conglomeration of five elements (skandhas), which are constantly changing (*anitya*) or momentary (*kṣaṇika*).

(*iv*) In Hy. emancipation (Nirvāṇa) is individualistic but at the same time, it should be noted that it is not annihilation but it is eternal state, peaceful, happy and excellent, while in My. it is the attainment of perfection of knowledge, i.e., Prajñāpāramitā or Buddhahood.

(*v*) In Hy. Nirvāṇa is attained by eradication of impurities due to ignorance (avidyā), while in My. emancipation is not only by the eradication of impurities due to ignorance but also the eradication of obscuration of the immutable calm, pure and eternal (jñeyāvaraṇa).

(*vi*) In Hy. its followers are known as Śrāvakas, who seek *arhathood*, and at the end of life-span, *Nirvāṇa*, while in My. its followers are known as Bodhisattvas, who are instructed to attain *Bodhi-praṇidhi-citta* and *Bodhi-prasthāna-citta*[1], i. e., by the former term it is meant that they are to take the vow that they want to attain Bodhi and ultimately become a Buddha, and by the latter term it is meant that the Bodhisattvas are to start attempts for attaining perfection in the six perfections (*pāramitās*) and *Daśa bhūmis.*[2] Their aim should be to realise the highest truth (*paramārtha-satya*), which is vast and of one taste like the ocean, in which all rivers lose their identities.

(*vii*) In Hy. the laity is mainly supporters of the Saṅgha by making gifts of food, robes and by erecting monasteries for the residence of monks. They are mere listeners to the discourses delivered by the monks and observers of the five precepts and occasionally of the eight precepts temporarily, while in My. the laity is designated as Bodhisattvas, whose duties have been mentioned above.[3]

1. *Bodhicaryāvatāra* (A. S.) of Śāntideva, pp. 23-5.
2. See infra.
3. The agreements and differences are based on Beatrice Suzuki's *Mahāyāna Buddhism.*

(*viii*) According to Hy., Buddhas appear only once in an aeon (*kalpa*), while, according to My., all beings possess Buddha-nature, technically known as the *Tathāgata-garbha* (womb of Tathāgatas), which is a mixture of both good and evil, and it is only when the evils of a being are totally eradicated, the particular being becomes a Tathāgata.

(*ix*) In Hy. there is no place for metaphysical conception of *Śūnyatā* of the Mādhyamikas nor for the conception of *Vijñana-mātra* of the Yogācāras. Both the Mādhyamikas and the Yogācāras regard that the worldly beings and objects are transient, momentary (kṣaṇika), and hence they are actually non-existent (*śūnya*) or absolutely pure consciousness.

It is now proposed to deal with the agreements between Hy. and My, These are.—

(*i*) to get rid of attachment, hatred and delusion (*rāga, dveṣa, moha*).

(*ii*) the world has neither beginning (*anamataggo ayaṃ saṃsāro*) nor end.

(*iii*) The four Āryasatyas, viz., duḥkha, samudaya, nirodha and mārga (=suffering, its origin, its decay and the eightfold path leading to its decay.)

(*iv*) All worldly beings and objects are transient (*anitya*), momentary (*kṣaṇika*) and are in a state of perpetual flux (*santāna*), and are without any real substance (anātmakaṃ).

(*v*) The law of causation (pratītya-samutpāda) is universally valid. It is thus explained in verse :—

Ye dharmā hetuprabhavā hetuṃ teṣāṃ Tathagataḥ hyavadat/ teṣāṃ yo nirodh' evaṃ vādī Mahāśramaṇaḥ//

(Transl. The worldly beings and objecls, which arise from a cause, the Tathāgata has explained it and their extinction has also been explained by the Great Ascetic.)

Nāgarjuna in his *Mādhyamika Kārikā* (pp. 6, 160, 503, 542) has identified the law of causation with the highest truth and its incarnation is Buddha in these words :

"yaḥ pratītyasamutpādaṃ paśyati, so dharmaṃ paśyati, yo dharmaṃ paśyati, so Buddhaṃ paśyati."

(The sense of this passage is that the worldly beings and objects, which arise out of causes, do not exist in reality. One, who realises this unreality of worldly beings and objects, visualizes the Truth, and therefore visualizes the Buddha, the embodiment of truth.)

CHAPTER IV

DASA BHUMI

Pre-Bodhisattva Stage

It has been mentioned above that there were two *gotras*, one of which was the Ārya-gotra, which included the Bodhisattvas.

A Bodhisattva's completion of the six Perfections (pāramitās) is also termed *Gotra-bhūmi*, in which the aspirant, who had developed *Bodhicitta* and completed the Pāramitās, was entitled to take up the course of spiritual progress as indicated in the ten Bhūmis, and was therefore qualified to take up the *Adhimukti-caryā*, i.e., he could make progress in the ten Bhūmis.

Bodhisattva's stages of spiritual progress.

The ten *Bhūmis* are briefly as follows :—

(i) PRAMUDITĀ (Joyous stage) when a Bodhisattva (henceforth abbreviated as Bs.) becomes conscious that he had perfected himself in charity (*dāna-pāramitā*) as he had realised voidness of self (*pudgala-nairātmya*) as well as voidness of the worldly beings and objects (*dharma-nairātmya*).

(ii) VIMALĀ (Immaculate stage). A Bs. realises that he was free from sin or evil deeds as he had perfected himself in *Śīla-pāramitā* (perfection in moral precepts) and had accumulated the roots or bases of ten good deeds (*kuśala-mūlas*). His thoughts were also freed from infection or defilement. He practises also meditation (*dhyāna*) and deep concentration of mind (*samādhi*).

(iii) PRABHĀKARĪ (Shining stage or the stage of illumination). The Bs. shined on account of his perfection in forbearance (*kṣānti-pāramitā*) because he had no anger or spirit of

1. For detailed treatment see the present author's edition of the *Bodhisattvabhūmī*.

vengeance. The Bs. also completed the four trances (*dhyānas*) and the four immesurables (*apramāṇas*) and acquired the five supernormal knowledge (*abhijñā*). He had freed himself from attachment, hatred and delusion (*rāga, dveṣa*, and *moha*).

(iv) ARCIṢMATĪ (Bright or Radiant stage) on account of his perfection in energy (*vīrya-pāramitā*), which helped also his moral and intellectual activities. He applied himself to the acquisition of virtues leading to Bodhi (37 Bodhipakṣiya-dharmas) (for enumeration, see Mahāvyutpatti).

(v) SUDURJAYĀ (Hard to win). In this stage, the Bs. practises meditation and deep concentration of mind (*dhyāna, samādhi*). He develops wisdom (*prajñā*) and comprehends the four Aryan truths (*āryasatyas*), and realises the two truths : relative or conventional and real or the highest (*saṃvṛti* and *paramārtha*).

(vi) ABHIMUKHĪ (Right in front or Turned towards Bodhi). In this stage he comprehends the dependent origination of worldly beings and objects (*pratītya-samutpanna*). In his mind predominates perfect knowledge (*prajñā*) on account of his realisation of *Śūnyatā* (voidness).

(vii) DŪRAṂGAMĀ (Far going stage). In this stage (a) the Bs. makes acquisition of compassion (*karuṇā*), (b) knowledge of the five elements of existence (*skandhas*), (c) aspiration for Bodhi, (d) immaculate sojourn in existence, (e) extreme energy (*vīrya-pāramitā*), (f) turns Śrāvaka-yānist to Mahāyāna by *upāyakauśalya-pāramitā*, i.e., expediency, and (g) ultimately leading them to enlightenment.

(viii) ACALĀ (Immovable stage) marks a definite advance of the aspirant, who now knows where and when he will become a Buddha by the usual prophecy (*vyākaraṇa*).

(ix) SĀDHUMATĪ (stage of good thoughts). He perfects himself in the *Bala-pāramitā*, i.e., the ten powers of Buddha (daśa-bala). The Bs. now possesses perfect wisdom. He now makes necessary preparation for leading all beings to Nirvāṇa.

(x) DHARMA-MEGHĀ (Cloud of the Law). In this stage the Bs. attains perfection in knowledge (*jñāna-pāramitā*). The Bs. attains the excellence and pre-eminence of a

Buddha. He receives consecration (*abhiṣeka*) from all Buddhas for Buddhahood. His body of Law (*Dharmakāya*) is now complete and he can exhibit the magical transformations. Thus, ends the career of a Bs. in the ten Bhūmis.

It is now proposed to give an account of the Bhūmis along with a comparison with the Hīnayānic spiritual stages of progress.

The difference between Hīnayāna and Mahāyāna, as we have already stated, centres round the conception of the highest truth, which, according to the Hīnayānists, is Pudgalaśūnyatā only, while, according to the Mahāyānists, it is both Pudgala- and Dharma-śūnyatā. This difference is also evident in the various stages of progress chalked out by the two schools. The Hīnayānists recognize four stages called Sotāpatti, Sakadāgāmi, Anāgāmi and Arahatta, and mention specifically the attainments of an adept as he passes from one stage to another, obtaining in the last stage complete knowledge, which, according to them, is Arhat-hood. The Mahāyānists likewise recognize ten (according to the *Bodhisattvabhūmi* twelve) stages of progress, through which a Bodhisattva passes in order to have complete emancipation and to become a Buddha.

As the Mahāyānists hold that an insight into dharma-śūnyatā is the only means of attainment of the highest knowledge and that an insight into pudgalaśūnyatā equips an adept for proceeding higher up aud realising dharma-śūnyatā, they divide their stages of progress into two sections. The first, comprising the first bhūmi, leads an adept to the realisation of Pudgalaśūnyatā, while the second, comprising the last four bhūmis, gives them the real knowledge, Dharmaśūnyatā or Dharma-samatā. Thus, the first satisfies the aspiration of the Hīnayānists and hence corrresponds to their four stages, while the second lies beyond their reach, as they do not admit Dharma-samatā or Śunyata.

Though this is essentially the relative position of the Hīnayānists and the Mahāyānists with regard to the stages of spiritual process, one must, however, add to it the various other features, which are so often repeated by the Mahāyānists about their chief aim being not so much to attain happiness and emancipation for their own selves as to enable the suffering millions of the world to attain happiness and escape from the miseries of the world, even at the cost of the adepts' lives and religious merits. So while detailing the attainments necessary for each bhūmi, the texts point out the progress made by a Bodhisattva in regard to Āśaya, Upadeśa, Prayoga, Upastambha and Kāla,[1] as also the Ākāra, Liṅga and Nimitta. If the additional features of the Mahāyānic account of the first six bhūmis be left out, one may reasonably say that the description of the six bhūmis is simply a Sanskritised form of the Pāli passages, which deal with the stages of sanctification. Hence, the real addition of the Mahāyānists is the last four bhūmis, viz., Dūraṅgamā, Acalā, Sādhumatī, and Dharmameghā.

Literature on the topic

Regarding the literature on the subject, we may state that in Pāli there are no works dealing exclusively with the stages of sanctification. The accounts are found scattered in almost all the Pāli canonical works as well as in the few available Sanskrit works of the Sarvāstivādins. Buddhaghosa follows the Hīnayānic scheme of spiritual progress in his *Visuddhimagga.*[2] He divides it into three sections, of which the first deals with Sīla (moral precepts), the full observance of which results in the attainment of the first two stages, sotāpatti and sakadāgāmi; the second deals with Citta or Samādhi, which results in the attainment of the third stage Anāgāmi; and the third treats of Paññā (knowledge), perfection in which leads the adept to the final state, Arahatta or complete emancipation. Vaśubandhu has dealt with the stages in various places in his *Abhidharmakośa,*[3] supporting mostly, as we shall see, later on, in the accounts of the Pāli works.

In Mahāyāna literature, there are a few treatises, dwelling exclusively with the stages of spiritual progress while there are

1. *Bodhisattvabhūmi*, p. 2.
2. *Vis. M.* p. 6.
3. *Kośa*, VI. 34 ff.

many, which deal with them incidentally. Of the works treating mainly of the Bhūmis, the most important and at the same time comprehensive treatise is the *Daśabhūmikasūtra*,[1] one of the nine recognised scriptural texts of the Nepalese Buddhists. The next in importance are the *Bodhisattvabhūmi*[2] and the *Madhyamakāvatāra*,[3] both following the *Daśabhūmika-sūtra* with minor variations. For works containing an incidental treatment of the Bhūmis, reference may be made to the *Laṅkāvatāra, Sūtrālaṅkāra* and other similar works. The *Prajñāpāramitās* (*Śatasāhasrikā* and *Pañcaviṃśatisāhasrikā*) devote a chapter exclusively to the treatment of the Bhūmis, though they do not omit to state that from the standpoint of the highest truth these are devoid of any reality and are mere matters of convention.[4] The *Pañcaviṃśati-sāhasrikā* again has a peculiar feature of its own. While speaking of the various practices followed by the Bodhisattvas in connection with their progress in the *Prajñāpāramitā*, it indicates many of the attainments by using expressions, which are current among the Hīnayānists, *e.g.* Kulaṅkula, Ekavīcika, Sotāpanna.[5] The *Śatasāhasrikā*[6] also gives a list of ten Hīnayānic bhūmis, which are not in use in the Pāli texts. These are Śuklavipaśyanā (or vidarśanā)-bhūmi, Gotrabhūmi, Aṣṭamakabhūmi, Darśanabhūmi, Tanu-

1. Edited by Dr. J. Rahder. 1926.

2. A portion of the *Bodhisattvabhūmi* [Cambridge ms.—Vihāra-Paṭala] has been published by Dr. Rahder as an Appendix to his *Daśa.* Dr. Rahder has very recently published an article '*La Carrière du Saint Bouddhique*' in the *Bullentin de la Maison Franco-Japonaise,* Tome II, no. 1—Tokyo 1920. In it he has presented us with some new materials from the Chinese sources.

3. The Tibetan version of this work has been edited by Prof. Poussin in the Bibl. Bud. Series, and a French translation of the first six chapters of the same has also been published by him in *Le Muséon,* vols. VIII, XI, and XII. A reconstruction of its Sanskrit text is now being published in the *Journal of Oriental Research,* 1929, 1930, Madras.

4. *Śata.*' ch. X ; *Pañca.*, Paris ms. fol, 122-8.

5. This is the peculiar feature of the *Pañca.*, the Sanskrit original of whieh is avaliable at present. It is a recast of the original *Pañca,* of which the Sanskrit original is lost. See the present author's Intro to *Pañca.* for details.

6. *Śata.*, pp. 1470, 1520=*Mvyut.* 50=Das's *Tib. Dict.*, p, 475.

bhūmi, Vītarāgabhūmi, Kṛtāvībhūmi, Pratyekabuddhabhūmi, Bodhisattvabhūmi and Buddhabhūmi. The names clearly indicate the stages, which these are intended to signify. The first two refer to the pre-sotāpanna stages, the third and the fourth to the sotāpattimagga and sotāpanna stages, *i.e.*, so long as the adept is in the darśanamārga, the fifth to sakadāgāmi, in which stage rāga, dveṣa and moha reach their minimum (tanutva), the sixth to the anāgāmi stage when the above three are completely eradicated, the seventh to the arahatta stage, when the adept completes all that is to be done, for which reason an Arahat is often described as kṛtakṛtya (having done what is to be done). The eighth, ninth and tenth are self-explanatory and need no comment. It should be noted that the treatment of the Bhūmis in the *Prajñāpāramitās* is much simpler than that of the *Daśabhūmikasūtra*, and very likely it represents a stage in the evolution of the Bhūmi conception, standing midway between the *Mahāvastu*[1] and the *Daśabhūmikasūtra.* The account of Bhūmis in the *Mahāvastu* appears to be the earliest. The names used are not the standard ones. From the names used in the *Bodhisattvabhūmi*, it seems that the writers on Bhūmis considered it a piece of literary skill to devise names indicative of the qualities attained by a Bodhisattva in a particular stage.[2] The description of

1. The names in the *Mtu.* are : (i) Dūrārohā, (ii) Baddhamānā, (iii) Puṣpamaṇḍitā, (iv) Rucirā, (v) Cittavistarā, (vi) Rūpavatī, (vii) Durjayā, (viii) Janmanirdeśa, (ix) Yauvarājya and (x) Abhiṣeka.

2. Dr. Rahder says in his paper on *La Carriére du Saint Bouddhique* that the Chinese *Avataṃsaka-sūtra* devotes a large section to the discussion of the career of a bodhisattva. He says that it speaks of 52 stages (or degrees), *viz.*, "10 especes de Foi + 10 Résidences (adhimukti) + 10 Conduites (ācāra) + 10 Déflexions + 10 Terres (Bhūmi) + Eveil égal + Eveil merveilleux." These, it seems from their details, are only a form of classification of the bodhisattvas according to their qualities and do not indicate the gradual stages of spiritual progress. It is in the fifth item that we find mention of the Bhūmis (stages of progress). These are as given by Dr. Rahder in French, (i) Joyeuse ; (ii) Immaculée ; (iii) Clarifiant ; (iv) Radieuse ; (v) Dure-ā-gagner ; (vi) Droit-en-face ; (vii) Va-loin ; (viii) Immobile ; (ix) Bon-Espirit ; (x) Nuage d'Essence. These are exactly the same bhūmis as mentioned in the *Daśa* and other works.

bhūmis in the *Mahāvastu* is very scanty and does not contain the details, which are important and even essential from the Mahāyānic standpoint. On the other hand, it mentions some disciplinary (vinaya) rules, which a Bodhisattva is expected to observe, and the non-observance of which not only impeded his progress but also brought about his fall to the next lower stage. In the accounts of the first three bhūmis, some traces of the description contained in the *Daśabhūmikasūtra* are found, but in the next seven, and specially in the last four, there is hardly anything more than a mere mention of the names of Buddhas and Bodhisattvas, who attained them. It is apparent that the conception of bhūmis was very hazy to the author of the *Mahāvastu*, who tried to supply the gaps by recounting some legendary lives of Bodhisattvas and fictitious names of Buddhas.

For our present purpose of comparison between the Hīnayānic and Mahāyānic stages, we shall follow the account of the *Daśabhūmikasūtra*, indicating at places its agreements and disagreements with the *Bodhisattvabhūmi* and the *Madhyamakāvatāra*, and referring in the footnotes to the accounts of the *Mahāvastu* and the *Prajñāpāramitās* ; while for the Hīnayānic stages, we shall depend mainly on the Pali works, supplementing them where necessary by the information supplied by the *Kośa*.

Pre-Bhūmi stages

Pre-Bodhisattva or Pre-Sotāpanna stage,
(*i.e., Pṛthagjanahood to Āryahood*)

The most difficult task of an adept both in Hīnayāna and Mahāyāna is the fulfilment of the conditions laid down for passing from the state of a pṛthagjana (common man of the world) to that of an Ārya (a man capable of attaining the highest knowledge). The Mahāyānists demand that one must develop Bodhicitta before he can be entitled to commence the practices of bhūmis,[1] while the Hīnayānists held that one must comprehend the Four Truths and have firm faith in the teaching of Buddha, or in other words, he must complete the fifteen kṣaṇas of the Darśanamārga to be able to drift himself along the stream (sota) of sanctification—the eightfold path.[2]

About the pre-Bodhisattva stage, it is found very often in the *Prajñāpāramitās* and other Mahāyāna works a general remark that a being, who has performed meritorious acts (avaropitakuśalamūla) served many previous Buddhas (pūrva-jina-kṛtādhikāra), and had many kalyāṇamitras (spiritual guides) is destined to attain Bodhi.[3] In a slightly different manner, the *Sūtrālaṅkāra*[4] says that a being, who has developed Adhimukti[5] (aspiration) through innumerable existences, furnished himself with merits as the sea is by water, completed the preliminary purification by the observance of the Bodhisattva discipline, became wise by learning śāstras, and made his mind soft and pliable,[6] was entitled to exert himself in bhāvanā (i.e. repeated darśana) and derive benefit from the teachings of Buddha.

Adhimukticaryābhūmi

It is in the *Madhyamakāvatāra* that there is mention of a pre-Bodhisattva stage called the Adhimukti-caryābhūmi. The *Madhyamakāvatāra*,[7] quoting the *Ratnamegha-sūtra*, states

1. *Bodhic.*, pp. 86 f.

2. *Saṃyutta*, V, 347: soto soto tīha Sāriputta vuccati ; katamo nu kho Sāriputta soto ti ? Ayam eva hi bhante ariyo a ṭṭhaṅgiko maggo seyyathīdaṃ sammā diṭṭhi pe. sammā samādhī ti.

3. *Pañca.* (A.S.B. ms.), leaves 201b, 223b, 332a. Cf. *Mtu.*, I, p. 57,

4. *Sūtrā*,, xiv. 1-3, p. 90. The *Sūtrā.* is mainly a treatise on the Bodhisattvacaryā. Its treatment is general and comprehensive. As we are here concerned mainly with the Bhūmis, we shall pase over the minor details.

5. For a note on Adhimukti, see Lévi, *Translation* of the *Sūtrā.*, p. 13.

6. For kalpacitta, read kalyacitta, see Lévi, *Transl.* of the *Sūtrā.*, p. 16 fn.

7. *Le Muséon.* VIII, p. 262.

that the bhūmi of the Bhaviṣyad (future) Bodhisattva is placed just before the first bhūmi and consists essentially of excessive (adhimātra-adhimātra) practices of adhimukti (aspiration). He is a future Bodhisattva because he has not yet developed Bodhicitta. He is therefore said to be in the Adhimukticaryābhūmi, *i. e.*, he has been aspiring to become a Buddha by following the doctrines of Mahāyāna. After hearing a religious discourse, or praises and accounts of the power of a Buddha, he has only passing thoughts that he would become a Buddha, but unless and until this thought stays permanently in his mind, he cannot be said to possess Bodhicitta and become an Ārya, a Bodhisattva.[1]

The *Bodhisattvabhūmi* is more explicit in regard to the pre-bodhisattva stage ; the technical name given by it is Prakṛticaryā.[2] It divides this stage into two : Gotravihāra[3] and Adhimukticaryāvihāra.[4] These two preparatory stages cannot be strictly called bhūmis. The *Daśabhūmikasūtra* and other treatises dealing with bhūmis do not therefore mention them in their list of bhūmis. These deal with or refer to the qualities needed in the pre-bodhisattva stage but do not reckon them as additional bhūmis as the *Bodhisattvabhūmi* does.

1. Cf. *E R,E.*, II, p. 745.

2. This is mentioned also in the *Mtu.* as the first of the four caryās.

3. Vihāra-bhūmi. The corresponding Hīnayāna term is Gotrabhū, which is reckoned as a pre-sotāpanna stage. See *Aṅguttara*, IV, p. 373. The first two bhūmis, Śuklavipaśyanā and Gotra, mentioned in the *Śata.* also correspond to this.

4. It is the same as the Adhimukticaryābhūmi of the *M. Ava.* The *Laṅkā.* (p. 65) speaks of the preparatory stage as Parikarma-bhūmi. (See *E.R.E.*, II p. 744 for Parikarma and Upacāra bhūmis). In the *Śata.* (ch. x), Parikarma refers to the duties to be performed by a bodhisattva in a bhūmi.

The *Mtu.* (I, 46f.) names the corresponding bhūmis as Prakṛticaryā and Praṇidhānacaryā. The former refers to the worldly virtues of a being e.g., respectfulness to parents, śramaṇas and brāhmaṇas ; performance of the ten kuśala-karmapathas, worship of Buddhas, etc. The latter (praṇidhānacaryā) refers to the aspiration made, by a bodhisattva to become a Buddha and to achieve the same at any cost. The *Mtu.* gives also the legends about the present Buddha as to when and in what circumstances, he made the resolution (praṇidhāna).

The Gotravihāra is thus described in the *Bodhisattvabhūmi* : A person who is gotrastha, *i.e.*, belongs by nature to a noble class of beings, is endowed with the qualities, high aims, and good dharmas of a Bodhisattva. These are apparent in his natural demeanour. He sets himself to perform good deeds naturally, and does not require persuasion ; he does the same with a certain amount of wisdom and charitable feeling. He possesses the seeds of Buddha-dharmas and is incapable of commiting evil deeds, not to speak of the deadly (ānantarya) sins.[1] The gotravihāra forms the root-cause (hetumātra) of the other eleven vihāras. It only makes it possible for one to exert himself for the attainment of the other bhūmis but does not carry him further.

The Adhimukticaryāvihāra is the name given to the first attempts made by a Bodhisattva to develop Bodhicitta, the noble aspiration. In this bhūmi the bodhisattva actually starts on his march to the Tathāgata-vihāra, while in the Gotravihāra he gives only an indication of same.[2] When he completes the duties of the Adhimukticaryā, he can be said to have done the work preliminary to the first bhūmi, the Pramuditā. In the Adhimukticaryāvihāra, a bodhisattva practises bhāvanās to a limited degree, and is incapable of retaining what is acquired. He makes only an attempt for nirnimitta-bhāvanā (*i.e.*, meditation of the Absolute, devoid of all signs)[3]. He is possessed of pratisaṃkhyānabala (power of discriminating knowledge) and applies himself to the duties of a bodhisattva with pratisaṃkhyāna-prajñā and not by natural *tanmayatā* (absorption). He cannot yet have the Bodhisattva-bhāvanās, which make one steadfast and non-receding. He is not above the five fears, viz., of livelihood, dispraise, death, evil destiny (durgati) and censure by the assembly[4]. With

1. For ānantarya sins, see *Kośa*, IV. 96 : *Vibhaṅga*, p. 378.

2. These two vihāras have a parallel in the two kinds of Bodhicitta, mentioned in the *Bodhic.*, viz., Bodhipraṇidhi and Bodhiprasthāna. The *Bodhic.* puts these two after the development of Bodhicitta, see *infra*,

3. *B. Bh.* p. 3.

4. Cf. *Aṅguttara*, IV, p. 394.

pratisaṃkhyā he exerts himself for the good of beings and not out of natural love and compassion. Sometimes, he explains things wrongly and sometimes he interests himself in improper spheres or in the material requisites of life. He may have reverential faith (śraddhā) but not innate knowledge of the truth. He possesses only limited śrutamayī and cintāmayī prajñā (knowledge derived through hearing and reflection),[1] which again sometimes gets bewildered. He follows the bodhisattva-path with great difficulty and sluggish knowledge (dhandha-abhijñā) and does not develop a very strong desire for bodhi. Now and then he forgets the right means, in which beings should be trained and even the Buddhavacanas. Occasionally he imparts teaching incautiously and fails to produce the desired result. At times he diverts his mind from bodhi and loses energy for the observance of Bodhisattva-saṃvaras (disciplines) or for rendering service to beings. Sometimes he also seekś his own happiness, though after reflection he seeks the happiness of others as well. Not unoften he notices his own failings but lacks sufficient energy to correct them. He likes instruction in the Bodhisattva-dharmas. These are the chief indications, by which it can be ascertaincd whether or not a person is in the Adhimukticaryābhūmi.

The idea underlying the preparatory stage is that these are beings, who possess to their credit such kuśalamūlas that they are destined to become Buddhas. These beings are called gotrasthas.[2] Just as a king's sons are different from those of a commoner by their inherent nature, demeanour and aspiration, so also those beings, who possess the germs of Buddhahood are known by their inherent nature.

The *Daśabhūmikasūtra*[3] furnishes us with the details of the pre-bodhisattva stage, which are on many points different from the account of the *Bodhisattvabhūmi*. Some of the

1. See *Netti.* pp. 8, 60 ; *Kośa*, VI. 5c. Cf. Rahder, *La Carriers du Sainte Bouddhique*, p. 5.

2. See *Sūtrā.*, p. 11 fer gotrāgratva. The *B. Bh.* devotes about six leaves to the details of the gotra ; see Camb. Ms. leaves 1-6

3. *Daśa.*, p. 11.

details, are : The pre-Bohisattvas develop bodhicitta after having accumulated enough merits, followed the prescribed practices, worshipped many Buddhas, possessed pure and sublime intention and aspiration, and held compassion always in the forefront of their mind. They are desirous of attaining the Buddha-knowledge, the ten powers, the four great Vaiśāradyas, realisation of the sameness of all dharmas (things), rescuing all beings from misery, acquiring every form of knowledge, and purifying all Buddha-kṣetras.

These accounts depict the wavering mind of a person, who is endeavouring to develop the Bodhicitta. It is by the actual development of the Bodhicitta[1] that a person gets rid of his pṛthagjana-hood and becomes an Ārya or the Elect to proceed along the stream of sanctification.[2] Bodhicitta, in short, means the vow or aspiration of a being to become a Buddha and to acquire all the qualities and powers of a Buddha. The *Bodhicaryāvatāra* divides it into two parts, Bodhipraṇidhicitta and Bodhiprasthāna-citta. The former is simply an aspiration to become a Buddha for saving worldly beings from misery without seriously thinking of the duties of making the highest gifts, and acquiring such other virtues. The latter refers to the resolution to observe the Bodhisattva-saṃvaras (disciplines) and to strive for the acquisition of merits. The former is compared to a traveller, who is thinking of going to another country, while the latter to one who has actually set out on his journey in order to reach the destination.[3] As soon as one develops bodhicitta, he is entitled to perform the duties connected with the first Bhūmi.[4]

---

1. The topic of Bodhiciita is of all-absorbing interest in most of the Mahāyāna works. The *Bodhic.* devotes to it its first three chapters, and its commentary quotes many sūtras throwing light on the same.

2. See *E.R.E.*, II, p. 744 ; *M. Ava.* in the *Le Muséon*, VIII p. 11 : yena cittotpādena sahotpannena bodhisattvo 'atikrānto bhavati pṛthagjanabhūmim avakrānto bhavati bodhisattva-niyāmaṃ, etc.

3. *Bodhic.*, pp. 23-5.

4. According to the *Mtu.* (I, 78) a bodhisattva in the first bhūmi is still a pṛthagjana but he is prāptaphala and dakṣiṇeya.

7

Hīnayānic treatment of the pre-sotāpanna stage

We have in the Hīnayānic works also an elaborate description of the qualities necessary for a person to pass from the puthujjana stage to the Ariya. Like the general statements in the *Prajñāpāramitās* about the previous kuśalamūlas of the bodhisattvas, we have also in the Pāli texts references to the previous merits (upanissaya) of a person seeking ordination or spiritual progress. It is often said in connection with the conversions made by Buddha that he delivered discourses after ascertaining the kuśalamūlas (merit-roots or previous merits) of persons, whose conversion he had in view. The usual passage is "Satthā paccusakāle lokam avolokento imassa kulaputtassa upanissayam addasa"[1] [the Teacher at dawn looked round the world and saw the previous merits (lit. bases) of the person]. This implies that the real benefits of discourses cannot be derived by everybody. It is only those, whose previous actions have raised them to a certain height, that they derive benefits from the discourses. There are many instances in the Pāli works showing that a person had to have to his credit sufficient merits entitling him to become a sotāpanna after hearing only one discourse; there are also cases of persons becoming sakadāgāmi, anāgāmi, arahat, paccekabuddha by virtue of their stores of previous merits. The implication in such cases is that the persons in their previous lives had died after attaining the stage of sanctification, or its corresponding qualities, just preceding the one obtained by them in this life. The Hīnayānists hold that a pṛthagjana must have some kuśalamūlas before he can expect to be an ārya, *i.e.*, a srotāpanna.[2]

A puthujjana is defined in the *Majjhima Nikāya* as one who labours under the delusion of "I-ness" and "Mine-ness" and thinks that he has rūpa, vedanā, etc. Not knowing the true law, he develops attachment to things which he should avoid, and thereby produces and increases the āsavas (inflowing impurities) of kāma (desire), bhava (desire for existence) and

1. *Jātaka,* VI, 70; *Petavatthu Cy.* p. 38.
2. The Kuśalamūlast or called Mokkhabhāgāīas in the *Kośa.*

avijjā (ignorance).[1] The *Puggala Paññatti*[2] simply says that a puthujjana is one who has neither got rid of the three saṃyojanas nor applied himself to get rid of them. The *Paṭisambhidāmagga*[3] tells us that the puthujjanas, who are striving to be ariyas, try to be indifferent to the saṅkhārās by looking upon them as anicca, dukkha and anattā but this indifference of theirs does not stay permanently in their minds and sometimes even appears distasteful to them.

The stage next to Puthujjana is Gotrabhū, corresponding in some respects to the Gotravihāra of the *Bodhisattvabhūmi.* The Gotrabhū represents the last state of a puthujjana, for a person becomes gotrabhū when he is just fit to commence the works, which make a person an ariya. The *Paṭisambhidāmagga*[4] takes gotrabhū not only as a stage prior to sotāpanna but also as an indication of a class of persons, who are on the way to arhathood and may be in possession of one of the eight maggas and phalas. Likewise the *Abhidhammatthasaṅgaha*[5] places the Gotrabhū stage after Paṭipadā-ñāṇadassana-visuddhi (the purity of insight in regard to the path)[6] and Vuṭṭhāna-gāmini-vipassanā-ñāṇam (discernment leading to uplift) and makes the Gotrabhū an ariya, *i.e.*, a sotāpatti-maggaṭṭha. In the two works mentioned last, Gotrabhū denotes those persons, who are on the path and are entitled to become Arhats, and hence persons in any one of the three stages, sotāpatti, sakadāgāmi, and anāgāmi.[7] The *Aṅguttara Nikāya*[8] and the *Puggala Paññatti*[9], however, do not

1. *Majjhima*, I, pp. 7,239. It will be observed that the fourth āsava is not mentioned here. An Arahat in contrast to puthujjana is called a khīṇāsava. See also *Paṭis. M.* pp. 117-8.

2. *Pug. P.*, p. 12. See *Comp. of Phil.*, pp. 40-50 for the four classes of Puthujjana.

3. *Paṭis. M.*, I, pp. 63, 64,

4. *Paṭis. M.*, I, pp. 66-8.

5. *Comp. of Phil.*, pp. 67-71, 29, 215 (treated in detail by Mrs. Rhys Davids in the Introduction.

6. Buddhaghosa also supports this. See *Vis. M*,, p. 672: Ito (Paṭipadā-ñāṇadassana-visuddhi) paraṃ gotrabhū-ñānaṃ hoti.

7. *Comp, of Phil.*, p. 68.

8. *Aiguttara*, IV, p. 378.

9. *Pug. P.*, p. 14: Aṭṭha ariya-puggalā, ariyā, avassesā puggalā anariyā.

consider the Gotrabhū an ariya and hence these distinguish Gotrabhū as a stage preceding the Sotāpattimagga.

Those, who are between Gotrabhū and Sotāpanna (*i.e.* sotāpattiphala-paṭipanna) are divided into two classes, called Saddhānusārī and Dhammānusārī.[1] They still practise the Darśanamārga. According to the *Kośa*, the former are of mild (mṛdu) and the latter of sharp (tīkṣṇa) faculties. The Saddhānusārīs are those who follow the dharma through faith in their spiritual guide, or in other words, they take the practice of smṛtyupasthāna, etc., and work for the realisation of the Truth by being incited by others (para-pratyayena), while the Dharmānusārīs are those who set themselves to practise the Bodhipakṣika dharmas through the study of the scriptures (dvādaśāṅga).[2] The *Puggala Paññatti* simply states that, of the persons, who are working for the realisation of sotāpattiphala, those who have saddhindriyaṃ (faculty of faith) in a great measure (adhimattam) are called Saddhānusārī, while those who have paññindriyaṃ (faculty of paññā) in a great measure are called Dhammānusārī. The persons of the former class, when established in the sotāpattiphala, are called Saddhāvimutta and those of the latter class are called Diṭṭhippatta. The only difference between these two classes is this that the former destroys some of his āsavas but not as much as the latter.[3] For progressing along the path to Nibbāna, there are (i) two dhūras (courses)—saddhā (faith) and paññā (knowledge) (ii) two abhinivesas (adherences), samatha (quietude)[4] and vipassanā (introspection), and (iii) two sīsas (heads)—ubhatobhāgavimutta (one who is free in both ways) and

1. *Pug. P.*, p. 15 ; *Kośa*, VI, 29, 6 ; III, p. 105 ; *Saṃyutta* V, pp. 200, 205 ; *Vis. M.*, p. 659.

2. *Kośa,* VI, 29. Prof. Poussin drew my attention to the fact that the Dvādaśāṅga is mentioned only in the *Vyākhyā* in explanation of the term 'Dharma' in the *Kośa.*

3. *Pug. P.*, 15 : paññāya c'assa disā ekacce āsavā, parikkhīnā honti na ca kho yathā diṭṭhippattassa. See also *Kośa*, VI, 63.

4. *Cf.* Geiger, *Saṃyutta Transl.*, II, p. 172. See also *DhP.*, *A.*, I, p.7. granthadhura (way of study) and vipassanādhura (way of contemplation).

paññāvimutta (free by reason of knowledge).[1] The followers of Paññādhura and Samathābhinivesa are called Dhammānusārī in the sotāpattimagga stage, Kāyasakkhī[2] in the next six, and Ubhatobhāgavimutta in the arhat stage ; the followers of Paññādhura and Vipassanābhinivesa are called Dhammānusārī in the sotāpattimagga stage, Diṭṭhippatta[3] in the next six, and Paññāvimutta[4] in the arhat stage. The followers of Saddhādhura and Samathābhinivesa[5] are called Saddhānusārī in the sotāpattimagga stage, Kāyasakkhī in the next six, and Ubhatobhāgavimutta[6] in the arhat stage ; the followers of Saddhādhura and Vipassanābhinivesa are called Saddhānusārī in the sotāpattimagga stage, Saddhāvimutta[7] in the next six, and Paññāvimutta in the arhat stage[8].

Those, who are either Saddhānusārī or Dhammānusārī, reach the second stage[9] of the ariyamagga called sotāpattiphala, also called sattakkhattuparama (*i. e.*, they are to have seven more births). Mention is made of specific qualities, which an adept must possess in order to become a sotāpanna. In the *Saṃyutta Nikāya*[10] Sāriputta asks Ānanda, "How many are the dhammas, which one must give up as well as one must acquire for being a sotāpanno avinipātadhammo niyato sambodhiparāyaṇo (a sotāpanna gone beyond the possibility of retrogression and destined to attain the highest knowledge)." The

---

1. *Pug. P. Cy.*, p. 194 ; *Dīgha*, II, p. 71.

2. Kāyasakkhī is defined in the *Aṅguttara* (IV, pp. 451-2) as implying those who realise within their own body (kāyena phassitayā) the eight jhānas or vimokkas) and also destroy āsavas by paññā.

3. Diṭṭhippatta is described in the *Pug. P.*, (p. 15) as referring to those who know truly the four truths, and put an end to āsavas by comprehending the dharma of the Tathāgata by paññā.

4. See *infra*.

5. *Pug. P. Cy.* reads samādhi for samatha. 6. See *infra*.

7. Saddhāvimutta (*Pug. P.*, p. 15) are similar to Diṭṭhippatta ; only the paññā of the former is not as much as that of the latter.

8. *Pug. P. Cy.*, pp. 194-5. See also *Kośa*, VI, 63, 64.

9. The first stage being sotāpattimagga comprised the two classes called Saddhānusārī and Dhammānusārī.

10. There is a chapter called Sotāpatti-saṃyutta in the *Saṃyutta*, V, pp. 264, 262-3, 388=*Dīgha*, III, p. 227.

reply of Ānanda was that one must have firm faith (pasāda) in Buddha, Dhamma, and Saṅgha[1] and must be endowed with all the sīlas, liked and praised by the wise. They are called the Sotāpattiyaṅgas[2]. One who has the four Sotāpattiyaṅgas is considered free of five sins, *viz.*, killing, stealing, misconduct, lying, and drinking.[3] The *Saṃyutta Nikāya* also tells us that when an ariyasāvaka knows the taste, the dangers and the way out of thc indriyas, *viz.*, sukha, dukkha, somanassa, domanassa and upekkhā, he is a sotāpanna.[4] In a discourse in connection with the illness of Ānāthapiṇḍika, it is said that the puthujjana was expected also to comply as far as possible with the eight conditions of the aṭṭhaṅgikamagga *plus* sammā-ñāṇa and sammā-vimutti,[5] besides the four sotāpattiyaṅgas. The sotāpattiyaṅgas, in fact, are merely preliminaries, though essential, to the actual commencement of practices for attaining the sotāpatti stage. The duties, entailed upon a candidate just after the sotāpattiyaṅgas, are further increase in pīti (pleasure), pāmojja (joy), passaddhi (calmness), samādhi (concentration) and the practice of the cha vijjā- (or nibbedha-bhāgīya-) dhammas (six dharmas leading to knowledge), *viz*, the

1. There is a formula for announcing the faith, see *Dīgha*, III, p. 227. The faith is called Saddhindriya, *Saṃyutta*, V, p. 196. *Paṭis. M.* p. 161 : Ye keci mayi aveccapasannā sabbe to sotāpannā. See *Kośa*, VI, 73b ; XXIV, p. 205 : La pureté de la conduite (prayoga) : régles de moralité (śīlāni) chéres aux Āryas ; pureté des sentiments (āśaya) and avetyaprasāda (firm faith).

2. The other four sotāpattiyaṅgas, very rarely found, are: (i) sappurisasaṃsevā, (ii) saddhammāsavañāṇam, (iii) yoniso manasikāro, and (iv) dhammānudhammapaṭipatti, *Saṃyutta*, V, pp. 345, 411 ; *Dīgha*, III, p. 227 ; *Paṭis. M.*, II, p. 17 show the connection between these and the indriyas.

3. *Saṃyutta*, II, pp. 61, 71.

4. *Ibid*, V, p. 207 ; *Paṭis. M.*, I, pp. 115-6. It says "Aññātaññāssāmītindriyam ekam ṭhānaṃ gacchati, sotāpattimaggaṃ and then tells of the position of the indriyas. It adds that in the sotāpattimaggakkhaṇa, except things already existing, all thoughts that arise are pure, transcendental, and lead to Nibbāna.

5. *Saṃyutta*, V, pp. 381-4.

realisation (anupassanā) of (i) transitoriness (anicca) of constituted things, (ii) unhappiness (dukkha), due to transitoriness, (iii) essencelessness (anattā) of things ; (iv) giving up (pahāṇa), (v) virāga (detachment, and (vi) nirodha (cessation.)[1]. The *Nikāyas* do not go into details about the attempts of a candidate in the sotāpanna stage to comprehend the anicca, anattā and dukkha or the four āryasatyas. In the *Dīgha Nikāya* there is only a bare mention of the four ñāṇas *viz.*, dukkhe ñāṇam, nirodhe ñāṇam, samudaye ñāṇam, and magge ñāṇam.[2] An exposition of these has been given in the *Paṭisambhidāmagga*,[3] which says that when one has "understanding, search, research, discernment, discrimination, etc. of each of the four truths, he is said to have comprehended the four truths. This topic has received special treatment in the *Kośa*,[4] which may briefly be stated : There are two mārgas, darśana and bhāvanā,[5] the latter commencing at the last stage of darśanamārga. The darśanamārga has sixteen kṣaṇas or moments of comprehension of the truths,[6] which are as follows :—

---

1. *Saṃyutta*, V, p. 345 ; *Dīgha*, III, p. 251 ; *Kośa*. Intro. to chs. V and VI, p. iv, as Prof. Poussin shows, puts the order of progress in the pre-sotāpanna stage thus :—

(i) Acquisition of the Mokṣabhāgiya-kuśalamūlas
(ii) Acquisition of the Ariyavaṃśas (*Kośa*, VI, 7c-d ; 8a-b ; *Aṅguttara*, II, p, 24 ; *Dīgha*, III, p. 224—rules relating to the requisites of a monk) ;
(iii) Aśubhabhāvanā, Ānāpānasmṛti ;
(iv) Practice of Smṛtyupasthānas ;
(v) Acquisition of the Nirvedhabhāgiyā dharmas ;
(vi) Satyābhisamaya (15 kṣaṇas)—darśanamārga.

There are many details which should be mentioned in an exposition of the path of spiritual progress, but as we are concerned here mainly with the comparison of the Hīnayāna and Mahāyāna stages, the details have been passed over.

2. *Dīgha*, III, p. 227.

3. *Paṭis. M.*, I, p. 119. See for translation of this stock passage, 'Mrs. Rhys Davids' *Buddhist Psychology*, p. 18.

4. Prof. Poussin has given a summary of it in the Intro. to his transl. of the *Kośa*, chs. V and VI ; *M. Vṛ.*, p. 479, n. 4.

5. Bhāvanāmārga is seeing the Truths again and again. See *Kośa*, Intro. to chs. V and VI, p. vi.

6. See *Kośa*, VI, 261 ; VII, 4.

1) Duḥkhe dharmajñāna-kṣānti 5) Samudaye do. 9) Nirodhe do. 13) Mārge do.	(faith producing the knowledge that things of the Kāmadhātu are full of duḥkha, are subject to samudaya and nirodha, and that there is also the mārga to the origin and cessation of things).
2) Duḥkhe dharmajñāna 6) Samudaye do. 10) Nirodhe do. 14) Mārge do.	(actual realisation of the Kāmadhāṭu are full of duḥkha, are subject to samudaya and nirodha, and that there is also the mārga leading to their origin and cessation).
3) Duḥkhe anvayajñāna-kṣānti 7) Samudaye do. 11) Nirodhe do. 15) Mārge do.	(faith producing the knowledge that things of the Rūpa and Arūpa dhātus are full of duḥkha, are subject to samudaya and nirodha, and that there is also a mārga leading to their origin and and cessation).
4) Duḥkhe anvayajñāna 8) Samudaye do. 12) Nirodhe do. 16) Mārge do.	(actual realisation of the fact that things of the Rūpa and Arūpa dhātus are full of duḥkha, are subject to samudaya and nirodha, and that there is also a mārga leading to their origin and cessation)[1].

The *Kathāvatthu* shows the stages of gradual progress of a srotāpattiphalapratipannaka while he is in the darśanamārga thus :

1. The order of the kṣaṇas is to be made out from the number prefixed to each of the sixteen kṣaṇas. For a list, see *Mvyut*. 56 ; and for detailed exposition, see *Kośa*, VII, 8, p. 13.

By Dukkhadassana, the srotāpatti-phala-pratipannaka gives up partially but not completely sakkāyadiṭṭhi, vicikicchā and sīlabbataparāmāsa and the kilesas involved in them.	He is not yet quite Srotāpanna or Sattakkhattuparama or Kolaṃkola or Ekabiji.
By Samudayadassana, he gives up sakkāyadiṭṭhi completely, and the other two partially, and so also the kilesas.	Do
By Nirodhadassana, he gives up vicikicchā completely and sīlabbataparāmarṣa partially and so also the kilesas.	Do
By Mārgadassana, he gives up sīlabbataparāmāsa completely and the kilesas partially.	He is now a srotāpanna

The *Kośa* tells us that a candidate while progressing along these kṣaṇas is called Śraddhānusārī, Dharmānusārī or Srotāpattiphala-pratipannaka up to the fifteenth kṣaṇa. It is in the sixteenth moment that he is considered established (sthita) in the srotāpattiphala, and he may now be said to have obtained Catusatyābhisamaya.[1] This attainment, or in other words, the completion of the Darśanamārga frees him from the avastuka-kleśas etc. and makes him an Ārya, i.e., a person entitled to let himself flow along the stream of sanctification—the eightfold path. He is no more to be called Śrāddhānusārī or Dharmānusārī. He is now a Srotāpanna.[2]

The pre-Ārya stage, in fact, decides the path which a candidate is to follow. If one aspires only to *mokṣa* or *Nirvāṇa* and accumulates kuśalamūlas of not a very high excellence as the Hīnayānist is to do, he is a Śrāvaka and if he aspires to Buddhahood in order to become the rescuer of the worldly

1 *Kośa*, I, p. 164 leaves this point as doubtful but all the passages mentioned there support the inferences drawn above.

2 *Kośa*, p. 25 n. VI,

beings, i. e., he develops *Bodhicitta* and accumulates kuśala-mūlas which only an exceedingly rare person can, he is a Bodhisattva.

I. Pramuditā

An adept as soon as he brings his mind up to to the path described above[1] goes beyond the pṛthagjanabhūmi (plane of an ordinary being) and becomes definitely a bodhisattva. He can now be regarded as a member of the Tathāgata family[2] becomes irreproachable (anavadya) by any taint relating to birth (sarvajātivādena), ceases from worldly existences, proceeds on in the transcendental existences, becomes established in the bodhisattva-dharmatā and well established in the rank of a bodhisattva, comprehends sameness (tathatā) and is destined to be in the family of tathāgatas of all times (past, present and future) and ultimately attains Sambodhi. Such bodhisattvas while in this bhūmi have prāmodya (joy), prasāda (faith), prīti (pleasure), utplāvanā (elation), udagrī (exaltation), uśī (fragrance), utsāha (energy), and become asaṃrambha (devoid of pride), avihiṃsā (devoid of malice) and akrodha (devoid of anger). The Jinaputras become joyous on remembering the Buddhas, their dharmas, the Bodhisattva practices, the pāramitā purifications etc.[3] They are pleased also because they know that they are out of worldly matters, nearing the Buddhabhūmi, the Jñāna-bhūmi, and cut off from births in hell or any lower form of existence. They are the refuge of all beings, and are always within the close view of the Tathāgatas. They are devoid of all sorts of fear[4] because they have no love for self or for things. They do not expect any service from others ; on the other hand, they are prepared to render service to all beings. As they have no conception of self, they cannot have any fear of death,

1 *Kośa*, VI. 31a-b : He is now either a kāyasākṣī or dṛṣṭiprāpta or śraddhāvimukta.

2 See *infra*.

3 Cf. *B. Bh.*, p. 7 ; ' Abhisamayālaṅkārāloka ' in the *Kośa*, VI. 26, p. 181 fn.

4 Cf. *Ibid.*, p. 7.

as they know that when they are dead, they will always be with Buddhas and Bodhisattvas.

Then the Bodhisattvas, having sublime aspiration and mahākaruṇā in their forethought, engage themselves in the attainment of further merits. On account of their having in a greater degree śraddhā, prasāda, adhimukti, avakalpanā, kṛpākaruṇā, mahāmaitrī and having a firm mind endowed with hrī, apatrāpya, kṣānti, sauratya and admiration for the doctrines, and being helped by spiritual guides (kalyāṇamitras) they become well-established in the first bhūmi. They now take the following mahāpraṇidhānas (resolutions)[1] :—

(i) to perform the worship of Buddhas in every possible manner and as completely as possible ;

(ii) to preserve and protect the doctrines of the Tathāgatas ;

(iii) to watch the Buddhotpādas of all the worlds and to accompany the Bodhisattvas in their last existence from their descent from the Tuṣita heaven up to their mahāparinirvāṇa.

(iv) to practise all the bhūmis along with the pāramitās ;

(v) to ripen all beings and help them in attaining omniscience ;

(vi) to purify all Buddhakṣetras by paying visits to them ;

(vii) to comprehend the endless distinctions that exist in the things of all lokadhātus ;

(viii) to persuade all bodhisattvas to develop the highest aspiration and collect merits therefor, to attend upon all Buddhas, to see Buddhotpādas whenever wished for, to pass through the various forms of existence with his own body, in order to be accomplished in the doctrines of Mahāyāna and to propagate the same ;

(ix) to perform the duties of a bodhisattva, to do righteous acts by body, speech and mind, to realise the Buddhadharma, to remove afflictions by faith, to obtain a body like that of the

1. See *Śikṣā.*, pp. 291-5=*Daśa.*, p. 14—18 ; *Sūtrā.* (Fr. transl.), p. 36n : Suzuki, *Outlines of Mahāyāna Buddhism*, pp. 308-310 ; *E.R.E.*, sv. Bodhisattva (bassed on the *Bodhisattvabhūmi*) and is not the same as *Daśa* : *Dharmasaṅgraha*, cxii : Praṇidhānaṃ trividhaṃ.

Mahābhaiṣajyarāja or be like the wish-fulfilling gem and to obtain speech which will never be fruitless ; and

(x) to attain Sambodhi in all lokadhātus, to make without moving a hair-breadth from the right path from his birth as an ordinary human being, to retire from the world, perform miracles, attain bodhi under the bodhi-tree, preach the dharma-cakra and attain ultimately mahāparinirvāṇa.[1]

While in the Pramuditā bhūmi, the Bodhisattvas take innumerable praṇidhānas, of which the ten mentioned above are the chief. They now pity the countless beings, who are led by wrong views and blinded by ignorance, desire and so forth, repeatedly take birth in the three worlds, and according to the law of causation, increase their stores of misery. They try to establish themselves in Nirvāṇa, the extreme happiness (atyantasukha).[2]

While in the first bhūmi they develop compassion and love and apply themselves to mahātyāga (*i.e.* giving up everything) of wordly wealth, sons, wives, etc. They seek again and again the worldly and transcendental things and thus become versed in all śāstras and are consequently able to judge what is good and what is evil for beings. They become lokajña.[3] By constant worship and observance of śāsana (doctrines), they possess the ten qualities needed for the purification of the ten bhūmis,[4] *viz.*, faith (śraddhā), compassion (karuṇā), love (maitrī), sacrifice (tyāga), patience to withstand distress (khedasahiṣṇutā), knowledge of the scriptures (śāstrajñatā), knowledge of the world (lokajñatā), modesty, bashfulness, steadiness and the ability of

---

1. *Cf. Mtu.*, I, pp. 47 ff.

2. *Daśa*, p. 18 ; *B. Bhumi*, p. 9. 3. *Cf. B. Bh.*, p. 9.

4. *Mtn.*, I, p. 78 has tyāga, karuṇā, aparikheda, amāna, sarvasādhyāyitā vikrama. lokānujñā, and dhṛti. *Śata.* (p. 1454) has adhyāśaya, sarvasattva-samacittatā, tyāga, kalyāṇamitrasevanā, dharmaparyeṣṭi abhīkṣṇa-naiṣkramya, buddhakāyaspṛhā, dharmavivaraṇa, mānastambhananirghātana, satyavacana. For an explanation of these terms. see *Śata.*, pp. 1458-1460. It will be observed that all the attainments mentioned in the *Mtu.* and *Śata.* appear in the account of the *Daśa*. *Cf*, *B. Bh.*, p. 9 : daśa vihārapariśodhakā dharmā.

performing the worship of the Tathāgatas.[1] They now see many Buddhas and worship them with all the necessary requisites, show respect to their Saṅghas and transfer the merit thus acquired to the attainment of Sambodhi.[2] They gain the power to ripen beings through gifts (dāna) and affable words (priyavāditā) and adhimukti (strong desire). Over and above these, they gain the other two saṃgrahavastus[3] (elements of popularity) but not yet the insight into the unlimited knowledge. Of the ten pāramitās,[4] their dānapāramitā is of an extraordinary nature. A bodhisattva, who has attained the first bhūmi, is entitled to become a king of Jambudvīpa and be a righteous ruler with mind always turned towards Buddha, Dharma and Saṅgha, the bodhisattva practices and omniscience. Wishing to become a leader of men, he renounces the worldly life, takes ordination[5] and in a moment enters into a hundred samādhis, sees a hundred Buddhas, traverses over a hundred lokadhātus and performs other extraordinary matters.

Correspondence of Bhumis with Maggas and Phalas

The Hīnayāna system does not offer any parallel to the first bhūmi of the Mahāyānists, for it has no concern with Bodhicitta, Praṇidhānas, Maitrī, Karuṇā, and the ten qualities needed by a bodhisattva for fortifying himself to proceed along the ten bhūmis. It is from the second bhūmi that the Hīnayāna system offers a parallel to the Mahāyānic stages of progress. The *Bodhisattvabhūmi*[6] and the *Madhyamakāvatāra*[7] notice this fact in their treatment of the bhūmis.

In the Hīnayāna system a very common way of speaking about the various stages of progress is that an adept by com-

1. *Daśa.*, p. 19 ; *B. Bh.*, p. 9. *Mtu.*, I, p. 78 mention these eight qualities in connection with the first bhūmi.

2. *Cf. B. Bh.*, pp. 9-10.

3. *Mvyut.* 25 : dānaṃ priyavāditā arthacaryā samānārthatā ; see also *Lal Vis.*, p. 38 ; *Daśa.*, p. 22 ; *B. Bh.*, p. 10.

4. *Mvyut.* 34 gives a list of ten. This is common in Pāli works.

5. *Cf. Śata.*, p. 1459 : Tathāgata-śāsane pravrajati.

6. See Rahder's edition in the App. to *Daśa.* p. I.

7. *M. Ava.*, ch. I (*Le Muséon*, VIII).

plying with the rules of Adhiśīla[1] (entire moral precepts) becomes a Sotāpanna and Sakadāgāmi, by complying with the rules of Adhīcitta, becomes an Anāgāmi, and by those of Adhipaññā, becomes an Arhat. So we can name the Hīnayāna stages also as (1) Puthujjana but Gotrabhū ; (2) Adhisīla, (3) Adhicitta and (4) Adhipaññā.[2] We may now compare with these the Mahāyānic bhūmis as named in the *Bodhisattvabhūmi* ; the relation of the Hīnayānic to Mahāyānic bhūmis becomes apparent. These are as follows : (1) Gotra-Vihāra, (2) Adhimukticaryā-Vihāra, (3) Pramuditā-Vihāra, (4) Adhiśīla-Vihāra,[3] (5) Adhicitta-Vihāra, (6), (7) and (8) Adhiprajñā-Vihāra, (9) Sābhisaṃskāra-sābhoga-nirnimitta-Vihāra, (10) Anābhoga-nirnimitta-Vihāra, (11) Pratisaṃvid-Vihāra, and (12) Parama-Vihāra. Of these twelve Vihāras, we have already dealt with the first two, the preparatory Bhūmis, which are, as a rule, not included in the usual list of bhūmis, and correspond to the Hīnayānic Puthujjana or pre-Sotāpanna stage. Hence, if these be left out, we have the usual ten bhūmis. Evidently the five bhūmis (4-8 of the *Bodhisattvabhūmi*, and 2-6 of the *Daśabhūmikasūtra*) correspond to the four Hīnayānic stages. The higher knowledge and attainments, which the Bodhisattvas claim and which, according to the Mahāyānists, are beyond the capacity of the Hīnayānists, are to be attained in the last four bhūmis.

II. Vimala or Adhisila

A Bodhisattva, who has well practised the first bhūmi and seeks the second, develops ten cittāśayas, *viz*., ṛju (plain), mṛdu (soft), karmaṇya (pliable), dama (submissive), śama (tranquil),

1. The Aṭṭhaṅgika Magga is arranged thus :
   Sīla=Sammāvācā, °kammanta, and °ājiva.
   Citta or Samādhi=Sammāsaṅkappa, °vāyāma, °sati. °samādhi.
   Paññā=Sammādiṭṭhi. See, *e.g.*, *Vis. M.*, pp. 4, 510 ; *Dīgha*, III, p. 219.
2. Three samanakaraṇīyas in the *Aṅguttara*, I, p. 229.
3. *B. Bh.*, p. 42 tells us that the Adhiśīla is the same as Vimalābhūmi of the *Daśa*.

kalyāṇa (beneficial), asaṃsṛṣṭa (unlogged), anapekṣa (indifferent), udāra (noble) and māhātmya (magnanimous).[1]

When these cittāśayas are developed, he is established in the second bhūmi, Vimalā. He then quite naturally refrains from prāṇātipāta (taking life), adattādāna (stealing), kāme mithyācāra (misconduet), anṛtavacana (telling lies), piśuṇavacana (malignant speech), paruṣavacana (harsh speech), sambhinnapralāpa (frivolous talks) and becomes anabhidhyā (non-avaricious), avyāpannacitta (devoid of malevolence), and comes to possess samyagdṛṣṭi (right view).[2] He then thinks that all beings suffer on account of not avoiding the said ten akuśalakarmapathas. He therefore must persuade them to follow the right conduct, and with that object in view, he must himself first observe them.[3]

He ponders over the fact that persons are graded according to their kuśalakarmapathas (good deeds performed) and other practices, by virtue of which they become men, gods, etc., and also Śrāvakas, Pratyekabuddhas, Bodhisattvas and Buddhas. He also ponders over the fact that by committing evil deeds (akuśalakarmapathas) beings are born in hell, the animal world or the Yama world, or as human beings with a short life and many diseases. So he decides that he

1. *B. Bh.*, p. 11 mentions ten samyagāśayas but does not enumerate them. The *Mtu.*, I, pp. 85-9 mentions twenty adhyāśayas and amplifies each of them by a stanza. This is followed by an enumeration of the evil consequences that follow their non-observance, making the Bodhisattvas go downwards. It is in connection with the third bhūmi (*Mtu.*, I. p. 101) that the *Mtu.* tells us daśa karmapathān kuśalān sevafe puruṣottamo.

2. *Daśa.*, pp. 23-5 ; in p. 26 the sufferings that follow each of the misdeeds are mentioned.

3. *B. Bh.*, pp. 11-12 refers briefly to the acquisition of kuśalakarmapathas and remarks that just as gold is purified by heating and other processes, so a Bodhisattva is purified by the practice of these karmapathas. The *Mtu.*, however, makes no reference to the kuśalakarmapathas in the second bhūmi. *M. Ava.* (ch. II) enumerates the kuśalakarmapathas in details, and also dilates on the purity acquired by the bodhisattva in this bhūmi, which is for this reason named Vimalā.

will observe the ten kuśalakarmapathas and persuade others to do so.[1] He therefore becomes loving and compassionate towards all beings and takes upon himself the duty of being a teacher and a guide, diverting them from the wrong to the right view. He observes that beings suffer on account of anger, avarice, desire, hatred, delusion, mental darkness, lack of energy and so forth, that they are tossed up and down by the waves of desire, love of existence, ignorance, that they are tied up by love and hatred, likes and dislikes, and labour under the misconception of 'I-ness' and 'Mine-ness', etc. Out of compassion, he resolves to rescue those beings and lead them to a suitable heaven of peace.

While in this bhūmi, he can see many Buddhas, worship them and transfer the merit thus acquired to the attainment of Bodhi. He receives the kuśalakarmapathas from the Buddhas and fulfils them in many kalpas. He gets rid of mātsarya (covetousness) and carries out fully the precept of liberality. Of the four saṃgrahavastus, he increases priyavadya (affability) to a great measure, and of the ten pāramitās, he improves the śīlapāramitā to a great degree but not so the other pāramitās.

Should a bodhisattva, after the attainment of the second bhūmi, desire material prosperity, he can become a righteous cakravartin with seven ratnas and so forth.[2]

This account of the second bhūmi leaves us in little doubt as to its similarity to the Adhiśīla practices of the Hīnayānists, without, of course, taking into account the adhyāśayas developed by the Bodhisattvas. In the *Visuddhimagga* it is stated that the sīla practices lead to the purification of all impurities relating to conduct,[3] and serve as the basis for

1. *Śata.*, p. 1455 refers to śīlas, but its account agrees to a great extent with that of *Daśa. Śata.* enumerates eight duties, śīlapariśuddhi kṛtajñatā, etc. For comments on them, see *Śata.*, pp. 1460-1. The *Mtu.* gives us very little information in regard to this bhūmi.

2. *Cf. B. Bh.*, p. 12. The *Mtu.* adds, in every bhūmi, the qualities which make a bodhisattva retrogress from a higher to a lower bhūmi but passes over other details.

3. *Vis. M.*: sīlena ca duccarita-saṅkilesa-visodhanaṃ pakāsitaṃ hoti.

the attainment of sotāpanna and sakadāgāmi stages. In the first chapter of the *Visuddhimagga*, Buddhaghosa dilates on the various sīlas to be observed by the householders, lay-devotees, monks and nuns, supplementing it by the second chapter on the thirteen dhūtaṅgas, which he considers necessary for the ascetics (yogī) to bring their sīlas to perfection.[1] The *Nikāyas* usually mean by the sīlas the commonly known ten sīlas and the 250 pātimokkha rules.[2] By the complete observance of sīlas and a little of samādhi and paññā[3] an adept becomes a sotāpanna and a sakadāgāmi. We know that a sotāpanna is free from the three saṃyojanas and the two anusayas, *viz.*, diṭṭhi and vicikicchā.[4] By bringing the three hindrances, rāga (attachment), dosa[5] (hatred), and moha (delusion) to their minimum (tanutta), and by getting rid of anusayas, kāma, rāga and paṭigha and by practising a little more of samādhi, and paññā, he becomes a sakadāgāmi. In the *Paṭisambhidāmagga*,[6] it is stated that an adept in sotāpattiphala, sakadāgāmimagga, etc., obtains aññindriya (the faculty of perfect knowledge), and the dhammas that were already existing in him become unmanifest (avyākata), and the new thoughts that arise in his mind are pure, transcendental and conducive to Nibbāna.[7] A sotāpanna also gets rid of diṭṭhāsava completely and the other three āsavas so far as they lead to hell, while a sakadāgāmi of oḷārika (gross) kāmāsava, and partially of bhavāsava and avijjāsava.[8] In addition to the attainments required in the sotāpattimagga, the adept must also think of the transitoriness and essencelessness of the five upādāna-khandhas.[9]

There are two sub-stages between sotāpatti (or sattakkhattuparama) and sakadāgāmi. These are called kolaṃkola

1. *Ibid.*, p. 59.
2. See, *e.g.*, *Aṅguttara*, I, pp. 229, 235.
3. It will be observed that an adept commences practising all the three : sīla, samādhi, and paññā, but he fulfils only one in this stage.
4. *Paṭis. M.*, II, p. 96
5. *Ibid.*, I, pp. 72-3 ; II, p. 96.
6. *Ibid.*, II, p. 96.
7. *Ibid.*, I, p. 116.
8. *Ibid.*, I, p. 24.
9. *Saṃyutta*, III, p. 168.

(kulaṅkula) and ekabīji (ekavīcika).[1] Any one who has got rid of the three saṃyojanas, completed the sīlas and practised a little (mattaso) of samādhi and paññā is usually called sotāpanna. He is also called sattakkhattuparama[2] because he will be re-born seven times more among men and gods before he can attain Nibbāna. He will never fall back into hell and is destined to attain Nibbāna after getting rid of two more avarabhāgīya (orambhāgīya=lower) fetters, *viz.*, kāmacchanda and vyāpāda, and five ūrdhvabhāgīya (uddhambhāgīya=higher) saṃyojanas (fetters), *viz.*, rūparāga, arūparāga, auddhatya, māna and moha.

A sotāpanna becomes a kulaṅkula by getting rid of the third and fourth categories of passions of the Kāmadhātu and by the acquisition of purer indriyas as opposed to the passions. He will be reborn twice or thrice either among the gods when he is called Devakulaṅkula or among men when he is called Manuṣyakulaṅkula.[3] The *Nikāyas* do not draw any clear difference between sotāpanna and kolaṃkola. The *Visuddhimagga* distinguishes them by stating that the Kolaṃkolas have vipassanā and indriyas of the medium order,[4] while the sotāpannas have those of mild (mṛdu) order.

The next stage Ekabīji (Ekavīcika) is put in the Pāli texts after Kolaṃkola and before Sakadāgāmi, but in the *Kośa* it is put after Sakadāgāmi.[5] The superiority of Ekabījis, as shown in the Pāli texts, is that they develop samādhi and paññā still more but cannot complete them.[6] The *Visuddhimagga*

---

1. *Aṅguttara*, I, p. 233 ; IV, pp. 380-1 ; *Saṃyutta*, V, p. 205 ; *Pug. P.*, p. 16 ; *Netti.*, p. 189 ; *Vis. M.*, p. 709 ; *Kośa*, VI, 34. For the two stages prior to sotāpanna, *viz.*, Dhammānusāri and Śaddhānusārī, see *ante*.

2. There are disagreements among the schools as to the number of existences ; some interpret seven existnces among men and seven among the gods, and some even more, though the texts cited by each clearly show that seven existences in all were meant. See, for details, *Kośa*, VI, 34, pp. 200-2.

3. *Kośa*, II, 30.

4. *Vis. M.*, p. 709, following *Kośa*.

5. *Kośa*, VI, 35, 36.

6. 'Na paripūrakārī' is used instead of 'mattasokārī'.

adds that they have sharp faculties (tikkhindriya). In consequence of this, they are reborn once more among men (mānuṣakaṃ bhavaṃ) for attaining Nibbāna. Quite similar is the description of a Sakadāgāmi ; only in this case, it is not mentioned whether the one (sakṛd) more rebirth will be among the gods or men ; the texts simply say "imaṃ lokam āgantvā", *i.e.*, they will be reborn in the Kāmadhātu, which includes both men and gods. In any case, the Sakadāgāmi reduce rāga, dosa, and moha to their minimum (tanutta).

The *Kośa* tells us that a Sakṛdāgāmi destroys passions (kleśas) up to the sixth category. Having been born among the gods, he will be reborn once more among men. In him rāga, dveṣa, and moha are brought to the minimum, and there remain only the three lower categories of passion, *viz.*, mṛdvadhimātra, mṛdumadhya and mṛdumṛdu. The Ekavīcikas are distinguished from them by the fact that they destroy seven or eight categories of passions and acquire the faculties opposed to these passions.[1]

The division of srotāpannas into three classes are mentioned also in the *Laṅkāvatāra.* It states that the srotāpannas are of ordinary (hīna), medium (madhya), and excellent (viśiṣṭa) classes[2]. The hīna class will undergo seven more rebirths, the madhya (*i. e.* kulaṅkula) three or five and the viśiṣṭa (*i. e.* ekavīcika[3]) only one. The saṃyojanas, *viz.*, satkāyadṛṣṭi, vicikitsā and śīlavrataparāmarṣa are mild, medium or sharp according to the class of srotāpannas. A srotāpanna by getting rid of the three saṃyojanas does not have rāga, dveṣa and moha.[4] While speaking of the sakṛdāgāmi, the *Laṅkāvatāra*

1. *Kośa*, VI. 36 says on the etymology of the word thus: vīci= interval, separation, *i e.*, they are separated from Nirvāṇa by one more birth. Quite different, however, is the etymology given in the Pāli texts, where bīja=seed.

2. *Laṅkā.*, p. 117.

3. *Ibid*, pp. 117-9 explains Satkāyadṛṣṭi as of two kinds, sahaja (natural) and parikalpita (imaginary), and then interprets Vicikitsā and Śīlavrataparāmarṣa as a Yogācāra text would do.

4. *Laṅkā.*, p. 119 ; on this point *Laṅkā.* differs from all Hīnayāna texts, which say that Sakṛdāgāmis bring rāga, dveṣa and moha to the minimum.

simply mentions that they require one more birth to put an end to duḥkha.[1] The stage next to sakṛdāgāmi is anāgāmi corresponding to the third bhūmi of the Mahāyānists.

III. Prabhakari or Adhicittavihara

A Bodhisattva, who has completed the second bhūmi and seeks the third, should develop the following ten cittāśayas :[2] śuddha (pure), sthira (firm), nirvid (world-disgustful), avirāga (non-detached), avinivṛta (non-returning), dṛḍha (strong), uttapta (energetic), atṛpta (never satisfied), udāra (noble) and māhātmya (magnanimous).

While in the third bhūmi the bodhisattva realises that the constituted beings and things are impermanent, full of suffering, have momentary origin and decay, are without beginning and end, and are subject to the causal law. He comprehends the misery and despair as issuing from attachment to saṃskāras, and so he applies his mind to the attainment of Tathāgatajñāṇa,[3] which he finds as unthinkable, immeasurable and above all misery and despair, and where there is neither fear nor trouble, and by attaining which one can save beings. He then develops ten more cittāśayas.

Realising this state of things, the bodhisattva again resolves to rescue beings and strive for their benefit. He then thinks over the means, by which he can rescue them and finds that it is possible only by anāvaraṇa-vimokṣa-jñāna (the unscreened knowledge of emancipation). He observes that it is attainable only by hearing and practising the dharma. So he turns his mind to perfecting himself in the dharma and resolves to sacrifice all earthly wealth and enjoyment, and undergo all sorts of suffering[4]. He now sees that mere purification in speech and action would not be sufficient and that he must observe the

1. *Ibid.*, p. 129.

2. *Cf. B. Bh.*, p. 12 ; *Mtu.*, I, pp. 89-90 mentions 28 factors, which send back a Bodhisattva from the 3rd to the 2nd bhūmi.

3. *Cf. B. Bh.*, pp. 12-3.

4. *Cf. Mtu.*, I, pp. 91-5 for ekā gāthā subhāṣitā, a Bodhisattva is prepared to sacrifice even his own life. This is followed by an enumeration of the evils, for which a Bodhisattva may retrogress.

dharmas and anudharmas.[1] With that end in view, he practises the dhyānas, the four brahmavihāras, *viz.*, maitrī, karuṇā, muditā, and upekṣā, and acquires the abhijñās, *viz.*, ṛddhividha (power of performing miracles), divyaśrotra (supernatural power of hearing), paracittajñāna (power of reading the thoughts of others), pūrvenivāsānusmaraṇa (power of remembering former births), and divyacakṣu (supernatural power of vision).[2]

He sees many Buddhas, hears their discourses, and follows their directions. He comprehends that all dharmas are non-transmigrating, non-decaying and are only subject to cause and condition. The fetters of Kāma, Rūpa, Bhava and Avidyā become weak, those due to wrong views (micchādiṭṭhi) having been already destroyed. He gets rid of rāga, dveṣa and moha, and the following āśayas are purified : kṣāntisauratya (forbearance with gentleness), akhilamādhurya (sweetness without hindrance), akopya (non-anger), akṣubhita (non-agitation), alubhita (non-covetousness), anunnānānavamāna (non-elation and non-depression), sarvakṛtapratikṛtānāṃ niṣkāṅkṣā (non-desire for remuneration for works done), aśāṭhyāmāyāvitā (non-deceit), and agahanatā (non-mysteriousness). Of the four saṃgrahavastus he increases arthacaryā to a great measure, and of the ten pāramitās, he improves kṣāntipāramitā, but not the rest.

In this description of the third bhūmi, it will be noticed that the bodhisattvas, apart from the extraordinary qualities peculiar to them, commence practising the eight dhyānas (jhānas), the four brahmavihāras, and the six abhijñās. Their fetters relating to Kāma, Rūpa, Bhava, and Avidyā become weak, and those due to dṛṣṭi are destroyed. Their rāga, dveṣa, and moha are completely destroyed.

In the Hīnayāna system also an adept after completing the sīlas, attempts to rise higher and higher in the training of mind through samādhi.[3] The *Visuddhimagga*[4] treats in detail of the

---

1. *Cf. B. Bh.*, p. 13 ; *Mtu.*, I, pp. 91-2 ; *M. Ava.* (*Le Muséon*, VIII, pp. 301 ff.)

2. *Śata.*, p. 1455 mentions only five dharmas in connection with the third bhūmi. Except the first there is very little agreement in the three works : *Mtu. Śata.*, and *Daśa.*

3. *Vis.* M., p. 84.

4. *Ibid.*, ch , II.

practices that are classed under samādhi. These are the four jhānas with the help of forty kammaṭṭhānas (bases of meditation), ten anussatis (objects of remembrance), four brahmavihāras, the four āruppa (higher) jhānas, two bhāvanās, ten iddhis, and six abhiññās, all of which, it will be observed, are included in the third bhūmi. The *Visuddhimagga* also tells us that an adept after completing the citta-practices becomes an Anāgāmi, *i.e.*, he will not be reborn any more in the Kāmaduātu.[1] He gets rid of the five orambhāgiyas (lower fetters) *viz.*, sakkāyadiṭṭhi, vicikicchā, sīlabbataparāmāsa, kāmacchanda and vyāpāda,[2] completely destroys rāga, dosa and moha, and removes wholly kāmāsava, and partially bhavāsava and avijjāsava.[3] He comes into existence as an upapātika (self-born)[4] and attains Nibbāna.

The Anāgāmis are divided into five sub-classes[5] called :

(1) Antarāparinibbāyi, *i.e.*, those who practise the path to destroy the five higher (uddhambhāgiya) saṃyojanas just after coming into being and before reaching the middle of their lives.[6]

(2) Upahacca (=Upapadya of *Kośa*)-parinibbāyi, *i.e.*, those who practise the path of destroying the five higher saṃyojanas after the middle and a little before the end of their lives.[7]

(3) Asaṅkhāraparinibbāyi, *i.e.*, those who attain parinibbāna by putting an end to kilesas with a little trouble and without great effort (appadukkhena adhimattaṃ payogam akatvā).[8]

---

1. *Pug. P. Cy.*, p. 198 ; oraṃ vuccuti kāmadhātu.
2. The first three are destroyed by the Sotāpattis and Sakadāgāmis ; so in this stage only the last two are destroyed.
3. *Paṭis. M.*, p. 118.
4. In the Suddhāvāsalokas (*Pug. P. Cy.*, p. 198).
5. *Vis. M.*, p. 710. The *Kośa* adds five more to this list. *Pug. P. Cy.*, p. 200 calculates 48 classes of Anāgāmis out of these five.
6. *Pug. P.*, p. 199 : āyukkhayassa āsanne ṭhatvā. It may be remarked in this connection that the length of lives in these existences is counted by thousands of kalpas. *Kośa*, VI, p, 211 explains it as those who attain sopādhiśeṣanirvāṇa-dhātu immediately after birth.
7. *Pug P. Cy.*, p. 199.
8. *Kośa*, VI, p. 211.

The *Kośa* explains it as those who attain Nirvāṇa without effort because they are not energetic.[1] The *Aṅguttara-Nikāya* gives a different interpretation. It states that those who complete the fourth Jhāna, develop the five balas and five indriyas, and attain parinibbāna in this life are called Asaṅkhāraparinibbāyi.[2]

(4) Sasaṅkhāraparinibbāyi, *i.e.*, those who attain parinibbāna by putting an end to kilesas with great trouble and great effort (dukkhena kasirena adhimattaṃ payogaṃ katvā).[3] The *Kośa* explains it as those who attain Nirvāṇa without relaxing the exercises because they are energetic. The *Aṅguttara Nikāya* explains it as those who look upon the body as evil (asubha), food as loathsome and all constituted things as disgusting. They cogitate on the transitoriness of beings and death, and make their minds steady. They develop greatly the five balas and five indriyas.[4]

(5) Uddhaṃsota Akaniṭṭhagāmi, *i.e.*, those Anāgāmis, who do not attain parinibbāna while they are in the Aviha heaven but rise higher and higher until they reach the Akaniṭṭha heaven where they attain Nibbāna.[5]

---

1. *Kośa*, VI. 2. *Aṅguttara*, p. 156.

3. *Pug. P. Cy.*, p. 198; see *Vis. M.*, p. 453; sasaṇkhāra-pubbapayoga.

4. *Aṅguttara*, II, p. 156, *Cf. Kośa*, VI, p. 212 fn. The Anāgāmis (1) and (4) are of sharp faculties, (2) and (3) of mild faculties. (3) and (4) practise the dhyānas while (1) and (2) are described without any mention of dhyānas. About the precedence of (3) to (4), see *Kośa*, VI, p. 212.

5. See *Kośa*, VI. 37, p. 213 for two kinds of Urdhvasrotas: (i) Akaniṣṭhagā and (ii) Naivasaṃjñānāsaṃjñāyatanagā.

The Akaniṣṭhagā are divided again into three sub-classes:

(*a*) Pluta (one who soars high) on account of dhyānas practised by him, he is born in the Brahmakāyika heaven and lastly he is born in the Akaniṣṭha heaven where he attains Nirvāṇa;

(*b*) Ardhapluta (one who soars only half-way); on account of dhyānas practised by him, he is born in the Brahmakāyika heaven, from which he passes to Suddhāvāsa and thence to Akaniṣṭha to attain Nirvāṇa there and

(*c*) Sarvacyuta; before entering into Akaniṣṭha heaven, he passes across all the heavens except Mahābrahmā. An Anāgāmi cannot have two existences in one heaven because he always rises higher and higher.

Thus we see that the Hīnayānic Anāgāmi stage is parallel to the Mahāyānic third bhūmi.

The practices of the fourth, fifth and sixth bhūmis correspond to the Adhipaññā practices of the Hīnayānists. In the *Bodhisattvabhūmi*, three bhūmis are put under Adhiprajñā vihāra, the reason being that the Bodhisattva acquires Prajñā by three different means (tribhir mukhaiḥ), *viz*., bodhipakṣika dharmas, the four truths, and the causal law. So it subdivides this Vihāra into three :

(i) Bodhipakṣyapratisaṃyuktādhiprajñāvihāra (practice of Prajnā with reference to the Bodhipakṣika dharmas) ;

(ii) Satyapratisaṃyuktādhiprajñāvihāra (practice of Prajñā with reference to the Truths) ; and

(iii) Pratītyasamutpādapratisaṃyuktādhiprajñāvihāra (practice of Prajñā with reference to the law of causation).

IV. Arciṣmatī or Bodhipakṣyapratisaṃyuktādhiprajñāvihāra

A Bodhisattva passes from the third to the fourth bhūmi after acquiring the ten dharmālokas[1], *i. e*., after obtaining insight into sattvadhātu (world of sentient beings), lokadhātu (various worlds), dharmadhātu (universe), ākāśadhātu (space), vijñānadhātu (world of consciousness), kāmadhātu (world of desires), rūpadhātu (world of forms), ārūpyadhātu (world of formlessness), udārādhyāśayādhimuktidhātu (spheres of noble intention and aspiration) and māhātmyādhyāśayādhimuktidhātu (spheres of magnanimous intention and aspiration).

He becomes an accomplished member of the Tathāgata family by acquiring the following ripeners of knowledge,—unbending aspiration, implicit faith in the three ratnas, clear perception of the origin and decay of saṃskāras, of the non-origination of things in reality, of the incoming and outgoing of the world, of saṃsāra (worldly existences) and nirvāṇa (cessation), and of the actions of beings of the various spheres.

He practises the four smṛtyupasthānas (earnest thoughts) and exerts to acquire further merits and preserve the merits already acquired and not to commit evil actions any more.

1. Cf. *B. Bh.*, pp. 14ff.

He practises the ṛdhipādas, the five indriyas[1] and balas, the seven bojjhaṅgas and the eight mārgas.[2]

In this bhūmi he gets rid of satkāyadṛṣṭi and its relevant factors and performs actions leading to sambodhi.

As he acquires the various qualities of this bhūmi, his mind becomes softer, aspiration stronger, compassion for the sentient beings greater, and consequently he becomes more and more energetic.[3] His doubts are removed and his cittāśaya becomes immeasurable.

He now takes ordination.[4] His kuśalamūlas become of the purest kind. Of the four saṃgrahavastus, he develops samānārthatā (feeling of equality) and practises the vīrya-pāramitā of the ten pāramitās.

V. Sudurjayā or Satyapratisaṃyuktādhiprajñā-vihāra

A Bodhisattva passes from the fourth to the fifth bhūmi by developing the cittāśayaviṣayaviśuddhisamatā[5] (uniformity and purity of intention) relating to the following matters : doctrines of the past, present and future Buddhas, mental discipline, removal of wrong views and doubts, knowledge of the right and wrong path, practice of the Bodhipakṣika-dharmas, and the duty of elevating beings morally.

In this bhūmi, on account of the repeated practice of the various Bodhipakṣika dharmas, the possession of a still more purified intention[6], the comprehension of *tathātva* (thatness) of

---

1. *Viz.*, Śraddhā, Virya, Smṛti. Samādhi and Prajñā.

2. Cf. *B. Bh.*, p. 15. 3. Cf. *B. Bh.*, pp. 15, 16. 4. See 1st bhūmi.

5. The fourth Bhūmi in the *Mtu.* is not clearly described. It mentions some evils, which retard the progress of a Bodhisattva and speaks about the *avaivartika* qualities, attained or to be attained. See *Śata.* 1' (pp. 1452, 1462-3), which gives a slightly different list.

6. Cf. *B Bh.* p. 16. The *Mtu.* (p. 110) states that the *citta* of a Bodhisattva, when passing from the fourth to the fifth Bhūmi, realises *ādīptaṃ* sarvabhavaṃ rāga-dveṣa-mohebhyaḥ". But this is mentioned in the *Daśa.*, in connection with the third bhūmi. The account of the *Śatai* Is also different and speaks only of some disciplinary rules, It says that in this bhūmi, a Bodhisattva avoids gṛhī-saṃsrava, bhikṣuṇī-saṃstava kula-mātsarya saṃganikā gaṇkā-sthāna, ātmotkarṣaṇa, vyāpāda, para-paṃsaṇa, daśākuśala-karmapatha, māna, stambha, viparyāsa, rāga, dveṣa, moha (*Śata.*, pp. 1450, 1463-5).

all dharmas, and further increase of his aspiration, compassion, love, etc., he comprehends the four Āryasatyas.

He becomes proficient in understanding the

(*a*) Conventional truth (*saṃvṛti satya*) on account of catering to the wishes of other beings ;

(*b*) Transcendental truth (*paramārtha-satya*) on account of following only one path ;

(*c*) Truth of signs (*lakṣaṇa*) by realising the generic and particular characteristics of things (*svasāmānyalakṣaṇa*) ;

(*d*) Truth of analysis (*vibhāga*) by knowing the various divisions of dharmas ;

(*e*) Truth of overcoming (*nistīraṇa*) on account of knowing the real condition of skandhas, dhātus, āyatanas, etc. ;

(*f*) Truth of things (vastu) by subjecting his body and mind to afflictions ;

(*g*) Truth of origin (prabhava) on account of births ;

(*h*) Truth of decay and non-origin (kṣayānutpāda) on account of the complete suppression of all sufferings ;

(*i*) Truth of the knowledge of the path (mārgajñātāvatāra) ; and

(*j*) Truth of the origin of Tathāgata knowledge (tathāgatajñānasamudaya) on account of attaining knowledge in all its details and for following the bodhisattvabhūmis.

Having known the truths he realises that all the constituted things are essenceless, false. He pities the ignorant beings, who undergo repeated births and the consequent sufferings for not knowing the truth, and he wishes that all his merits be transferred to them for their happiness, training, and ultimate emancipation.

In this bhūmi he becomes smṛtimān, *i. e.*, does not get bewildered, matimān for having clear knowledge, gatimān for knowing the sense in which a sūtra is uttered, hrīmān for preserving himself as well as others, dhṛtimān for practising the disciplinary rules, and buddhimān for being proficient in ascertaining what is proper and improper and such other things.[1] His desire and energy for acquiring further

1 Cf. *B Bh.*, p. 17.

merits and rendering service to beings become greater and greater. He pleases the beings by means of all the four saṃgrahavastus, by showing his rūparāga, by giving discourses on the doctrines, on the Bodhisattva practices, on the greatness of Tathāgatas, on the evils of the world, on the virtue of acquiring Buddhajñāna, and by performing miracles. For establishing the Buddha-dharma he also acquires the secular sciences, *viz.*, mathematics, medicine, poetry, drama, metallurgy, astronomy, etc.

A Bodhisattva on the completion of the mārgas, passes to the sixth bhūmi and realises the ten kinds of sameness,[1] *viz.*, the sameness of all dharmas on account of being (i) animitta (baseless), (ii) alakṣaṇa (signless), (iii) anutpāda (originless), (iv) ajāta (unborn), (v) vivikta (detached), (iv) ādiviśuddha (pure in the very beginning), (vii) niṣprapañca (inexpressible), (viii) anāyūha-niryūha (non-taken and non-rejected), (ix) māyā-svapna-pratibhāsa-pratisśrutakopama (similar to dream, illusion, or echo), and (x) bhāvābhāvādvaya (identity of existence and non-existence).

Looking upon all things in this manner, the bodhisattva, through his deep faith, reaches the sixth bhūmi but does not yet attain the anutpattikadharmakṣānti (faith in the non- origination of things by nature). As mahākaruṇā predominates in his mind, he pities the beings who, on account of their ignorance, think of the things of the world as originating, decaying and possessing a soul (ātman). Not knowing the truth, they walk along the wrong path, are moved by merits and demerits, and thus have some abhisaṃskāras (thought-constructions). The thought-seed (citta-bījam) thus produced by the abhisaṃskāras becomes contaminated (sāsrava), being full of upādana (attachment to existence) and productive of birth, old age, death and rebirth. Then by the thought creation of karma-kṣetra (fields of action), ignorance and desire, a net of views is woven, from

1 Cf. *B. Bh.*, p. 18. The *Mtu.* (I, p. 120) does not speak of anything particular in this bhūmi. It simply states that a bodhisattva by associating with the meditating ascetics (yogācāras) and by developing śamatha and vipaśyanā passes from the 5th to the 6th bhūmi.

which appear name and form (nāma-rūpa) ; from them arise in succession the five means of sense, contact, feeling (vedanā), abhinandana (enjoyment) combined with tṛṣṇā (thirst), attachment (upādāna), desire for existence (bhava), and five skandhas distributed into five classes of beings (gatipañcaka). These beings fade into old age, despair, etc. The bodhisattva comprehends that there is really no doer of these, which being by nature are uncreated by any power (anābhoga, śāntilakṣaṇa), disappear and there is no destroyer of them. The bodhisattva further realises that the non-comprehension of the highest Truth is avidyā (ignorance) and this avidyā is the source of saṃskāras, which produce the first citta-vijñāna with its concomitant (sahaja) the four upādāna-skandhas, from which arise name and form and gradually the mass of sufferings. The tree of suffering grows without any doer, or feeler (kārakavedakarahita). So he realises that these three worlds are all mere thought-constructions (cittamātraṃ asad idaṃ traidhātukaṃ).[1]

Through his comprehension of the law of causation from the ten different standpoints and on account of his being convinced of the fact that there is no doer or feeler, and no creator (asvāmika), and that all things are subject to cause and condition, and devoid of any essence, detached from everything else, and essentially non-existing, the bodhisattva realises the śūnyatā-vimokṣamukha (release of essencelessness).[2] Then by comprehending that the bhavaṅgas (the links in the chain of causation) are by nature extinct (svabhāva-nirodha), he does not notice any dharmanimitta (basis of dharmas) and thus he attains animitta-vimokṣamukha (release of baselessness). Lastly, on account of his understanding the śūnyatā and animittatā of all bhavaṅgas, he does not really seek any vimokṣa, though he keeps up the appearance of doing so out of compassion for the innumerable beings ; hence he obtaining apraṇihita-vimokṣamukha (release of desirelessness). Keeping mahākaruṇā before his mind, he completes the bodhyaṅgas, which are still incomplete,

1 The Pratītyasamutpāda is explained here from ten different standpoints, see *Daśa.*, pp. 48-51.

2 Cf. *B. Bh.*, p. 18.

and being convinced of the fact that the saṃskāras proceed from the assemblage of, or connection with, materials that are by nature non-originating and non-decaying, he turns his mind to asaṅgajñāna (knowledge free from attachment) called Prajñāpāramitāvihāra[1] and develops it greatly. He now practises all the śūnyatā, animitta and apraṇihita samādhis and develops ten āśayas for rising higher and higher in the spiritual attainments and goes beyond every possible chance of fall to Śrāvaka or Pratyeka-buddha stage. Of the ten pāramitās he greatly develops the prajñāpāramitā.[2]

A bodhisattva by passing through these bhūmis attains all the qualities of an arhat besides those which are indispensable to a bodhisattva. He is now an arhat because as the *Laṅkāvatāra* states that he is now free from the thought-constructions (vikalpa), of dhyāna (meditation), dheya (objects of meditation), samādhi (concetration), vimokṣa (release), bala (powers), abhijñā (higher knowledge), kleśa (afflictions) and duḥkha (misery).[3]

We have seen that, accorinng to the Hīnayānists, an adept, on completion of the paññā practices, becomes an arhat. Buddhaghosa devotes the last twenty chapters of the *Visuddhimagga* to the elucidation of the various matters which comprise the Paññābhūmi. In this bhūmi[4] the adept is accepted to examine analytically the five skandhas (constituents of the body), the twelve āyatanas (fields of the organs of sense), twenty kinds of indriyas (faculties), four truths and the twelve-linked chain of causation. These are only the preliminary practices of the Paññābhūmi. These help the adepts to complete the bhāvanāmārga. We have seen[5] that the bhāvanāmārga commences in the sixteenth moment, *i.e.*, the last srotāpanna stage. So the adepts, while progressing along the stages of sanctification, complete

1. Cf. *B. Bh.*, p. 19.

2. *Śata.*, p. 1456 states that a Bodhisattva in this bhūmi completes the six pāramitās and avoids the following six thoughts: śrāvakacittam, pratyekabuddhacittam, paritarṣaṇacittam, anabalīnacittam, durmanaskacittam and vikṣepacittam.

3. *Laṅkā.*, p. 120.

4. *Vis. M.*, p. 443.

5. *Vis. M.*, pp. 443, 587ff.

the sīla and citta-visuddhis and partially the visuddhi relating to paññā. These visuddhis, as classified in the *Visuddhimagga*[3] and the *Abhidhammatthasaṅgaha*[1] are "(i) diṭṭhivisuddhi (purity of views), kaṅkhāvitaraṇa-visuddhi (purity by which all the sixteen classes of doubts with reference to the past, present and future are transcended) ; maggāmaggañāṇadassanavisuddhi (purity consisting in distinguishing the actual path from that which is not the path) ; paṭipadāñāṇadassanavisuddhi (purity of insight during the progress of the practice of discernment), and ñāṇadassanavisuddhi (purity-insight or path-insight).[2] In the arhat stage, the adept gets rid of the five remaining saṃyojanas (uddhambhāgiyas), all kilesas (afflictions), āsavas (impurities) and comprehends finally the real sense of the four truths, *i. e.*, he obtains perfect knowledge and his mind is completely freed. He will have no more rebirth and will attain Nibbāna. This also is borne out by the description of the arhats that we find in the *Prājñāpāramitās* and other Mahāyāna texts. It generally runs thus : An arhat is kṣīṇāsrava (devoid of the four āsravas), niṣkleśas (free from afflictions), vaśībhūta (with a well-controlled self), suvimuktacitta (with the mind completely freed), suvimuktaprajña (with knowledge cleared up), ājāneya (well-bred), kṛtakṛtya (doer of all that is to be done) ; apahṛtabhāra (relieved of the burden of five skandhas), anuprāptasvakārtha (successful in achieving the object of life) and parikṣīṇabhavasaṃyojana (free from the fetters of rebirth).

Corresponding to the two classes of sotāpannas called Saddhānusārī and Dhammānusārī, the arhats are also divided into two classes : Ubhatobhāgavimutta and Paññāvimutta.[4]

---

1. Mrs. Rhys Davids has lucidly explained these visuddhis in her Intro. to the *Compendium* ; her English rendering has been adopted here ; for further details, see *Comp. of Phil*., pp. 65ff.

2. *Vis. M.*, p. 672 . sotāpattimaggo sakadāgāmimaggo anāgāmimaggo arahattamaggo ti imesu pana catusu maggesu ñāṇaṃ ñāṇadassana-visuddhi nāma.

3. Buddhaghosa calls these five visuddhis 'sarīra' while the sīla and citta-visuddhis 'mūla.' See *Vis. M.*, p. 443.

4. *Dīgha*, II, pp. 70-1 (up to saññāvedayitanirodha).

The former comprises those who realise the eight vimokkhas (releases) and destroys their āsavas (impurities) by paññā (knowledge) while the latter comprises those who do not realise the eight vimokkhas but destroy their āsavas by paññā.[1]

All the arhats, it seems, did not possess the paṭisambhidās, which a bodhisattva acquires among others in the ninth bhūmi. It is often found that an arhat, who possessed paṭisambhidā also, was specially described as sahapaṭisambhidā arahattaṃ pāpuṇi (*i.e.*, attained arahathood with paṭisambhidā).[2]

With the sixth bhūmi, our comparison of the Hīnayānic and Mahāyānic stages end. The accounts of the remaining four bhūmis have nothing to do with the Hīnayānic practices, and besides, the attainments for which a bodhisattva performs the tasks of these bhūmis were unknown to the Hīnayānists. From the seventh bhūmi really commence the attempts of the bodhisattva to realise the dharmaśūnyatā, the nirnimittatā of things cognised, and the four bhūmis only indicate the gradual development of this knowledge of bodhisattvas until the Tathāgatabhūmi, in which he becomes a perfect Tathāgata and one with all the other Tathāgatas. The Hīnayānists, of course, accord a very high position to Buddha with the extraordinary power and attributes, some of which are found mentioned in connection with the last four bhūmis.

VII. *Dūraṅgamā or Sābhisaṃskāra-sābhoga Nirnimitta-vihāra*

A Bodhisattva after completing the bodhisattvamārga enters into the seventh bhūmi. He now commences practising a

1. *Dīgha*, II, p. 71 ; *Pug. P.*, p. 14; *Aṅguttara*, IV, p. 453 ; *Kośa*, VI. 63. The *Aṅguttara*, IV, pp. 452-3, however states that the Paññāvimutta attains the eight vimokkhas, and omits the words "kāyena phassitvā" which are mentioned in connection with the Kāyasakkhins and Ubhatobhāgavimuttas.

2. *Mil.*, p. 18 ; *DhP. A.*, II, pp. 58, 93 ; *Aṅguttara*, II, p. 160 : Sāriputta attained it within a fortnight after his ordination ; *Mahāvaṃsa*, pp. 3-6 : pabhinnatthādiñāṇaṃ pitakattayadhāriṇaṃ......arhantānaṃ ; p. 54 : chaḷabhiññe tepiṭake pabhinnapaṭisambhide, etc.

different and superior part aided by the ten kinds of knowledge of expedients (upāyaprajñā).[1] The ten kinds are as follows: He

i. (*a*) possesses a mind well-trained by the meditations of śūnyatā, animitta and apraṇihita: (*b*) appears as if acquiring a collection of great merits and knowledge;

ii. (*a*) comprehends the essencelessness (nairātmya-niḥsattva) of all dharmas; (*b*) does not give up the four apramāṇa-vihāras, *viz*., karuṇā, maitrī, muditā and upekṣā;

iii. (*a*) collects the best of all merits: (*b*) does not cling to any dharma;

iv. (*a*) remains detached from the three dhātus; (*b*) shows also his doings in the three dhātus;

v. (*a*) frees himself absolutely from all afflictions (kleśas); (*b*) performs actions needed for eradicating rāga, dveṣa etc. of beings;

vi. (*a*) realises the non-duality (advaya) of all things which are like mirage, echo, etc.; (*b*) shows also his various actions, discriminations, and immeasurable aspirations;

vii. develops a mind well aware of the sameness of all Buddhakṣetras;

viii. (*a*) merges himself in the dharmakāya of all Buddhas; (*b*) shows also his rūpa-kāya with its major and minor lakṣaṇas[2];

ix. acquires the voice of the Tathāgata; and

x. (*a*) comprehends the time distinguished as past, present and future as one moment (ekakṣaṇa-tṛpadhvānubodham); (*b*) shows also for the sake of the world his existence in the various kalpas.

---

1. *B. Bh*, p. 19. It should be noted that there are two sections in each of the ten kinds of knowledge or activities of the bodhisattva, the first section being indicated as (*a*) representing his actual, and the second as (*b*) the expedients (upāyakauśalya) adopted by him for the sake of ordinary human beings.

2. *Laṅkā*., p. 192, states that the bodhisattvas in this bhūmi cannot see the manomaya-dharmakāya of the Tathāgata.

For even a moment he does not remain dissociated from mārga-abhinirhāra (activities relating to the path), and jñānābhirhara (activities relating to jñāna). He completes all the ten pāramitās[1] and the four saṃgrahavastus, four adhiṣṭhānas and thirty-seven bodhipakṣika-dharmas.[2] He is now endowed with kāyakarma and vākkarma, pure according to the aspiration of the bodhisattva, the ten kuśalakarmapathas practised by Samyaksambuddhas and performs spontaneously the functions connected with the worldly arts and crafts (śilpasthāna-karmasthāna), which were mastered by him in the fifth bhūmi,[1] and is now the teacher of beings of the three thousand worlds[2] and has no equal in āśaya (aspiration) and exertion (prayoga) excepting, of course, those bodhisattvas who are in the higher bhūmis. He has now in front of his mind all dhyānas, samādhis, samāpattis, abhijñās and vimokṣas, which will be completed in the following bhūmis. He now practises many samādhis and goes beyond the Śrāvaka and Pratyekabuddha bhūmis and approaches the Prajñā-jñāna-vicaraṇabhūmi[3].

He attained nirodha in the sixth bhūmi, and in the seventh, he entered into and arose out of it but it should not be thought that he is subject to nirodha because he is above that delusion (vitarkadoṣa) of the Śrāvakas, *viz*, that nīrodha is saṃskṛtātyanta vyupaśama (the ultimate cessation of the constituted things).[4] It is one of the excellences of bodhisattvas that they rise up to, and remain in, the bhūtakoṭi-vihāra

1. *Daśa.*, pp. 56-7. It will be observed that the pāramitās are counted here as ten, *i.e.*, adding to the usual six (7) Upāyakauśalya, (8) Praṇidhāna, (9) Bala and (10) Jñāna.

2. *Daśa.*, pp. 57-8 gives briefly a comparative statement of the previous six bhūmis aud the seventh bhūmi. All the attainments acquired hitherto up to the seventh bhūmi are completed spontaneously (anābhogena) by the bodhisattvas in the later bhūmis.

3. *Daśa.*, p. 60 accounts for the reasons of Bodhisattva's repeating the performances of the first or other bhūmis. Cf. *B. Bh.*, p. 20.

4. In fact this shows the line of demarcation between the Śrāvakas and the Bodhisattvas.

(*i.e.*, ultimate possible state of sentient existence)[1] but are never subject to nirodha.

Armed with a great power, meditation and knowledge of expedients, he manifests himself in the world, shows his aspiration for Nirvāṇa and surrounds himself with a large number of followers but he remains mentally detached from everything. According to his praṇidhāna, he appears in the tridhātu to rescue beings from misery, but he is not contaminated by the worldly impurities. Though he has the Buddhajñāna, he shows himself as belonging to the class of Śrāvakas or Pratyekabuddhas, or even as subject to the snares of Māra and the influences of heretical teachers, going even so far as to sever himself from the Buddhadharma, take to worldly rites, or the enjoyments of the worlds and heavens.

He sees many Buddhas, hears from them the law, and acts according to their directions. His faith in the abstruse dharma (gambhīradharmakṣānti) is purified. He greatly develops the upāyakauśalya-pāramitā[2].

VIII. Acalā or Anābhoga-nirnimitta-vihāra

A Bodhisattva after completing the seven bhūmis and purifying the mārga by means of knowledge and expedients, collecting merits, forming the great resolution (mahāpraṇidhānas), establishing himself in the four adhiṣṭhānas (*viz.*, satya, tyāga, upaśama and prajñā), and so forth, he comprehends that all things are without origin, growth, decay, change and are by nature non-existent, and that their beginning,

1. Cf. Bhavāgraparama—Nevasaññānāsaññāyatana. *Kośa* VI, 37 fn. Cf. also *Dīgha*, II, p. 156: When Buddha was attaining parimibbāna, it was said that he "nevasaññānāsaññāyatana-sanāpattiyā vuṭṭhahitvā saññā-vedayita-nirodhaṃ samāpajji." Then he comes down from there and attains parinibbāna in the fourth jhāna.

2. The *Mtu.* (I, p. 127) states nothing in particular about this bhūmi except that a bodhisattva practises self-control for doing good to beings.

The *Śata.* (p, 1457) speaks of forty dharmas relating to the non-existence of soul and other worldly things, and the realisation of śūnyatā and allied matters. Hence, it gives the gist of the practices mentioned in the *Daśa.*

middle and end are all the same, in short, he comprehends the tathatā (thatness) of all thing.[2] He goes beyond the thought constructions due to citta and manovijñāna and knows that all dharmas are same like ākāśa (that is the faith that things have no orgination).[2] As soon as he acquires śānti, he is established in the eighth bhūmi (Acalā) and is above all enjoyments. He is possessed of dharmas which are spontaneous (anābhoga), and hence, has no anxiety for matters relating to kāya, vāk and citta, is free from all thought-constructions produced by the movements of thought and is established in the vipāka-dharmas (completion). He does not, in fact, practise the rules of conduct (samudācāras) of Bodhisattvas and Śrāvakas.[3]

He is now asked by the Buddhas to exert for acquiring the ten balas and four vaiśāradyas, which he up till now has not acquired, and also to take into consideration the ruffled, afflicted, deluded state of mind of the ignorant people. He is then reminded of one of his previous resolutions that dharmatā (*i.e.* dharmas being without origin continuity and decay) is not for Tathāgatas only but that the Śrāvakas and Pratyekabuddhas should also be made to realise it. He is then asked by Buddhas to exert for possessing like them immeasurable body, knowledge, worlds, refulgence, purity of mind and limbs, dharmālokas, kṣetras, sattvas and the variety of dharmas of the ten corners of the universe. The possession of immeasurables is of great value, far surpassing all the merits and knowledge acquired in the previous seven-bhūmis, because the merits and knowledge acquired hitherto were by means of exertion (sābhoga-karmaṇā) while in the present bhūmi the merits and knowledge are acquired spontaneously.

On account on his acquiring spontaneously the upāyakau-

1. Cf. *B. Bh.*, p. 21. The *Mtu.* (1, p. 136) simply tells us that the Bodhisattva develops mahākarṇṇāsamprayuktaṃ cittaṃ for going from the seventh to the eighth bhūmi and completes the account of the eighth bhūmi by mere enumeration of some legendary names.

2. Cf. *B. Bh.*, p. 22 ; see also pp. 49, 273.

3. Cf. *Laṅkā*, pp. 221-2, 226

śalyajñāna (knowledge of expedients) and as the result of his efforts to acquire omniscience, he comes to know how and when a world comes into being, continues to exist, and then disappears, and which karma is responsible for it. He understands the smallness, greatness, *i.e.*, every minute detail of the four elements, of the various classes of sentient beings, and their fields of action. Such detailed knowledge is needed by a bodhisattva, because he must appear among those sentient beings just as one of them in order to make them feel that he is same as them and that it is possible for every sentient being to become a Buddha.[1]

He develops ten vaśitūs[2] (control) over āyu (span of life), cetas (mind), pariṣkāra (requisites), karma (action), upapatti (origin, *i.e.*, birth), adhimukti (aspiration), praṇidhāna (resolution), ṛddhi (miracles), dharma (doctrines) and jñāna (knowledge).

The bodhisattva at this stage can be said to possess inconceivable, incomparable, immeasurable knowledge and all actions are always faultless. He now possesses the praṇidhānas, adhiṣṭhānas, pāramitās, mahāmaitrī, mahākaruṇā, dhāraṇī, pratibhāna, etc., in short, all dharmas, which make a Buddha. Hence, this bhūmi is called Acalā and there is no possibility of his going back from this bhūmi (avaivartyabhūmi). He is now a member of the Buddha family, and may be said to possess the Buddha gotra. He is henceforth constantly attended by all the gods and Vajrapāṇi.[2]

IX. *Sādhnmatī or Pratisaṃvid-vihāra*

A Bodhisattva after acquiring and developing the apramāṇa jñānas, dhāraṇīs, samādhis, abhijñās, minute knowledge of the lokadhātus, balas, and the vaiśāradyas of the Tathāgata

1. *Daśa.*, pp. 67-70 refers to the minute details of this knowledge, which is called Sarvākāratā. The details are passed over here. See also *Kārikā* (Bibl. Buddhica), p. I.

2. *Śata.*, p. 1458 gives the attainments of this bhūmi.. These are similar to those described in the *Daśa*, Cf. *Laṅkā.*, p. 192.

mentioned in the previous bhūmi, enters into the ninth bhūmi.[1] At this stage, he knows truly whether the dharmas are good, bad or indifferent, pure or impure, worldly or transcendental, conceivable or inconceivable, definite (niyata) or indefinite (aniyata), constituted or unconstituted. He knows the duties of the Śrāvakas, Pratyekabuddhas, Bodhisattvas, and the Tathāgatabhūmi. By the intelligence thus derived, he knows correctly the habits or the nature of thoughts of beings, their affliction (kleśa), actions (karma), faculties (indriya), aspiration (adhimukti), elements (dhātu), desire and intention (āśayānuśaya), birth according to desires (vāaānusandhi) and the rāśis (*i.e.*, gotras). He knows the multifarious nature (nānātva) of thoughts (citta), afflictions, karma, etc.

The bodhisattva in this bhūmi is in a position to have a very minute knowledge of the aims and qualities of every being and so he is now capable of deciding the way, in which a being is to be guided to the goal. He therefore modifies his teaching according to his judgment.

He also takes the form of a dharmabhāṇaka[2] (preacher of dharmas) in order to preserve the doctrines of the Teacher. On account of his immeasurable knowledge, he preaches the dharma in various ways, adopting the four pratisaṃvids (branches of logical analysis).[3] By the practices of these pratisaṃvids and working as a dharma-preacher, he becomes a receptacle of dharma utterances. Possessed of dhāraṇīs and pratibhānas he preaches the dharma to beings of all lokadhātus and does the same in an infinite number of ways.

Even in this bhūmi he continues his own spiritual practices and never gets out of the sight of Buddhas. He greatly develops

1. *Mtu.*, I, p. 141 mentions only some legendary names in this bhūmi and speaks of nothing else.

2. Cf. *B. Bh.*, p. 23.

3. *Viz.*, Dharma (nature or condition), Artha (analysis), Nirukti (etymological analysis) and Pratibhāṇa (context). It is difficult to find suitable expressions for the Pratisaṃvids. An idea, however, can be formed from the illustrative passages given in the *Daśa.*, pp. 77-8.

the bala-pāramitā. If he wishes, he can now become a Mahābrahmā.[1]

X. *Dharmameghā or Parama-Vihāra*

A bodhisattva on completion of the duties of the ninth bhūmi passes to the tenth.[2] Now he masters countless samādhis, and as the result, a lotus of infinite splendour and size appears and he is found to be seated on it with an equally resplendent body and established in the samādhi of omniscience (sarvajñānaviśeṣābhiṣeka)[3] surrounded by countless bodhisattvas, who are not yet in any one of the nine bhūmis and all looking at him. The rays of light issue forth from his body and make all beings happy.[4] While he is thus seated on the lotus, rays come forth from the Tathāgatas and consecrate him as a Samyaksambuddha possessed of omniscience, and hence this bhūmi is called Abhiṣekabhūmi.

He now knows thoroughly how the world and its dharmas appear and disappear, the innumerable functions of a Buddha, the countless bodhisattva-vimokṣamukhas, samādhis, dhāraṇīs, etc. He is now possessed of such smṛti-kauśalya (expedients of memory) that he can hold all dharmas showered on him (dharmameghā) by infinite Buddhas.[5] He can peaform any kind of miracle. In this bhūmi he greatly develops the jñānapāramitā.[6]

---

1. See *Śata.*, p. 1458. It speaks of quite different matters, some of which appear in *Mtu.*, I, p. 142, in connection with the tenth bhūmi.

2. The *Mtu.*, I. p. 142, has nothing corresponding to the account of the *Daśa.* It mentions something connected with the Bodhisattva's descent from the Tuṣita heaven and birth in the world of mortal beings.

3. Cf. *B. Bh.*, p. 24.

4. The wonders of the lotus rays described here are found as well as in the *Prajñāpāramitās* and other Mahāyāna works.

5. Cf. *B. Bh*,, p. 24.

6. *Śata* p. 1472 says that the bodhisattva in this bhūmi obtains, besides the pāramitās, Tathāgata-balas, four vaiśāradyas and four pratisaṃvids, eighteen āveṇikadharmas, sarvākārajñatā, sarvavāsanākleśānusandhiprahāṇa and sarvabuddhadharmaparāyaṇa.

It is after the tenth bhūmi that a bodhisattva becomes a Tathāgata, and so the *Laṅkāvatāra* calls this stage Tathāgata-bhūmi.[1] The *Śatasāhasrikā*[2] also remarks that a bodhisattva in the tenth bhūmi can be called a Tathāgata.

In the Hīnayāna literature one does not expect any account corresponding to that of the last four bhūmis. The conception of Buddha among the Hīnayānists is more or less hazy and that is due to the fact that the introduction of the Bodhisattva conception in their literature was only an afterthought, suggested undoubtedly by the Mahāyānic speculations. They carefully avoided all metaphysical conceptions introduced by the Mahāyānists in connection with the Bodhisattva and Buddha conceptions, though they could not offer a similar treatment to the devotion-inspiring stories of the lives of the bodhisattvas. The Hīnayānists, consistent with their doctrinal principles incorporated in their literature a life of Buddha preceeded by a short account of the Bodhisattva lives under the headings *Dūrenidāna* and *Avidūrenidāna*.[3] These two *Nidānas* are nothing but the gist of stories current among the Mahāyānists and possess trace, though very slight, of borrowings. Apart from the expressions like Buddhabīja[4] and Abhinirhāra,[5] the passage in which Sumedha brāhmaṇa says, "I have no need of nibbāna by destroying the kileśas, like Dīpaṅkara Dasabala, I shall attain the highest sambodhi and by means of the boat of dharma, I shall lead the men across the sea of transmigration and attain parinibbāna,"[1] shows clearly Mahāyānic, or at least, semi-Mahāyānic traces. But the Hīnayānists rejected not only the metaphysical speculations but also the stereotyped list of pāramis of the Mahāyānists. The *Jātaka* as well as the *Mahābodhivaṃsa*[6] states that the Buddhakārakadhamma is only ten pāramis, *viz.*, dāna, sīla, nekkhamma, paññā, viriya, khanti, sacca, adhiṭṭhāna, mettā and upekkhā. This is a list of their own making and does not agree with the Mahāyanic list.[7]

1. *Laṅkā*, p. 227.
2. *Śata* p. 145
3. *Jāt.*, I, p. 2.
4. *Ibid*, I, p. 16.
5. *Ibid*. I, p. 7
6. *Jāt*. I, p. 14.
7. *Ibid.*, p. 25; *Mahābodhivaṃsa*, p. 9.

Of the extraordinary spiritual powers attained by a Buddha, the Hīnayānists say very little. We have in the *Nikāyas* the remark that Buddhas (including Paccekabuddhas) attain perfect knowledge by themselves, and by following the dharma unheard before.[1]. A Samyaksambuddha preaches the dhamma and becomes the founder of a religion, and the leader of men and gods. He is sabbaññu (omniscient) and his knowledge of any matter whatsoever does not require any āvajjanā (reflection); he possesses ten balas[3] and four vesārajjas. In the *Kathāvathu*[2] there is a discussion on this topic, *viz.*, whether the powers of a Tathāgata are the same as those of a Sāvaka—a point raised by the Andhakas on the basis of the *Anuruddha-saṃyutta*[4]. Among the powers of Buddha referred to there is nothing véry special except the few mentioned above, and the Theravādins were driven to an uncomfortable position by the question of the Andhakas. In their literature Hīnayānists try to prove that Buddha is a rare being and superior to men and gods, but they mention also that there is hardly any distinction between an Arhat and a Buddha except that the latter is a founder and teacher of a religion.[5]

1. *Aṅguttara*, III, p. 9 ; *Pug.*, *P.* p. 14.
2. *Majjhima*, I, p. 482 sabbaññu sabbadassāvī aparisesaṃ ñāṇadassanaṃ paṭijānāti.
3. *Kvu.*, III, 1. 2.
4. *Saṃyutta*, V, p. 304.
5. For a comparison of Śrāvakas, Pratyekabuddhas and Buddhas see above and also *Dialogues of Buddha*, II, 1-3 ; III. 6.

TABULAR STATEMENT SHOWING THE CORRESPONDENCE BETWEEN HINAYĀNIC AND MAHĀYĀNIC BHUMIS

Hīnayānic Stages ...	*Daśabhūmikasūtra, Śata-sāhasrikā* and other Mahāyāna works	*Bodhisattvabhūmi* ...	*Śatasāhasrikā* (p. 1473) =*Mvyut.* 50 (śrāvakabhūmis) =*Tib. Dict.* (p. 475) of S. C. Das	*Mahāvastu*
Pre-sotāpanna or Puthujjana (up to completion of the 15 kṣaṇas of the darśanamārga, see above.	No name but there is a description of the practices.	A. Prakṛticaryā sub-divided into	I. Śuklavipaśyanābhūmi but see Rahder, *Daśa*, pp. xi, xvii.	A. Prakṛticaryā Śukla
Gotrabhū (Acc. to *Aṅguttara* and *Pug.P.* it precedes Sotāpattimagga but according to other works, adepts in one of the maggas and phalas are Gotrabhū).	...	(*a*) Gotravihāra and	II. Gotrabhūmi	...
...	Adhimukticaryābhūmi (in the *Madhyamakāvatāra*). See pp. 243-4.	(*b*) Adhimukticaryāvihāra or Śuddhāśaya-bhūmi	...	B. Praṇidhānacaryā
... Sotāpattimagga :— (i) Saddhānusārī (ii) Dhammānusārī	I. Pramuditā	III. Pramuditā	III. Aṣṭamakabhūmi [*Tib. Dic.* makes it the seventh bhūmi (?)].	I. Durārohā

I. Sotāpanna (or Sattakkhat-tu-parama) :— (i) Saddhāvimutta (ii) Diṭṭhippatta (see above. (*a*) Kolaṃkola (i) Devakolaṃkola (ii) Manussakolaṃkola (*b*) Ekavīcika or Ekabījī *Kośa* puts this after Sakadāgāmi.	II. Vimalā ...	B. Caryāpratipatti-bhūmi comprising IV. Adhiśīlavihāra	IV. Dharma-bhūmi	C. Anulomacaryā comprising II. Baddhamānā
II. Sakadāgāmi :— (i) Saddhāvimutta (ii) Diṭṭhippatta (see above).	...	...	V. Tanubhūmi...	...
III. Anāgāmi :— (i) Saddhāvimutta (ii) Diṭṭhippatta (see above). (*a*) Antarāparinibbāyi (*b*) Upahaccaparinibbāyi (*c*) Asaṅkhāraparinibbāyi (*d*) Sasaṅkhāraparinibbāyi (*e*) Uddhaṃsoto Akaniṭṭha-gāmi. The last mentioned is again subdivided into (1) Akaniṭṭhagā (i) Pluta	III. Prabhākarī ...	V. Adhicittavihāra ...	VI. Vītarāga-bhūmi	III. Puṣpamaṇḍitā

Hīnayānic stages ...	*Daśabhūmikasūtra*, *Śatasāhasrikā*, and other Mahāyāna works.	*Bodhisattvabhūmi* ...	*Śatasāhasrikā* (p. 1473) =*Mvyut.* 50 (śrāvakabhūmis) =*Tib. Dict.* (p. 475) of S.C. Das.	*Mahāvastu*
(ii) Ardhapluta (iii) Sarvacyuta (2) Naivasaṃjñānāsaṃjñāyatana-upagā (see above).				
IV. Arahatta :— (i) Ubhatobhāgavimutta (ii) Paññāvimutta	IV. Arciṣmatī ...	VI. Bodhipakṣya-pratisaṃyuktādhiprajñāvihāra	VII. Kṛtāvībhūmi	IV. Rucirā V. Cittavistarā VI. Rūpavatī
	V. Sudurjayā ...	VII. Satyapratisaṃyuktādhiprajñāvihāra	[The *Mvyut*, and *Tib. Dict*, stop here].	
	VI. Abhimukhī ...	VIII. Pratītyasamutpādapratisaṃyuktādhiprajñāvihāra		
Pratyekabuddha ...	...	...	VIII. Pratyekabuddhabhūmi	...
...	...	...	IX. Bodhisattvabhūmi	VII. Durjayā. D. Anivartanacaryā comprising VIII. Janmanirdeśa

...	VII. Dūraṅgamā ...	IX. Sābhisaṃskāra-sābhoga-nimitta-vihāra		...
	VIII. Acalā or Avaivartika	X. Anābhoga-nirnimittavihāra (or Niyatā		
...	IX. Sādhumati ...	XI. Prattsaṃvidvihāra (or Niyata-caryā)		IX. Yauvarājya
Samyaksambuddha ...	X. Dharmameghā (or Abhiṣeka-bhūmi)	XII. Parana-vihāra (or Niṣṭhāganana) or Tathāgata-bhūmi	X. Buddhabhūmi	X. Abhiṣeka *N.B.*—The powers and qualities attained in the various bhūmis according to the *Mahāvastu* do not tally with those mentioned in other works.

CHAPTER VI

Conception of Kāya

The first point of difference between the Hīnayāna and Māhāyana schools noticed in the *Saddharama-Puṇḍarīka*, viz., that Buddha makes a show of his existence in the three dhātus leads us to an examination of the question of the Kāyas of Buddha as conceived by the Hīnayānists and the Mahāyānists. Of the Hīnayāna schools, the Sthaviravādins had very little to do with the kāya conceptions, as Buddha was to them an actual man living in this world like any other human being and subject to all the frailties of a mortal body. Metaphorically they sometimes spoke of Buddha as identical with Dhamma without any metaphysical implication but these remarks gave an opportunity to the Sarvāstivādins and the Mahāyānists to put forth their theories of Dharmakāya.

The Sarvāstivādins commenced speculating on the kāya of Buddha, but it was the school of the Mahāsaṅghikas that took up the question of kāya in right earnest and paved the way for the speculations of the Mahāyānists.

The early Mahāyānists, whose doctrines are mostly to be found in the *Aṣṭādaśasāhasrikā Prajñāpāramitā*, along with the school of Nāgārjuna (i.e., Mādhyamika) conceived of two kāyas : (i) Rūpa (or Nirmāṇa) kāya, denoting bodies, gross and subtle, meant for beings in general, and (ii) Dharmakāya, which was used in two senses, one being the body of Dharma (*i. e.*, collection of practices), which makes a being a Buddha, and the other the metaphysical principle underlying the universe—the Reality (*Tathatā*).

The Yogācāra school distinguished the gross rūpakāya from the subtle rūpakāya, naming the former Rūpa- or Nirmāṇa-kāya and the latter Sambhoga-kāya. The *Laṅkāvatāra*, representing the earliest stage of the Yogācāra, conceives the Sambhoga-kāya as Niṣyanda-buddha or Dharma-niṣyanda-buddha (the Buddha produced by the Dharma). The

Sūtrālaṅkāra[1] uses the term Sambhogakāya for Niṣyanda-buddha and Svābhāvikakāya for Dharmakāya. In the *Abhisamayālaṅkārakārikā* and the recast version of the *Pañcaviṃśati-sāhasrikā Prajñāpāramitā*, Sambhogakāya denotes the subtle body which the Buddhas adopted for preaching the doctrines to Bodhisattvas, and Dharmakāya the body purified by the practice of the bodhipakṣika and other dharmas, which constitute a Buddha. For the metaphysical Dharmakāya these texts use the term Svabhāva or Svābhāvika-kāya. The *Vijñaptimātratāsiddhi* retains the conception of the *Kārikā* but adopts a new term Svasambhogakāya to denote the Dharmakāya of the *Kārikā* and distinguishes the Sambhogakāya by naming it Parasambhogakāya.

Realistic conceptipn of Buddha in the Nikāyas

In a land where the tendency to deify saints is so strong, that it lies to the credit of the early Hīnayānists that they were able to retain the human conception of Buddha even a century or two after his actual existence, when the scriptures may be regarded as having been put into a definite shape. They gave expression to their conception of Buddha in the following words :

Bhagavā arahaṃ sammāsambuddho vijjācaraṇasampanno lokavidū anuttaro purisadammasārathi satthā devamanussānaṃ buddho bhagavā. So imaṃ lokaṃ sadevakaṃ sabrahmakaṃ sasamaṇa-brāhmaṇaṃ pajaṃ sadevaṃ sayaṃ abhiññā sacchikatvā pavedeti. So dhammseti ādikalyāṇaṃ, etc.

[The Blessed One is an arhat, a fully awakened one, endowed with knowledge and good conduct, happy, a knower of the world, unsurpassed, a leader able to control men, a teacher of men and gods, the awakened, the blessed. He knows thoroughly the worlds of gods, māras, recluses, brahmins and men, and having known them he makes his knowledge known to others. He preaches the dhamma (doctrines), which is excellent in the beginning, middle and end, etc.][2]

1. *Sūtrā.*, pp. 45, 188.
2. *Dīgha*, I, pp. 87-88 ; *cf. Lal. Vis.*, p. 3 ; *Sad. P.*, pp. 144, 376.

A description like this does not suggest that Buddha was originally more than a man, a mortal. In the cosmology of the Buddhists, the gods of the various heavens, the highest of which is Brahmaloka,[1] are only beings of superior merit and power, but they are inferior, in the matter of spiritual attainments, to the saints or arhats. So in this description, the Hīnayānists do not attribute any transcendental or theistic element to Buddha. All they say is that Śākyamuni, by pure and simple spiritual culture in this life and as a result of the accumulated merits of his previous lives, reached the highest stage of perfection and attained not only knowledge and power superior to any man and god but also the highest knowledge and power attainable. In the *Majjhima Nikāya*, Ānanda explains why Buddha should be considered superior to the Arhats as well, although both arrived at the same goal. He says that there is not a single bhikkhu, who can be regarded as endowed with all the qualities in all their forms as possessed by Buddha. Moreover, a Buddha is the originator of the path not existing before, a knower and promulgator of the mārga, which is only followed by the sāvakas.[2]

Nikāya passages admitting a non-realistic conception

In the face of such descriptions of Buddha, it would have been difficult for the later Hīnayāna schools to sublimate the human elements in him, had it not been for certain expressions in some of the earlier works of the Piṭaka, which lent themselves to other interpretations. Some of these expressions are :—

(1) Yo vo Ānanda mayā dhammo ca vinayo ca desito paññatto so vo mam' accayena satthā.

(Buddha said to Ānanda just before his parinibbāna 'the dhamma and vinaya that have been preached by me will be your teacher after my death').[3]

1. In the Mahāyānic works also, as for instance, in the *Daśa.*, it is stated that a Bodhisattva can become a Mahābrahmā in the ninth bhūmi if he so wished.

2. *Majjhima*, III, p. 8.

3. *Dīgha*, II, p. 154 ; *Mil.*, p. 99. This passage occurs in many places of the *Nikāyas*.

The dhamma and vinaya clearly refer to the collection of doctrines and disciplinary rules delivered by Buddha. It is also evident from the conversation of Ānanda with Gopaka-Moggallāna, in which the former explains why the monks after Buddha's death should not be regarded as without refuge (appaṭisaraṇa). He says that they have now a refuge in Dhamma (dhamma-paṭisaraṇa), which, he points out, are the doctrines and disciplinary rules.[1]

(2) Bhagavato'mhi putto oraso mukhato jāto dhammajo dhammanimmito dhammadāyādo iti.[2] Taṃ kissa hetu? Tathāgatassa h' etam adhivacanaṃ. Dhammakāyo iti pi Brahmakāyo iti pi, Dhammabhūto[3] iti pi ti.

Just as a brāhmaṇa would say that he is born of Brahmā, through his mouth—Brahmuno putto oraso mukhato jāto brahmajo brahmanimmito brahmadāyādo—so a Śākyapuittiya-samaṇa may say that he is born of Bhagavā, through his mouth, born of his doctrine, made of his doctrine, etc. Though in this passage Dhamma is equated to Brahmā, the context shows that there is no metaphysical sense in it; it is only to draw a parallel between a brāhmaṇa and a Śākyputtiya-samaṇa that Dhammakāya is equated to Brahmakāya.

(3) Vakkali on his death-bed became very eager to see Buddha in person; so Bhagavā came to him and said,

"Alaṃ Vakkali kiṃ te pūtikāyena diṭṭhena. Yo kho Vikkali dhammaṃ passati so maṃ passati. Yo maṃ passati so dhammaṃ passati."

Just after saying this, Buddha referred to his dhamma of impermanence (anicca). There are in the Nikāyas many

1. *Majjhima*, *Gopaka-Moggallāna Sutta* (No. 108). *Cf. Saddhamma Saṅgaha* (*JPTS.*, 1890), ch. x, p. 65: Buddha says "84,000 dhamma-kkhandhas have been preached by me in 45 years, I alone only pass away while there are 84,000 dhammakkhandhas, which like 84,000 Buddhas (Buddha-sadisa) will admonish you."

2. *Saṃyutta*, II, p. 221; *Majjhima*. III, p. 29 has the identical passage with the addition "no āmisadāyādo" after "dhammadāyādo." For the interpretation of "dhammadāyādo" see *Majjhima*, I, pp. 12f.

3. *Majjhima*, II, p. 84; *Dīgha*, III, p. 84; *Majjhima*, III, pp. 195, 224 has "Bhagavā jānaṃ jānāti passaṃ passati cakkhubhūto ñāṇabhūto. dhammabhūto."

passages of this import, which may well be taken as precursors of the later Mahāyānic conceptions and probably formed the basis of their speculations. But the passages, when read as they stand, do not appear to bear any metaphysical sense. In this passage Buddha refers to his body as *putikāya* (body of impure matter), and to lay stress on his doctrines, he says that his dhamma should be looked upon with the same awe and reverence by his disciples as they regarded his person.[1]

(4) The passage in the *Aṅguttara Nikāya*,[2] where Buddha says that he is neither a god, nor a gandhabba, nor a man, has been taken by Prof. Masson-Oursel[3] as showing trace of the Mahāyānic kāya conceptions. It is not impossible to read some metaphysical ideas into the passage, though probably the compiler of the Suttas did not mean to convey them. Droṇa brāhmaṇa, noticing the sign of wheel in the feet of Buddha, enquired of him whether he was a deva, a gandhabba, a yakkha or a mortal. Buddha replied that he was none of these beings as he had got rid of the āsavas (impurities) by the continuance of which one remains a deva, gandhabba, yakkha or a mortal. Just as a lotus is born in water, grows in it but it remains above and is apart from it, so also Buddha was born in the world, grew up in it but overcame it (abhibhuyya) and lived unaffected by the same.

---

1. *Saṃyutta*, III, p. 120; *Majjhima*, I, pp. 190, 191: Yo paṭiccasamuppādaṃ passati so dhammaṃ passati, yo dhammaṃ passati so paṭiccasamuppādaṃ passati. For other references, see Prof. Vallée Poussin's article "Notes sur les Corps du Buddha" in *Le Muséon*, 1913, pp. 259-290. Compare the remarks in the later Pāli works,—

Saddhamma Saṅgaha (*JPTS.*, 1890), p. 61:

Yo me passati saddhammaṃ so maṃ passati Vakkali,
Apassamāno saddhammaṃ maṃ passe pi na passati.

Milinda, p. 71: yo dhammaṃ passati so bhagavantaṃ passati, nidassetuṃ dhammo hi maharāja bhagavatā desito ti.

Ibid., p. 73: Dhammakāyena pana kho mahārāja sakyā bhagavā nidassetuṃ, dhammo hi mahārāja bhagavatā desito ti.

2. *Aṅguttara*, II, p. 38.

3. Prof. Masson-Oursel's article "*Les trois Corps du Bouddha*", *J.A.*, 1913, pp. 581ff.

Therefore, he asked the brāhmaṇa not to regard him as anything but the Buddha.

There are other passages referring to the miraculous powers of Buddha, *viz.*, his ability to live a kalpa or to assume different forms and perform such other miracles, but it should be noted that these powers were attributed not to Buddha alone but also to his disciples in general, who had been able to attain the higher stages of sanctification.[1]

Kāya-conception of the Theravādins remains unchanged

Even if it be assumed that the Mahāyānic ideas are latent in the above-mentioned expressions, though not adequately expressed, the discussion in the *Kathāvatthu*[2] to establish the historical existence of Buddha as against those who denied it, and the manner in which references were made to the events of Buddha's life as depicted in the *Nikāyas* leaves no vestige of doubt about the opinion of the Theravādins regarding the kāya of Buddha.

Though the terms rūpakāya and dharmakāya found their way into the later Pāli works[3] from Mahāyāna or semi-Mahāyāna works, these did not bring with them any non-realistic sense. Buddhaghosa even as late as the fifth century A. D. refers thus to the kāyas :

Yo pi so Bhagavā asīti anuvyañjana-paṭimaṇḍita-dvattiṃsa-mahāpurisalakkhaṇa-vicitra-rūpakāyo sabbākāraparisuddha-sīla-kkhandhādi-guṇaratana-samiddha-dhammakāya yasamahatta-puññamahatta............appaṭipuggalo arahaṃ sammāsam-buddho.

(That Bhagavā, who is possessed of a beautiful rūpakāya, adorned with eighty minor signs and thirty-two major signs of a great man, and possessed of a dhammakāva purified in

1. See *Kośa*, II, 10 (also for references to the *Nikāyas*.

2. *Kvu* , xvii, 1 : The Vetulyakas held on the basis of the passage cited above that "it is not right to say that the exalted Buddha lived in the world of mankind." The Theravādins did not agree with them. Buddhaghosa also pointed out how the passage should be interpreted.

3. See, *e.g.*, *Sad. Saṅ.* (*JPTS.*, 1893), p. 69 :

Sambuddhānaṃ dve kāyā rūpakāyo sirīdharo,
Yo tehi desito dhammo dhammakāyo ti vuccati.

every way and glorified by sīla, samādhi, etc.,[1] full of splendour and virtue, incomparable and fully awakened).[2]

Though Buddhaghosa's conception was realistic, he was not immune from the religious bias of attributing super-human powers to Buddha. In the *Atthasālini*[3] he says that during the three months of his absence from the world while Buddha was engaged in preaching Abhidhamma to his mother in the Tusita heaven, he created some *Nimmita-buddhas* as exact replicas of himself. These Nimmitabuddhas could not be distinguished from the real Buddha in voice, words and even the rays of light that issued forth from his body. The created Buddha could be detected only by the gods of the higher classes and not by the ordinary gods or men of the world.

In short, the early Hīnayānists conceived Buddha's *rūpakāya* as that of a human being,[4] and his *dhammakāya* as the collection of his dhammas, *i.e.*, doctrines and disciplinary rules collectively.

Conception of the Sarvāstivādins

The other school, the Sarvāstivādins, who retained the realistic conception of Buddha, differed a little from the Theravādins. Unfortunately their original Piṭakas in Sanskrit are lost beyond recovery and we have to depend for our information about them on the few fragmentary pieces of their literature discovered in Central Asia, or in the Chinese translations of their Āgamas, in which again very little spadework has yet been done.[5] Our main source of information at present is the *Abhidharamakośa*, made accessible to us from Chinese by the monumental French translation of Professor

1. The five khandhas referred to here are sīla, samādhi, paññā, vimutti and vimuttiñāṇadassana. See *Mil*,, p. 98.

2. *Vis. M.*, p. 234 ; *Jātaka*, I, p. 84 ; Rūpakāyasirī.

3. *Attha.*, p. 16.

4. See Prof. La Vallée Poussin's *Bouddhisme*, pp. 232f.

5. Dr. Chizen Akanuma (*Eastern Buddhist*, II, p. 7) quotes some passages from the Chinese Aṅguttara and Saṃyukta Āgamas and shows that the *dharmakāya* of Buddha denoted the collection of dharmas (teachings).

La Vallee Poussin. The *Kośa*, again, it should be noted, is the work of a systematiser and the production of a time much later than that of the Āgamas, to which it bears the same relation as the *Visuddhimagga* does to the Pāli Piṭakas. As the present state of our knowledge indicates that the *Divyāvadāna* and the *Lalitavistara*[1] originally belonged to this school, though these were recast by the Mahāyānists, we should examine with caution some of the statements found in them regarding the kāya conception.

I. *Divyāvadāna*

There are a few passages in the *Divyāvadāna* throwing light on the rūpakāya and dharmakāya of Buddha and bearing the identical sense of the Pāli works. On the occasion Śroṇa Koṭikarṇa said that, through the grace of his teacher, he had seen the dharmakāya of Buddha, but as he was anxious to see the rūpakāya, he wanted to go to the place where Buddha was living at the time.[2] Upagupta once said to Māra that he had seen the dharmakāya only and requested him to show him the rūpakāya. Māra thereupon made an image (vigraha) of Buddha replete with all the major and minor signs of great men.[3] In the answer that king Rudrāyaṇa gave to Bimbisāra that "na rājan kṛpaṇo loke dharmakāyena saṃspṛśet" [let not, O King, an irreligious person[4] attain (lit. touch) the dharmakāya], the word "dharmakāya" may bear a metaphysical interpretation but the context does not warrant it.[5] The remark made by Aśoka, after Upagupta had pointed out to him the stūpa of Ānanda, makes the sense of dharmakāya quite explicit. It runs thus : 'That body which you all call pure, excellent and made of dharma (dharmātmano dharmamayo) was borne (dhāritaṃ) by him called Viśoka (=Ānanda) and therefore his stūpa deserves great honour. The lamp of dharma, the

---

1. Winternitz, *Geschichte etc.*, II, p. 194.
2. *Divyā.*, p. 19.
3. *Ibid.*, p. 360.
4. *Ibid.*, p. 560 : kṛpaṇa is defined thus :
   yas tu dharmavirāgārtham adharme nirato nṛpaḥ,
   sa rājan kṛpaṇo jñeyas tamastamaḥparāyaṇaḥ.
5. *Ibid*, p. 560.

dispeller of darkness of afflictions that shone still among men was due to the power of him, the son of Sugatendra, and therefore, should be worshipped with special reverence.[1]

There are, however, Avadānas in the *Divyāvadāna*, which were not without some Mahāyānic tint, for, we read in the *Rudrāyaṇāvadāna*,[2] as we usually find in the Mahāyānic works, that rays of light issued forth from Buddha's mouth when he smiled, irradiating the beings of heaven and hell. It is noteworthy that the *Atthasālinī*[3] also speaks of raśmis (rays of light) of six colours issuing out of Buddha's body. It seems that the Mahāyānic ideas were percolating gradually into the rocky soil of the conservative Theravādins.

II. Lalitavistara

The *Lalitavistara* gives us a picture of Buddha more superhuman than human and yet far from the Mahāyānic conceptions of the Sambhogakāya and Dharmakāya, though in the last two chapters it dwells on the doctrine of Tathatā. In the *Lalitavistara* Buddha is deified but there are no traces of the Trikāya conception. It says in many places that Buddha appears in the world of men for *lokānuvartana*[4] (*i.e.* to follow the ways of the world), which, if he so desired, he could avoid by remaining in one of the heavens and attaining emancipation there. The running account of Buddha's life is interrupted at times—probably these are afterthoughts of the compiler—by dialogues between Buddha and Ānanda, in order to make the treatise appear Mahāyānic and not Hīnayānic. At one place Buddha explains to Ānanda that, unlike human beings, he did not stay in the filth of mother's womb but in a jewel-casket (ratnavyūha)[5]

1. *Divyā.*, pp. 366-7. Cf. Przyluski, *Asoka*, p. 408 : In connection with the destruction of the law, Mahāmāyā exclaimed "Ceuxqui sont nés du Corps de la Loi (dharmakāya), ou sont-ils allés ?'
2. *Divyā.*, xxxvii, p. 568.
3. *Attha*, p. 16.
4. E.g., *Mtu.*, I, pp. 168, 170.
5. *Vis.*, *M.* pp. 88, 105, 106. This formed one of the points of contention of the Mahāsaṅghikas. See Masuda, *Early Origin etc.*, in the *Asia Major*, Vol. II.

placed in the womb, which was as hard as adamant but soft to the touch like the down of a Kācilindika bird, and that his birth and other events connected with it were all superhuman. At the same time, he prophesied that there will be, in the future, men unrestrained in act, thought and speech, ignorant, faithless, proud, believing without deliberation what is heard by them, who will not believe in the superhuman nature of his birth.[1] One can perceive through the poetical exaggerations of the *Lalitavistara* that it has in view the historical Buddha endowed with the major and minor signs —a human being after all, who requires to be reminded by the heavenly musicians of the acts of his past lives and his resolution to become a Buddha and rescue beings from misery, and who needs a stimulus to renounce the world in order to fulfil his resolution.[2] In connection with the offer of houses, which were made by the gods to the Bodhisattva when he was in the womb, it is said that in order to please all the gods who offered houses, he caused his appearances by means of the Mahāvyūha samādhi. This does not clearly reflect any idea of the Nirmāṇakāya—it appears more like some of the miracles mentioned in the *Nikāyas*. In the last chapter of the *Lalitavistara* where Buddha's attributes are mentioned, he is called the great tree (mahādruma), because he possessed a body of Dharmakāyajñānaa (knowledge of Dharmakāya).[3] As this chapter is very likely a Mahāyāna addition, we may reasonably say that the *Lalitavistara* in its original form was a treatise of the Sarvāstivādins, who viewed Buddha as a human being with superhuman attributes.

III. Abhidharmakośa

We may now consider the writings of Vasubandhu, the great exponent of the Sarvāstivāda school. In his *Abhidharmakośa* he imparted a new meaning to the words Dharma-

1. *Lal. Vis*, pp. 87ff. This goes against the Sarvāstivāda and Theravāda conception.

2. The descriptions gave opportunity to the Mahāyānists to invent Upāyakauśalya Pāramitā, the duties of Adhyeṣaṇā, Yācanā, etc.

3. *Lal. Vis.*, p. 428.

kāya and Rūpakāya. In examining the three Śaraṇas, he tried to bring out the real sense of Buddha, Dharma, and Saṅgha, in which a devotee takes refuge. He said that those who take refuge in Buddha do, in fact, take refuge in the dharmas (qualities), which constitute a Buddha (buddhakāraka), *i. e.*, the dharmas by the acquisition of which a person is called a Buddha, or in other words, the dharmas by the acquisition of which a person understands all things. These dharmas are kṣayajñāna (knowledge of the destruction of misery), anutpādajñāna[1] (knowledge of the further non-origination of misery) and samyagdṛṣṭi (right view) of the Aśaikṣas together with the dharmas attendant to the jñāna, *viz.* the five pure skandhas. A dharmakāya is formed of these dharmas. In another place, while showing the sameness of the Dharmakāyas of all Buddhas, he explained the Dharmakāya as a series of pure dharmas, or rather a renewal of the psycho-physical organism of the substratum (anāsravadharmasaṃtāna, āśrayaparāvṛtti).[2] The Dharmakāya then signified a new purified personality or substratum (āśraya), but it is pointed out that such a dharmakāya is possessed also by an arhat.[3] In the *Sūtrālaṃkāra*[4] such a dharmakāya is attributed to the mother of

1. *Kośa*, VII, 67 explains that Kṣayajñāna with Anutpādajñāna makes Bodhi. On account of difference among saints in the acquisition of these jñānas, Bodhi is said to be of three kinds: Śrāvakabodhi, Pratyekabudhabodhi and Anuttarasamyaksambodhi. By the above two jñānas one completely abandons ignorance (aśeṣāvidyāprahāṇāt); by the first, one realises the truth that his task is accomplished (*i.e.*, duḥkha has been realised by him); by the second, one realises that his task is no more to be accomplished (*i.e.*, duḥkha has been realised by him and he will not have to exert any more.)

The samyagdṛṣṭi of the Aśaikṣas is to see things as they are really, to know truly the general character (sāmānyalakṣaṇa) of dharmas. See *Kośa*, VI, 50 fn. For a note on the Kṣayajñāna, see Masuda, *Early Origin etc.*. in *Asia Major*, Vol. II, Fasc. I.

2. Kośa, VII, 34 for the sense of āśraya, see *Ibid*, viii 34, fn. cf. aśraya-pariśuddhi in *Sūtrā.*, p. 286.

3. *Kośa*, IV, 56.

4. Huber, *Sūtrālaṃkāra*, pp. 217, 390, 390 quoted in the *Kośa*, VII, 32. p. 81.

Śākyamuni or to an advanced upāsaka. Thus, it is seen that the *Kośa* has two interpretations of the Dharmakāya, one being the qualities adhering to a Buddha and the other being the purified personality (āśraya) possessed by him. The *Kośa*, in fact, replaces the concrete conceptions of the Dharmakāya found in the *Nikāyas* and the *Divyāvadāna* by an abstract one. In the last two works the Dharmakāya signified only the doctrines, *viz.*, the Bodhipakkhiya dharmas or Anicca, Dukkha and Anattā, together with the *Vinaya* rules contained in the *Pātimokkha*, while to Vasubandhu it meant the qualities adhering to a Buddha as well as the purified personality (āśraya).

Referring to the formulæ of the Śaraṇas, Vasubandhu says that as the physical body (rūpakāya) of Buddha does not undergo any modification by the acquisition of the quality of Buddha, one should not take refuge in the rūpakāya of Buddha, which is, in fact, the rūpakāya of the Bodhisattva and hence sāsrava (impure). Just as a man would respect a monk for the qualities adhering to him and not for his person, so a devotee should take refuge in Buddhatva and not in Buddha the person. In the same way, Vasubandhu explains the two śaraṇas, *viz.*, Dharma and Saṅgha, the former being explained as Nirvāṇa, or the three Truths—Duḥkha, Samudaya and Mārga, or Sukha, Duḥkha and Asukha-aduḥkha—and the latter as the qualities that a saṅgha of monks is expected to possess.[1]

The *Vibhāṣā* informs us that there are some, who believe that to take refuge in Buddha is to take refuge in the body constituted by the head, nape of the neck, belly, back, hands and feet of the Tathāgata. Some say that as the body is born of parents, it is impure (sāsrava) and therefore it should not be a place of refuge. The refuge should be the Aśaikṣa dharmas, which make a Buddha, *i. e.*, the Dharmakāya[2]. Apparently the *Vibhāṣā* refers in the first

1. Compare the formula of Saraṇa in the Nikāyays, *e.g.*, *Dīgha*, III, p 227.

2 *Kośa*, VI, p. 32 ; IV, p. 76n. ; VIII, p. 34.

instance to the earlier Hīnayāna schools and in the second to the Sarvāstivādins and their offshoots.

Allied Dharmakāya Conception among the Satyasiddhis and the Mahāyānists

The Satyasiddhi school takes almost the similar view of the Dharmakāya as the Sarvāstivādins. According to it, the Dharmakāya is made of śīla, samādhi, prajñā, vimukti and vimuktijñānadarśana. Buddhaghosa, Nāgārjuna and the author of the *Milindapañha* also refer to such a dharmakāya[1]. It means that the body of Buddha was purified by the practices of these five skandhas stated above, and hence it can be called Dharmakāya. But as these purifications are obtained by Arhats also, Harivarman, the propounder of the Satyasiddhi school, distinguished the Dharmakāya of Buddha by saying that his Dharmakāya consisted not only of the above five purificatory practices but also of ten powers (daśa bala), four proficiencies (vaiśāradya) and the three recollections (smṛtyupasthāna), which the Arhats cannot obtain.[2]

The *Abhisamayālaṅkārakārikā*[3] and *Pañcaviṃśatisāhasrikā-prajñāpāramitā*,[4] important text-books of the Yogācāra school, define the Dharmakāya in a similar sense. These state that the various dharmas, *viz.*, Bodhipakṣikas, Apramāṇas, Vimokṣas, Samāpattis and so forth, constitute Sarvajñatā (omniscience) and Sarvajñatā is the Dharmakāya. It should be noted that the *Kārikā* and the *Prajñāpāramitā* use this expression in a sense different from that current in the Mahāyāna texts. They really mean the Svasambhogakāya of the later Vijñānavādins.

The *Prajñāpāramitās* also maintain the conception that the Dharmakāya is produced by dharmas, the highest of which is, according to them, the prajñāpāramitā, *i. e.*, the knowledge, which helps a person to realise the dharma-śūnyatā. The

1. *Vis. M.*, p. 234 ; *M. Vṛ.* (as opinion of non-Mādhyamikas), p. 423 ; *Mil.*, p. 98,
2. Sogen, *Systems* etc , pp. 181, 182.
3. *Kārikā*, ch. viii.
4 *Pañca.*, (ASB. ms.) leaf 224a.

Aṣṭādaśasāhasrikā takes up the question, whether the honour shown to the relics of the Tathāgatakāya is more meritorious than the honour shown to the *Prajñāpāramitā, e.g.*, by making a copy of it. The answer given is that the relics depend on the body purified by the prajñāpāramitā, and therefore it is the source of Buddhas. The source deserves more honour than the remnants of the fruit (*i.e.*, relics of Buddha) produced therefrom, and therefore it is more meritorious to honour the Prajñāpāramitā than the relics[1]. It adds that all teachings of Buddha issue from the Prajñāpāramitā, and the Dharmabhāṇakas preserve and propagate them; so the Dharmabhāṇakas should also be respected. They are protected by the Dharmakāya, the Prajñāpāramitā. *Sarvajñatā* (omniscience) is pervaded (paribhāvita) by the prajñāpāramitā; from *sarvajñatā* issues the body of Tathāgata, the relics of whom are worshipped; hence prajñāpāramitā deserves greater honour.[2]

Hīnayānic speculations : (a) Whether Rūpakāya is vipākaja ?

The *Kośa* maintains that the rūpakāya of Buddha endowed with the major and minor signs is the result of the excellent karmas of his previous lives. According to it, even the Buddhas cannot escape the effects of their karma. The schism created by Devadatta in the saṅgha is attributed to a deed in one of the previous lives of Śākyamuni. The *Vyākhyā* and the *Vibhāṣā* explain that it happened to Śākyamuni only, and not to the other Buddhas, because in one of his former lives he sowed dissensions among the disciples of an ascetic, possessed of five abhijñās.[3] That the Buddhas enjoy or suffer the effects of karma is also maintained by the *Divyāvadāna*[4] and the *Majjhima Nikāya.*[5] The *Divyāvadāna* refers to a saying of Śākyamuni that even the Jinas themselves are not free from their karmas, while the *Majjhima Nikāya*[5] says that a Tathāgata performs good deeds in his previous lives, and as a result of these, he enjoys

1. *Aṣṭa*, ch. iv.

2. *Ibid.*, p. 99. It is from this conception that the Prajñāpāramitā is addressed as the mother of Buddhas.

3. *Kośa*, VII, 34, p. 8 fn., 84; IV, 102, p. 212 fn. 2.

4. *Divyā.*, p. 416. 5. *Majjhima*, III, p. 227.

in the present, pure and pleasant sensations (vedanā) only. Tradition says that when Buddha was hurt by the splinter of stone thrown by Devadatta, he said that ninety-one kalpas ago he had hurt a person by a spear, as the result of which evil deed, he now received a wound.

The *Milindapañha*, however, takes a different view of this matter. Admitting that Devadatta created a schism in the saṅgha, it says that as the schism was not created by any act of Buddha's own, and as it was caused by an external influence, it should not be said that Buddha as the result of his *karma* had a divided assembly (bhejjapariso). In a similar way it explains away the wound or the illnesses, from which Buddha suffered. First it asserts that Buddha attained omniscience after uprooting all roots of evil (akusalamūlas) ; so he could not have any more sufferings through *karma.* It then says that apart from *karma,* there are other causes like the three humours, seasons, etc., which produce vedanā (feelings). According to it, the wound that Buddha received was due to an opakammika (accidental) cause and his illnesses to causes other than *karma.*[1]

(*b*) *Was Buddha a Jarāyuja or Upapāduka* ?

In order to remove doubt from the minds of the people as to the nature of the birth of so great and meritorious a being as the Bodhisattva in his last existence—a doubt expressed also in the *Lalitavistara,* where a ratnavyūha has been devised for the Bodhisattva's abode in his mother's womb—the *Kośa*[2] proceeds to show that the Bodhisattvas possess the power of choosing the manner of their birth (upapattivaśitva), and that Śākyamuni chose birth in a womb (jarāyu) with two objects : one was to benefit the Śākya clan and at the same time not to give an opportunity to the people to consider him a magician or a god or a demon, and the other was to leave some relics of his body, by worshipping which men and other beings would go to heaven by thousands, or attain deliverance.

The Mahāsaṅghikas and their followers[3] assert that

1. *Mil.*, pp. 134f. 2. *Kośa*. III, 9. 3. *E g.*, the Vetulyakas.

Śākyamuni was an upapāduka (self-born), and that even his son Rāhula was also an upapāduka, for Bodhisattvas cannot have *kāma.* They assert that the Bodhisattvas are possessed of 'ādhiṣṭhāniki ṛddhi' (*i.e.*, the miraculous power of appearing anywhere and in any form), and that by the power Śākyamuni made a show of his existence in the womb of Māyā. They conceived Buddha as *lokottara* (transcendental), and Śākyamuni as only a created body (Nirmāṇakāya). The transcendental Buddha has a rūpakāya, which is limitless, everlasting, free from all sāsrava dharmas. He is always in samādhi,[1] never sleeps or dreams, and can know everything in an instant of thought. He knows neither fatigue nor rest, and is ever busy in enlightening sentient beings. His power and his life are limitless. For the benefit of sentient beings, he appears at will in any one of the six gatis. Whatever he utters relates to the truth, though people may understand him differently. In short, the Mahāsaṅghikas conceived Buddha as a totally supramundane being with illimitable powers and knowledge, who never desired to attain Nirvāṇa.[2]

Kāya conception at the beginning of Mahāyāna

The Mahāyānists incorporated the Nirmāṇakāya conception of the Mahāsaṅghikas into their Trikāya theory, adding the two others, Sambhogakāya and Dharmakāya, the former approaching the Mahāsaṅghika conception of the transcendental Buddha, and the latter being a new metaphysical conception of the Mahāyānists.

These new Kāya conceptions, it seems, did not make much of an appeal at the beginning of Mahāyāna. The *Saddharma-Puṇḍarīka* and the *Suvarṇāprabhāsa* tried to erase from the minds of the people the lingering impression about the historical existence of Śākyamuni. In the *Puṇḍarīka*[3] we find

1. Cf. *Laṅkā.*, p. 240 ; sadā samāhitāś ca tathāgatāḥ.
2. For deiails see Masuda's *Origin and Doctrines of Early Indian Buddhist Schools*, *Asia Major*, vol. II, fasc. I ; Anesaki's article in the *ERE.*, sv. *Docetism* (Buddhist) ; Suzuki's *Outliues of Mahāyāna Buddhism*, pp. 249-251. See also *Kośa*, III, 9 referring to *Mtu,*, I, pp. 145, 154.
3. *Sad. P.*, pp. 311ff.

Maitreya assuming the role of a sceptic and enquiring how Buddha could, within a short space of forty years after the attainment of Bodhi at Gayā, perform the innumerable duties of a Tathāgata and lead incalculable bodhisattvas to Buddhahood. It appears like the paradox of a man of twenty-five years claiming centenarians as his sons and the latter calling him their father. Similarly Buddha's pointing to Bodhisattvas, who had been performing the various duties conducive to Buddhahood for many millions of years as his disciples appears paradoxical. Maitreya says further that in the minds of those Bodhisattvas, who recently became Mahāyānists (navayānasamprasthitāḥ), there may be doubts of this nature; so the Tathāgata should explain the paradox for the welfare of the religion. Buddha then asks his audience thrice to believe his words (avakalpayadhvam abhiśraddaddhaṃ), and says "It is not to be considered (naiva draṣṭavyam), that Bhagavān Śākyamuni lately leaving his family life attained Bodhi at Gayā, said "I attained sambodhi incalculable ages ago, and since then I have been preaching the dharma. All that I have said about the previous Tathāgatas, Dīpaṅkara etc., and their parinirvāṇa were all my own creations. These were only my expedients for imparting the dharma (upāyakauśalya-dharma-deśanābhinirhāra-nirmitāni). All that I have said to the effect that I was young, recently born, left home, and attained Bodhi, was to appeal to a class of people, who otherwise would not have been convinced of the excellence of the religion and derived benefits therefrom. But all that I said was not untrue, as the Tathāgatas know that the three dhātus really are; they know that the dhātus are neither born nor non-exist; neither they are the same nor different, and they are neither true nor false. "All that the Tathāgatas say is true, but people devoid of right knowledge construe different meaning out of it. "Though I have not attained parinirvāṇa, I say that I have attained it. In order to rouse curiosity in the minds of the people and a desire to see Buddha, I say that the appearance of a Buddha is an exceedingly rare event. I made a show of Nirvāṇa, but did not enter into it, but people with distorted views could not see my real self, and busied themselves with the worship of my relics. But this also produced a good effect, for they thereby became righteous and gave up their passions. From among them I formed my śrāvakasaṅgha, and showed myself at Gṛdhrakūṭa, and explained to them how to attain the agrabodhi".

In the *Suvarṇaprabhāsa*[1] Ruciraketu and Kauṇḍinya the brāhmaṇa play the role of sceptics. The former enquires why Śākyamuni, who performed so many meritorious deeds, should have such a short span of life as eighty years. The latter seeks a mustard-like relic of Buddha's body to worship and thus go to heaven. Ruciraketu is told by the Buddhas of all lokadhātus that they did not know any man or god who could calculate the length of Śākyamuni's life. They said that it might be possible to count the drops of water in a sea but it would be impossible to ascertain the length of his life. Kauṇḍinya brāhmaṇa, who only feigned ignorance, was told by Litsavikumāra that, just as it is absurd to expect cocoanuts from a rose-apple tree, so it is absurd to expect a relic from the Buddhakāya. The Tathāgatas have no origin, they are ever existing and inconceivable. It is only the Nirmitakāya that is shown by them. How can a baby, in which there is no bone or blood, leave a dhātu (relic)? Buddhas have only Dharmakāya and there is only the Dharmadhātu.

Nirmāṇakāya

The Mahāyānic texts tried to show, on the one hand, that the Hīṇayānists were wrong in their belief that Śākyamuni was really a man of flesh and blood and that relics of his body existed, while on the other hand, they introduced the two conceptions of Nirmāṇakāya and Buddhakāya. Whatever is said to have been done by Śākyamuni is accounted for by those texts as the apparent doings of a created body of the Buddhakāya, a shadowy image created to follow the ways of the world (lokānuvartana),[2] in order to bring con-

1 *Suvarṇaprabhāsa* (B.T.S. ed.), pp. 4-8.

2. Cf. *Mtu.*, I. pp. 168, 170.

viction in the hearts of the people that the attainment of Buddhahood was not an impossibility. As the Buddhas possess the knowledge of all that is to be done (kṛtyānuṣṭhānajñāna),[1] they can take any form they desire for the enlightenment of the various classes of beings. The Mahāyānic conception of Nirmāṇakāya is essentially the same as that of the Mahāsaṅghikas.

The *Prajñāpāramitās* in their quaint way refer to the Nirmāṇakāya or Rūpakāya. The *Pañcaviṃśati.* says that a bodhisattva, after acquiring all the necessary dharmas and practisting prajñāpāramitā, becomes a Sambuddha. He then renders service to beings of all lokadhātus (worlds) of the ten corners at all times by Nirmāṇamegha (Nirmāṇa clouds). This is called the Nairmāṇika-kāya.[2].

From the Chinese sources[3] we are informed that Nāgārjuna, in his commentary on the Prajñāpāramitā, names it as *Mahāprajñāpāramitā śāstra*, and speaks of two kāyas, rūpakāya and dharmakāya. The former is the body born of parents, possessing the qualities of sentient beings, and is subject to human frailties. It was born in Kośala while his dharmakāya was born at Rājagṛha. The material body was neeessary for "earthly truth". It was for the deliverance of beings that Buddha assumed different kāyas, different names, birth-places and the ways of emancipation. This interpretation of rūpa and dharma-kāyas is also followed in the Chinese *Parinirvāṇasūtra* and *Sandhinirmocanāsūtra.*[4]

Some of the Yogācāra texts furnish us with the following information regarding the conception of Nirmāṇakāya as prevailing among the Yogācārins :

(i) The *Sūtrālaṅkāra*[5] explains the Nirmāṇakāya to be those forms, which are assumed by Buddhas to render service to beings of the various worlds. It generally refers to the

1. One of the four jñānas peculiar to Buddha, see *Mvyut.*, p. 2
2. *Pañca.* (Cambr. ms.), leaf 343c.
3. C. Akanuma, *E. B.*, II, pp. 17ff. ; Masuda, *Die Individualistische etc.*, p. 60.
4. *E. B.*, II, pp. 21f.
5. *Sūtrā.*, p. 45.

human form that Buddha takes in order to make a show of his acquiring the ordinary arts and crafts required by an average man, living a family life and then retiring from it, and ultimately attaining Nirvāṇa by recourse to ascetic practices.

(ii) The *Vijñaptimātratāsiddhi* tells us that the Nirmāṇakāya is meant for Śrāvakas, Pratyekabuddhas, Pṛthagjanas (common men) and Bodhisattvas, who are not yet in one of the ten bhūmis. It may appear in all lands whether pure or impure.[1] The Chinese commentaries on the *Siddhi* mention the various ways, in which Buddha can transform his body or another's body or voice, and his oı others' mind, to suit his purpose. Not only could he transform himself into Śākyamuni, or Śāriputra into a young girl, but also could create an altogether new apparitional body, not, of course, a living, thinking being. Often he assumed the voice of Brahmā or expressed himself through the mouth of Śāriputra or Subhūti, and it was for this reason that we find Śāriputra or Subhūti explaining some of the abstruse Mahāyāna teachings, which they themselves were not expected to understand.[2] The third way in which he could transform his voice was to produce sounds from the sky. His thoughts were supramundane (lokottara) and pure (anāsrava). He could produce in mind any thought he liked ; in fact, he appeared in his Nirmitakāya as Śākyamuni with a mind (citta) suited to the ways of the world. He could also impose his thoughts on the minds of others.

(iii) The *Abhisamayālaṅkārakārikā* states that there are four kāyas, of which the Svābhāvikakāya is real, and the three others, *viz.*, Dharmakāya (=Svasambhogakāya), Sambhogakāya (=Parasambhogakāya) and Nirmāṇakāya are sāṃvṛta (*i. e.* unreal) ; these are meant for Bodhisattvas and Śrāvakas respectively. According to it, the Nirmāṇakāya was intended for Śrāvakas and Bodhisattvas

1. Masuda, *Die Individualistische etc.*, p. 60.
2. See *Aṣṭa.*, pp. 14, 33, 414,

who are not yet in one of the ten bhūmis. It describes the Nirmāṇakāya as a body unsevered from the real kāya, and as the actions performed by it are similarly unsevered from the kāya, they should be regarded as asaṃsāra (transcendental, *i.e.*, not worldly). Then it proceeds to show that the thirty-seven kinds of purificatory actions performed by the Nirmāṇakāya are really the actions of the Dharmakāya. The thirty-seven actions, explained by it, are the thirty-seven steps, through which a Nirmāṇakāya passes after its inception. These are as follows[1] : A Nirmāṇakāya (i) is unmindful of good or bad forms of existence ; in other words, takes birth as an animal, human being or god as necessities require—this is called *gatipraśama* ; (ii) practises the four *saṃgrahavastus* (elements of popularity) ; (iii) enlightens himself about matter opposite and similar, good and evil, by the *śrutamayi* and such other means of knowledge, and then applies himself to the service of others, keeping himself unconcerned (*i.e.*, having no *anunaya*, like a magician for the things made by him magically) ; (iv) practises the six pāramitās purified in three ways *trimaṇḍalaviśuddha*) ; (v) performs, and persuades others to perform the ten *kuśalakarmapathas* (moral duties) and thus establish all in the path leading to Buddhahood ; (vi) exerts for realising the non-existence in reality of all things ; (vii) comprehends the non-duality of things and the all-pervasiveness of the dharmadhātu, and so on, until he reaches the Tathāgatabhūmi after realising the absence of difference between things constituted and unconstituted.[2] In short, the *Kārikā* wants to say that the whole course of life of a Bodhisattva, extending through incalculable births, is nothing but the Nirmāṇakāya, a thing not separate from the Dharmakāya, as, in fact, according to the Mahāyāna philosophy, all creations are neither the same as, nor different from, the dharmadhātu.

(iv) The *Laṅkāvatāra* explains the relation of Nirmāṇakāya

1. *J. A.*, 1913, p. 604.
2. *Kārikā*, ch. viii ; also *J. A.*, 1913. pp. 599, 600.

to Dharmakāya in the same way as the *Kārikā*. It states that Nirmitabuddhas are not produced by actions ; the Tathāgata is neither in them nor outside them (sarve hi nirmitabuddhā na karmaprabhavā na tesu tathāgato na cānyatra tebhya tathāgatā).[1] It is only when the sons of the Jina realise the visible world to have no existence apart from the *citta* that they obtain the Nirmāṇakāya free from *kriyā* and *saṁskāra*, and endowed with *bala*, *abhijñā* and *vaśitā*[2]. Like the *Siddhi*, it says that the Tathāgatas by creating Nirmāṇakāya perform the various duties of a Tathāgata (Tathāgatakṛtya).[3] It gives also the interesting information that Vajrapāṇi serves as an attendant on the Nirmitanirmāṇabuddhas, and not on the real Buddhas.[4] and that the function of such a Buddha is to preach and explain the characteristics of dāna, śīla, dhyāna, samādhi, citta, prajñā, jñāṇa, skandha, dhātu, āyatana, vimokṣa, and vijñāna.[5]

Sambhogakāya

We have seen that the Rūpakāya or Nirmāṇakāya was meant for the Śrāvakas, Pratyekabuddhas, Pṛthagjanas and Bodhisattvas, who were not in one of the ten bhūmis, so another kāya had to be devised, a very suitable kāya for the benefit of all Bodhisattvas. This is called Parasambhogakāya, as distinguished from Svasambhogakāya, a similar subtle body perceived by the Buddhas alone. It is this Parasambhogakāya, which plays the role of a preacher of the various Mahāyāna sūtras, the scenes being mostly laid either at Gṛdhrakūṭa, the only place in the three dhātus considered pure and suitable for the appearance of a Sambhogakāya, or in the Sukhāvati-vyūha, or in one of the heavens.

It will be observed from the description of the appearance of Buddha and his manner of preaching the Sūtras that the Mahāyānists were not yet able to forget or rise above the human conception of Buddha of the Hīnayānists. They still gave Śākyamuni the role of the presiding Buddha of the universe,

1. *Laṅkā.*, p. 242.
2. *Ibid.*, p. 73.
3. *Ibid.*, p. 240.
4. *Ibid.*, p. 242.
5. *Ibid.*, p. 57.

to whom flocked reverently with flowers, incense, etc., all the Bodhisattvas, Śrāvakas and Gṛhapatis of the various lokadhātus of the ten directions, to hear from him the *Prajñāpāramitā*, the *Saddharmapuṇḍarīka*, or the *Gaṇḍavyūha*. These Bodhisattvas again had their own tutelary Buddhas, who, according to the Mahāyāna metaphysics, possessed the same Dharmakāya as that of Śākyamuni. They also came or were sometimes sent by their Buddhas, with messages of greetings and flowers as tokens of their regard, to Śākyamuni Buddha, whose Buddhakṣetra was then the Sahā lokadhātu. Sometimes the descriptions go so far as to say that the Buddhas themselves came to hear discourses from Śākyamuni Buddha, and the concourse of Buddhas and Bodhisattvas became so great that the Sahā lokadhātu had to be cleared of all oceans, mountains, seas, rivers, and cities, as well as of gods, men and other beings. As we read in the Hīnayāna texts that monks used to come to meet Buddha, bringing with them one or two sāmaṇeras, so also we read in the *Saddharma-Puṇḍarīka* that on account of insufficiency of space the countless Buddhas could not have with them more than one or two Bodhisattvas as attendents (upasthāpakas).[1]

Now let us see what was their conception of the Kāya of this Buddha. According to the *Śatasāhasrikā* and the *Pañcaviṁśatisāharikā*,[2] it is an exceedingly refulgent body, from every pore of which streamed forth countless brilliant rays of light, illuminating the lokadhātus as innumerable as the sands of the Ganges. When this body stretched out its tongue, innumerable rays of light issued forth from it, and on each ray of light was found a lotus of thousand petals on which was seated a Tathāgatavigraha (an image of the Tathāgata, a sort of Nirmāṇakāya), preaching to Bodhisattvas, Gṛhasthas (householders), Pravrajitas (recluses) and others the dharma consisting of the six pāramitās. After a Siṃhavikrīḍita samādhi his body illuminated the trisāhasra-

1. *Sad. P.*, pp. 244-245.

2. *Śata.*, pp. 8-29 ; *Pañca*,, pp. 6ff. ; for 'Āsecanaka' sce *Samādhirājasūtra* (B.T.S. ed.) p. 10.

mahāsāhasra lokadhātu just as the bright clear Sun or the full Moon illuminates the world. Buddha then shows his *Prakṛtyātmabhāva* (real form) to all the worlds. The several classes of gods as well as the men of the four continents, Jambudvīpa, Aparagodāna, etc., see this *Prakṛtyātmabhāva* and think that the Tathāgata is sitting before them and preaching the doctrine. From this body again issue forth some rays of light, by which all beings of all lokadhātus see Śākyamuni Buddha preaching the *Prajñāpāramitā* to his saṅgha of monks and congregation of Bodhisattvas.

Though this conception of the refulgent body of Buddha found currency in the *Prajñāpāramtiās*, the expression Sambhogakāya was still unknown to them. It was usually called by them Prakṛtyātmabhāva (natural body) or Āsecanaka ātmabhāva (all-diffusing body). As a matter of fact, the *Aṣṭasāhasrikā* is not even aware of the *Prakṛtyātmabhāva* or *Āsecanaka-ātmabhāva*, showing clearly its priority to the other *Prajñāpāramitās*. It speaks only of Rūpakāya and Dharmakāya[1] and the long glorious description of Buddhakāya, which appears in the *Śata* and *Pañcaviṁśati-sāhasrikā* as nidāna (introduction to the text), is totally absent from it. It is only in the recast version of the *Pañcaviṁśati* that the expression Sāṃbhogika-kāya was introduced by way of giving a gist of the topic.[2] In it the Sambhoga-kāya is described thus : Bodhisattvas, after attaining bodhi by means of the prajñāpāramitā, take a body endowed with thirty-two major and eighty minor signs with a view to preach the doctrines of Mahāyāna to the bodhisattvas and at the same time to arouse in their minds joy, delight and love for the excellent dharma. The original *Prajñāpāramitā* regarded this refulgent kāya as nirmita (created) and as such it included it in Rūpakāya and did not feel the necessity of introducing the conception of a third kāya, the Sāmbhogika.

In keeping with this dvikāya theory of the *Prajñāpāramitās*, Nāgārjuna also did not refer to, or probably was not

1. *Aṣṭa.*, pp. 338, 497, 513.
2. *Pañca.*, (A.S.B. ms.) leaf, 359a : Iti Sāmbhogika-kāyaḥ.

aware of, the third kāya, the Sāṁbhogika. Both Drs. Akanuma and Masuda could not trace the conception of Sambhogakāya in Nagārjuna's *Mahāprajñāpāramitā-śāstra.* Dr. Akanuma also mentions his disinclination to accept the "Hymns of the Triple Body (Trikāya)" ascribed by the Tibetans to Nāgārjuna as a work of the famous author.[1] If the *Kārikās* of Nāgārjuna on the Tathāgatakāya[2] be examined, it also becomes apparent that Nāgārjuna was interested in giving an exposition of the real kāya (*i.e.*, Dharmakāya or Svabhāvakāya) only. To him the distinction of Sambhogakāya and Rūpakāya was unimportant, as both of them were unreal.

Thus, it is seen that up to the time of Nāgārjuna, the conception of Sambhogakāya was not distinguished from that of Rūpa- or Nirmāṇa-kāya. The *Laṅkāvatāra* presents us first with this conception, calling it Niṣyanda- or Dharmatā-niṣyanda-Buddha, and it seems that the term Sambhogakāya was not yet current. We have seen that in Hīnayāna works also, it is pointed out that the super-excellent body of Buddha, endowed with the major and minor signs of great men, was due to the countless meritorious deeds performed by him in his countless meritorious deeds performed by him in his previous lives.[3] The Chinese rendering of Sambhogakāya by *pao sheny*[4] in which *pao* means fruit or reward, also indicates that Sambhoga had no other sense than 'vipāka or niṣyanda'. The later Yogācārins called it Parasambhoga-kāya in order to distinguish it from the other kāya called by them Svasambhoga. Though the *Aṣṭasāhasrikā* does not distinguish Sambhogakāya from the Nirmāṇakāya, it refers to the super-excellent body of Buddha as the result of his meritorious acts in previous lives.[5] The *Laṅkāvatara*, by using

1. *Eastern Buddhist*, II, pp. 17ff.
2. *M. Vṛ.*, Ch. XXII.
3. *Laṅkā.*, pp. 28, 34; see ante.
4. Sakaki, *Mvyut.* 117.
5. *Aṣṭa.*, p. 515. Buddhānāṃ kāyaḥ kāraṇasamutpannaḥ pūrve-karmavipākād utpannaḥ, etc.

the expression Vipākaja or Vipākastha, shows a stage of transition from the Hīnayānic conception of Vipākaja-kāya to that of the Mahāyānic Parasambhogakāya.

(*i*) The *Laṅkāvatāra* says that the function of the Niṣyanda-Buddha is to teach the *parikalpita* (imaginary) and *paratantra* (relatively existent) nature of things to those persons, who weave a net of thought-constructions around themselves, being unaware of the dream-like nature of things.[1] This is also the function of Śākyamuni of the Sahā lokadhātu when he imparts the teaching of the *Prajñāpāramitās* or the *Saddharma-Puṇḍarīka.*[2]

(*ii*) The *Sūtrālaṅkāra* also does not distinguish Sambhoga-kāya into Svasambhoga and Parasambhoga. It says that with this body Buddhas enjoy the dharmas and it is different according to the different lokadhātus, implying thereby that a Buddha of each lokadhātu has his own Sambhogakāya, which is different from those of other Buddhas of other Buddhakṣetras[3].

(*iii*) The *Suvarṇaprabhāsa* and (*iv*) the *Abhisamayālaṅkā-ra-kārikā* tells us that the Sambhogakāya is a very subtle body of Buddha. It is endowed with all the mahāpuruṣa signs and is generally assumed by Buddhas for imparting the higher and metaphysical truths to the advanced bodhisattvas. The *Suvarṇāprabhāsa*[4] also does not speak of the two forms of Sambhogakāya, as found in the *Siddhi*.

(*v*) The *Siddhi* says that there are two Sambhogakāyas called Parasambhogakāya and Svasambhogakāya. The former is seen by bodhisattvas, while the latter is seen by the Buddhas of the various lokadhātus, and not by bodhisattvas. As regards refulgence, illimitability and immeasurability there is no difference between these two kāyas. Both of them have colour and form (varṇa-rūpa-saṃsthāna) as well as voice (śabda). On

1. *Laṅkā.*, p. 57.

2. The function of Nirmitabuddha is to teach dāna, śīla, etc., see ante.

3. *Sūtrā.*, pp. 45-6.

4. Suzuki, *Outlines etc.*, p. 257; in the published portion of the Sanskrit text (B.T.S.) this passage does not appear.

account of the knowledge of sameness (samatā) obtained by Buddhas, the body is anāsrava (pure). It can appear only in a pure land like the Sukhāvatīvyūha or Gṛdhrakūṭa. The difference between the Parasambhogakāya and the Svasambhogakāya is that the former has the mahāpuruṣalakṣaṇas while the latter has not, and that the *citta* of the former is as unreal as that of the Nirmāṇakāya, while the *citta* of the latter is real, and besides, this *citta* possesses the four jñānas, *viz.*, ādarśajñāna (mirror-like knowledge),[1] samatā-jñāna (knowledge of the sameness of all things), pratyavekṣaṇā-jñāna (knowledge of distinguishing subject, object and the varieties of things) and kṛtyānuṣṭhāna-jñāna (knowledge of doing all that is to be done).[2] The rūpa of both the Sambhogakāyas is exceedingly subtle and expansive without limit, yet it is *sapratigha* (possessed of the quality of obstruction). Nevertheless the subtle bodies of countless Buddhas are interpenetretable.

The recast version of the *Pañcaviṃśati*[3] refers to the Sambhogakāya, and does not like the *Kārikā*, distinguish between Dharmakāya (=Svasambhoga) and Parasambhogakāya, the reason being that in the original version of the *Pañcaviṃśati*, there must have been, as in the other *Prajñāpārmitās*, the conceptions of only two kāyas, and not of three or four. The *Kārikā*, in fact, supports the *Siddhi* in regard to ihe conception of kāyas, using only somewhat different names. The conception of the Svasambhogakāya shows a tendency of the Yogācāra school to posit something like the Īśvara of the Upaniṣads behind the phenomenal universe. The Dharmakāya corresponds to the impersonal Absolute of the Vedānta. the Brahman, and the Sambhogakāya to the Iśvara when Brahman assumes name and form. Every Buddha, it should, however, be noted, has his own Sambhogakāya but all Buddhas have one Dharmakāya. The *Laṅkāvatāra* also gives hints to this effect. It says that *abhāva* (absence of anything) is not Tathāgata, and again, as Tathāgata

1. Cf. *Dīgha*, II, p. 93 : Dhammādāsa.
2. Explained in detail in the *Sūtrā.*, pp. 46ff ; *Mvyut.* 5.
3. *Pañca.* (A.S.B. ms.), leaf. 359a. Cf. *Śikṣā.*, p. 159 ; *Bodhic.*, pp. 1, 4 ; *Mtu.*, III, pp. 344, 452.

is describsd as 'Anutpāda-anirodha', it has some meaning. It then denotes the Manomaya-dharmakāya.[1] It cannot be seen by the non-Buddhists, Śrāvakas, Pratyeka-buddhas and even Bodhisattvas in one of the first seven bhūmis. Just as different names of one thing or one person like hasta, kara, pāṇi, or Indra, Śakra, Purandara indicate dlfferent aspects of the same thing so also the different names of Śākyamuni Buddha in the Sahā lokadhātu, *e.g.*, Svayambhū, Nāyaka, Tṛṣabha, Viṣṇu, Īśvara, Pradhāna, Kapila, Soma, Bhāskara, Rāma, Vyāsa, or Śūnyatā, Tathatā, Bhūtakoṭi, Nirvāṇa, Sarvajña, etc., indicate the different aspects of Śākyamuni Buddha.[2] People being subject to the conceptions of two extremes 'is' or 'is not' (dvayāntapatitayā) do not know that Buddha is like a reflection of the Moon on water neither appearing nor disappearing, In this passage there is a clear hint that this Manomaya-dharmakāya, existing in the Sahā lokadhātu, is the same as the Svasambhogakāya of the *Siddhi* and the Āsecanka-ātmabhāva or Prakṛtyātmabhāva of the *Prajñāpāramitās*, and it corresponds to the *Upaniṣadic* conception of Īśvara.

Dharmakāya

The three kāyas, of which we have so far spoken, belong strickly, to the realm of Saṃvṛti, worldly and transcendental, and as such they were treated as Rūpa or Nirmāṇa-kāya by the early Mahāyānists, including Nāgārjuna. The only real kāya of Buddha is the Reality as conceived by the Mahāyānists, and is not different from the things or beings of the universe.[3] Though an attempt to define it by the current words and expressions is bound to be not only incorrect but misleading, the Mahāyānic texts tried to give an idea of it as far as the language permitted. The *Kārikā* and the *Siddhi* call it Svābhāvika or Svabhāva kāya. It is, according to them, immeasurable and illimitable. It fills all space. It is the basis

1. For the definition of Manomayakāya and its three sub-divisions see *Laṅka.*, p. 81 ; Suzuki, *E.B.*, iv, pp. 284-5.

2. *Laṅkā.*, pp. 192-3 ; cf. *Daśa.*, p. 55.

3. In a Buddhist inscription of Battambang, a stanza in salutation of Buddha brings out this idea. See *Le Muséon*, vol. VII.

of the Sambhoga and Nirmāṇa-kāyas. It is devoid of all marks (*i.e.*, mahāpuruṣalakṣaṇas) and is inexpressible (niṣprapañca). It is possessed of eternal, real and unlimited guṇas. It has neither citta nor rūpa, and again Dharmakāya Buddhas may have their individual Sambhogakāyas but they have all one Dharmakāya.[1] It can only be realised within one's own self (*pratyātmavedya*) and not described, for that would be like the attempt of a blind man to describe the Sun, which he has never seen.[2]

It is often questioned whether the conception of Dharmakāya can be traced in the *Prajñāpāramitās*, and the works of Nāgārjuna, and whether the *Prajñāpāramitās* and the works of Nāgārjuna admit of such a reality, or rather preach only pure and simple negativism ? To put it in another way, was it the object of the *Prajñāpāramitās* and Nāgārjuna's works to point out only the incongruities of the world and worldly knowledge and avoid making any statement about the Reality or the Truth ?

The *Aṣṭasāhasrikā*[3] and other *Prajñāpāramitās*, though unrelenting in their negation of every possible statement about the reality, never assert that Tathatā or Śūnyatā or Dharmakāya in its real sense is also non-existing. The statements like 'tathatāvikārā nirvikārāvikalpā nirvikalpā' (Suchness is immutable, unchangeable, beyond concept and distinctions)[3] show rather a positive conception of the Reality than a purely negative one. In regard to the Dharmakāya also the *Aṣṭasāhasrikā* makes similar statements. It says that he who

---

1. Cf. *Vis. M.*, p. 508 : Nirvāṇa is one for all Buddhas.

2. Masuda, *op. cit.*, p. 59 ; Suzuki, *Awakening of Faith*, p. 62.

3. *Aṣṭa.*, p. 307 ; cf. the passage : yā ca tathāgata-tathatā yā ca sarvadharma-tathatā ekaivaiṣā tathatā'dvayā'dvaidhīkārā'dvayatathatā na kvacit tathatā na kutaścit tathatā na kasyacit tathatā yataḥ sā na kasyacit tathatā tataḥ sā tathatā'dvayā'dvaidhīkāradvayatathatā.

(That which is Tathāgata-tathatā and that which is all-things-tathatā are non-dual, one and the same. Tathatā is neither anywhere nor arises from anywhere, nor belongs to anything, hence as Tathatā does not belong to anybody, it is non-dual and one).

For other passages of similar import, see *M. Vṛ.*. Ch. xxii.

knows that the dharmas, existing in the world or preached by the Tathāgata, have no more existence than things seen in a dream and, does not enquire whence the Tathāgata comes and where he goes, realises the Tathāgata through Dharmatā.[1] The Buddhakāya, that people speak of, arises through cause and condition like the sound of flute ; it involves really no appearance or disappearance. Those, who run after the form and voice of the Tathāgata and conceive of his appearance and disappearance are far from the Truth.[2] No further statements than this can be made about the Reality, for that would be again *prapañca.* When the *Aṣṭasāhasrikā* asserts that the Tathāgata does not exist, it refers to that Tathāgata as conceived by one on reading the Mahāyāna texts. Even the Bodhisattvas, unless and until they reach the tenth bhūmi, cannot extricate themselves from a conception of the Tathāgatakāya, however, subtle it may be (*e.g.*, the Svasambhogakāya). They are still under a delusion and it is this delusion that the *Prajñāpāramitās* endeavour to remove by asserting that there is no Tathāgata.

Nāgārjuna by denying the existence of a so-called Tathāgata does nothing more than what the *Prajñāpāramitās* endeavour to establish. His point is that, if *bhavasantati* (series of existence) be admitted then the existence of a Tathāgata should also be admitted,[3] for the Tathāgata represents the ultimate state of this *bhavasantati* ; it is a state attained by a being after a long series of existence. As in reality (paramārthataḥ), there is no bhavasantati, there is also no Tathāgata—that being who is supposed to have become a Tathāgata after practising mahākaruṇā and other virtues, and thereby attaining omniscience. If the Tathāgata had really existed, he would either be the same as five skandhas or different from them, or the skandhas would be in him or he in the skandhas, but as he is none of these nor any one of these is he, he cannot have

1. *Aṣṭa.*, p. 514 : te dharmatayā tathāgataṃ prajānāti. Cf. *M. Vṛ.*, p. 448 : dharmato buddhā draṣṭavyāḥ.

2. *Aṣṭa.*, p. 513.

3. *M. Vṛ.*, p. 431 : vidyata eva bhavasantatis tathāgata-sadbhāvāt ; *Ibid.*, p. 432. Na hy ekena janmanā śakyaṃ tathāgatatvam anuprāptum.

any real existence. By these and other similar arguments Nāgārjuna asserts that there is no Tathāgata. By such denial he only establishes that the Tathāgata as the ultimate state of bhavasantati does not exist.[2]

Candrakīrti, in support of Nāgārjuna's arguments, quotes a passage from the *Aṣṭasāhasrikā* (p. 472) in which Buddha and his dharma are compared to *māyā* or *svapna*, but at the same time he says "we do not assert the non-existence (nāstitva) of the Tathāgata in every way, for then we would be guilty of *apavāda* (denial), and yet being desirous of describing the Tathāgata by means of vyavahāra-satya (conventionally) and by taking recourse to super-impositions (samāropa) we say that he is śūnya or aśūnya, śūnyāśūnya or naiva śūnya nāśūnya. But he who endeavours to realise the true Tathāgata by having recourse to statements and denials will never know him. Candrakīrti, in support of the above, quotes the verses from the *Vajracchedikā*, to which the *Aṣṭsāhasrikā* as well as the *Bodhi-caryāva-tara* (P. 42) refer, *viz.*, "he who endeavoured to see me through my form and voice could not see me because

dharmato buddhā draṣṭavyā dharmakāyā hi nāyakāḥ,
dharmatā cāpy avijñeyā na sā śakyā vijānitum.

[A buddha is to be seen in the sense of dharmatā (nature of dharmas), for the leaders (of men) have only Dharmakāya. That dharmatā is unknowable (so also is the Tathāgata)].[1]

Nāgārjuna concludes his examination of the Tathāgatakāya by identifying Tathāgata with the world (jagat),[2] or nature itself, and asserting that the Tathāgata, whom people or even Bodhisattvas have in view, is only a *bimba* (image) of kuśala-dharmas and is not the real Tathatā or Tathāgata.[3] A dialectician like Nāgārjuna cannot go further than this to establish the Reality. It is by denial of the existence of unreal

---

1. *M. Vṛ.*, p. 448 ; cf. *Aṣṭa.*, pp. 513, 514 ; *Vajra.*, p. 43.
2. Tathāgato yatsvabhāvas tat svabhāvam idaṃ jagat,
Tathāgato niḥsvabhāvo niḥsvabhāvam idaṃ jagat.
3. *M. Vṛ.*, pp. 448-9.

things, including the so-called Tathāgata, that he points towards the Reality—the real Tathāgatakāya, the Dharmakāya.[1]

The conception of Dharmakāya was of special interest to the Yogācārins. The *Laṅkāvatāra*[2] in describing it says that (Dharmatā) Buddha is without any substratum (nirālamba) and lies beyond the range of functioning organs of sense, proofs or signs and hence beyond the vision of Śrāvakas, Pratyekabuddhas or the non-Mahāyānists. It is to be realised only within one's own self. The *Sūtrālaṅkāra*[3] calls it Svābhāvika-dharmakāya. It is one and the same kāya in all Buddhas, very subtle, unknowable and eternal. The *Triṃśika*[4] explains the Dharmakāya as the transformed āśraya (substratum)—the ālayavijñāna—the transformation being effected by knowledge (jñāna) and the suppression of the two evils (dauṣṭhulyas), *viz.*, kleśāvaraṇa and jñeyāvaraṇa. The *Āloka*[5] on the *Abhisamayālaṅkārakārikā* also explains the Dharmakāya in a similar way. According to it, there are two kinds of Dharmakāya, one being the Bodhipaṣika and the other dharmas, which are themselves pure and productive of clear knowledge (niṣprapañcajñānātmanā) and the other the transformed āśraya of the same, which is then called Svabhāvakāya. Professor Stcherbatsky[6] supplies us with nearly the same information that we find in the *Āloka* from some source, which he does not mention. He says that "according to the early Yogācāras, the Dharmakāya is divided into Svabhāvakāya (ño-bo-ñid-sku) and jñānakāya (ñe-śes-kyi-sku) ; the first is the motionless (nitya) substance of the universe, the second is anitya, *i.e.*, changing, living". Evidently what the Professor means by Jñānakāya is the Dharmakāya, consisting of the Bodhipakṣika and other dharmas, of the *Āloka*. That the Svabhāvakāya is the

---

1. Prapañcayanti ye budhaṃ prapañcātītam avyayaṃ,
Te prapañcahatāḥ sarve na paśyanti Tathāgataṃ.
See also *M. Vṛ.*, p. 534.

2. *Laṅkā.*, pp. 57, 60.

3. *Sūtrā.*, p. 45.

4. *Triṃśikā*, p. 44.

5. *J. A.*, 1913.

6. *Con. of N.*, p. 185n.

nityakāya, as pointed out by him, is also supported by the *Suvarṇaprabhāsa* and other texts.[1].

The Chinese commentators on the *Siddhi* state that Dharmakāya is the metaphysical principle of real *citta* and *rūpa* of the Tathāgata. It is the real nature of things, and can be equated with Tathatā, Dharmadhātu or Tathāgatagarbha.[2]

The goal of Bodhisattvas is to realise the Dharmakāya. Every being has the Dharmakāya, or the Dharmakāya comprises all beings of the world, but as they are blinded by avidyā, they do not realise this fact. What the Bodhisattva aims at is the removal of this avidyā and the realisation of the fact that he is the same as the Dharmakāya. The *Āloka* on the *Kārikā*[3] enumerates the steps through which a Bodhisattva passes and points out that the last step of a Bodhisattva is to realise the Dharmakāya (dharmakāyābhisambodhena bhaviṣyati), after which it becomes easy for him to assume any one of the four kāyas. In the *Laṅkāvatāra* we notice that Mahāmati is anxious to know how are Bodhisattvas, after completing the ten bhūmis, can attain the Tathāgatakāya or Dharmakāya and go to any one of the Buddhakṣetras or heavens. The *Laṅkāvatāra* also describes in rosy colours the prospect of attaining the Mahādharmamegha in the ninth bhūmi, is adorned with many jewels, and sits on a lotus in a jewelled palace surrounded by other Bodhisattvas of his status. He comprehends there the illusory nature of all things. He is anointed (abhiṣeka) by Vajrapāṇi and a son of Buddha. He then goes beyond the bhūmi of Buddhasutas by realising within himself the dharma-nairātmya and confronts the Dharmakāya.[4] The *Triṃśikā* says that just as Vimuktikāya is the goal of the arhats, so Dharmakāya is the goal of the Bodhisattvas. It shows that as the arhats by getting rid of kleśāvaraṇa obtain a purified

1. *Suvarṇaprabhāsa* (B.T.S.), p. 8 ; *Laṅkā.*, p. 78 ; *Sūtrā.*, p. 46.

2. I have derived the information from Professor La Vallée Poussin. In *Laṅkā.* (pp. 77, 78) the Tathāgatagarbha is described as nitya, dhrūva, śāśvata, śiva, etc., just as the non-Buddhists speak of their great soul as nitya, kartā, nirguṇa, vibhū, and avyaya.

3. *J. A.*, 1913,

4. *Laṅkā.*, pp. 51, 70.

kāya, so also a Buddha by getting rid of both kleśāvaraṇa and jñeyāvaraṇa obtains the Dharmakāya.[1]

The world of experience is phenomenal. It may be compared to a magical illusion or dream. In the *Aṣṭasāhasrikā Prajñāpāramitā* (R. Mitra's edition, p. 39) appears the following passage,—

> Āyuṣmān Subhūtiḥ tān devaputrān etad avocat. māyopamās te sattvāḥ. svapnopamās te sattvāḥ. Iti hi māyā ca sattvāś ca advayā advaidhīkārā. Evaṃ sakṛdāgamīm pi....arhattam pi ... Samyaksambuddham pi māyopamā svapnopamāḥ.

[Transl. Āyuṣmān Subhūti said to the Devaputras that all worldly beings are illusion, dream. Illusion and worldly beings are one and the same.

It should be noted that not only worldly beings but also saints like the Once-returners (*Sakṛdāgāmi*) and the Perfect (*Arhat*) and even the worldly figure of Gautama Buddha are illusion or dream.]

The Absolute, *i.e.*, the *Dharmakāya* of Buddha is indescribable. It is the only reality that Buddha realised at Bodh-Gaya.

All things of the world has three aspects : *viz.*, (i) quintessence, (ii) attributes and (iii) activity. Take, for instance, an earthen jar ; it is subject to origination and disintegration, while the earth is indestructible, *i.e.*, unconditioned while the latter two are destructible *i.e.*, conditioned.

Another simile may be useful. Take for instance, an ocean and the waves of the ocean. The latter may be high or low, according to the force of wind of ignorance but the water of the ocean neither increases nor decreases. It is unfathomable and immeasurable, *i.e.*, unconditioned. The whole universe has two aspects, *i.e.*, changed and unchanged. The latter is known as the *Bhūta-tathatā*, the absolute. It presists through all space and time, the basis of all, the universal and eternal substratum.

---

1. *Triṃśikā*, p. 44.

It corresponds to the conception of Brahman of the *Upaniṣads*. This is identical with the *Dharmakāya* of Buddha. *Dharma* is the supreme principle of life. Ādi-Buddha happens to be the first conception of the personification of Dharma. It is a metaphysical conception. It is not in active touch with the world.

The leaders of men possess true body or nature, which is unknowable, it cannot be known (except within one's own self) (*pratyātmavedya*). In the *Aṣṭasāhasrikā Prajñāpāramitā* (R. Mitra's ed. p. 94) appears the following passage,—

> Mā khalu punar imaṃ bhikṣavaḥ satkāyaṃ kāyaṃ manyadhvaṃ. Dharmakāyo pariniṣpattito māṃ bhikṣavo drakṣyanti.

[Transl. O monks, you should not think that this individual body is my body. O monks, you should see me from the accomplishment of the Dharma-body).

Again, in the same text (p. 513) appears the following passage :—

> na hi tathāgato rūpakāyato draṣṭavyaḥ. dharmakāyas tathāgatā. na hi kulaputra dharmatā āgacchati vā gacchati vā. Evam eva kulaputra na hi tathāgatānāṃ āgamanaṃ vā gamanaṃ vā. Tad yathāpi nāma kulaputra puruṣaḥ svapnāntargat' ekaṃ tathāgato paśyet dvau vā trīn vā sahasraṃ tato vā uttaraṃ, na prativibuddhaṃ san ekam eva tathāgataṃ na paśyet....Tad yathāpi nāma kulaputra vīṇāyāḥ śabdaṃ utpadyamāno na kutaścit āgacchati niruddhamāne'pi na kvacit gacchati...hetupratyayā sāmagrīsy'utpadyate. hetvādhīnaḥ pratyayādhīnaḥ.

[Transl. The Tathāgatas cannot be seen in his form (*rūpa*) *i.e.*, material body. The Dharma bodies are the Tathāgatas. There is no coming or going of Dharmatā. Similarly, there is no coming or going of the Tathāgatas. A sleeping man might see in his dream one Tathāgata or two or three up to one thousand or still more. On waking up, he would, however, no longer see even one Tathāgata or two or three up to one thousand or still more. These Tathāgatas do not come from anywhere nor go to anywhere. They are eternal and ever existing.]

Buddha appears in this world with high intelligence and unlimited amity (*maitrī*) and compassion (*karuṇā*) to rescue beings from their lives of misery on account of birth and death.

In the *Saddharma-puṇḍarīka* (Ch. III) appears an episode as to the ways and means (*upāya-kuśalya-pāramitā*) adopted by Buddha. It is as follows :—

There was a fabulously rich man, who had an old, large and unused house, which became a haunt of birds, worms and reptiles. It had a tottering roof of straw and had only one door for exit. The house suddenly caught fire. The owner of the house had a number of children playing within the house. He was very much frightened on account of the fire as well as of the venomous reptiles existing in the house and thought of taking out the children by his strong arms but the difficulty was that they could not be brought together and would not listen to their father's warning about the raging fire. The father knew his children's inclinations and so he came out of the house and collected beautiful toy-carts drawn by goats, deer and bullocks and tempted the boys to come out and take them, after coming out of the burning house. The boys struggled among themselves to come out first in order to take the best cart. The father then felt relieved at the safety of his sons. When the boys asked for the toy-carts, the rich father gave them not the cheap types of carts but expensive, fast carriages, replete with all the conceivable furnishings and drawn by sturdy bulls.

Buddha then asked Śāriputra whether he would consider the father guilty of lieing. When Śāriputra answered in the negative, Buddha told him that he himself may be likened to the rich father and the house to the world of existence of senses and desires, and the sons to the men of the world, unmindful of the fire burning the world. The wooden cheap toy-carts were the various disciplihary and meditational practices prescribed in the Śrāvakayāna, Pratyekabuddhayāna and Bodhisattva-yāna, which were held out as the bait for the men of the world to come out of the three worlds (Kāmadhātu, Rūpadhātu and Arūpa-dhātu). The bait was the attainment of eternal happiness through perfection in Balas, Bodhyaṅgas, Dhyāna, Vimokṣa, Samādhi, Samāpatti, etc.

Some of the men of the world, who relied on Buddha's words, retired from worldly life. Of them again some became interested in attaining salvation (nirvāṇa) for himself only by listening to the teaching of, and following the practices prescribed in the formula of the Āryasatyas. They were the Śrāvakayānists and they might be compared to the boys seeking carts drawn by goats (aja). There were also those who aspired for omniscience like that of the Buddha by self-acquired perfect knowledge and wished to help all beings to attain parinirvāṇa and also exerted to attain the qualities, which make a Buddha. These were the Mahāyānists, seeking exit from the Tridhātus, and might be compared to those boys seeking carts drawn by bulls, not only, toy-carts but also actual vehicles of a very high class. Likewise, Buddha gave his disciples Buddhayāna. In fact, all the four yānas were of one nature and realise that Buddha could not have told a lie by taking recourse to the expedients (upāyakauśalya) of teaching his dhamma in different ways, *viz.*, Śrāvakayāna, Pratyeka-buddhayāna and Bodhisattvayāna.

CHAPTER VI

EXPOSITION OF NIRVANA

The second fundamental point of difference between the doctrines of Hīnayāna and Mahāyāna, mentioned in the *Saddharma-Puṇḍarīka*, lies in the conception of Nirvāṇa.

Hīnāyānic Nirvāṇa : (*i*) *Liberation from Duḥkhatā*

The Hīnayānist considers himself afflicted with three kinds of misery (duḥkha), viz., (a) suffering due to mental and physical causes (*duḥkha-duḥkhatā*), (b) that inhering in caused and conditioned existences (*saṃskāra-duḥkhatā*) subject as they are to origin and destruction, and (c) that due to transformation of pleasurable sensations into painful ones (*vipariṇāma-duḥkhatā*)[1]. He seeks release from these miseries incidental to life in any of the three worlds Kāma, Rūpa, and Arūpa[2] (including the six ordinary forms of existence[3]) by realising the formula of the law of causation (pratītyasamutpāda) and the four āryasatyas, and the transitoriness (anityatā) and essencelessness (anātmatā) of the things of this world and the miseries to which these lead. The *Puṇḍarīka* concedes that many of the disciples of Buddha attained Arhatship or Nirvāṇa by perceiving the non-existence of anything corresponding to soul (ātmā) in any of the five categories of mental and physical elements (skandhas)[4]. The Hīnayānists admit that

---

1. *Sad. P.*, p. 109 : *M. Vṛ.*, p. 475 ; *Mvyut.* 3 ; *Kośa*, vi, 3 ; Poussin, *Nirvāṇa*, p. 174 ; Burnouf, *Lotus etc.*, p. 68 ; *Dīgha*, III, p. 216 ; *Saṃyutta*, IV, p. 259, V, p. 56. In the *Vibhaṅga-Aṭṭhakathā* (pp. 93-94) seven kinds of *dukkhas* are mentioned : dukkha-dukkham, vipariṇāmad., saṅkhārad., paticchannad., appaticchanad., pariyāyad., and nippariyāyad.

2. *Sad. P.*, pp. 100, 117, 132-3, *Samādhirāja* (B.T.S. ed.), p. 13 ; *Sūtrā.*, pp. 94, 128.

3. *Sad. P.*, pp. 135-6 ; for the six gatis, see *Dīgha*, III, p. 264 ; *J.P.T.S.*, 1884, p. 152 ; *Annals du Mutsé Guimét*, V, pp. 514-528 ; *E.R.E.*, sv. Cosmogony and Cosmology.

4. Cf. *Paṭis. M.*, I. p. 146.

their Nirvāṇa consists in liberation from the three kinds of *duḥkhatā,* incidental to existence in the three laukikadhātus. Thus, according to the Hīnayānic conception, beings obtain liberation by attaining nibbānadhātu without any residue.[1] The Pāli works, canonical or post-canonical, agree on the point that this release is obtained by realising anityatā, duḥkhatā and anātmatā as well as pratītyasamutpannatā of the world.

What the Mahāynāists endeavour to point out is that the Hinayānists concern themselves with the realisation of the non-existence of a permanent entity like soul (*Pudgala-nairātmya*) and not of the non-existence of anything whatsoever supposed to exist (*i.e. Dharma-nairātmya*)[2]. According to the Mahāyānists, this realisation attained by the Hīnayānists cannot lead them to the ultimate Reality ; it carries them only some distance towards the Truth, and hence Nirvāṇa, in the real sense of the term, cannot be said to have been attained by them[3]. The Hīnayānists, however, consider that they reach Nirvāṇa when they know that they will have no more birth as they have led the life of holiness (brahmacarya) and realised the pudgala-nairātmya. Some think, as the *Laṅkāvatāra*[4] puts it, that Nirvāṇa is attained by comprehending what is really soul or personality ; some others think that it is attained by penetrating into the truth that things are dependent on causes. But, in fact, the *Laṅkāvatāra*[5] adds, there is no real emancipation (*mokṣa*) without the realisation of Dharma-nairātmya. So the Hinayānists do not actually reach mokṣa ; they are only tossed up and down by the properties (*lakṣaṇa*) of things like a log of wood tossed by the waves.

(*ii*) *Passage from Nimitta to Animitta*

The Hinayānists, according to the *Sūtrālaṅkāra*[6], have

1. *DhP.*, 26 : saṅkhāradukkhatāyā loko anupādisesāya nibbānadhātuyā muñcati.

2. *Sūtrā.*, pp. 154-160 ; *Laṅkā*, pp. 68-69.

3. Cf. *Bodhic.*, p. 442 : without the realisaton of *Śūnyatā*, there may be *nivṛti* (quietude) but it is not permanent.

4. *Laṅkā.*, pp. 63-4. 5. *Laṅkā.*, p. 135. 6. *Sūtrā.*, p. 140.

only personality as their basis (*pudgala-nimitta*) for meditation, and so they reach only Śrāvaka-bodhi or Pratyeka-buddha-bodhi and not Samyak-sambodhi, which can only be attained by making all *dharmas* (existent things and conditions) the basis (*nimitta*) for meditations[1]. The Śrāvakas distinguish between a thing with signs (*nimitta*) and a thing without signs (*animitta*) and try to draw away their minds from all nimittas and apply themselves to the attainment of animitta, which they attain in due course. The Mahāyānists think that the dual conception of things cannot lead to mokṣa. They do not know of anything other than *Tathatā* (thatness of things) ; so to them a nimitta is equally an animitta, and consequently their knowledge, derived as it is on the basis of Tathatā alone, is free from all differentiations or dualism (*dvayagrāha-vivarjitam*).[2] By the remark that the Hīnayānists distinguish between *Nimitta* and *Animitta* and consider that a person attains Animitta (=Nibbāna) by cogitating on the Animitta-dhātu and dissociating his mind from all things with signs, the *Sūtrālaṅkāra*[3] refers in a general way to the practice of the Hīnayānists to avoid rāga, dveṣa, moha, and such other nimittas[4] by which a being becomes entangled in worldly things. There are in the Nikāyas many passages of this import, *e.g.*, in the *Dīgha* and *Aṅguttara Nikāyas*[5] it is said that a person by inattention to all signs (of allurement) develops such a mental concentration that it may be described as animitta (without

1. *Sūtrā.*, pp. 169-170.

2. For the exposition of *Dharma-tattva* as *satataṃ dvayaṃ rahitaṃ*, see *Ibid*, pp. 58 ff.

3. *Sūtrā.*, p. 169 : Sarvanimittānām amanasikārād animittasya ca dhātor manasikārād animittaṃ samāpadyante (as done by the Śrāvakas and not by Bodhisattvas.

4. *Mahāniddesa*, I, p. 198 : rūpanimitta, saddan., gandhan., rasan., phoṭṭhabban., and dhamman.

5. *Aṅguttara*, III. pp. 292, 397 ; *Dīgha*, II, 100 : Yasmiṃ samaye tathāgate sabbanimittānam amanasikārā ekaccānaṃ vedanānaṃ mirodho animittaṃ cetosamādhim upasampajja viharati : *Paṭis, M.*, I, p. 91 ; Nimittaṃ bhayato sampassamāno animitte adhimattattā pavattamajjhupekkhitvā nirodham nibbānam animittam āvajjittvā samāpajjiati ; see also *Vis. M.*, p. 672 ; *Mahāniddesa*, I, p. 198.

sign). But the prevalent meaning of Animitta in Pāli works is Nibbāna, the goal to be reached through the meditations (samādhis or vimokkhas) called suññata, appaṇihita and animitta. These vimokkhas help the adept to comprehend that the things of the world are essenceless (anattā), unpleasant (dukkha) and impermanent (anicca)[1]. The *Aṅguttara Nikāya*[2] hints that a person puts an end to his āsavas (impurities) by dwelling on these three nimittas, while the *Atthasālini*[3] states that the five khandhas appear as frightful to a man as a dead body hung round his neck, if he understands the three lakkhanas (anicca, dukkha and anattā).

(iii) Removal of Kleśāvaraṇa and not Jñeyāvaraṇa

The *Laṅkāvatāra*[4] while explaining the position of the Hīnayānists says that they believe in the reality of saṃsāra (worldly existence) and are frightened by its attendant miseries, from which they seek release ; this is only due to their ignorance of the non-existence of any difference between *saṃsāra* and *nirvāṇa*. The standpoint of the Hīnayānists is that the world or things around us are produced out of the five skandhas or seventy-two elements having real existence. The constituted things which originate through some causes and conditions (pratītya-samutpanna) are in a constant state of flux and devoid of any substance.[5] The mental and physical constituents undergo momentary (kṣaṇika) changes and there is no permanent entity apart from them. It is by the removal of the notion of the existence of an ātman

1. These three are called also lakkhaṇas (properties of worldly things). Cf. *Jāt*,, I, p. 48 : Buddhānañ ca dhammadesanā tilakkhaṇamuttā nāma natthi, tesām anicca, dukkham, anattā ti . . .

2. *Aṅguttara*. III, p. 319.

3. *Attha*., p. 225.

4, *Laṅkā*., p. 61.

5. *Paṭis. M.*, II, p. 177 devotes a chapter to the exposition of *Suññatā* The general definition offered by it is that the things of the world are devoid of attā or attanīya. Then it says that Suñña can be explained in 24 ways, *viz.*, suññasuññam, saṅkhārasuññam, vipariṇāmasuññam, etc., up to paramatthasuññam (=Nibbāna). The various suññas may well be compared to the 18 kinds of Śūnyatā of the Mahāyāna scriptures.

as identical with one of the skandhas or something apart from them that a person attains Nirvāṇa.

The Mahāyānists do not admit the real existence of the skandhas or elements composing a being. They assert that the skandhas exist only in imagination (*vikalpa*) or the illusory conception (*māyā*) held by the so-called beings suffering from a defective vision due to ignorance. So the Truth, according to the Mahāyānists, is *Śūnyatā* or *Dharma-nairātmya*. The *Puṇḍarīka*[1] therefore says that he who knows the *dharmas* as devoid of *ātman* knows the truth. It is because one does not possess this knowledge of the essencelessness of dharmas (*śūnyajñāna-vihīnatvāt*) that one is called a Śrāvaka. The *Kāśyapa Parivarta* sarcastically compares the Pudgala-śūnyatā of the Śrāvakas with the whole made by a termite, and the Dharmaśūnyatā of the Bodhisattvas with the infinite space (ākāśa).[2] Of the seven reasons adduced by the *Sūtrālaṅkāra* to show why Mahāyāna should be considered superior to Hīnayāna, one is that the knowledge of the Mahāyānists is on a higher level, for it penetrates into both Pudgala-nairātmya and Dharma-nairātmya[3]. The *Triṃśikā*[4] brings out very clearly the difference between Pudgala- and Dharma-nairātmya. It says that the realisation of the two forms of Nairātmya is needed for the removal of the two screens (*āvaraṇa*) *viz.*, that of passions (*kleśa*) and that hindering true knowledge (*jñeya*). The passions or desires, attachment, etc. arise on account of a belief in a self; so when one realises the non-existence of self, the egoism is destroyed, and as a result his passions are eliminated. The realisation of the non-existence of the things of this world (dharma-nairātmya) removes the screen over true knowledge. The removal of both the screens is needed for the attainment of emancipation (*mokṣa*) and omniscience (*sarvajñatva*). The passions are obstacles to the attainment of emancipation (*mokṣaprāpterāvaraṇaṃ*) ; hence the removal of passions leads

---

1. *Sad P.*, p. 38 ; *Kāś. P.*, pp. 115f.
2. *Kāś. P.*, 114, *Pañca.*, leaves 77, 78,
3. *Sūtrā*, p. 171.
4. *Siddhi*, p. 15 : cf. *Sūtrā.*, p. 94.

to mokṣa. The screen of *jñeya* works as a hindrance to the functioning of knowledge (jñāna), *i.e.*, in the apperception of things through knowledge. When it is removed, knowledge penetrates unhindered into all objects of knowledge in detail (*sarvākāra*) without, however, causing attachment of any kind and this is called the attainment of omniscience or Bodhi.

The Hīnayānists, however, do not admit that they shake off only the kleśāvaraṇa and not jñeyāvaraṇa as stated by the Mahāyānists. They contend that by the removal of the screen of actions (karmāvaraṇa), of the effects of karma (vīpākāvaraṇa) and of afflictions (kilesāvaraṇa),[1] the Arhats attain full knowledge without any veil (anāvaraṇa).[2] They completely eradicate from their minds the āsavas including the avijjāsava. Of the three branches of their spiritual culture, *viz.*, sīla, samādhi and paññā, the last, according to them, brings home to an Arhat the Truth[3], which is the same for Arhats and Buddhas. The function of Paññā consists in destroying avijjā, the veil of ignorance, the source of worldly existences, and therefore, of all miseries (dukkha). It is avijjā, which (i) causes experience of things which ought not to be experienced, *e.g.*, evils through thoughts words and deeds; (ii) veils things which ought to be known, *e.g.*, the merit of observance of good conduct and so forth; (iii) acts as a hindrance to the realisation of the fact that the five khandhas are in reality an undifferentiated heap (rāsaṭṭham), and that the perceptions of the organs of sense are senseless and that the truths are the same tathaṭṭham,[4] (iv) drives (javāpeti) beings into the various

1. The Mahāyānists perhaps made capital out of the statements very often found in the Hīnayāna works like "Arahattamaggena sabbakilesehi vimuccatīti". *Paṭis. M.*, II, p. 243,

2. *Paṭis. M*,, I, pp. 124, 131.

3. *Ibid.*, II, pp. 31, 244: arhattamaggena sabbakilese saṃvaraṭṭhena sīlavisuddhi, avikkhepaṭṭhena cittavisuddhi, dassanaṭṭhena diṭṭhivisuddhi.

4. *Paṭis., M.*, 104 explains *tathaṭṭham* thus: Cattāro dukkhassa dukkhaṭṭhā tathā avitathā anaññathā; dukkhassa pīlanaṭṭho saṅkhataṭṭho santāpaṭṭho vīpariṇāmaṭṭho...Evaṃ dukkhaṃ tathaṭṭhena saccaṃ. In this way the other truths are also explained.

forms of existence in the Kāma, Rūpa, and Arūpa worlds without cessation ; (v) cause one to discriminate between things, which, in the ultimate analysis, have no real difference and clouds one's vision from the real nature of the khandhas ; and (vi) blinds one to the relative nature of the world, *i.e.*, its dependence on causes and conditions (paṭiccasamuppana).[1] By the complete removal of Avijjā through paññā, a person becomes an Arhat and reaches the state which is beyond change, beyond destruction—the state of immortality. There can be no state higher than this. The Hīnayānists acknowledge that the Buddhas, by their extraordinary merits accumulated in the past, acquire omniscience (sabbaññutañāṇa)[2] and many other powers unattainable by Arhats,[3] but they do not admit that the Nibbāna of Buddha is different from that of an Arhat. The knowledge (ñāṇa) acquired by Arhats and Buddhas is *anāvaraṇa* (without any veil) with this difference in the case of a Buddha that his knowledge is detailed and superior in some respects to that of the Arhats.[4]

(*iv*) *Transition from Laukika to Lokottara*

It is stated in the *Puṇḍarīka* that the Hīnayānists conceive of Nirvāṇa as passing from the worldly (*laukikadhātu*) to the transcendental sphere (*lokottaradhātu*), *i.e.*, the Hīnayānic Nirvāṇa is a transcendental state beyond the three dhātus, free from every kind of affliction and beyond any possibility of retrogression to lower stages. The *Laṅkāvatāra*[5] points out that ordinary knowledge (laukikajñāna) of the people of the world has reference to the existence and non-existence of things (sad asat pakṣābhiniviṣṭa) while the transcendental knowledge (lokottarajñāna) posseesed by the

1. *Vis. M.*, p. 526. 2. *Kvu.*, xxi, 3 ; i. 2.

3. For a comparison of the powers (bala) of Arhats and Buddhas, see *Paṭis. M.*, II, pp. 173 ff.

4. *Paṭis. M.*, I, pp. 131 ff. 11, pp. 31, 32. The Buddhas possess 14 jñānas, of which eight are common to the Arhats and Buddhas.

5. *Laṅkā.*, p. 157.

Srāvakas and Pratyekabuddhas has reference to the particular and generic characteristics of things (svasāmānyalakṣaṇa-patitāśayābhiniviṣṭa)[1] penetrating through the notion of existence and non-existence of things. The distinction between laukika and lokottara as drawn in the *Puṇḍarīka* and *Laṅkāvatāra* find support in the Hīnayāna scriptures. There it is stated that the puthujjanas (non-sotāpannas) labour under the notion of individual existence in the worlds while the arhats are free from such notion, as they know that all beings are made of five skandhas devoid of an underlying permanent entity and owing their origin to causes and conditions (pratītyasamutpanna), and that the common characteristics of beings are anityatā, duḥkhatā and anātmatā.

The *Paṭisambhidāmagga*, *Vibhaṅga* and other works speak of four dhātus, *viz*., Kāma, Rūpa, Arūpa and Apariyāpanna or Lokottara.[2] *Kāmadhātu* is the world of beings having vatthukāma (desire for existence in any of the three worlds) and kilesakāma (proneness to passion). It comprises the eleven spheres of existence from the Avīci hell to the Paranimmita heaven.[3] In Kāmadhātu, the beings possess 5 khandhas, 12 āyatanas, 18 dhātus, 32 indriyas, 9 hetus, 7 kinds of phassa, vedanā, saññā, cetanā and citta, are conversant with the 3 truths and dependent on 4 āhāras.[4] *Rūpadhātu* is the world of beings without kāma (passion), their actions being subtle (sukhuma)[5] in contrast to those of kāmadhātu, whose actions are oḷārika (gross). It comprises sixteen planes of existence from Brahmaloka to

1. *Kośa*, VI, 14c, d. ; svalakṣaṇa=les caractéres propre ; sāmānyalakṣaṇa=les caractéres genéraux.

2. *Vis. M.*, p. 493 ; *Paṭis. M*, I, p. 83.

3. *Attha.*, pp. 61-2 ; *Paṭis. M.*, I, p. 83. The eleven spheres are the six Devalokas, Manussaloka, Petaloka, Tiracchānayoni and Niraya.

4. *Vibh.*, p. 404.

5. *Vis. M.*, p. 475.

Akaniṭṭhas[1], 6 āyatanas, 9 dhātus, 14 indriyas, 8 hetus, and 4 kinds of phassa, vedanā, saññā, cetanā and citta, are conversant with 3 truths and dependent on 3 āhāras. *Arūpadhātu* is the world of beings without kāma (passion) and rūpa (material constituents of a body). It contains the gods residing in the four spheres from the ākāsānañcāyatana to nevasaññā-nāsaññāyatana.[2] In this dhātu the beings possess 4 khandhas, 2 āyatanas, 2 dhātus, 11 indriyas, 8 hetus, one kind of phassa, vedanā, saññā, cetanā and citta are conversant with 4 truths and dependent on 3 āhāras.

These three dhātus contain all the beings of the universe from the lowest to the highest plane of existence. The aim of Hīnayāna Buddhism is to reach a plane beyond the three dhātus, called the Apariyāpanna- or Lokottara-dhātu (the unincluded or transcendental sphere.) According to the *Paṭisambhidāmagga*[3] it contains those beings, who have reached the four maggas and had obtained the four maggaphalas or the Asaṅkhata, *i.e*, Nibbāna. The *Vibhaṅga*[4] explains that the beings of Apariyāpannadhātu possess khandhas and āyatanas similar to those of Arūpadhātu with the difference that the former are conversant with two truths (nirodha and magga), possess one additional power, *viz.*, anaññātaññāssāmītindriya and 6 hetus.[5] Evidently, the texts have in view those sentient

---

1. These are called *Rūpabrahmalokas.* By practising the first jhāna, an adept develops a state of mind which is similar to that of the denizens of the first three Rūpabrahmalokas. Should the adept die after perfecting himself in this jhāna, it is believed that he will be reborn in one of those lokas, which are therefore called *Paṭhamajjhānabhūmi.* Applying the same reason, the second three Rūpabrahmalokas are called *Dutiyajjhānabhūmi,* the third three *Tatiyajjhānabhūmi,* the tenth and eleventh *Catutthajjhānabhūmi,* and the remaining five Suddhāvāsabhūmi.

2. These four are called *Arūpabrahmalokas.* The adepts, as above, by practising the Ākāsānañcāyatana and other jhānas rise to the same level as gods of the Akāsānanta and other āyatanas.

3. *Paṭis. M.*, I, p. 84. 4. *Vibh.*, p. 407.

5. Buddhaghosa points out that in reality one cannot speak of lokottarāṇi viññāṇāi.

beings of the first three dhātus, who come to possess one of the stages of sanctification including Arhathood. The texts, however, do not explain how a being belonging to the Kāma- or Rūpa-dhātu and possessing one of the stages of sanctification can be without the rūpakkhandha and how one possessed of the Asaṅkhata or Nibbāna can continue to have the khandhas, dhātus, āyatanas, etc.,[1] which are the attributes of the members of Apariyāpānna- and Arūpa-dhātus. Thus we find that the Hīnayānists seek release from the three laukikadhātus by attaining the lokottara- or apariyāpanna-dhātu, which includes the Asaṅkhata- or Nibbāna-dhātu.

Nirvāṇa according to the early Mahāyāna works

The Hīnayānic Nirvāṇa thus, according to the *Puṇḍarīka*[2], is a haven of peace and rest and is a vimukti (emancipation) so far as the kleśas[3] (afflictions) are concerned. It further says that there may be people who may look upon this form of existence as Nirvāṇa and regard the Hīnayānists as right in their ways of thinking and practising. In order to counteract such a supposition, it states that there is one and only one Nirvāṇa, not two or three, and that one is, and, can be attained only by a thorough comprehension of the sameness of all things (*sarvadharma-samatāvadhāt*)[4] The conception of *Samatā* (sameness) has been developed in the *Sūtrālaṅkāra*, which gives five meanings of the same. It says that a being after comprehending *Dharmasamatā* (sameness of things) is realising the non-substantiality of things (dharma-nairātmya) sees that in the series of existences whether of himself or of others, there is no difference as regards nairātmya (essencelessness) and duḥkha (misery);

---

1. *Vis. M.*, p. 545.
2. *Sad. P*, pp. 129, 136-7.
3. *Sūtrā.*, p. 119 : *M. Vṛ.*, p. 519 : Tatra niravaśeṣasyāvidyārāgādikasya kleśagaṇasya prahāṇāt sopādhiśeṣaṃ nirvāṇam iṣyate.
4. *Sad. P.*, p. 133 ; see also p. 143 :
   śarvadharmāḥ samāḥ sarve samāḥ samasamāḥ sadā,
   Evaṃ jñātvā vijānitvā vijānāti nirvāṇam amṛtaṃ śivaṃ.

that the desire for the removal of misery from himself as well as from others is the same : that the remedy applicable is the same for himself as well as for others ; and that the knowledge attained by the bodhisattvas is the same as that attained by him.[1] The *Laṅkāvatāra*[2] explains samatā (sameness) by saying that is the sameness of the world (*saṃsāra*) and its cessation (*nirvāṇa*), *i.e.*, saṃsāra bears to nirvāṇa the same relation as waves bear to water. The *Pañcaviṃśati*[3] explains *samatā* by the illustration of *Ākāśa* (space). It is that Ākāśa has no direction like east or west, no past, present or future, no increase or decrease, no contamination nor purification. It has no origin, continuity or decay. It cannot be a subject of thought. It can neither be heard nor seen ; it is neither known nor unknown. It has nothing to do with the Kāma, Rūpa or Arūpa dhātus, with attachment or non-attachment, with hatred or non-hatred and so forth. It has no concern with the various *cittotpādas* (*i.e.*, the development of citta for the attainment of bodhi), *bhūmis* (stages of spiritual progress), *phalas* (fruits of spiritual sanctification), or any conceptions like happiness (*sukha*), misery (*duḥkha*), quietude (*śānta*), excellence (*praṇīta*), etc. This is what is called the samatā (sameness) of Ākāśa. It is in this light that the things of the world are to be seen. What the *Pañcaviṃśati* contends for is that, from the standpoint of reality, the things seen, heard or known by us are, in fact, the outcome of our imagination. What we should do is to regard these things as our fancies, because they are really the same as Tathatā, of which nothing can be predicated, just as nothing can be predicated of Ākāśa.

---

1. *Sūtrā.*, p. 94 : see also p. 48 : samacittatā sarvasattesv ātmaparasamatayā.

2. *Laṅkā.*, p. 42 : saṃsāra-nirvāṇa-samatā ; *M*„ *Vṛ.*, ch. xxv : na nirvāṇasya saṃsārāt kiñcid asti viśeṣaṇaṃ. For an exposition of Saṃsāra and Nirvāṇa as one, see Suzuki's *Outlines of Mahāyāna Buddhism*, pp. 352-6 ; Y. Sogen's *Systems etc.*, pp. 40-1.

3. *Pañca.* (A.S.B. ms.), leaves 114 ff ; *Śata.*, pp. 1560 ff.

According to the *Puṇḍarīka*, the real Nirvāṇa is that state, in which one sees things without any differentiation or dichotomy, and for the description of which all the expressions that can be used by man, relative as they are, are inadequate. The *Laṅkāvatāra*[1] describes the jñāna of Bodhisattvas as the *lokottaratama-jñāna* (super-transcendental knowledge), as distinguished from the *lokottarajñāna* of the Śrāvakas and Pratyekabuddhas and *laukika-jñana* of pṛthagjanas (common persons). It consists in the realisation of all dharmas as mere reflections, having no origin and decay. Hence, no question of existence and non-existence can arise in regard to this (nirābhāsadharmapravicayād anirodhānutpādadarśanāt sad asat pakṣavigatam).

The Mahāyānists, however, concede the point that the Arhats can remain at peace in the state called by the Hīnayānists Arahathood or Nirvāṇa but, according to them, it is a lower ideal, a selfish end, devoid of love (*sneha*)[2] and charity. The *Puṇḍarīka*[3] states that the arhats after attaining (Hīnayānic) Nlrvāṇa do not, in fact, wish to stay there for ever ; it is only a temporary rest (viśrāmo'yaṃ na nivṛtiḥ)[4]. At this stage, they become capable of realising the nature of the Truth and the powers and privileges appertaining to a Buddha, who is indistinguishable from that Truth. Then they set themselves to the performance of the duties still remaining and ultimately becoming Buddhas, *i.e.*, attain Nirvāṇa properly so called. They now realise that the three dhātus, from which they have so long struggled to extricate themselves, had no existence whatsoever,[5] and

1. *Lankā.*, p. 157.

2. *Sūtrā.*, pp. 127-8 : Niḥsnehānāṃ śrāvaka-pratyekabuddānāṃ sarvaduḥkhopaśame nirvāṇe prrtiṣṭthitaṃ manaḥ.

3. *Sad. P.*, pp. 132-3, 138, 140 ; cf. *Pañca.* (A.S.B. ms.), leaf 70b.

4. *Sod. P.*, pp., 142, 188. Cf. 5 kinds of Nirvaṇa in the Brahmajāla Sūtta. Dr. E. J. Thomas, in his *Lsfe of Buddha,* p. 200, refers to it thus, "They hold that Nirvāṇa consists in the enjoyment of this life in five ways either in the pleasures of sense or one of the four trances".

5. *Sad. P.*, p. 318.

were merely imaginary superimpositions (parikalpanā).[1] The three dhātus that are seen in the ten directions are only appearances like a mirage ; hence, they cannot have origination, destruction or transformation, bondage or freedom, light or darkness. As they are non-cxistent like things seen in a dream or a mirage, any statement about them would be inappropriate. Unless one realises that the things of this uviverse in this way, he cannot obtain Nirvāṇa (sarvadharmā na prāptāḥ kutas tasya nirvāṇam iti).[2] One who has developed bodhicitta never thinks of himself as existing either in saṃsāra or in nirvāṇa. Hence, an Arhat, aspiring to comprehend the ultimate truth, should not think of himself as having gone beyond Saṃsāra and established himself in Nirvāṇa. Thus, the *Puṇḍarīka* brings out clearly the difference between the Hīnayānic and Mahāyānic Nirvāṇa.

Existence of Soul is denied but Nirvāṇa is not annihilation

Of late, many scholars have tried to elicit from the various passages of the *Nikāyas* dealing with Nirvāṇa the sense, which Buddha had in his mind, or at least the sense with which the earliest Buddhism started. Most of the earlier scholars, who did the pioneering work in the field of

1. *Sūtrā.*, p. 94 ; sa traidhātukātmasaṃskārān abhūtaparikalpanāmātrān paśyati.

2. Cf. Das Gupta's *Indian Philosophy*, pp. 425. 426, 428 referring to Gauḍapāda's definition of the Absolute. The close agreement between the views of the *Sad. P.*, and Gauḍapādā's *Māṇḍukyakārikā* will be evident from the following passages :—

Sad. P., p. 318 Dṛṣṭaṃ hi tathāgatena traidhātukaṃ yathābhūtaṃ na jāyate na mriyate na cyavate nopapadyate na saṃsarati na parinirvāti na bhūtaṃ nābhūtaṃ na sattvaṃ nāsattvaṃ na tathā nānyathā na vitathā nāvitathā. Traidhātukaṃ tathāgatena dṛṣṭaṃ yathā bālapṛthagjanā na paśyanti . . .

Māṇḍūkhya, ii. 32 : Svapnamāye yathā dṛṣṭe gandharvanagaraṃ yathā, tathā viśvam idaṃ dṛṣṭaṃ Vedānteṣu vicakṣaṇaiḥ. Na nirodho na cotpattir na baddho na ca sādhakaḥ, na mumukṣur na vi mukta ity eṣā paramārthatā.

Muṇḍūkya, ix. 68 ; Yathā svapnamayo (māyāmayo or nirmitako) jīvo jāyate mriyate' pi ca, tathā jīvā amī sarve bhavant na bhavanti ca.

Buddhism, namely, Childers, Burnouf, Hardy were inclined to interpret Nirvāṇa as *annihilation* or to use the common Indian term *Ucchedavāda,* a dogma which was opposed to the view of the early Buddhists.[1] Professor La Valée Poussin suggests that this conclusion of the scholars was an inevitable consequence of the denial of soul by the early Buddhists.[2]

The conception of soul and the denial of its existence in the early Buddhist literature constitute as complicated a problem as the interpretation of Nirvāṇa. As the conception of one largely depends on the other, we shall state here briefly the position of the early Buddhists as to their conception of *Pudgala* (soul). The Theravādins are explicit in their statement that the five khandhas, *viz.*, rūpa (material aggregates), vedanā (feeling), saññā (perception), saṅkhārā (impressions) and viññāṇa (consciousness) are the ultimates, to which the composition of the world can be reduced. The mass (khandha or saṅgaha) or material aggregates, feeling, etc., would have remained in their original state dissociated from each other if avijjā (ignorance) had not stepped in and constituted (saṅkhata) out of them a being (sattvā) with the sense of 'I'. When and how this avijjā of the truth—that the five khandhas remain ever dissociated[3] from each other and do not form an individual—came into existence and brought endless miseries had not been told by any teacher,

---

1. Cf. *Saṁyutta*, iii, p. 109 : Yamaka harboured the wrong view that Buddha taught that a khīṇāsavo bhikkhu kāyassa bhedā bhijjati vinassati na hoti param maraṇā.

2. *Nirvāṇa*, pp. vii f.

3. Ususally the Pāli texts speak of Avijjā as ignorance of the four ariyasaccas.

In the *Vis. M.*, (pp. 198, 525) it is equated to bhavataṇhā (desire for existence) and in another place (p. 526) it is explained as "khandhānaṃ rāsaṭṭhaṃ, āyatanānaṃ āyatanaṭṭhaṃ. dhātūnaṃ suññaṭṭhaṃ, indriyānam adhipatiyaṭṭhaṃ, saccaānaṃ tathaṭṭham aviditaṃ karotī ti pi avijjā. Paramatthato avijjamānesu itthipurisādīsu javati, vijjamānesu pi khandhādīsu na javatī ti avijjā. Api ca cakkhuviññāṇādinaṃ vatthārammaṇaṃ paṭiccasamuppāda-paṭiccasamupannā ca dhammānaṃ chādanato pi avijjā.

not even by Buddha (purimā koṭi na paññāyati avijjāya).[1] Evidently, the five khandhas alone constitute a being and there is nothing as the sixth, which can be regarded as *Attā* or soul. But still one cannot deny the fact that of the five khandhas *viññāṇa*[2] (consciousness) is the most active constituent and is mainly instrumental in the formation of a being (nāma-rūpa). It is produced from Saṅkhārā,[3] which again issue out of avijjā.[4] According to Buddhaghosa, the belief in a self arises with the ninth link (*viz.* upādāna)[5] of the chain of causation. Hence, on upādāna hinge the origin and cessation of worldly existence. The belief in a self (ahaṅkāra) is nothing but the false notion of the undisciplined men of the world[6] that one of the five khandhas is soul (attā). It corresponds to the false notion of Ahaṅkāra as conceived by the teachers of Sāṃkhya and Vedānta. The Buddhist conception of self (attā) is therefore as much imaginary as the notion of ahaṅkāra in the Brāhmanic systems of philosophy.

Vasubandhu's appendix to the eighth chapter of the *Abhidharmakośa*[7] and the first section of the *Kathāvatthu* throw a flood of light upon the early Buddhist theory of soul. In fact, in the Nikāyas the existence of soul is not categorically denied in answer to direct questions on that point.[8]

1. *Vis, M.*, p. 525.
2. Viññāṇa=six froms of consciousness through the six organs of sense, *vis.*, cakkhu, sota, ghāṇa, jivhā, kāya and mano.
3. *Viz*, puññābhisaṅkhāro apuññābhisaṅkhāro āneñjābhisaṅkhāro, kāyasaṅkhāro vacisaṅkhāro cittasaṅkhāro. *Vibhaṅga*, p. 135.
4. For a full explanation of Avijjā, see *Vis. M.*, p. 526.
5. *Vis. M.*, p. 569 : Upādāna is of four kinds ; kāmupādānam, diṭṭhupā°, sīlabbatupā° and attavādupā°.
6. *Dh. S.* 1217 ; *Vibh.*, p. 375.
7. Stcherbatsky, *Soul Theory of the Buddhists* (published by the Royal Academy of Sciences, St. Petersburg) ; La Vallée Poussin, Fr. translation of the *Kośa*, ch. ix.
8. *E.g.*, *Dīgha*, I, pp. 185ff ; Stcherbatsky, *Soul Theory of the Buddhists* (p. 864) shows that Buddha would have said 'taṃ jīvaṃ taṃ sarīraṃ' if the questioner had not meant by *Jīva* a soul "as a real living unit, controlling our actions from within". As an answer in the positive or negative about such a soul would be like the discussion about the hardness or softness of the hair of a tortoise, Buddha had to be silent on the point (avyākata).

What the early Buddhists held was that there was no such thing as soul in the sense, which had come to be widely accepted previous to the advent of Buddhism, *viz.*, as a persisting, unchangeable entity. "In Buddhism", says Mr. Shwe Zan Aung, "there is no actor apart from action, no percipient apart from perception. In other words, there is no conscious subject behind consciousness...Subject, in Buddhism, is not the self-same permanent conscious object but merely a transitory state of consciousness".[1] This conception is identical with Bergson's conception of mind or soul, spirit or ego. Mind or soul, according to Bergson, is not "some sort of permanent substantial reality, on which the various states of consciousness are each of them the entire mind in one of the phases of its continuous movement... They are not parts or fragments of the mind, members in an endless series which, for no reason, we choose to regard as a unity and call by a single name".[2] In Buddhism, the conception of soul as a permanent entity is not only wrong but works as an obstacle to the comprehension of the unreality and transitoriness of things of this world. When Buddhism arose, the term *ātman* had become so very common, and so much associated with the attributes ascribed to it by the teachers of the early Upaniṣads that the Buddhists had no other alternative than to deny its existence as far as possible in order to wipe out from the minds of the people the deep-rooted ideas. Besides, Buddhism started with the premises that everything whatsoever except Nirvāṇa is unreal;[3] so there could not be any real soul. But it could not do away with the word *ātman*, for the Budahist texts tell us that the early expositors could not help using the current expressions in propounding the doctrines. They wanted to impress on the minds of the

1. *Comp. of Phil.*, pp. 7, 8.

2. *Philosophies. Ancient and Modern, Bergson* by J. Solomon (Constable and Co., 1911), p. 36.

3. The nature of unreality varies with the two forms of Buddhism. Hīnayāna and Mahāyāna; for a discussion of this, see *infra*.

people that there is a continuity of the skandhas kept up by action (*karma*) but there is no persisting, unchangeable and indestructible entity to keep up that continuity. Professor Stcherbatsky puts it thus: "A personality (pudgala), in which other systems imagine the presence of a permanent spiritual principle, a soul (ātman), is in reality a bundle of elements or forces (saṃskārasamūha) and a stream of thought (santāna). It contains nothing permanent or substantial, it is anātman".[1] This definition of soul struck at the root of the supposition of any permanent entity and served fully the purpose of Buddhism, *viz.*, to show that there is nothing in the world, to which one can cling as real and permanent and so he must develop a state of mind in which he must drift to the ultimate, real state called Nirvāṇa, without having anything to cling to in the intermediate process.

Four lines of interpretation in the Nikāyas

Scholars who took the passages in the Buddhist literature on the denial of soul too literally, without considering the motive for the denial of soul made at a particular place and in reply to the query of a particular person, believed that the early Buddhists did not admit the existence of soul and that hence the finality reached by perfect beings was complete annihilation, the absence of existence altogether. There were also some scholars, not very many among the earlier group, who were inclined to the view that Nirvāṇa was not annihilation but an inexpressible state corresponding to the Vedāntic Brahman. All these scholars, although they held one or other of the two views, *viz.*, either complete annihilation or eternal, inexpressible existence, often admitted that Buddha was an agnostic and did not give a definite answer to any of the queries of a metaphysical character, *viz.*, whether there is a soul, or what really is Nirvāṇa. Thus, the opinions of scholars can be classified as follows:—

1. *Con. of N.*, p. 8.

(i) That Nirvāṇa is annihilation ;[1]

(ii) That Nirvāṇa is an inconceivable and inexpressible eternal state ;

(iii) That Nirvāṇa has been left undefined (avyākṛta) by Buddha.[2] To these may be added the interpretation of Buddhaghosa,

(iv) That Nirvāṇa is eternal, pure and infinite consciousness.

Nikāyas, a mosaic of materials of different times and places

It should be observed that all those scholars, who arrived at these conclusions, cited passages from the texts of the Nikāyas in support of their findings, and that the views taken by them in most cases followed naturally from those passages. In these circumstances, we have to admit that the Nikāyas as a whole do not present a coherent system of philosophy and doctrine, but the question is whether, in view of the fact that the Nikāyas took centuries to grow and attain a definite shape, we are not entitled to expect from them a coherent system. The Nikāyas are, in fact, a mosaic made up of materials of various times and places, wide apart from each other ; hence, it would not be reasonable to expect from them a coherent interpretation of Nirvāṇa. The ancient teachers, too, were puzzled in regard to the correct interpretation of Nirvāṇa, but they never attempted to discover a consistency in the passages of the Nikāyas as a whole. It will be seen from the discussions preserved in the *Kathāvatthu* and the *Abhidharmakośa* that the disputants cited a set of passages in support of their

1. Suzuki, *Outlines of Mahāyāna Buddhism*, p. 351 quoting the *Vimalakīrtisūtra* : "Non-activity and eternal annihilation were cherished by the Śrāvakas and Pratyekabuddhas".

2. See La Vallée Poussin, *Nirvāṇa*, pp. 9, 87 ff. ; also *E. R. E.* II, p. 3 and his *Way to Nirvāṇa*, p. 134 ; Beal, *Cateua etc.*, p. 172.

According to Colebrooke, Nirvāṇa = profound calm ;

" " Hardy, Burnouf, Childers, Nirvāṇa = extinction ;

" " Max Müeller, Nirvāṇa = rest ;

" " Oldenberg, Nirvāṇa = supreme happiness.

contentions, and not any particular Nikāya or Sūtra. To these ancient disputants each saying was independent, and carried the weight, which a number of sayings would do. It is, however, striking that the disputants never questioned the authenticity of the passages cited by their opponents. This shows that a disputant only preferred one set of passages to another and built his theories on that set. The Nikāyas evidently are only a collection of these various passages put in a uniform setting and given the garb of the sūtras. Attempts, of course, are now being made to sift these sūtras and find out the various strata, but it is doubtful how far the efforts will be fruitful in the absence of new evidences. It may be contended that a Piṭaka is a collection of texts made by a particular school of Buddhist thought, and that consistency should be apparent or dicoverable in the passages of that Piṭaka. The contention seems reasonable, but the facts are against it. Professor Poussin has discovered in the Nikāyas many passages cited by the Sarvāstivādins in the *Kośa* in support of their contentions, while Mrs. Rhys Davids and Mr. Aung have identified many of the citations of the opponents of the Theravādins in the Pāli Piṭaka, the collection of the Theravādins. This fact indicates that the collection of Pāli sūtras was not made with any sectarian motive and that the cempilers of the Tripiṭaka included in it all the sayings that they could find out, excepting, very probably, some, which went directly against their creeds and dogmas,[1] and for the rejection of which they took the plea of unauthenticity. It is now fairly well known that each Nikāya developed by itself under the special attention of a group of reciters called *Bhāṇakas*, who confined themselves exclusiveiy to the preservation of that particular collection.[2] Buddhaghosa, although an orthodox adherent of the Theravāda school, had to acknowledge that even these bhāṇakas differed among themselves regarding the use and sense of certain technical

1. A hint to this effect is seen in the *Dīpavaṃsa*, ch. iv.
2. *Sum. Vil.* p. 15.

expressions.[1] Thus, we see, that even the orthodox supporters of the Pāli Tripiṭakas believed that the Nikāyas did not agree in all their interpretations. We should also bear in mind the significant remark found in the *Kośa*[2] that many sūtras were lost, that many of the sūtras underwent slight changes, and that new ideas and expositions were woven around them in such a way that the accretions conveyed a sense different from that of the kernel around which they were set.[3]

Nirvāṇa, the inconceivable state, the infinite consciousness

On account of this admixture of materials, it is possible to make a selection of passages of the Pāli Nikāyas in such a way as to substantiate any one of the four interpretations of Nirvāṇa, to which we have referred. The passages, which give the impression that Nirvāṇa is annihilation, if read in the light of other passages, which interpret Nirvāṇa as an inconceivable existence, may convey a sense different from annihilation.

Prof. Keith has, for instance, shown that the simile of the extinction of the flame, which is one of the many important similes relied on by scholars favouring the view of annihilation, has been worked out in the *Aggivacchagotta sutta* to show that it is not extinction but disappearance in the "deep, immeasurable, difficult to fathom" state of existence.[4]

1. *Vis. M.*, p. 95 : Majjhima-bhāṇaka Revata thera ; p. 275 : idaṃ tāva Dīghabhāṇaka-Saṃyuttabhāṇakānaṃ matam. Majjhimabhāṇakā pana etc. See also pp. 286, 431.

2. *Kośa*, ii. 55, p. 278 fn. sūtrāni ca bahūny antarhitāni mūlasaṅgītibhraṃśāt.

3. Cf. Prof. Poussin's remark in his *Nirvāṇa*, p. 9 : "La vieille tradition scripturaire (Petit Véhicule), codifiée, renouvelée, amplifiée par les écoles, est mal datée, en partie tradive, point toujours claire, contradictoire sinon dans ses dogmes du moins dans ses tendences". See also p. 133.

4. Keith, *B. Phil.*, pp. 65-6 : "The comparision is indeed significant, for there is no doubt that the Indian idea of the extinction of fire was not that which occurs to us of utter annihilation, but rather that the flame returns to the primitive, pure, invisible state of fire, in which it existed prior to its manifestation in the form of visible fire".

Buddhaghosa has drawn our attention to one or two passages in the *Dīgha*[1] and *Majjhima*[2] *Nikāyas*, which present us with quite a new interpretation of Nibbāna. The passage runs thus :

Viññāṇam anidassanam anantaṃ sabbato pabhaṃ.
Ettha āpo ca paṭhavī tejo vāyo na gādhati,
Ettha dīghañ ca rassañ ca aṇuṃ thūlaṃ subhāsubhaṃ,
Ettha nāmañ ca rūpañ ca asesam uparujjhati,
Viññāṇassa nirodhena etth' etam uparujjhatīti[3].

[On a certain occasion a bhikkhu was advised by Buddha to put his question thus :—"What is that place where (distinctions like) water and earth, fire and air have no footing, where long and short, fine and coarse, good and bad, or name and form cease absolutely ?" instead of asking "Where do the four elements earth, water, fire and air disappear absolutely ?". (The answer quoted above was given to it is) "It is viññāṇa (consciousness), which is signless, infinite[4], radiant on all sides (sabbato pabham)[5] where all the distinctions mentioned above,

1. *Dīgha*, I, p. 323 ; *Sum. Vil.* in the *I.H.Q.*, II, i.

2. *Majjhima*, I, p. 329 ; *Papañcasūdanī*, I, p. 413.

3. Cf. *Majjhima Nikāya* (I, p. 329) passage : Viññāṇam anidassanam anantaṃ sabbato pabhaṃ, taṃ paṭhaviyā paṭhavittena ananubhūtaṃ, āpassa āpattena ananubhūtaṃ, etc. The *Papañcasūdanī* (I, p. 413) comments on it as follows :—Padadvayena (i.e., *viññāṇam anidassanam*) pi nibbānam eva vuttaṃ. *Anantan* ti tayidam uppāda-vaya-antarhitattā anantaṃ nāma. . . .*Sabbato pabhan* ti sabbato pabhāsampannaṃ. Nibbāṇato hi añño dhammo sappabhataro vā jotimattaro vā parisuddhataro vā paṇḍarataro vā n'atthi, etc.

4. Buddhaghosa says that it is infinite (ananta) because it has no origin, no decay, no duration (sthiti) and no change.

5. J. d'Alwis' suggestion of 'pabham' for 'paham' has been preferred here. For a note on this, see *Sacred Books of the Buddhists*, II, p. 282n. Buddhaghosa, it seems, preferred the word "Papam" (from Sanskrit Prapā=a shed on the roadside for providing passerbys with water Aufrecht, *Abhi. Ratnamālā*, p. 283) to "Pabham" more for maintaining the analogy between Nibbāna and sea just mentioned before this passage. He says that just as in a great sea no landing-place is provided for seafarers, so also in Nibbāna there is no particular name corresponding to the 38 kammaṭṭhānas (bases for meditation), through which a monk aims at Nibbāna, i.e., through whatever kammaṭṭhānas (compared

cease, and where the (constituted viññāṇa, after cessation, disappears". Buddhaghosa in commenting upon this passage says that the first viññāṇa is another name for Nibbāna[1] while the second viññāṇa is one of the five khandhas. His interpretation, it seems, is based upon a few Nikāya passages. In the *Saṃyutta Nikāya*[2], Buddha referring to the parinibbāna of Vakkali bhikkhu said that the wicked Māra was searching for the viññāṇa (consciousness)[3] of Vakkali, who had been just dead, and predicted that Māra's attempt would not be successfull because Vakkali had passed away (parinibbuto) with viññāṇa, which cannot be localised (*apatiṭṭhita*). The sense of *apatiṭṭhita-viññāṇa* is given elsewhere in the *Saṃyutta Nikāya*[4], where it is explained as consciousness, which requires no support (patiṭṭhā or ārammaṇa) for its origin. It arises only when the attachment (rāga) to rūpa (material elements of the body), and the other four khandhas is removed. It is unconstituted, devoid of growth and independent of any cause and condition and hence free. Being free it is steady ; being steady it is happy ; being happy it is without any fear of change for the worse ; being fearless it attains parinibbāna.

here to landing-places) one may reach Nibbāna, there is nothing to distinguish it in Nibbāna.

For Prof. O. Franke's notes see his *Dīgha Nikāya* (Quellen der Religions Geschichte), Leipzig, p. 166n.

1. *Sum. Vil.* (*I H. Q.*, II, i), p. 33 : Tattha viññātabban ti viññāṇaṃ ; nibbānass' etaṃ nāmam. With regard to the second 'viññāṇa' Buddhaghosa says "Tattha viññāṇan ti carimaka-viññāṇam pi abhisaṅkhāra-viññāṇan ti" (Cf. *Vis. M.*, p. 689). He holds that the viññāṇa, the last consciousness of an arhat is abhisaṅkhāra (constituted) and that it ceases like the flame of a lamp to pass into a state of indistinguishability (apaṇṇakabhāve). Cf. Keith, *B. Phil.*, pp. 47, 48 where Prof. Keith points out that Prof. Franke's attempt to prove that there is much of negativism in early Buddhism favours the view that Nibbāna of early Buddhism was more idealistic than negativistic. See alss O. Franke's notes on Nibbāna in *Z. D. M. G.*, lxix, pp. 475-481.

2. *Saṃyutta*, III, p. 124 ; *Dhp. A.*, I. p. 432 : appatiṭṭhitena ca viññāṇena Godhiko Kulaputto parinibbuto.

3. *i. e.*, Paṭisandhiviññṇa, see *Vbh. A.*, pp. 161, 192f. ; *Dhp. A.*, I, p. 432

4. *Saṃyutta*, II, p. 65 ; III, pp. 53-61.

In commenting on this passage, Buddhaghosa further says that an arhat never has any maññanā (thought-construction)[1] in regard to the four elements or Nibbāna or anything whatsoever, which a puthujjana or a khīṇāsava[2] (but not yet an arhat) has. Buddhaghosa thus tries to show that Nibbāna is inexpressible, infinite and that any attempt to establish a relation between it and a being is a delusion of the mind. He is also constrained to say that such a description of Nibbāna had to be given as a set-off to the arguments of Brahmā,[3] hinting thereby that even such statements are not permissible as Nibbāna is inexpressible. From such interpretations of the Nikāya passages as well as from his exposition of Nibbāna in the *Visuddhimagga*, treated later on,[4] it will be apparent that he, far from supporting nihilism, held that Nibbāna was a transcendental, indescribable state. In fact, there was hardly any school of Buddhism, which favoured the view of annihilation, and so it seems that the opinions of scholars, who supported annihilation do not rest on very sure foundations. Prof. La Vallée Poussin has criticised in detail the views of these scholars. He has given the gist of their views, showing the weak points in them along with his learned dissertation on the interpretation of Nirvāṇa (Études sur l'histoire de religions, 1925). As in his work he has reviewed most of the writings of his predecessors on Nirvāṇa, we need not deal with them again. For our present purpose, it is sufficient to state his opinion and those of Prof. Berriedale

1. The Nikāya passages referred to here (*Majjhima*, I, p. 4) were not in harmony with Prof. Stcherbatsky's theory and so these did not appeal to him. See his remarks in *Con. of N.*, p. 42n. The "maññanā" of Buddhaghosa reminds us of one of the passages of the *Prajñāpāramitās*, in which it is asserted that all dharmas are like dream and that Bodhisattvas 'svapnam api na manyante, svapnena na manyante, etc.; *e.g.*, *Pañca*, (A.S.B. ms.) leaves 225, 399b : saṃsāraṃ saṃsārato na vikalpayati, nirvāṇaṃ nirvāṇato na vikalpayati and ss forth.

2. For distinction between an Arhat and a Khīṇāsava, see *Papañcasūdanī*, I, p. 42.

3. *Papañcasūdanī*. II, p. 413.

4. See *infra*.

Keith and Prof. Stcherbatsky, the three latest exponents of the subject.

Prof. La Vallée Poussin on Nirvāṇa

Prof. La Vallée Poussin starts with the statement that it is possible to distinguish Buddhism on the one hand as popular and devotional, and on the other hand as clerical and mystic.[1] The former is meant for the laity and the latter for the monks. The popular and devotional form of Buddhism holds out the prospect of paradise to the laity. It is only a means to an end, for the layman in one of his later lives is to become a monk and take to the clerical and mystic side of Buddhism and ultimately attain Nirvāṇa. Prof. Poussin then proceeds to define Nirvāṇa. He says that Nirvāṇa is undoubtedly the highest happiness, putting a stop to duḥkha and transmigration. It implies the absence of merit as well as of demerit. It requires a purely ascetic discipline to bring the desires or passions to an end.[2] The monks unlike the laity do not seek paradise, for even the life in paradise ends with the exhaustion of one's good karma.[3] They therefore seek a state which affords eternal (dhruva) beatitude (sukha).[4] The very common appellation to denote this state is *Amatapadam* (immortality), which Prof. Poussin considers to be a very old and characteristic expression used to describe Nirvāṇa. He thinks that the notion of deliverance has been made precise in the early Buddhist literature. It is an *abode*, supreme and definite but yet this notion has not been coloured by any positive philosophic doctrine or by speculation upon God, soul, or

1. *Nirvāṇa*, pp. 1, 7. 8. Cf. Karma and Jñāna of Brāhmanic philosophy; the former leads to svarga (heaven) while the latter to mokṣa (emancipation).

2. *Nirvāṇa*, p. 4.

3. Cf. *Chāndogya*, 8, 1, 6: Tad yatheha karmajito lokaḥ kṣīyate, evam evāmutra puṇyajito lokaḥ kṣīyate (just as the things produced by efforts of people are exhausted by their use, so also heavenly lives, etc., earned by sacrifices, merits, etc., are exhausted by their use).

4. *Nirvāṇa*, pp. 48, 63.

being in itself.[1] He, as also Dr. E. J. Thomas[2], refer to the fact that the early Buddhists did not speculate about such Upaniṣadic doctrine as the Parabrahman, which was developed by the Vedāntists long after Buddhism. They knew only of the highest heaven called Brahmaloka. Dr. Thomas remarks in connection with the *Brahmajāla Sutta* that "among all these views there is no expressed contradiction or even recognition of the Vedāntic theory of Ātman or Brahman as the one ultimate reality"[3]. Prof. Poussin also points out that it is not correct to hold that Buddhism originated purely in opposition to the Brāhmanic theories. He says that there is nothing, which permits us to affirm that Nirvāṇa was conceived in opposition to any Brāhmanic theory. Nirvāṇa, Immortality, or Deliverance appears to be a rudimentary idea free from all metaphysical speculations. It is connected more with myths than with metaphysics. Nirvāṇa is an invisible abode where the saint disappears, often as the middle of a flame, or in a kind of apotheosis.[4] In short, the Hīnayāna Buddhism from the time of the *Mahāvagga* to Buddhaghosa emanated, so to say, from the Yoga almost without any mixture. The Immortal State, the Inexpressible is what a saint aims at, because it is the deliverance from birth and death. It is, however, not possible to establish any relation, philosophical or ontological, between the Immortal and the world of beings, who transmigrate. Immortality is the name given to Nirvāṇa; in other words, perfect happiness, extinction, detachment are terms, which are devoid of doctrinal complexities, and which, in fact, appear to signify merely the extinction of the fire of desire, or, to put it in another way, constitute the road to the Immortal State, or the Immortal State itself.[5] It is obvious that Prof. Poussin wants to contradict the long-

---

1. *Nirvāṇa*, p. 49: "La notion de la deliverance était précise: l' ascéte ne doute pas que la déliverance ne soit un séjour supréme et definitif".
2. *Life of Buddha*, p. 200.
3. *Ibid.*
4. *Nirvāṇa*, p. 57.
5. *Ibid.*, pp. 53-4.

advocated view that Nirvāṇa is annihilation. He cites several passages to show that the self-originating fire, in which a saint consumed himself, as also the saint hīmself was not annihilated.[1] While summarising his views, he gives the following different uses of the term Nirvāṇa :

(i) The Nirvāṇa, the Absolute, the Uncaused, which is by itself the destruction of passion, of duḥkha.

(ii) The complete possession of Nirvāṇa, which reduces all passions and all new existences to the quality of *anutpattika* (not being capable of reproducing) ; in other words, that which constitutes the saintship, the deliverance from thought (or conceptions), the *Sopādhiśeṣa Nirvāṇa* (Nirvāṇa with corporal residue).

(iii) The consciousness of the possession of Nirvāṇa, consciousness obtained in ecstasy, which is beatitude, and which is the best form of Nirvāṇa in the world, and properly speaking, the only Nirvāṇa.

(iv) The possession of the Samādhi of the cessation of ideas and sensations (*saṃjñāvedayitanirodha*), a possession obtainable by saints, perfect or imperfect, a samādhi which appears like entering into Nirvāṇa, and of which one becomes conscious through the body only, since the thought is then stopped.

(v) The entering into Nirvāṇa at the last moment of thought, the end of duḥkha, the entering into *Anupādhiśeṣa Nirvāṇa* (Nirvāṇa without any corporal residue).

(vi) The possession of Nirvāṇa relating to such and such a passion, which carries with it the quality of not being able to reproduce itself for such passion and such future existences ; an incomplete sanctity which one enjoys in ecstasy.[2]

Prof. Poussint has endeavoured to show that the Nirvāṇa of the early Buddhists is not annihilation ; it is a state which may well bear comparison with the paradise of the laity but it is free from the implication of a life in paradise, *i. e.*, unlike the life in a paradise, it is eternal (*dhruva*), it is beatitude, but without any sensation even of

1. *Nirvāṇa*, p. 58. 2. *Ibid.*, p. 43.

bliss.[1] It is beyond merit and demerit, a quiescent state, which is obtainable in this life by saints when they establish themselves in the samādhi of *saṁjñāvedayitanirodha* (cessation of ideas and senations). In this state as the thought is completely stopped, the saint feels only by his body the supreme bliss. He, however, warns us not to identify the supreme state of bliss with the Vedāntic Parábrahman, for the Buddhists had not yet arrived at that conception. His reason for holding this opinion is, chiefly, that the early Buddhists were not interested, to any appreciable extent, in metaphysical speculations, but were rather busy with myths. Hence, their conception of Nirvāṇa was not of a metaphysical nature but just the utmost possible extension of the conception of paradise.

Prof. Stcherbatsky on Nirvāṇa

Prof. Stcherbatsky protests strongly against the view of Prof. Poussin that Nirvāṇa is a sort of ultimate conceivable existence—a view suggested by the expression *Amatapadam*,[2] often used to describe Nirvāṇa, and by the descriptions of the same found in the *Milindapañha* and the *Nikāyas*. Prof. Stcherbatsky does not examine the various passages of the Piṭakas and other works, which influenced Prof. Poussīn's conclusions. It would appear from the *Conception of Nir-*

1. Cf. *Dhammasaṅgīṇi*, 1389, 1579 ff. : Nībbāṇa is not to be taken as accompanied by pīti (delight), sukha (happiness), or upekkhā (equanimity). In the *I. H. Q.*, IV, p. 247, Prof. Poussin says, "Nirvāṇa from the beginning is perfect happiness. the *summum bonum*, much better than any paradise, not a paradise (of course) without any conceivable relations with any form of existence. The canonical literature states clearly that the happiness of Nirvāṇa, end of suffering, is blissful because it is not vedita".

2. In this connection, we may mention that Amatapadam does not always necessarily mean "heavenly state". The word 'mṛtyu' (pāli maccu), in the lines of the *Taitt. Upa.* 2. I, I : Brahmavid āpnoti param, na punar mṛtyavo, and *Chānd Upa.* 7. 26. 2 : Tad ekaṃ paśyati na paśyo mṛtyuṃ paśyati, is explained by the commentator as neither heavenly existence nor eternal death but as pramāda (negligence, error) and moha (delusion). This comment is supported by the *Dhammapada* line : Pamādo maccuno padam. See *P. T. S. Dict.*, sv. Maccu.

vāṇa as well as from his earlier work the *Central Conception of Buddhism* that Prof. Stcherbatsky bases his finding purely on the study of the *Abhidharmakośa* of Vasubandhu, and ignores the fact that the *Kośa* does not present us with the original doctrines, which the Piṭakas are supposed to preserve. He also does not attach importance to the fact that the Theravādins and Sarvāstivādins do not agree as to the nature of distintegration of constituted elements (saṁskṛtavastus), which is clearly hinted at in the discussion in the *Kathāvatthu*[1] on the theory of the Sarvāstivādins that "all exists".[2] In his treatment of the discussion of this topic, however, he refers to the the fact that the Vibhajyavādin (=Theravādins) did not always agree with the Sarvāstivādins.

In view of the fact mentioned above, it is doubtful how far Prof. Stcherbatsky was right in attributing to Buddha the views found in the *Kośa* that "(i) Buddha was led to a denial of every permanent principle, (ii) that the originality of Buddha's position consisted in denying substantiality altogether, and (iii) that forsaking the Monism of the Upaniṣads and the Dualism of the Sāṃkhya, he established a system of the most radical pluralism".[3] These might have been the views of the later Vaibhāṣikas but were certainly not those of the early Buddhists, not to speak of Buddha himself. Many passages can be, and have been, cited from the Piṭakas[4] to show that Nirvāṇa is a reality, that it is unspeakable and possesses the sign of peacefulness, the taste of immortality, that it offers consolation, that it is unborn, uncreated, and indestructible. In the face of the glowing descriptions that are to be found of the state of Nirvāṇa in early post-canonical works,[5] it is difficult to agree with Prof. Stcherbatsky that Nirvāṇa is

1. *Kvu.*, I, 6, pp. 115 f.

2. *Central Concepiion of Buddhism,* pp. 43, 76 ff. ; Keith's *B. Phil.*, p. 168 ; *Con. of N.*, pp. 3, 27 ; for bibliography on the topic "All exists" see *Kośa*, v. 24, pp. 49, 50 fn.

3. *Con. of N.*, p. 3.

4. See besides Prof. Poussin's *Nirvāṇa,* Heiler's *Die buddhistische Versenkung, Muenchen*, pp. 36-42 ; *P, T. S. Dict.* sv. Nibbāna.

5. *e.g.*, *Thera-* and *Theri-gāthā* ; *Milindapañha.*

nothing but eternal death and that it is an unconstituted element (asaṃskṛta-dhātu), because it is tantamount to the absolute annihilation of the constituted elements (saṃskṛta-dharmas)—"a kind of entity where there is no consciousness".[1] In faci, Prof. Stcherbatsky's opinion makes it resemble one of the heretical doctrines condemned by Buddha, *viz.*, Asaññi attā hoti arogo param maraṇā (the soul remains after death as an unconscious but healthy entity).[2] Without multiplying instances, we can refer to the last few lines of the *Kevaddha Sutta*[3] to show that there are passages in the early Buddhist works which go directly against the conclusions of Prof. Stcherbatsky. If Nibbāna is extreme happiness (paramasukha), a place of perfect peace[4] (santivarapadam), an object of realisation (sacchikiriyā),[5] it is safer to accept the opinion of Prof. Poussin that Nirvāṇa is the highest conceivable paradisical existence than to agree with Prof. Stcherbatsky that Nirvāṇa is simply an end of the saṃskṛta dharmas—a stone-like life without a vestige af consciousness.

In short, Prof. Stcherbatsky makes Buddha a materialist and annihiiationist (Ucchedavādin) so severely condemned by Buddha. Prof. Stcherbatsky admits this anomalous position of his exposition, and endeavours to extricate himself from the anomaly by stating that Buddha's materialism and annihilationism were of a modified nature, because, as he says, the elements constituting a being were not only material, but both material and spiritual, and hence, according to him, Buddha was not an out-and-out materialist like the Cārvākas, or like Ajita Kesakambalin and Pakudha Kaccāyana, but was partially so. Then, as regards Buddha being not an out-and-out annihilationist he points to the moral law, the strength and importance of which were recognised by Buddha ; Buddha meant that the being, which is only a conglomeration

1. *Central Conception of Buddhism*, p. 53
2. *Majjhima*, II, pp. 230 f.
3. *Dīgha*, I, p. 223 : for its commentary see *Sum. Vil.* in the *I. H. Q.*, vol., II.
4. *Majjhima*, I, p. 257.
5. *Ibid.*, I, pp. 56, 63, 510.

of "evanescent elements" passes through a series of existence governed by the moral law, ultimately to be annihilated or, in other words, to attain Nirvāṇa or eternal death. Hence, according to Prof. Stcherbatsky, Uccheda or annihilation takes place not after one life but a series of lives.

Nirvāṇa as viewed by Prof. Keith

Prof. Keith on the basis of the Nikāya passages where there is an emphatic assertoin of the existence of Nirvāṇa as something unfathomable, unborn, uncreated, unconstituted, and so forth,—a description echoed in the works of Nāgārjuna,—and also on the strength of the discussions in the Buddhistic literature on the existence of the Tathāgata during his life-time or after his decease, thinks that the Madhyamaka view can be traced in the Nikāyas, and that there are "positive assurances of the reality of something over and above the empirical world".[1] He says further that "the great sermon at Benares on the characteristic of that which is not self does not deny in express terms that there may exist another realm of existence which is exempt from empirical determination, and which, therefore, must be regarded as absolutely real".[2] Though Prof. Keith thinks that the view a section of the early disciples about the "existence of an absolute reality admits of serious support" and that passages or expressions can be traced in the Nikāyas having the colour or flavour of the Brāhmanic *Upaniṣads* or the *Mahābhārata*, he puts forward the proviso that on the basis of these coincidences, it would not be proper to say that the Buddhist Nirvāṇa is "essentially the absolute parallel with the Brahman", for the Buddhists "like every new belief were largely compelled to put their wine in old bottles".[3] He also does not ignore the fact that there are ample evidences in the Nikāyas to show that "Buddha was a genuine agnostic",[4] though he himself is not much in favour of the view. In short, Prof. Keith is of the opinion that the Nikāyas do not teach annihilation, or eternal

1. Keith, *B. Phil.*, p. 67.
2. *Ibid.*, p. 61.
3. *Ibid.*, p. 68.
4. *Ibid.*, p. 63.

death. He finds in Nirvāṇa only a negative aspect of the Absolute or the Void and wouid nor recognize it to be the same as Brahman of the Upaniṣads or the Vedāntists. Prof. Poussin also would suscribe to this view if it be taken as the Mahāyānic conception of Nirvāṇa, for according to him, the Hīnayānic Nirvāṇa is something definite and real, a tangible reality. Prof. Stcherbatsky rises above all hesitations and asserts that the Hīnayānic Nirvāṇa is eternal death, while the Mahāyānic Nirvāṇa is eternal life, and that the latter is the same as the Monism, or Advaita Brahman of the Vedāntists.[1] Though he may be partial to Vasubandhu and Nāgārjuna, he cannot he justified in ignoring and explaining away the passages of the Nikāyas, which interpret Nirvāṇa differently from Vasubandhu. The opinion of Prof. Poussin that there is a great deal of Mādhyamika philosophy in the Pāli canon",[2] and the reference of Prof. Keith to passages or suttas of the Nikāyas is indicative of the reasonableness of holding such an opinion, appears startling to Prof. Stcherbatsky, and against them he holds without mentioning any authority or citing any passage, that "it is quite impossible to maintain that Hīnayāna is an advaita systems"[3] and that it is going too far to see a "full-fledged *Prajñāpāramitā*" in the *Majjhima Nikāya.*

Now that we have stated the views of the latest exponents of the Buddhist conception of Nirvāṇa, we shall proceed to examine some of them in the light of evidences yielded by the Pāli works.

Is saṃjñāvedayitanirodha a foretaste of Nīrvāṇa ?

It is, however, striking that both Profs. Stcherbatsky and Poussin have tried to form an idea of Nirvāṇa on the basis of the quiescent state attained by a yogin at the highest altitude of his meditation. Both agree that it is this quiescence which

---

1. Dr. F. Otto Schrader in his article on *Nirvāṇa* in the *J. P. T. S.* (1904-5) favours the metaphysical conception of the Absolute as the real interpretation of Nlrvāṇa of the early Buddhists.

2. *E. R. E.*, sv. Nirvāṇa. Prof. Poussin has also traced Vijñānavāda ideas in the *Aṅguttara* ; see his *Nirvāṇa*, p. 65.

3. *Con. of N.*, p. 42 fn.

is aimed at by all saints, including the arhats. To Prof. Stcherbatsky, Nirvāṇa is the highest form of quiescence imaginable, and hence it is a condition where there is no vestige of cosciousness—an absolute annihilation of life,[1] while to Prof. Poussin, it is a condition where the mind (*citta*) does not function, but the body is pervaded by an extremely pleasant feeling ; the mind, being inactive, does not enjoy the pleasure.

Prof. Poussin formed his impresssion mainly from the utterances of perfected saints in the *Udāna* and the *Thera-* and *Theri-gāthā.* His conception of Hīnayānic Nirvāṇa appears to my mind to be the magnified form of the pleasant sensation felt by saints in the second and third trances. The *Nikāyas* often speak of the pleasant sensation in the second and third tranees as similar to that of a person when his body is besmeared with fine powder by an expert bath attendant ; but they do not speak about the sensation felt by a saint while in Nirvāṇa. Prof. Poussin is justified in regarding the highest meditation of Saṃjñāvedita- (or vedayita-) nirodha as a foretaste of Nirvāṇa in this world, but his view that the body of saint is pervaded by blissful sensation is unwarranted.[2] The Pāli texts are quite clear about their definition of this highest meditation. In the *Mahāparinibbāna Sutta,*[3] Buddha entered into meditation before attaining parinirvāṇa and rose from the lowest to the highest samādhi, the *Saññāvedayitanirodha,* when Ānanda, imperfect as he was, took him to be dead (parinibbuta). This is the highest meditation, to which an adept can reach.[4] The condition of a person in this meditation is almost the same as that of a dead man. The *Saṃyutta Nikāya*[5] explains the differences thus : There is a complete cessation of the activities in a dead man as well as in a person in the

1. *Con. of N.*, p. 28.

2. *Nirvāṇa*, pp. 83-4 - la possession du recueillement de la cessation de l'idée et de la sensation, possession réservée aux saints complets on incomplets, recueillement semblable ā l'entrée dans l' Nīrvāṇa et dont on a coineidence pas le corps puisque la pensée est interrempue.

3. *Dīgha*, II, p. 156.

4. *M. Vṛ.*, p. 48.

5. *Saṃyutta*, IV, pp. 293 f. cf. *Majjhima*, I, p. 301.

highest samādhi,—*i.e.*, of the (i) physical activities (kāyasaṅkhāro), *e.g.*, inhalation and exhalation, (ii) vocal activities (vacisaṅkhāro), *e.g.*, reflection and deliberation (vitakka-vicārā), and (iii) mental activities (cittasaṅkhāro), *e.g.*, ideation and feeling (saññā ca vedanā ca)[1]. The life (*āyu*) of the men engaged in meditation is not exhausted as also his internal heat (*uṣmā*), and his organs of sense remain in a placid condition, while in a deceased person there is no life (*āyu*) and no internal heat (*uṣmā*) and his sense-organs are defunct. In the Saññāvedayitanirodha, a saint cannot at will rise from it. Before entering into the samādhi, he fixes the time-limit after which he would revert to the ordinary state of consciousness and he does so at the fixed moment. This meditation in which the mind, the body, and the power of speech completely cesae to function may be likened to the condition of deep sleep (suṣupti) of a man. It is similar to the Upaniṣadic conception of "deep-sleep consciousness" in which there is no consciousness either of the objective world or of the self.[2] The Pāli texts nowhere mention a blissful sensation enjoyed by the body apart from the mind. The feeltng of ease enjoyed by an ascetic in the highest trance is generated within the body, and not by any contact with an external material thing[3]. The verses in the *Thera-* and *Therī-gāthā* and the passages in the *Mahāparinibbāna sutta* describing the last trance of Buddha only express the ecstasy experienced by a perfected saint when he is in the highest trance. It is really the foretaste of what he is going to experience permanently. At the Arhat stage, *i.e.*, on the attainment of the anupādisesa-nibbānadhātu, he is assured of the fact that the supreme bliss in the inexpressible form of

1. Cf. *Patañjali Yoga-sūtra*, I. 2 : Yogaścittavṛttinirodhaḥ.
2. Ranade, *Constructive Survey of Upaniṣadic Philosophy*, p. 260.
3. There are passages in the Nikāyas, in which it is said that "vimokkhe kāyena phassitvā viharati" (*Aṅguttara*, II, 90). The Vimokkhas do not refer to Nibbāna but to the eight meditations (*Dīgha*, III, pp. 261-2) or to the three Samādhis called Animitta, Appaṇihita, and Suññata vimokkhas (*Vis. M.*, p. 658). These refer only to experiences of meditating saints felt within themselves and not by coming into contact with something external.

existence is going to be permanently his after the dissolution of his physical body, or in other words, he is going to be established in the Anupādisesa-nibbānadhātu permanently. The close relation between the meditation of Saññāvedayitanirodha and Nibbāna will be apparent from the verses of the *Udāna* describing the parinibbāna of Dabba Mallaputta :

Abhedi kāyo nirodhi saññā vedanā pi 'ti dahaṃsu sabbā,
vupasamiṃsu saṅkhārā viññāṇam attham agamā ti.

[The body is disintegrated, perception stops, all sensations are burnt away, the (three) activities cease and the (constituted) consciousness disappears.]

The Saññāvedayitanirodha, therefore, is very similar to parinibbāna. The *Majjhima Nikāya*[1] adds that a perfect saint not only attains it but also destroys his āsavas (impurities) by knowledge and thus goes beyond the clutches of Māra. Hence, the Saññāvedayitanirodha of a saint is tantamount to a foretaste of Nibbāna only when it is accompanied by the other necessary conditions, *viz.*, destruction of āsavas, insight into the truth and so forth.

Is Nirvāṇa eternal death ?

Prof. Stcherbatsky thinkt that Nirvāṇa, being allied to Saṃjñāvedayitanirodha may be regarded as a state without a vestige of consciousness. In the accoont of Buddha's parinirvāṇa, Buddha enters into the Saṃjñāvedayitanirodha but he does not stay there permanently. He comes down to the lowest and then rises again to attain parinirvāṇa in the fourth dhyāna.[2] If Nirvāṇa had been a permanent form of Saṃjñāvedyaitanirodha, then Buddha would have remained there and attained mahāparinirvāṇa.

To prove his contention that Nirvāṇa is eternal death, Prof. Stcherbatsky takes support from another statement in the *Mahāparinibbāna-sutta* commented upon in the *Mādhyamiko-Vṛtti.*[3] The passage is :

Pradotyasy' eva nirvāṇaṃ vimokṣas tasya cetasaḥ.

---

1. *Majjhima*, I, p. 160 ; III, p. 45.
2. *Dīgha*, II, p. 156.
3. *M. Vṛ.*, p. 525.

He attributes to the Vaibhāṣikas the comment, which follows this passage in the *Vṛtti*. The Vaibhāṣikas,[1] as is supposed by him, assert in refuting the *abhāva* theory of the Sautrāntikas that there is something 'in which desire is extinct', and that it is not merely 'extinct desire' as the Sautrāntikas think.[2] In the Sanskrit text there is no word or hint about the extinction of consciousness. All that is said is about *tṛṣṇā*. Prof. Stcherbatsky, however, in his translation says that every desire (also consciousness) is extinct (at final Nirvāṇa).[3] Probably his addition "and consciousness" in the line was suggested by the line that follows, *viz.*, "yasmin sati cetaso vimokṣo bhavati." He translates *cetaso vimokṣah* as "consciousness is quite extinct." It is difficult to accept his English rendering and it is not at all clear why he should prefer "consciousness" to "mind" as the English equivalent of cetas. The Pāli version of the line, "Pajjotass' eva nibbānaṃ vimokkho cetaso ahū ti"[4] was uttered by Anuruddha to describe Buddha's Nirvāṇa. Buddhaghosa in commenting upon this passage says that *vimokkho* means the removal of all screens hindering vision, and that the extinction of the flame indicates the state of non-manifestation.[5] Prof. Stcherbatsky may have other reasons for such an opinion, but it is difficult to agree with him in regard to the fact that the early Buddhists generally, including the Theravādins, regarded Nirvāṇa as an inanimate reality. In the *Kathāvatthu* and the *Dhammasaṅgaṇi*, Nibbāna has been qualified as *acetasika*, the English rendering of which, according to Mrs. Rhys Davids, should be "not a property of the mind", or according to Prof. Poussin, "where

1. *Con. of N.*, p. 191.

2. Nirvāṇa as Kṣayamātra is discussed in the *Vis. M.*, p. 508; see *infra*.

3. *Con. of N.*, App., p. 191.

4. *Dīgha*, II, p. 157 ; see Otto Franke, *Z.D.M.G.*, xlix, p. 476.

5. *Sum. Vil.* (Burmese ed., Rangoon, 1903), p. 158 : Vimokkho ti kenaci dhammena anāvaraṇo vimokkho, sabbaso apaññattibhāv'upagamo pajjotanibbānasadiso jāto.

mind does not function any more."[1] Here *acetasika* does not mean inanimate substance, but it is a state where the individual *citta* (=manovijñāna) or the *abhisaṅkhāraviññāṇa* of Buddhaghosa[2] ceases to exist ; hence Nirvāṇa is not eternal death,

Prof. Stcherbatsky, in interpreting Nirvāṇa as an eternal state of death, has attached too much importance to the influence of Sāṃkhya on Buddhism.[3] He almost identifies the Vaibhāṣikas with the Sāṃkhya School excepting for the conception of Puruṣa in the latter.[4] He says tnat Nirvāṇa is a lifeless reality corresponding to the undifferentiated matter (*Prakṛti*) of Sāṃkhya.[5] The position of Prof. Stcherbetsky reduces to this, that the phenomenal world issued out of Nirvāṇa to return to it again by the removal of Avidyā (ignorance), and that Nirvāṇa is the same as the five skandhas in their original undifferentiated state. This is not supported by the canonical as well as the non-canonical texts. The Sarvāstivādins in enumerating the various 'elements' mention Nirvāṇa as an Asaṃskṛta-dhātu existting side by side with the elements constituting a being. The Theravādins also hold that the five khandhas[6] are nothing but masses of five kinds of elements, out of which a being is constituted through Avidyā. Both the Sarvāstivādins and the Theravādins are emphatic in theia statement that a being once constituted out of the seventy-two elements or five khandhas passes through innumerable existences, until by the removal of Avidyā, he enters into the

1. Also "Unmental, automatic" see *Points of the Controversy*, pp. 57ff., 249.

2. See *ante*. Prof. Stcherbatsky himself writes elsewhere (*Central Con. of B.*, p. 15) that citta=mano=manovijñāna.

3. See his *Soul Theory of the Buddhists*, p. 824.

4. *Con. of N.*, pp. 27-8. 5. *Ibid.*

6. Nowhere in the Buddhist texts, any statement is made that the five khandhas were originally in an undifferenıiated state. All that they say is that the material elements of all beings of all times of the Kāmadhātu and Rūpadhātu are collectively called Rūpakkhandha, so also Vedanā, Saññā, Saṅkhārā, and Viññāṇa of all beings taken together are called Vedanākkhandha, Saññākkhandha, Saṅkhārākkhandha and Viññāṇakkhandha. *Vis. M.*, pp. 443, 452.

Asaṃskṛtadhātu or Nirvāṇa, which is an element existing by itself. According to the Sāṃkhya School of Philosophy, the mokṣa (emancipation) of a being consists in his realisation of the fact that Puruṣa and Prakṛti remain ever apart (viveka-khyāti) and not by a being passing from the constituted to the unconstituted state. In Sāṃkhya, the emancipated being is one of the innumerable Puruṣas while in Buddhism he is after death indistinguishable from Nirvāṇa. The agreement between Sāṃkhya and early Buddhism lies in the fact that the undifferentiated matter (Prakṛti)[1] of Sāṃkhya corresponds in its differentiated form to the five khandhas and not to Nirvāṇa as inferred by Prof. Stcherbatsky. If an analogy for Nirvāṇa be sought for in Sāṃkhya, we may say that it could have been found in Puruṣa if the innumerable Puruṣas were one Asaṃskṛtadhātu.

Is Nirvāṅadhātu a vastu?

On the basis of the *Visuddhimagga* and the *Abhidharmakośa*, Prof. La Vallée Poussin remarks that Nirvāṇa is a *vastu*[1] (material substance), a reality, which the body touches when in the highest trance (saṃjñāvedayita-nirodha), while Prof. Stcherbatsky, in consonance with his interpretation of Nirvāṇa, says that it is a "reality (dharma or vastu) in the sense of a materialistic lifeless reality" similar to the Prakṛti of Sāṃkhya. The inclusion of Nibbāna in Asaṅkhata-dhātu along with Ākāasa and the comparison drawn between Ākāsa and Nibbāna makes us think that Nibbāna is a substance (vastu, dhātu) similar to Ākāsa.[3] But the expression

1. Buddhaghosa refers to Pakati-Purisa but does not compare them with the Buddhist khandhas. See *Vis. M.*, pp. 518, 525.

2. See *P. T. S. Dictionary*, p. 176 sv. dhātu-nibbāna. Drs. Rhys Davids and Stede have drawn attention to the fact that dhātu in connection with Nibbāna or Amata does not convey the sense of any thing. It is only a state—the state of Nibbāna, for which they coined the word "Nibbāna-dom or Nibbāna-hood". On the various meanings of *Vastu*, see *Kośa*, II, p. 285.

3. The conception of Ākāśa as made by the Sarvāstivādins may be similar to that of the Sāṃkhya. Dr. B. N. Seal thinks that "Ākāśa corresponds in some respects to the ether of the physicists and in other, to what may be called proto-atom." See Ray's *Hindu Chemistry*, p. 88.

'dhātu' is used in the Buddhist works in senses as varied as some of the other terms like dhamma, khandha, or saṃkhāra ; so it is not safe to interpret the dhātu of Nibbāna-dhātu as a vastu or dravya (thing). As for the reason of the Buddhist writers for selecting Ākāsa as an object of comparison with Nibbāna, it may be said that it was done only because many aspects of Ākāsa were identical with those of Nibbāna, but it does not follow that because Ākāsa is a dhātu, Nibbāna is also a dhātu. Like Ākāsa, Nibbāna is inexpressible ; it is beyond empirical determination but not a material substance. In the Buddhist works, the term 'Nibbāna-dhātu' has been used in such a way that one is likely to take it for a substance like Ākāsa or Samudda. In the *Mahāniddesa*,[1] a large number of bhikkhus is described as attaining Nibbāna without residue (anupādisesa-nibbāndhātu) but causing no perceptible increase or decrease in the 'Nibbānadhātu'. The *Milindapañha*[2] compares Nibbāna to Ākāsa or Samudda, implying thereby that it exists but its form, location, age, or measure cannot be ascertained. It is like space (Ākāsa) without origin, life or death, rise or fall. It is uncovered and supportless and is infinite. Just as birds fly about in the Ākāsa or animals float about in the sea so also the perfect (Ariyas) move about in the Nibbāna-dhātu. It is like fire without a continued objective existence. Just as fire remains latent unless and until two pieces of wood are rubbed to make it patent, so Nibbāna, which is without any continued objective existeuce, is called forth into being when the necessary conditions are put

The Vaiśeṣikas define Ākāśa as "a simple, continuous, infinite substance and is the substratum of sound." See Prof. Radhakrishnan, *Ind Phil.*, II, pp. 192-3.

1. *Mahāniddesa,* I, p. 132 ; *Kvu.*, p. 124 ; *Mil.*, pp. 316 : Atthi dhammassa nibbānassa rūpaṃ va saṇṭhānaṃ va vayaṃ va pamāṇaṃ apaññāpanaṃ. Cf. *Saṃyutta* II, pp. 124-6.

2. *Mil.*, p. 320 : Yathā Mahārāja ākāso na jāyati na jīyati na miyati na cavati no uppajjati duppasaho acorāharaṇo anissito vihagagamano nirāvaraṇo ananto evam eva kho mahārāja nibbānaṃ na jāyati............ ariyagamanaṃ.........anantaṃ.

together. The *Kathāvatthu*[1], in connection with the discussion of 'Amatadhātu' maintains the same position. It shows that the Theravādins declined to agree with the Pubbaseliyas, who held that Nirvāṇa (Amata) is a material object. This inference of the Pubbaseliyas was based, as pointed out in the text, on the well-known passage of the *Majjhima Nikāya*.[2]

Nibbānam nibbānato sañjānāti, nibbānaṃ nibbānato saññatvā nibbānaṃ maññati, nibbānasmiṃ maññati, nibbānato maññati, nibbānam me ti maññati, nibbānam abhinandatī ti. [He knows Nibbbāna as (an object) nibbāna ; having so known, he thinks of it ; thinks (that he) is in it or away from it ; that it is his and that it is worth praising.][3]

Buddhaghosa, in commenting upon this discussion, says that the opinion of the Pubbaseliyas is due to the drawing of a careless inference and that the passage cited above refers to earthly Nirvāṇa[4] and not to the real Nirvāṇa and hence it is not conclusive. Buddhaghosa's view may not be acceptable to all but it makes it quite clear that according to the Theravādins, Nirvāṇa though denoted by Amata, must not be taken as a *dravya* (thing), though it may be serve as an *ārammaṇa* (basis) for meditations.[5]

1. *Kvu.*, ix. 2.

2. *Majjhima*, I p. 4.

3. For a comment on this passage, see Keith, *B. Phil.*, p. 49 ; La Vallée Poussin, *Nirvāṇa*, pp. 126, 127. See *ante*.

The sense of the passage is that a person, who has not truly realised Nibbāna may labour under the delusion that Nibbāna is an object, which he has known, and with which he stands in some relalion, namely, that he has entered into it or that he is away from it, or that Nibbāna is his or that Nibbāna is an object to be praised.

4. *Kvu. A.*, p· 116 ; diṭṭhadhamma-nibbānaṃ saṃdhāya bhāsitaṃ tasmā asādhakaṃ, Cf. *Papañcasūdani*, p. 38 : Tattha Nibbānan ti "yato kho bho ayam attā pañcahi kāmaguṇehi samappito samaṅgibhūto paricarati, ettāvatā kho bho ayam attā paramadiṭṭhadhammanibbānam patto hotī ti" : see *Dīgha*, I, 36.

5. *Vis. M.*, pp. 680, 681.

Resume : *Early Conception of Nirvāṇa*

The results of our examination of the expositions of Nirvāṇa in Hīnayāna and Mahāyāna works, and of the discussions of same by modern scholars, may be summarised thus :

The texts of the early Buddhists present a threefold conception of Nirvāṇa, *viz.*, ethical, psychical, and metaphysical :

(i) *Ethical.* The ethical conception of Nirvāṇa has received the largest amount of attention in the Pāli texts as well as in the writings of modern scholars. The Nikāyas abound in terms and passages expressive of the ethical conception of Nirvāṇa so much so that Dr. Stede wrote as late as 1923 that "Nibbāna is purely and solely an *ethical* state to be reached in this birth by ethical practices, contemplation, and insight. It is therefore not transcendental".[1] This opinion is not supported by facts. Throughout the Nikāyas, Nibbāna is described as the destruction (khaya) of attachment (rāga), hatred (dosa) and delusion (moha), of desire (taṇhā), impressions (saṅkhārā), and firm grasp of wrong views (upādāna), of impurities (āsava) and afflictions (kilesa), and of desire for existence (bhava), birth (jāti), old age, death (jarāmaraṇa), and thus of misery (dukkha). In describing the positive aspect of Nibbāna, the Nikāyas state that it is a condition which is very happy (accantasukha), imperishable (accuta), steady (acala, dhīra), tranquil (santa) and free from fear (akutobhaya). It is the state of the highest bliss (amata). The ethical conception of Nirvāṇa appealed so much to the Buddhist authors that they wrote literaey pieces of great poetical excellence in order to pay glowing tributes to the attainment of same.

(ii) *Psychical.* Many scholars have dealt with the psychical aspect of Nirvāṇa but without laying sufficient emphasis upon its significance. This aspect of Nibbāna is generally brought out in those passages of the Nikāyas, which treat of the

1. See *P. T. S. Dict.*, sv. Nibbāna. The part of the Dictionary, containing the article on Nibbāna was published after the death of Dr. Rhys Davids, *i. e.* by Dr. Steda.

Jhānas (contemplation). The object of Jhānas is to bring the mind into such a state that it will be above worldly pleasure and pain. It can be effected by dissociating the mind completely from all worldly matters. This is achieved by means of the trances, the highest of which is the Saññāvedayitanirodha. From the foregoing discussion about the highest trance, it is evident that Nibbāna is psychically Saññāvedayitanirodha provided that the adept complies with the other necessary conditions of Arhathood. In course of our exposition of the various dhātus, it has been shown that an adept in the first Jhāna rises mentally to the same level as that of the denizens of the Rūpabrahmaloka, and gradually proceeding higher and higher, develops a mental state corresponding to that of the beings of the Nevasaññānāsaññayatana—the highest plane of existence in the three worlds. He acquires the five transcendental powers (abhiññā), *viz.*, performing supernatural feats (iddhividha) such as visiting the Brahmaloka ; acquiring divine ear (dibbasota) and divine vision (dibbacakkhu), knowing others' thoughts (paracittavijānana), and remembering former existences (pubbenivāsānussati). According to the Buddhist conception, an adept, who is capable of rising up as high as the eighth trance (nevasaññānāsaññāyatana), is as powerful as the gods of the highest Arūpabrahmaloka. The stage of Nibbāna being still higher, he has to rise further in trance and attain the Saññāvedayitanirodha, where his mind stops functioning, and hence there is no perception or sensation. He is now fit to stay in the Apariyāpannadhātu or Lokuttaradhātu. While in this trance, he has a foretaste of Nibbāna, which is going to be his permanently. He acquires the sixth abhiññā, *viz.*, knowledge of the destruction of his impurities (āsavakhayakāraṇañāṇa)[1] and of the consequent attainment of emancipation. His mental faculties then become so very clear[2] that

1. The usual expression is, āsavānaṃ khayā anāsavaṃ cetovimuttiṃ paññāvimuttiṃ diṭṭhe va dhamme sayaṃ abhiññā sacchikatvā upasampajja viharati. *Dīgha*, III, p. 281.

2. See *Jātaka*, I, p. 106 *Vaṇṇupatha Jāt.* : Obhāsamattam=supernatural illumination while striving to attain jhāna. Cf. *Dīgha*, II, p. 33 ; *Saṃyutta*, II, pp. 7, 105 : cakkhum udapādi ñāṇam udapādi paññā uda-

he understands with a moment's thought all that is happening around him. He is now possessed of full illumination, *i.e.*, he is enlightened.

(iii) *Metaphysical.* The metaphysical aspect of Nibbāna presents the greatest difficulties to the students of Buddhism and has been the source of many controversies. There is no end of metaphorical terms and passages in the Nikāyas to describe Nibbāna admitting of a metaphysical interpretation. The notable passage of the *Itivuttaka*[1] : 'Atthi, bhikkhave, abhūtam akatam asaṅkhataṃ' shows that the early Buddhists conceived of Nibbāna not as annihilation but as something positive,[2] which is, however infinite and indescribable like Ākāsa. It is called a dhātu (realm) beyond the three dhātus,—the Apariyāpanna- or Lokuttara-dhātu. It is a state to be realised (sacchikātabba) within one's own self (paccattaṃ veditabbo viññūhi). It is homogeneous (ekarasa) and in it there is no individuality. It is like the disappearance of flame in the fathomless state of existence in the infinite.

The few passages of the *Dīgha* and *Majjhima Nikāyas*, in which Nibbāna has been equated to infinite consciousness (ananta-viññāṇa) do not, however, find support in other portions of the same works, which throw light on the conception of Nibbāna. All that can be said in the circumstances is that these passages were later interpolations made at a time when the *Saṃyutta Nikāya* was being compiled. The account of the death of Vakkali with apatiṭṭhita-viññāṇa and not paṭisandhi-viññāṇa hints that the constituted viññāṇa of an Arhat passes away and mixes up indistinguishably with an ever existing infinite consciousness. This seems to be an anticipation of the Vijñānavāda school of philosophy, but we cannot deny the existence of a trend of thought like this among the early Buddhists. The more accurate conception of Nibbāna would certainly be that it is a state beyond the domain of word and thought and possible of realisation only within one's own self.

---

pādi vijjā udapādi *āloko* udapādi ; *Paṭis. M*, II, p. 150 : "Āloko udapādī ti" obhāsaṭṭhena.

1. *Itiv.*, p. 37. 2. *Kvu*, p. 124 ; see also *Mil.* p. 316.

The Pāli Nikāyas, as already pointed out, are a mosaic composed of materials of various times and regions : hence these yield divergent opinions regarding the conception of Nibbāna. But the one presented above is supported by mosi of the suttas of the Nikāyas and can be treated as the earliest. We shall now pass on to some of the later Buddhist works and ascertain from them how far the early conception of Nibbāna was retained in later times and what changes, if any, were introduced.

The Kathāvatthu on Nirvāṇa

Before we deal with the *Visuddhimagga*, we may well examine the few remarks scattered here and there in the *Kathāvatthu* regarding the conception of Nibbāna.[1] While discussing the existence of puggala, the *Kathāvatthu* makes a remark showing that it conceived Nibbāna as a real and eternal state. It states that if puggala (soul) be taken as not disintegrating with the disintegration of khandhas, this will entail sassatavāda, for the soul becomes eternally existent like Nibbāna.[2] Buddhaghosa in commenting upon this states : Yathā hi nibbānaṃ na uppajjati na bhijjati evaṃ hi puggalo[3] (just as Nibbāna does neither originate nor decay so would be the soul). Thus it is seen that the *Kathāvatthu*, supported by Buddhaghosa, takes Nibbāna as an eternal state without origin and decay, and does not consider a parinibbuta puggala as sassata.[4] In other connections too, the *Kathāvatthu* remarks that Nibbāna is eternal and unchangeable (nibbānaṃ dhuvaṃ

1. Though according to the orthodox tradition, it is canonical, it may also be treated as non-canonical as it was composed after the canon had been closed. For the present purpose, we leave out of account the various aspects (guṇa or ākāra) of Nibbāna. It has been dealt with by Prof. Poussin in his *Nirvāṇa*, pp. 158 ff.

2. *Kvu.*, I. i. 170 (p. 34): Khandhesu bhijjamānesu no ce bhijjati puggalo, puggalo sassato hoti nibbāna-samasamo.

3. *Kvu. A.*, p. 25.

4. *Kvu.*, p. 61.

sassatam aviparināmadhammaṃ).[1] It also says that Nibbāna unlike ñāṇa (knowledge) exists by itself like rūpa or cakkhu and does not require any ārammaṇa (basis) to arise.[2] Unlike sīla (morality), phassa (contact) and vedanā (feeling), it is acetasika (not a property of the mind)[3] and is unconnected with mind (citta-vippayutta).[4] It is asaṅkhata (unconstituted)[5] because it possesses the three signs, *viz.*, no origination (uppāda), no destruction (vayo) and no change (na ṭhitānam aññathattaṃ paññāyati).[6] The *Kathāvatthu* thus conceived Nibbāna as existing eternally without origin, decay and change, and is beyond all description.

The Visuddhimagga on Nirvāṇa

In the *Visuddhimagga*,[7] Buddhaghosa retains the conception found in the *Kathāvatthu* and selects only those passages from the Nikāyas, which lend support to his view. In describing its guṇas, he comments on a passage of the *Aṅguttara Nikāya* (ii. 34) where Nibbāna is described as suppressing pride, removing lust, destroying ālaya (of the five kāmaguṇas), and arresting the cycle of existence in the three worlds. While commenting on the etymology of the word Nibbāna,[8] he says that it is the going out of the 'vana' which is a synonym of taṇhā and is so called because it acts as a hindrance to the four kinds of birth (yonis), five forms of existence (gatis), seven viññāṇa existences (*i.e.* the planes of existence above the Arūpa worlds) and nine srttāvāsas (abodes of sentient beings). This shows only the

---

1. *Kvu.* I. 6 (p. 121); see also the note of the commentator in the *Points of the Controversy*, p. 63 fn.

2. *Kvu.*, IX. 5; cf. *Dh. S.* 1408. 1415, 1418: Rūpañ ca nibbānañ ca anārammaṇā.

3. *Kvu.* IX. 7; cf. *Dh. S.* 1513: Katame dhammā acetasikā? Cittañ ca rūpañ ca nibbānañ ca.

4. *Ibid.* XIV. 6; cf. *Dh. S.* 1515: Katame dhammā cittavippayuttā? Rūpañ ca nibbānañ ca.........

5. *Dh. S.* 1439.

6. *Ibid.*, p. 60. cf. *Dh. S.* 1416: Nibbānaṃ na vattabbam uppannan ti pi anuppannan ti; see also 1534, 1535.

7. *Vis. M.*, pp. 293, 294.

8. *'Ibtd.*

aspect of quietude (upasama) of Nibbāna. He then takes up the well-known passage of the *Saṃyutta Nikāya* (iv. 362, 369 ff.)[1] to show that Nibbāna is truth, transcendental, difficult to be seen, without decay, eternal, indescribable, immortal, happy, peaceful, wonderful, healthy, pure and is an island of refuge. It appears from the selection of passages made by Buddhaghosa that he is a supporter of the view that Nibbāna is eternal and that it is a lokottara[2] state beyond the Kāma, Rūpa and Arūpa dhātus.

Buddhaghosa's conception of Nibbāna is well brought out also in his arguments against the Sautrāntika view of the non-existence (*abhāva*) of Nibbāna.[3] He starts with the assertion that Nibbāna brings peaee of mind (santi). and has the taste of imperishableness (accuti) and solace (assāsakaraṇa), and brings one to a state of mind, which is inexpressible (nippapañca), and in which difierentiations disappear (animitta). He then takes up the view of his opponents, evidently the Sautrāntikas, that Nibbāna does not exist like the horn of hare because of its non-perceptibility (anupalabbhanīyato), and meets it by saying that Nibbāna does exist and is realisable if the right path be followed—the realisation being similar to the cognizance of others' thoughts in the transcendental plane (lokuttara-citta)[4] by the power of knowing the thoughts of others (cetopariyāyañāṇa).[5] One is not justified in saying that a thing does not exist because it cannat be perceived by ordinary men. He states further in support of his contention that if the existence of Nibbāna be denied, the practices of Sammādiṭṭhi, etc., become fruitless (vañjhābhāvo āpajjati). To this the opponent answers : The practites are

1. Also dealt with by Prof. Poussin in his *Nirvāṇa*, pp. 153, 154.
2. Cf. *Dh. S.* 1447 ; *Laṅkā.*, p. 157 see *ante.*
3. *Vis. M.*, pp. 507-9.
4. See Shwe Zan Aung's *Comp. of Phil.*, p. 12 : transcendental consciousness beyond Kāma, Rūpa and Arūpa dhātus.
5. It is one of the Abhiññās possessed by Arhats, see *Vis. M.*, p. 431,

not really fruitless since they lead to the realisation of abhāva (*i.e.*, Nibbāna as total absence of every thing).

Buddhaghosa : If Nibbāna be merely abhāva, then the absence (abhāva) of past and future would also be Nibbāna, but it is surely not.

Opponent : The absence of the present might be Nibbāna.

Buddhaghosa : The absenee of the present (vattamāna) is not possible, for it is self-contradictory, because it must be either past or future. Besides, it would also be incorrect to say that the absence of the present is Nibbāna, for in the present life at a certain moment (vattamānakkhandha-nissita-maggakkhaṇe)[1] one obtains the sopādisesa-nibbānadhātu (*i.e.*, Nibbāna with eorporal residue).

Opponent : Would it not be equally incorrect to say that at that moment there was the non-presence of kilesas (impurities) ?

Buddhaghosa : To deny the non-presence of kilesas would be to deny the efficacy of the Ariyamagga, and that is impossible.

This reply of Buddhaghosa did not, it seems, convince his opponent, who passed on to the next argument as to whether the khaya, *i.e*,, destruction of attachment (rāgakkhaya), etc. should be taken as Nibbāna.[2] Buddhaghosa answered in the negative, saying that in that case arhathood would also be mere extinction. Besides to take Nibbāna as khaya (destruction) of something would make Nibbāna impermanent, constituted, and disconnected with sammāvāyāma, etc. To this the opponent replied : It would not be wrong to say that because a thing after its decay has no more origination, it has attained Nibbāna.

Buddhaghosa : Decay of this sort does not enter into the quesiion ; even if it be so considered, it would not

1. For Maggakkhaṇa see *Paṭis.*, *M.*, I, pp. 69f ; *Vis. M.*, pp. 681, 682. For Phalakkhaṇa see *Vis. M.*, p. 680.

2. Cf. *M. Vṛ.*, p, 525 : Sautrāntikas say : Nanu ca yo'sya nandirāgasahagatāyās tṛṣṇāyāḥ kṣayo virāgo nirodho nirvāṇam ityuktam.

support the contention of the opponent, for it is the ariyamagga which produces (lit. turns into) the state of Nibbāna (bhāva), and it is the ariyamagga which dsstroys evil and prevents its reappearance, because it is the stage (upanissayatta) for final destruction without the possibility of further origination (anuppattinirodhasaṅkhatassa khayassa); that of which it forms the basis (upanissaya) is destroyed by conduct.

The opponent then took up the third argument enquiring why Nibbāna had not been given a description (sarūpen' eva kasmā na vuttan ti ce ?).

Buddhaghosa : Because it is exceedingly subtle ; so extremely subtle, indeed, that Buddha even once thought of not preaching it at all ; it can be seen by ariyacakkhu only (*i.e.*, realisable by Arhats only). Being associated with the magga, it is extraordinary (asādhāraṇa), and its beginning being absent, it is devoid of origin.

Opponent : It is not without origin because it originated out of the magga.

Buddhaghosa : It was not originated by the magga ; it can be attained only by following the magga ; hence it is originless, and consequently decayless and deathless : being without origin, decay and death, it is eternal (nicca).

A fourth argument was put forward by the opponent, which is as follows :

Opponent : Would it not be objectionabie to regard Nibbāna as eternal like the aṇu (atom) ?

Buddhaghosa : No. Nibbāna has no hetu (cause) as aṇus have ; so it cannot be compared to aṇu.

Opponent : Is Nibbāna eternal on account of its eternal nature (*i.e.*, does any quality of eternalness adhere to Nibbāna) ?

Buddhaghosa : That cannot be, in view of the fact that the aṇu, etc., are not realised (asiddhatta) by the magga.

Buddhaghosa in conclusion said that for the reasons he

had put forward Nibbāna is eternal and, being devoid of the nature of form, is formless (arūpa). There is only one Nibbāna, and not different Nibbānas for different Buddhas. He then showed that it is called sopādiseasa-nibbāna when there remains a corporal residue (upādisesa), though a complete destruction of impurities has been effected by meditation (bhāvanā). It is called nirupādisesa-nibbāna[1] on the disappearance of upādisesa, which happens on account of the absence of any kind of manifestation after the last thought of kammaphala. This is due to the stopping and uprooting of samudaya (causes of origin). In short, it cannot be said that Nibbāna does not exist in view of the fact that it is attainable by means of special knowledge obtained by unflagging zeal ; that tts existence is indicnted by the words of the omniscient Buddha ; and lastly that it exists in reality (paramatthena sabhāvato) is indicated by the words : Atthi bhikkhave ajātam abhūtam akatam asaṅkhataṃ (*Itiv.*, p. 37 ; *Ud.*. p. 80).

The *Paramatthamañjusā*,[2] in commenting upon this portion of the *Visuddhimagga*, argues in its own way for the existence of Nibbāna. It starts by saying that Buddha can never utter an untruth ; so when he says "atthi bhikkhave ajātam etc.", it has to be admitted that the unconstituted dhātu, Nibbāna, in the highest sense, does exist. It cannot be abhāva (absence of anything) because of the fact that Buddha described Nibbāna as deep, immeasurable, difficult to be understood, etc. These can be said only of an existent state or object, and not of anything non-existent. Anything non-existent must in every way be non-exlstent. The following question may, however, arise as to the nature of abhāva of kilesas, to which attention is drawn by the Theravādins as an aspect of Nibbāna : Whether the abhāva of kilesas existing in beings is one or many. If the *abhāva* be one, then it should be

1. For sopādisesa and nirupādisesa nibbāna, see also *M. Vr.*, p. 519.

2. *Visuddhimagga ṭīkā* of Ānanda (Burmese ed.) edited by Saya U. Pye, 1910, vol. II, pp, 618-620.

effected by one path (magga) and there is no need of many maggas (evidently referring to the four maggas : sotapatti sakadāgami, anāgami, and arahatta), and all beings should attain Nibbāna at the same time. This objection is answered thus : If the abhāva be taken as one, then it is the abhāva of kilesas which is effected by the realisation of Nibbāna. It is in fact not an effect of magga, it is a thing to be envisaged. The opponent may say that there is no need of maggas, as it is not necessary to give up the kilesas, and there being no question of giving up kilesas and putting an end to dukkha, what is the use of the realisation (sacchikiriyā) of kilesabhāva. The objection is answered thus : Each magga has some definite function to perform. The sotapattimagga removes the first three saṃyojanas, the sakadāgamimagga reduces rāga, dosa and moha to their minimum, while the anagāmimagga eradicates them, and lastly the arahatta puts an end to all saṃyojanas. Abhāva is really one, and should not be inferred that there are many abhāvas because many kinds of kilesas are eradicated, *i.e.*, it does not follow that because there are sakkāyadiṭṭhi-abhāva, rāga-abhāva and moha-abhāva, there are so many abhāvas. Abhāva is really one and does not vary according to the nature of the object, of which, there is abhāva ; so the abhāvas are not to be regarded as five. because the five saṃyojanas are removed. It is only the common usage of the term that implies the existence of many abhāvas. The state of abhāva (absence of anything) cannot but be one, so Nibbāna is not many but one. The *Tīkā* concludes its argument by saying that the abhāva is effected by maggas, each magga producing its own effect, and that abhāva is not to be envisaged (na sacchikātabbo), while Nibbāna is to be envisaged ; hence, the abhāva of kilesas is not identical with Nibbāna.

The Abhidharmakośa on Nirvāṇa.

In the *Abhidharmakośa,* Vasubandhu expatiates on the Vaibhāṣika conception of Nirvāṇa. He first asserts that Nirvāṇa is one of the Asaṃskṛtas (unconstituted), and as against the objection of the Sautrāntikas that it might be a result produced by the mārga, he says that the mārga leads to the attainment or possession of Visaṃyoga (disconnection) or Nirvāṇa and that it is self-existent and not the fruit of mārgas.[1] In answering to the question of the Sautrāntikas as to the nature of the dharma called Visaṃyoga or Pratisaṃkhyā-nirodha, the Vaibhāṣikas state that it is the dharma nature, which is real and inexpressible ; only the Āryas realise it inwardly and individually. It is only possible to indicate its general characteristics, when the Pratisaṃkhyā-nirodha is said to be an entity (dravya), real, good, eternal, and distinct from others, it is called the Visaṃyoga.

The Sautrāntikas in their zeal to establish that Nirvāṇa is abhāva (absence of passions, etc.) argue that the Asaṃskṛtas (the unconstituted) are not real like the entities rūpa (form), vedanā (feeling), etc. They cite the instance of Ākāśa, which is, according to the Sarvāstivādins, an Asaṃskṛta-dhātu, and point out that Ākāśa (space) is nothing but the absence of something tangible, or in other words, of any resisting substance. Just as a man in darkness says it is ākāśa (vacuity or space) when he is not cognisant of the existence of anything tangible or resistible, so also the Ākāśa of the Saivāstivādins should be understood. Analogically they assert that the second Asaṃskṛta-dhātu of the Sarvāstivādins, namely, the Pratisaṃkhyā-nirodha, is really the destruction of anuśayas (desires) and existence already produced, and the non-origination of any further anuśayas ; and as this is achieved by means of knowledge (partisaṃkhyā), it is called Pratisaṃkhyā-nirodha. The third Asaṃskṛtadhātu, the Apratisaṃkhyā-nirodha, is the absence or non-origination of dharmas on account of the complete absence of causes[2], independent of the force of knowledge (apratisaṃ-

1. See *Kośa*, ii. 55. Cf. *Vis. M.*, p. 508 dealt with before for a similar argument against the Sautrāntikas,

2. Yamakami Sogen prefers "condition" (pratyaya) to causes. See his *Systems etc.*, p. 164. He explains Apratisaṃkhyānirodha (p. 167) as the "non-consciousness of dharmas or things which would have forced their way into our consciousness but for the engrossment of our

khyā), *e.g.*, when death before its time interrupts the existence, it is said that there has been Apratisaṃkhyā-nirodha of dharmas which would have been born in course of this existence, if the existence had continued.[1]

In this connection the Sautrāntikas mention the opinion of Sthavira Śrīlābha, also a Sautrāntika teacher, who interpreted the pratisaṃkhyā-nirodha as the future non-origin of passions due to knowledge (prajñā), and the apratisaṃkhyā-nirodha as the future non-origin of duḥkha, *i.e.*, of existence due to the disappearance of passions and not directly due to knowledge. The former, it is said, refers to sopādiśeṣa and the latter to anupādiśeṣa-nirvāṇadhātu.[2] The Sautrāntikas did not approve of the distinction made by Śrīlābha between Pratisaṃkhyā and Apratisaṃkhyā. According to them, the future non-origin of duḥkha implies pratisaṃkhyā; so, in fact, apratisaṃkhya-nirodha is included in the pratisaṃkhyā-nirodha.

The Sautrāntikas considered also the opinion of another school, supposed to be the Mahāsaṅghikas according to the Japanese editor of the *Kośa*. The Mahāsaṅghikas define apratisaṃkhyā-nirodha as the posterior non-existence (paścād abhāva) of dharmas already born by virtue of their spontaneous destruction. In this definition, apratisaṃkhyā-nirodha is not eternal in view of the fact that it does not arise as long as the anuśayas do not perish.

The object of the Sautrāntikas is to show through these definitions that the pratisaṃkhyā-nirodha implies an antecedent, *viz.*, pratisaṃkhyā and hence it cannot be eternal (nitya), because, if the antecedent be wanting, the consequence also becomes wanting. The Sarvāstivādins met this by arguing that the Sautrāntikas were not entitled to say that pratisaṃkhyā is anterior and the non-origin of unborn dharmas posterior. The

attention by something else. Apratisaṃkhyānirodha, accordingly, is a thing of daily occurrence in everybody's life."

1. *Kośa-vyākhyā* (B. Buddhica), pp. 16-18.

2. *Cf. Vis. M.*, dealt with above. See Prof. La Vallée Poussin's article on the two Nirvāṇadhātus according to the Vibhāṣā in *I. H. Q.*, vol. vi, pp. 39-45.

fact is, as the Sarvāstivādins thought, that the non-originated always exist by themselves ; so when the pratisaṃkhyā is lacking, the dharmas are born ; if and when pratisaṃkhyā arises, the dharmas are not born absolutely. The efficacy (sāmarthya) of pratisaṃkhyā in regard to the non-origin of dharmas is shown thus :

(i) before pratisaṃkhyā there is no obstacle in the way of the origin of dharmas ; and

(ii) after pratisaṃkhyā, *i.e.* pratisaṃkhyā being given, the dharmas, the origin of which has not been stopped previously (akṛtotpattipratibandha), are not born.

(1) Then as against the view of the Sautrāntikas that Nirvāṇa is simply non-production (anutpāda) of dharmas, the Sarvāstivādins cite a sūtra from the *Saṃyukta Āgama* (26.2), in which it is stated that the practice and culture of the five faculties, faith etc., have for their result the abandonment of duḥkha, past, present, and future. In fact, this abandonment (prahāṇa) refers to nothing else other than Nirvāṇa and is solely of a future dharma and not of a past or present dharma. The Sautrāntikas cannot accept it and interpret this passage somewhat differently, saying that the "abandonment" refers to the abandoning of passions (kleśas) relating to duḥkha, past or present, and citing some other passages from the *Saṃyukta Āgama* in support of their contention. They argue that the passions, past and present, produce in us some germs to originate future passions ; when these germs are destroyed, the passions, past and present, are abandoned. It is with reference to this fact that one says that the action (karma) and the result (phala) have been destroyed. Therefore by the abandonment of a future duḥkha or future passion, one understands that the duḥkha or passion will not be born any more owing to the absence of germs.

(2) The Sarvāstivādins then take up a second argument, found also in the *Visuddhimagga*,[1] which enquires why it has been stated in the *Saṃyukta Āgama* (31.12) that "of all dharmas, constituted or unconstituted, virāga (detachment) is the

1. *Vis. M.*, p. 507.

best". If a dharma be non-existing, how can a statement like the above be made ? The Sautrāntikas explain this by asserting that they admit its existence, as they admit that of a sound which has no existence before it is produced and after it has died away. The quotation praising "virāga" may well refer to a non-existent unconditioned thing, the absolute non-existence of everything evil.

(3) The third argument of the Sarvāstivādins is that if the Pratisaṃkhyā-nirodha or Nirvāṇa be non-existent, why is it mentioned as one of the Truths. The Sautrāntikas answer that truth (satya) is taken in the sense of "not-inexact" (aviparīta). The Āryas realize what exists and what does not exist in a "not-inexact" manner ; in that which is suffering (duḥkha) they see only duḥkha : in the non-existence of duḥkha, they realize the fact of the non-existence of same. Really, there is no contradiction in taking the "non-existence of duḥkha" or the pratisaṃkhayānirodha as a Truth. And this non-existence is the third Truth, because the Āryas see and proclaim it immediately after the second.

(4) The Sarvāstivādins then have recourse to the fourth argument that if the asaṃskṛtas be non-existent, how is it that knowledge has non-existent things as its basis (ārammaṇa). The Sautrāntikas dismiss this objection by remarking that they find in it nothing against their theory, and say that they will explain it in connection with the discussion of the past and the future.[1]

(5) The fifth argument of the Sarvāstivādins relates to the nature of the consequence found by the Sautrāntikas in the maintenance of their theory that the unconditioned really exists. The Sautrāntikas point out the unreasonableness of regarding the existence of a non-existent thing as real. In fact, they say that the unconditioned can neither be apprehended by the senses (pratyakṣa) like rūpa (form), vedanā (feeling), etc., nor can they be known by inference (anumāna) from their activities, *i.e.*, through the organs of sense.

(6) In the sixth argument, the Sautrāntikas become the

1. For which see *Kośa*, v. 25.

questioners and inquire how, if Nirodha be a thing in itself, a genitive construction like 'duḥkhasya nirodhaḥ' can be justified. The Sautrāntikas understand by Nirodha (destruction of a thing) the "non-existence of a thing", so also by the "destruction of duḥkha" they understand the "non-existence of duḥkha". They do not admit the existence of any relation of cause and effect between two things existing by themselves. To this the Sarvāstivādins reply, that, according to them, destruction is a thing in itself. Nevertheless one can specify the relation between "destruction" and the "thing destroyed", for, according to them, nirodha with reference to a thing indicates "obtaining possession" (prāpti) of the "destruction" at the moment when one is dispossessed of the thing. The Sautrāntikas would however inquire, what is that which determines or specifies the taking of possession of the "destruction".

(7) The seventh argument of the Sarvāstivādins is : if Nirvāṇa be non-existence, if it be only abhāva, what is that thing which is obtained by a bhikṣu in this life, the Sautrāntikas explain by saying that a bhikṣu in Nirvāṇa attains a stage (āśraya) in which neither passion (kleśa) nor a new existence is possible.

(8) In the eighth argument the Sautrāntikas cite a passage from the *Saṃyukta Āgama* (13·5) where Nirvāṇa is described as a disappearance (vyantibhāva), a decay (kṣaya), a destruction (nirodha), an appeasement (vyupasama) of duḥkha, and as a non-reproducer (apratisandhi) of duḥkha, and infer therefrom that Nirvāṇa is abhāvamātra. The Sarvāstivādins do not accept this interpretation, stating that the passage refers to Nirvāṇa as a thing in itself, in which there is no appearance (aprādurbhāva) of duḥkha. The Sautrānitikas do not agree with the Sarvāstivādins regarding the force of the locative case used in the passage.

(9) The ninth argument put forward by the Sautrānitkas is that the simile of the flame used in the famous line, "Pajjotas' eva nibbānaṃ vimokkho cetaso ahu" (as the nirvāṇa of the flame, so is also the deliverance of thought)[1], suggests only the

1. See above for a discussion of this passage.

passing away (atyaya) of the flame, and not a thing existing by itself.

(10) The tenth and the last argument advanced by the Sautrāntikas is that the Abhidharma, on which the Vaibhāṣikas rely most, contains the statement : "What are the *avastuka* dharmas ? These are the Asaṃskṛtas". In this, the term "avastuka" signifies to the Sautrāntikas "unreal", without true nature", but it is differently interpreted by the Vaibhāṣikas. According to them the term "vastu" is employed in five different senses, *viz.*, (i) svabhāva vastu (a thing in itself), (ii) ālambana vastu (object of knowledge), (iii) saṃyojanīya (cause of attachment), (iv) hetu (cause), and (v) parigraha (act of appropriation). In the present passage, vastu has been used in the sense of hetu ; here "avastuka" signifies "that which has no cause'. The unconditioned, although real, being always devoid of any activity, has neither any cause which produces them nor any fruit produced by them.

Kathāvatthu, Visuddhimagga and Abhidharmakośa analysed

It is now proposed to consider the expositions of Nirvāṇa as found in the *Kathāvatthu, Visuddhtmagga* and *Abhidharmakośa.* The last two also present a fairly good view of the Sautrāntika standpoint. These may be analysed thus :

(1) As against the Sautrāntika view that Nirvāṇa is unreal, that it is merely abhāva (absence) of kleśas, mere destruction of rāga, etc., all the texts mentioned above maintain that Nirvāṇa has real existence, their grounds are that

(i) It is realisable if the right path be followed (*Vm.*) ; it is realised by the Āryas (*A.* and *Vm.*)[1] ;

(ii) The arhats realize it in this life. It is known as the attainment of sopādiśeṣa-nirvāṇa-dhātu (*A.* and *Vm.*) :

(iii) The existence of Nirvāṇa has been described by Buddha in statements like "atthi bhikkhave ajātam abhūtam, etc." (*Vm.*), or, with reference to its subtlety or depth or excellence in statements like "duddasaṃ duranubodhaṃ, etc." (*Vm. ṭīkā*), "virāga is the best of all dharmas" (*A.*) or by mentioning it as

1. *A.=Abhidharmakośa ; Vm.=Visuddhimagga ;* and *K.=Kathāvatthu.*

one of the Four Truths (*A.*) or the ārammaṇa (basis) of knowledge (*Vm.*, *K.* and *A.*).

(2) As against the Sautrāntika view that Nirvāṇa, being only abhāva, cannot be eternal, existing by itself like rūpa (form) or aṇu (atom), or that it cannot be asaṃskṛta since it is the result of magga, these texts maintain that

(i) Nirvāṇa is eternal, exists by itself like rūpa or aṇu[1] (*Vm.* and *A.*): does not require any ārammaṇa (basis) like jñāna for its origin (*Vm.* and *K.*), and is unconnected with citta (acetasika, cittavippayutta) (*Vm.*, *K.* and *A.*), but it should be distinguished from rūpa and aṇu by the fact that it is uncaused (*Vm.* and *A.*) and requires the practice of magga for its realisation (*Vm.*);

(ii) Nirvāṇa is eternal but not the parinibbuta puggala, *i.e.*, individuality ceases in Nirvāṇa (*K.*): and that Nirvāṇa is one and not different for difierent Buddhas (*Vm.*);[2]

(iii) Nirvāṇa is asaṃskṛta as it has no origin, no decay, and no change (*Vm.* and *A.*);

(iv) The āryāṣṭāṅgika-mārga leads only to the cessation of kleśas: nirvāṇa is not produced by mārga, but exists by itself eternally (*Vm.* and *A.*).

(3) The Sautrāntikas understand the comparison of Ākāśa and Nirvāṇa in the sense that as ākāśa is really the absence or non-cognition of any resistible thing so Nirvāṇa is also the absolute absence of kleśas. The texts comment on it as follows:—

Nirvāṇa is infinite, immeasurable and inexpressible like ākāśa (*Vm.*, *K.* and *A.*): it has a positive existence, but the kleśas work as an āvaraṇa (screen) to the vision of beings, and so when the mārga removes the kleśas it is visualised (*A.*). The attainment of Nirvāṇa means the possession of the Visaṃyoga (disconnection) or Nirvāṇa (*A.*).

(4) To the question why if Nirvāṇa exists, Buddha did not define its nature (svarūpa), the texts answer that it is very

1. *Cf.* Belvalkar, *Brahma Sūtra* (Poona), II, 2, pp. 61-64.

2. Cf. Dharmakāya of the Mahāyānists; see *ante*.

subtle (*Vm.* and *A.*), so much so that even Buddha at first hesitated to preach it (*Vm.*).

(5) Buddhaghosa inclines towards the view that Nirvāṇa is inexpressible, indistinguishable, eternal and blissful. In the sopādiśeṣanirvāṇa, the Arhat obtains inwardly a vision of the same and actually gets it when he enters into nirupādiśeṣa-nirvāṇa.

(6) Vasubandhu emphasises the fact that Nirvāṇa is still a dhātu, a dravya (a thing in itself) but endowed with all the qualities mentioned above. The atoms or ions composing a being are continually changing, and ultimately, by the force of mārga, which he has been following, the individual reaches the immaculate state and becomes indistinguishable from the eternal and immaculate elements called Nirvāṇa-dhātu. Professor Poussin, on the basis of the available descriptions of this Nirvāṇa-dhātu, prefers to find in it a perfectly blissful and eternal life while Professor Stcherbatsky, following the strict logic of the atomic theory, concludes that the Nirvāṇa-dhātu is "eternal death", or the Sāṃkhya's non-differentiated matter.

As to the difference of opinion between Buddhaghosa and Vasubandhu, it should be observed that Buddhaghosa is untrammelled by the atomic theory, the consistency of which has all along been maintained by Vasubandhu in his arguments. Buddhaghosa states unequivocally that Nirvāṇa transcends every conceivable form of existence (beyond all sattāvāsas or viññāṇaṭṭhitis), and is an infinite and inconceivable state. This looks very much like the metaphysical conception of the Vedāntic Brahman, though not strictly so, as has been pointed out by Profs. Poussin and Belvalkar.[1] But it is clearly not advaya brahman, for it involves the conception of innumerable beings having separate existences of their own and only losing their identity when they are parinibbuta-puggalas.

1. *Brahma Sūtra* (Poona, 1924), II. 2, p. 57; "Hīnayāna has not developed any special aptitude for metaphysical theories and logical subtleties." Cf. *Śribhāṣya*, ed. by Durgācaraṇa Sāṅkhya-Vedāntatīrtha, p. 176: Nirvikāra-svaprakāśa-caitanyamaya-brahma.

The Prajñāpāramitās on Nirvāṇa

The conception of Nirvāṇa assumed a totally different form in the Mahāyānic works. It has been observed that the *Saddharma Puṇḍarīka* understands by Nirvāṇa the realisation of the sameness of all dharmas. The sameness (samatā), as explained in the *Prajñāpāramitās* and the *Sūtrālinkāra*, means, from the standpoint of the highest reality (paramārthataḥ), the non-distinguishability between any two things and the impossibility of particularizing a thing. The *Prajñāpāramitās* develop this idea of sameness a little further and show that everything perceived or known in this world is really an illusion (māyā) to the unenlightened mind. So when any one speaks of Nirvāṇa or the attainment of Nirvāṇa, he imagines, because of imperfect vision, the existence of a man and his nirvāṇa, and thinks that the man after practising the disciplinary rules attains the ultimate state called Nirvāṇa.[1] In reality, all these are merely his fancies (parikalpanā). One of the similes to show this unreality runs thus : Suppose a magician (māyākāra) or his disciple, expert in performing magical feats, creates the five kinds of enjoyable things (pañca-kāmaguṇā) and shows himself as enjoying these things.[2] Does he, in fact, enjoy them ? So also a Bodhisattva or Buddha speaks of the so-called worldly pleasures (kāmaguṇā). A Bodhisattva practises, skandhas (*e.g.* śīla, samādhi, etc.), the eightfold path, etc. These, in fact, do not exist at all ;[3] they are mere names invented to denote things, the existence of which is conceived by the unenlightened, *e.g.*, something which has no real existence is called a sattva (being) or rūpa (form),[4] but sattva or rūpa is only a form, a mere designation. That which

1. *Pañca.* (A.S.B.Ms.), leaf 399b : A bodhisattva does not seek Nirvāṇa because he "saṃsāraṃ saṃsārato na vikalpayati nirvāṇaṃ nirvāṇato na vikalpayati".

2. *Śata.*, p. 117.

3. *Śata.*, p. 432 : Atyantayā bodhisattvo nopalabhyate ; p. 613 : Prakṛtiśūnyāḥ sarvadharmāḥ.

4. See *Śata.*, pp. 325ff, for sattva may be put a man, a doer, a form, a bodhisattva, etc.

is a designation has no origin or decay ; it is used only as a symbol ; its interior, or exterior, or both cannot be perceived. The *Prajñāpāramitās* carry it further by stating that even the designation (nāmadheya) must not be taken as having any form of existence[1]. There being no such thing as entrance (āya) and exit (vyāya) of anything whatsoever, not excluding sarvadharmatathatā or Buddha, it should not be said that there is an Arhat or Buddha[2], or any kind of relation between them. If Buddha creates some māyāpuruṣas (illusory men) and makes them pass through all the stages of sanctification and attain omniscience, no one inquires about the existence of the māyāpuruṣas, their practices or attainments.[3] Similarly we should not trouble ourselves with the definition of either a monk or his nirvāṇa. On ultimate analysis a monk and nirvāṇa do not exist ; they are hallucinations, and both being unreal (śūnya), the monk and nirvāṇa are the same in character. So we should remove all misconceptions about the world and make the realisation of advayam advaidhīkāam (non-duality) of everything whatsoever as our aim.[4]

Nāgārjuna on Nirvāṇa

Nāgārjuna also supports this conception but his arguments are those of an expert logician or philosopher. He takes into account the views of the Hīnayānists, mainly of the Sarvāstivādins and shows the weak bases of their views. The Hīnayānists, he says, speak of two kinds of Nirvāṇa, sopādiśeṣa and nirupādiśeṣa, and think that Nirvāṇa is the nirodha (extinction) of kleśas (defiling elements) and skandhas (constituents) existing in a being. They wonder how the Mahāyānists can concieve Nirvāṇa if they think that everything is unreal (śūnya) without origin and decay, what is it then, from which Nirvāṇa confers

1. *Śata.*, p. 522 : Nāmadheyaṃ na sthitaṃ na viṣṭitaṃ nādhiṣṭhitaṃ. Tat kasya hetoḥ ? Avidyamānatvāt tasya nāmadheyasya.

2. *Śata.*, p. 552.

3. *Śata.*, pp. 886ff.

4. *Ibid.*, p. 825 : Sarvākārajñatā advayā advaidhīkārā sarvadharmā. bhāvasvabhāvatām upādāya.

release. Nāgārjuna answers : If kleśas (defiling elements) and skandhas (constituents) be elements existing by themselves, how can they be destroyed ?[1] The Śūnyatāvādins do not seek a Nirvāṇa where there is an end of kleśas and skandhas. Their Nirvāṇa is

Aprahīṇam asamprāptam anucchinam aśāśvataṃ,
Aniruddham anutpannam etan nirvāṇam ucyate.

(Nirvāṇa is that which is neither discarded nor attained ; it is neither a thing destroyed nor a thing eternal ; it is neither suppressed nor does it arise). Candrakīrti, in commenting upon this verse, says that it is not to be eradicated like rāga (passion) etc. nor to be attained like the fruits of a saintly life (*e.g.*, srotāpatti, sakṛdāgami, etc.). It is not eternal like aśūnya (real elements).[2] It is by its nature without origin and decay, and its lakṣaṇa (characteristic) is that it does not admit of any description.[3] In such an indescribable thing, how can an imagination (kalpanā) of the existence of kleśas and skandhas, and their eradication through Nirvāṇa find a place ? So long as those activities of our imagination continue to exist, there can be no Nirvāṇa. Nirvāṇa is realised only when all prapañcas, i.e., attempts at particularization or definition cease. To the argument of the Sarvāstivādins that even admitting the non-existence of kleśas and skandhas at the stage where Nirvāṇa is reached, it may be that they exist in saṃsāra, i.e., before the attainment of Nirvāṇa,—the Mahāyānists give the forcible reply that there is not the slightest difference between Nirvāṇa and Saṃsāra. So, in fact, Nirvāṇa requires no process of eradiction. Nirvāṇa is really the complete disappearance (kṣaya) of all figments of the imagination. The kleśas, skandhas,

1. The arguments of Nāgārjuna are found in the *Mādhyamika Vṛtti*, Ch. XXV translated by Professor Stcherbatsky as an Appendix to his *Con. of N.* In places, however, there are differences between Stcherbatsky's interpretation and the one that is given here.

2. Prof. Stcherbatsky suggests in the footnote that Aśūnya=Nirvāṇa of the Hīnayānists=Pradhāna of Sāṃkhya.

3. Prof. Stcherbatsky translates 'prapañca' by plurality and then sometimes even stretches this sense of the word.

etc., the disappearance of which is generally supposed to be necessary in Nirvāṇa,[1] have, according to the Mādhyamikas, no real existence whatsoever. Those who cannot get rid of the conception of "I-ness" or "Mine-ness" usually assume the existence of non-existent things. The sufferings of those, who are in a stage, in which they recognize the existence and non-existence of things, will never end. Candrakīrti includes in the category of such sufferers the schools of Kaṇāda, Kapila, etc, and also the Vaibhāṣikas, who believe in the existence of real entities : he also includes the Atheists (Nāstikas[2]) who deny their existence, the Sautrāntikas who deny the existence of the past, the future and the citta-viprayuktas[3] but admit that of all else, and the Yogācāras who do not believe in the existence of parikalpita (imaginary) things but admit the reality of the parinispanna (the ultimate)—the pure consciousness (vijñaptimātratā).[4] Nāgārjuna says that Nirvāṇa does not consist in the eradication or destruction of anything. It is really the avoidance of all imagination (kalpanā), of eradiction, destruction, etc. Just as a man imagines that he has taken poison and faints, though in fact, the poison has not entered into his stomach, so also a being in this world, not knowing really what the ego is, conceives of 'I-ness" and "Mine-ness." and suffers on that account. Nirvāṇa is beyond the limits of existence (bhāva) and non-existence (abhāva). A being fancies that something exist and that Nirvāna is the end of it, while, in fact, that something does not exist and therefore there can be neither its continuance nor extinction. Nirvāṇa really consists in the avoidance of the conception that something exists.[5]

According to Nāgārjuna, there are some (referring to the Vaibhāṣikas, etc.) who contend that Nirvāṇa does exist, for it

1. *M. Vṛ.*, p. 445.

2. Prof. Stcherbatsky prefers to call the Nāstikas, Materialists.

3. *M. Vṛ.*, pp. 444-5 : Sautrāntikamate atītānāgataṃ śūnyam anyad aśūnyaṃ, viprayuktā vijñaptiḥ śūnyā.

4. *M. Vṛ*, p. 445. In the enumeration of schools it will be observed that the Sthaviravādins have been omitted, as also the Vedāntists.

5. Cf. the *Prajñāpāramitā* view, *ante.*

works as a bar to the current of passions (kleśas), deeds (karmas), and births (janmas) like a dam arresting the course of a stream, and that a thing which is non-existent cannot be an effective barrier like a dam. In reply to this, it is argued (by the Sautrāntikas) that Nirvāṇa has been defined as the effacement (kṣaya) of desires together with pleasures (nandī) and passion (rāga), so what is mere extinction cannot have any existence. It is like the extinction of the flame of a lamp. This argument does not convince those who conceive Nirvāṇa as a real object, for, according to them, the extinction of desires happens in the Dharma called Nirvāṇa.[1]

Nāgārjuna refutes the opinion that Nirvāṇa is a bhāva (real thing) on the following grounds :

(i) that a really existent entity like vijñāna (consciousness) must suffer decay and death which Nirvāṇa cannot, and therefore that which has no decay and death cannot be said to have any form of existence ;

(ii) that an existent entity like vijñāna is necessarily constituted (saṃskṛta) but Nirvāṇa is unconstituted (asaṃskṛta) and hence cannot have existence ;

(iii) that an existent entity requires for its origin a causal substratum (svakāraṇasāmagrī), but Nirvāṇa does not require any, for it must be without a substratum (anupādāya).

As against the opinion that Nirvāṇa is merely abhāva (non-existence), an opinion held by the Sautrāntikas, Nāgārjuna adduces the following reasons :

(i) Nirvāṇa is not what is said to be the absence of defiling element (kleśa), birth (janma), etc., for, that would make transitoriness (anityatā) of kleśa, janma, etc. the same as Nirvāṇa. Transitoriness is the absence of kleśa and janma and nothing else, and so if Nirvāṇa be the absence of kleśa and janma then it must be the same as transitoriness of kleśa and janma, and in that case no exertion would be required to attain Nirvāṇa—which is not admitted.

(ii) If Nirvāṇa be abhāva (non-existence), how can it be spoken of as being without any substratum and without any

1. This controversy is given also in the *Kośa*, see *ante*.

reference to a bhāva (existent thing)? For no question of substratum (upādāna) can arise in regard to a non-existent thing. Against this may be raised the objection that the son of a barren woman or the horn of a hare is also said to be an abhāva (absence) without any positive counterpart. Nāgārjuna meets this by saying that abhāva (non-existence) implies a change (anyathābhāva) undergone by a thing which is existent,[1] while the son of a barren woman or the horn of a hare is only imagination (kalpanā) without implying the existence of any object. As there can be no abhāva (absence) without a positive counterpart, so Nirvāṇa is not abhāva.

Nāgārjuna now proceeds to state his conception of Nirvāṇa, which is neither bhāva nor abhāva. He says that coming and going, birth and death, are regarded sometimes as existing relatively, either antithetically like long and short, or as cause and effect like the lamp and its light, or the seed and its sprout. In both cases, they are shown to be a complex of causes and conditions. Everything whatsoever must therefore have a cause and a condition, but Nirvāṇa, in which birth and death have ceased, is uncaused and unconditioned and hence not produced (apravṛtti). Existence or non-existence cannot be predicated of what is not produced; so Nirvāṇa is neither existence nor non-existence. Those (*i.e.*, the Sarvāstivādins and the Sthaviras) who believe in the transmigration of constituents (saṃskāras) state that the group of constituents has for origin and decay a causal basis. When there is no causal basis, the group is no longer produced (apravartamāna). Then it is called Nirvāṇa. Those (*i.e.*, the Sāṃmitīyas), who believe in the transmigration of pudgala (personality), say that permanence (nityatva) or impermanence (anityatva) cannot be predicated of personality. Its coming and going happen through its corresponding upādāna (substratum) and are dependent on it. When the substratum of this personality ceases to exist, then it is called Nirvāṇa. Nāgārjuna contends that the presence (bhāva) and absence (abhāva) of the mere non-appearance (apravṛttimātrakam) of constituents (saṃs-

1. *M. Vr.*, Ch. XV, 5, p. 267.

kāras) or the personality (pudgala) cannot be conceived; similarly the existence (bhāva) and non-existence (abhāva) of Nirvāṇa cannot be affirmed. In support of his contention he quotes the saying of Buddha that desire for both existence (bhava) and non-existence (vibhava) should be given up, and points out that Buddha did not say that desire for Nirvāṇa should be given up. If Nirvāṇa has the nature of existence (bhāvarūpa) or the nature of non-existence (abhāvarūpa), then, according to Buddha, it must be given up; so existenee and non-existence cannot be predicated of Nirvāṇa.

There are again some (*i.e.*, the Vaibhāṣikas) who contend that Nirvāṇa is both existence (bhāva) and non-existence (abhāva). It is abhāva because in it there is absence of passion, birth, etc. It is bhāva because it exists by itself. Nāgārjuna refutes this on four grounds, saying that Nirvāṇa cannot be both bhāva and abhāva, for, in that case,

(i) Mokṣa (deliverance) would be bhāva and abhāva, and this would mean that the presence of saṃskāras as well as their extinction represent deliverance (mokṣa). But the former cannot be mokṣa, and therefore Nirvāṇa is not both bhāva and abhāva.

(ii) Nirvāṇa would be a dependent existence, for both bhāva and abhāva exist or arise through cause and condition. But as it is not so dependent, it is without any substratum.

(iii) Nirvāṇa would be caused and conditioned (saṃskṛta), for bhāva and abhāva cannot but be uncaused and unconditioned.

(iv) In Nirvāṇa, both bhāva and abhāva would exist together but this is impossible, for light and darkness cannot be simultaneously present at the same place. Hence Nirvāṇa cannot be both bhāva and abhāva.

Lastly, Nāgārjuna takes up the question whether Nirvāṇa is the negation of both bhāva and abhāva and shows that it cannot be so by two arguments:

(i) If bhāva and abhāva could have been realized, the negation of them would have been conceived as Nirvāṇa but

16

as what is really bhāva and abhāva is not known, it is inconsistent to describe Nirvāṇa by negation.

(ii) If it be imagined that Nirvāṇa is neither not-bhāva nor not-abhāva, it is impossible to ascertain the knower of such Nirvāṇa. If it be admitted that beings in the phenomenal world cognize it, it may be asked whether they cognize it empirically by vijñāna (consciousness) or metaphysically by jñāna (knowledge). Vijñāna (empirical consciousness) needs signs (nimitta) for cognition but Nirvāṇa is animitta (signless). Jñāna (transcendental knowledge) has śūnyatā (essencelessness) as its basis. It is originless (anutpāda) and formless (arūpa). How then with the help of this knowledge, which is indefinable, and escapes every attempt at clear expression, can it be cognized definitely that Nirvāṇa is neither not-bhāva nor not-abhāva? What cannot be cognized or understood (lit. grasped) cannot be said to have existence.

Nāgārjuna then points out that the fourteen problems, which Buddha did not think worth answering (avyākṛtaṃ),[1] prove only the non-existence of things in reality and the identity of saṃsāra and nirvāṇa.

If everything be non-existent, some may question, why it is said that Buddha preached his dharma, and for whose benefit he preached it. Nāgārjuna answers this question by saying that the Mādhyamikas define Nirvāṇa as the cessation (upaśama), and of not being in process (apravṛtti) of prapañca (expressibility) and nimitta (signs) and as a state the nature of which is upaśānta (quiet) and śiva (peaceful).[2] When Buddha is in Nirvāṇa (a state as described above), how can he be expected to have preached doctrines to men and

1. See, *e.g.*, *Dīgha*, I, pp. 187 ff. *M.Vṛ.*, p. 536.

2. *M. Vṛ.*, P. 538 :

Prapañcopaśama = vācām apravṛttiḥ	Śiva = cittasya apravṛttiḥ
„ = kleśānām apravṛttiḥ	„ = janmanoapravṛttiḥ
„ = kleśaprahāṇena	„ = niravaśeṣa-vāsanāprahāṇena
„ = jñeyānupalabdhyā	„ = jñānānupalabdhyā.

gods ? In the *Tathāgataguhya-sūtra* it is said that not a single word was uttered by Buddha between the attainment of bodhi and mahāparinirvāṇa,[1] but people, according to their individual tendencies and aims of life, conceived Buddha as giving discourses.

Conclusion of the Prajñāpāramitās and Madhyamakakārikā

Nāgārjuna, we see, leads us through a maze of arguments to the same conclusion that the *Prajñāpāramitās* have reached by every possible negation. Candrakīrti quotes a stanza from the *Prajñāpāramitā*[2] itself in support of Nāgārjuna's contention that Nirvāṇa or the Truth is the inexpressible absolute and is different from the Tathatā or Tathāgata, descriptions of which are to be found in Mahāyānic works. The stanza runs thus :

Tathāgato hi pratibimbabhūtaḥ
kuśalasya dharmasya anāsravasya,
Naivātra tathatā na tathāgato 'sti
bimbaṃ ca saṃdṛśyati sarvaloke.[3]

[Tathāgata is an image of good and pure dharma, there is (in reality) no Tathatā or Tathāgata ; only images are visible in all the worlds.]

In connection with the discussion on the existence and non-existence of saṃskāras, Nāgārjuna likewise points out that if Tathatā be equated with 'tathābhāvo 'vikāritvaṃ sadaiva sthāyitā' (sameness, changelessness and ever-existence), as is done by the Yogācārins, then he would also assert that Tathatā is non-existent. By all these negations Nāgārjuna only tries to show that the difference between the Mādhyamikas and the Yogācārins[4] consists in

1. *M. Vṛ.*, p. 539 : Avāca'nakṣarāḥ sarvaśūnyāḥ śāntādinirmalāḥ,
Ya evaṃ jānāti dharmān kumāro buddha socyate.

Cf. *Laṅkā.*, p. 194 : Uktaṃ deśanāpāṭhe mayānyaiś ca buddhabodhisattvair yathaikam apyakaṣaraṃ tathāgatā nodāharanti na pratyāharantī ti.

2. *M. Vṛ.*, pp. 449, 540. 3. *Ibid.*, p. 265.

4. *Ibid.*, p. 275 ; Madhyamakadarśana evāstītva-nāstitva-dvaya-daranasyāprasaṅgo na Vijñānavādidarśanādiṣviti vijñeyaṃ.

the fact that the former, unlike the latter, do not enter into the question of existence and non-existence of the Reality. Candrakīrti, however, apprehends that such a denial of the existence of Buddha or Tathāgata might lead people to the belief that Nāgārjuna preached pure and simple negativism ; so he says, "we do not assert the non-existence (nāstitva) in every way of the inexpressible Tathāgata, for in that case we should be guilty of apavāda (denial)".[1] The Mādhyamikas assert that the Reality is beyond determination, *i.e.*, statements like śūnya, aśūnya, both śūnya and aśūnya or not both śūnya and aśūnya cannot be made about it. These statements are used in the texts for the sake of prajñapti (communication). We should bear in mind that whenever Nāgārjuna negatives the existence of Tathatā or Tathāgata or any other synonym of it, he attributes to it the sense commonly accepted by the imperfect bodhisattvas or the Yogācārins. So, in fact, Nāgārjuna does not teach pure and simple negativism. But it should be remembered that there were among the followers of Nāgārjuna some who interpreted Nāgārjuna's principle as absolute nihilism and we may regard Bhāvaviveka as a prominent exponent of this view. But from this fact it does not follow that Nāgārjuna himself or his followers in general denied a supreme and ineffable reality, Tathatā or Śūnyatā and at least such negativism is not supported by the *Mahāprajñāpāramitāśāstra* of Nāgārjuna. The object of the *Prajñāpāramitās* as well as of the *Madhyamakakārikā* is to establish a Unity corresponding to the Vedāntic Absolute. The most characteristic mark, however, of the Vedāntic Absolute is that it is of the nature of pure intelligence (cit) and bliss (ānanda). In the Unity of Nāgārjuna bliss at least is totally absent. Śānta and śiva are the two terms which find place in Nāgārjuna's conception of the Reality ; hence it would be assuming too much to find in his conception a full-fledged Vedāntic Brahman—an all-pervading

1. *M. Vṛ.*, p. 443 : Na ca vayaṃ sarvathaiva niṣprapañcānāṃ tathāgatāāṃ nāstitvaṃ brumo yad asmākaṃ tad apavādakṛto doṣaḥ syāt.

'I' which Buddha categorically denies.[1] According to Dr. Das Gupta, it approaches more to the Nyāya-Vaiśeṣika conception of mukti, *i.e.*, a state entirely devoid of quality of any sort, either abstract or attributive, in which 'the self remains in itself in its own purity, unassociated with pleasure, pain knowledge, willingness, etc."[2] The Mādhyamika conception reality or Nirvāṇa may well, therefore, be said to have a resemblance to the impersonal aspect of the Vedāntic Brahman but not to its other aspects.[3]

The Laṅkāvatāra on Nirvāṇa

We conclude our examination of Nirvāṇa by ascertaining what the *Laṅkāvatāra*, an authoritative and early text of the Yogācārins, says about it. At the outset it may be said that the Yogācārins agreed with the Mādhyamikas so far as the unreality of the things of this world and the nonduality (advaya)[4] of saṃsāra and nirvāṇa is concerned. The Mādhyamikas were not prepared to establish any relation between the phenomenal world and the absolute except by remarking that from time immemorial beings have been subject to delusion, rendering them unable to realise the Truth unless and until they become Buddhas, after going through the processes prescribed in Mahāyāna works. The Yogācārins differed from the Mādhyamikas in attempting to find a relation between the absolute and the individual, and in doing so they asserted that there exists only citta (cittamātra) or vijñāna

1. Cf. Beal, *Gatena etc.*, pp. 175 ff (from Chinese sources); *Laṅkā.*, p. 78 in connection with Tathāgatagarbha: Reischauer, *Studies in Japanese Buddhism* (1925), p. 63: "Nothing is more striking than the similarities between the Vedānta philosophy and the speculations of Mahāyāna Buddhism; the one is as characteristically metaphysical in its mould as the other".

2. Das Gupta, *Ind. Phil.* p. 366 quoting *Nyāyamañjarī*, pp. 499ff.

3. Cf. Dr. Barnett's remarks in his Intro. to the *Path of Light*, pp. 29-30: "The Vedāntic metaphysicians could find no term to predicate of Brahman, the absolute, transcendental Reality but 'nay, nay'! And it is rather in this sense that we should interpret the negations of the Mahāyāna philosophers".

4. Cf. *e. g. Laṅkā.*, p. 76; *M. Vṛ.*, p. 537.

(vijñānamātra).[1] This citta or vijñāna, better known as Ālaya-vijñāna (store of consciousness, the substratum of saṃsāra), though originally pure, becomes polluted by delusions and dichotomizes itself into 'me' and 'not-me', subject and object, former becoming mind (manas) and the latter the external world. So, according to the Yogācārins, Nirvāṇa consists in the ceasing of the mind to dichotomize and in realising that there exists only citta and that the phenomenal world is only a delusion of the citta. *The Laṅkāvatāra* says that Nirvāṇa consists in the removal of the imagining intellect (vikalpasya manovijñānasya vyāvṛttir nirvāṇam ity ucyate),[2] the source of seven vijñānas and that it is not any one of the following four as conceived by the heretics :[3]

(i) absence of any real existence (bhāva-svabhāvābhāva) ;

(ii) absence of the various forms of existence (lakṣaṇa-vicitrabhāvābhāva) ;

(iii) realisation of the absence of the existence of one's own signs (svalakṣaṇabhāvābhāvāva-bodha) ; and

(iv) destruction of the chain of continuity of the general characteristics (svasāmānyalakaṣaṇa-saṃtati-prabandha-vyuccheda).[4]

According to the *Laṅkāvatāra*,[5] Nirvāṇa is the transformation (parāvṛtti) of vijñānas, mind, etc. It is devoid of the mental distinctions of existence and non-existence, and of eternal and non-eternal. It is not eternal, because it has no distinct generic characteristics, and it is not non-eternal because it can be realized by saints (āryas). It resembles neither death nor destruction.[5]

The *Laṅkāvatāra*[6] then proceeds to elucidate its position by enumerating the different conceptions of Nirvāṇa current among the non-Yogācārins, and remarks in a general way that all these conceptions are defective, because they fall

1. For criticism of this, see *M. Vṛ.*, pp. 274ff.

2. *Laṅkā.*, p. 126. 3. *Ibid.*

4. *Laṅkā.*, p. 157 : The Śrāvakas are referred to as svasāmānya-lakṣaṇa-patitāśayābhiniviṣṭāḥ.

5. *Ibid.*, pp. 98-9. 6. *Ibid.*, p. 66.

under either of the two extremes of 'is' and 'is not'[1]. The conception of Nirvāṇa, mentioned last among the non-Yogācāra conceptions, however, appears to be Mahāyānic. It runs thus: There are some who declare that Nirvāṇa is the removal (vyāvṛtti) of citta, manas and manovijñāna by passing from one bhūmi to another till the attainment of the Tathāgatabhūmi, and practice of the samādhi of Māyā, etc., appertaining thereto by (i) realising that everything is a fancy of one's own mind, (ii) not occupying oneself with the existence and non-existence of external things, (iii) ascertaining the true nature (yathābhūta) of things, (iv) non-perceiving subject and object without being deluded by the two extremes which follow from one's own thought-constructions, (v) realising the ineffectiveness of having recourse to proofs, (vi) knowing that the truth is a matter only of self-realisation, (vii) comprehending two nairātmyas, and (viii) removing the two kinds of kleśas (intellectual and habitual) and the two screens (āvaraṇas: kleśa and jñeya). The various conceptions which non-Buddhists hold in regard to Nirvāṇa are their imaginations. Mokṣa (emancipation) and mokṣopāya (means of emancipation), about which they speak, do not really exist but the teachers have vikalpa (thought-construction) about them and think of the action and the actor, existence (sat) and non-existence (asat), and busy themselves in jalpa (useless talks) and prapañca (diffuse talks). Just as forms in a mirror are seen but do not exist there, so also in the mirror of vāsanā[2] foolish people see the citta as twofold (dvidhā)[3]. Not knowing cittadṛśya (citta-image) truly, the ignorant forms vikalpas of the seen and the seer, whereas in fact there is only one citta, devoid of lakṣya and lakṣaṇa (percipient and percept). The

1. *Ibid*, pp. 182-7: for a summary see *E.B.*, IV, pp. 226ff.

2. Vāsanā = knowledge derived from memory = present consciousness of past perceptions, or an impression remaining unconsciously in the mind froms past good or evil actions and hence producing pleasure and pain (saṃskāra). See Monier Williams' *Dict*. sv. Vāsanā.

3. *Laṅkā.*, p. 182.

Laṅkāvatāra then goes into details of this exposition, asserting that the Tathāgata or Buddha is beyond predications and cannot be said to be made (kṛtaka) or unmade (akṛtaka), cause or effect, for such predication would be doubly faulty. If the Tathāgata be kṛtaka, he would be anitya and identical with all actions, which are by nature impermanent, and if he be akṛtaka, he would be non-existent,[1] and the merits so far collected by him become useless, and he becomes non-existent as a sky-flower. So the Tathāgata should be regarded as beyond four-fold limitations and hence beyond proofs, and is only to be realised within one's own self. When Buddha speaks about things as nirātma, he refers to phenomenal things and not to the Tathāgata. A Tathāgata is neither the same nor different from the skandhas ; hence he is neither nitya nor anitya. Similarly he is not the same nor different from mokṣa. In this way, if no statement can be made about the Tathāgata, and if he is beyond proofs, he turns into a word without any origin and destruction and can be equated with ākāśa, having nothing to rest upon (nirālamba) and beyond prapañca.[2] Though the Tathāgata is called Anutpāda-anirodha, it must not be supposed that 'Tathāgata' means only absence (abhāva) of something ;[1] this Anutpāda- anirodha is really the name of the Manomaya-dharmakāya[3] (=Svasambhogakāya) and is not in fact the Reality, the real Tathāgata (=Dharmakāya).

Points of agreement and difference re. Nirvāṇa in Hīnayānic and Mahāyānic works

Without going into the discussion on the conception of Nirvāṇa, which Buddha had in his mind, and which is to be found in the Piṭakas—a topic ably discussed in many works, the latest of which is Professor La Vallée Poussin's *Nirvāṇa*—we shall compare here the conceptions as found in the *Kathāvathu*, *Visuddhimagga* and *Abhidharmakośa* on the one

1. Alabdhātmakāḥ=na lakṣaṇataḥ kalpyāḥ, see *Laṅkā.*, p. 19.
2. Cf. *M. Vṛ.*, p. 536.
3. *Laṅkā.*, p. 191.
4. See *ante*.

hand, and the *Prajñāpāramitā*, *Mādhyamika Vṛtti*, and *Laṅkāvatāra* on the other.

All these texts agree in regard to the following points :—

(i) Nirvāṇa is inexpressible (niṣprapañca) ; it is unconstituted, and has no origin, no decay and no change.

(ii) It is to be realised only within one's own self—the pratyātmavedya of the Yogācārins and the paccattaṃ veditabbaṃ (viññūhi) of the Hīnayānists.

(iii) It is not abhāva (absence of anything) as maintained by the Sautrāntikas.

(iv) It is one and the same for all Buddhas, past, present and future.

(v) Mārga leads to Nirvāṇa.

(vi) Individuality ceases in Nirvaṇa.

(vii) The Hīnayānists, in agreement with the Mahāyānists, hold that Buddhas possess extraordinary powers and knowledge, far superior to the Arhats. But they do not consider that the Nirvāṇa attained by Buddha is different from that attained by the Arhats.[1] They thus object to the assertion of the Mahāyānists that the Nirvāṇa of the Arhats is a lower and not a perfect state.

(viii) Vimukti (freedom) from afflictions (kleśa) as an aspect of Nirvāṇa is the same for Arhats and Buddhas.[2]

The points of difference regarding the conception of Nirvāṇa as found in the works mentioned above are :—

(i) The *K.*, *V.* and *A.*[3] mention that Nirvāṇa is existing, eternal (nitya), blissful (sukha) and pure (śuci). The Yogācārins subscribe to this statement when they identify Apratiṣṭhita Nirvāṇa with Dharmakāya.[4] Strictly speaking both the Mādhyamikas and the Yogācārins do not predicate of Nirvāṇa anything like eternal or non-eternal (nıtya or anitya), blissful or withont bliss (sukha or asukua), pure or impure (śuci or

1. *Jāt.*, I, Dīpaṅkara Buddha is said to have attained anupādisesanibbānadhātu.

2. *Sūtrā.*, p. 36.

3. *K.* stands for *Kathāvatthu* ; *V.* for *Visuddhimagga* and *A.* for *Abhidharmakośa.*

4. Suzuki, *Outlines of Mahāyāna Buddhism*, p. 354.

aśuci), for Nirvāṇa to them is beyond all predication and hence cannot be stated as nitya, anitya and so forth.

The Mahāyānists following the warning of Buddha against the two extremes of śāśvata and uccheda decline to apply the predications to everything, including Nirvāṇa, but the *K.* and *V.* state that Buddha's warning refers only to the conception of soul, and not to Nirvāṇa.

(ii) The *K.*, *V*, and *A.* consider that Nirvāṇa is a thing to be acquired (prāptam) while the *M.* and *L.*[1] consider it to be unobtainable (asamprāptam).

(iii) The *K.* and *V.* maintain that Nirvāṇa forms an ārammaṇa (basis) for meditation and knowledge of monks. The *M.* and *L.* do not distinguish between Nirvāṇa and the monk, knowable and the knower, object and subject.

(iv) The *K.*, *V.* and *A.* define Nirvāṇa as a lokottara (transcendental) state, and as really the highest possible state conceivable by them.

The *L.* and *M.* recognise a state higher than lokottara (*L.* names it lokottaratama) and identify it with Nirvāṇa, remarking that in this state sarvajñatā (omniscience) is obtained a state unattainable by the Hīnayānists.

The Yogācārins are of the opinion that the Hīnayānists attain only Vimuttikāya or Mokṣa, while the Mahāyānists attain Dharmakāya and Sarvajñatva. The Hīnayānists subscribe to this view, for, according to them, Buddha is far superior in knowledge and powers to an Arhat and is omniscient while an Arhat is not.

(v) The Hīnayānists know only two forms of Nirvāṇa, sopādiśeṣa and nirupādiśeṣa, or pratisaṃkhyā and apratisaṃkhyā. The Yogācārins add to them Prakṛtiśuddha nirvāṇa[2] and Apratiṣṭhita nirvāṇa.[3]

---

1. *M.* stands for *Mādhyamika Vṛtti* and *L.* for *Laṅkāvatāra.*

2. Cf. *M. Vṛ.*, p. 541 ; atyantaparinirvṛta.

3. The Apratiṣṭhita Nirvāṇa is the state of one who after obtaining sopādisesa-nibbānadhātu, develops maitri, benevolence or charity for the suffering millions and chooses not to be let himself automatically pass, as he would otherwise, to anupādisesa-nibbānadhātu [Cf. *Pañca.* (A.S.B.ms.) leaf 157a : Śrāvakā nirupādiśesanirvāṇadhātau pratiṣṭhitāḥ].

(vi) The Mādhyamikas consider that Nirvāṇa is the impersonal absolute immanent in nature, and the only reality, everything else being mere thought-construction. It appears like the Absolute of the Vedānta, but lacks the *cit* (consciousness) and *ānanda* (bliss) of the latter.

From this it follows that there is the dharma-samatā or the sameness of all things, even of nirvāṇa and saṃsāra. These are related to each other as the sea and the waves.

(vii) The Mādhyamikas hold with the Yogācārins that Nirvāṇa is advaya (non-dual), *i.e.*, in it there is no duality of subject and object, or positlve and negative ; and that all worldly things are mere illusions.

(viii) The Mahāyānists conceive two 'screens' called kleśāvaraṇa and jñeyāvaraṇa[1] which operate as hindrances to the

---

He is then said to be possessed of Nirvāṇa tinged with charity or benevolence. The *Sūtrālaṅkāra* (pp. 126-7) puts it very clearly : The Śrāvakas and Pratyekabuddhas, being devoid of love, fix their minds on Nirʌāṇa, consisting in the cessation of all misery. The Bodhisattvas, however, being full of compassion, do not like to fix their minds on Nirvāṇa : hence they are said to be in the Apratiṣṭhita Nirvāṇa. It will be noted that the Arhats are not entitled to seek the Apratiṣṭhita Nirvāṇa : they pass directly from sopadiśeṣa to nirupadiśeṣa-nirvāṇadhātu. The Apratiṣṭhita Nirvāṇa can be obtained by Buddhas only, and hence it is a state superior to that of the Arhats. The *Vijñaptimātratā* adds that Buddhas in the Apratiṣṭhita Nirvāṇa rise above the idea of Saṃsāra and Nirvāṇa (cf. *Sūtrālaṅkāra*, p. 36) ; hence Śākyamuni was not really influenced by love or charity after the attainment of Nirvāṇa. The Hīnayānists conceive him as one without love (cf. *Milindapañha*, p. 160 ; vigataṃ tathāgatassa pemaṃ vigato simeho), though in fact, they repeatedly mention that he preached the Truth out of compassion for the innumerable sufiering being (lokānukampāya bahujanahitāya sukhāya). Compassion presupposes the exsistence of love, which may be, and in fact in the case of Buddha (but not of Bodhisattvas) was purely unselfish and, as the Mahāyānists say. devoid of kleśa. For a detailen treatment of the Apratiṣṭhita Nirvāṇa sce Masuda, *Die individualistische Idealismus der Yogācāra* Schule, pp. 49 f. : Stcherbataky, *Con. of N.*, pp. 185, 215-6 ; Lévi, *Mahāyāna Sūtrālaṅkāra*, •ii, pp. 21, 27 ; Keith, *B. Phil.*, pp. 557-8 : *Bodhic.*, p. 75 ; *Vijñaptinātratā*, x, pp. 99 (ed. of Saeki Kiokuga).

1. For details, see *ante.* Also *Laṅkā.*, pp. 97, 241.

attainment of Nirvāṇa. They hold that the Hīnayānists can get rid of only the kleśāvaraṇa, while they themselves get rid of both.

Conclusion

The agreements and disagreements in the accounts of Nirvāṇa, as noticed above, point to the following conclusions :

The Hīnayānic Nirvāṇa, *i.e.*, the Nirvāṇa as described in the literature of the Theravāda school, clearly refers to a Unity eternally existing beyond the three worlds (Kāma, Rūpa and Arūpa dhātus). It is infinite, inexpressible, unborn, and undecaying. It is homogeneous (ekarasa) and knows no individuality. In it, all discriminations or dichotomy cease. Many of the aspects of Ākāśa (space) and the ocean bear comparison with those of Nirvāṇa.

Every being is a conglomeration of elements, which can be classified under five heads : rūpa, vedanā, saññā, saṅkhā ā and viññāṇa ; hence one being is not essentially different from another, an ordinary man is not different from a perfected saint. But if the nature and proportion of each of the five constituents existing in an individual be taken into account, then one being is different from another, an ordinary man is different from a perfected saint. It is in this way that the Buddhist saying 'n'eva so na ca añño' (neither the same nor different) is explained.

The combination of elements is the outcome of Karma (past deeds) and is happening every moment (kṣaṇika), implying that the disintegration of elements always precedes it. The elements in a combined state pass as an individual, and from time immemorial he labours under the misconception of a self and of things relating to a self. His vision being distorted or obscured by ignorance of the truth he cannot perceive the momentary combination and disintegration of elements. On the other hand, he is subject to an inclination for them. A perfect man with his vision cleared by the Buddhistic practices and culture realises the real state of things, *viz.*, that an individual consists of the five elements and does not possess a permanent and unchanging entity called soul.

The elemeuts, combined under the force of karma, pass as an individual, who becomes deluded by misconceptions. He weaves a net of fancies around himself and believes that he is related in some way or other to things or individuals. Because of such illusions he experiences endless sufferings, or according to the Mahāyānists, thinks of himself as suffering, on account of his supposed separation from people or things near and dear to him, or though supposed disorders or derangements of his mental and physical system.

It is for these deluded so-called individuals that Buddhism prescribes the eightfold path. By following it an individual ultimately realises the transitoriness of things, to which he has nitherto attributed some form of existence, and finds that the elements, by which he thought himself constituted, are ultimately not constituents peculiar to him but common to all other so-called beings. He is then said to have attained Nirvāṇa, *i.e.*, a mental state in which he can no longer distinguish himself as an individual different from the infinite elements constituting the universe. In other words, all individuality ends in it. In that state of Nirvāṇa Gautama Buddha is not different from Śāriputra—all are one and the same.

The Mahāyānic conception of Nirvāṇa is completely different from the Hīnayānic. The fundamental point of difference is that the Mahāyānists deny the existence of elements altogether. They do not know of any other reality but the truth, the Dharmakāya or Dharmadhātu. Many of the aspects of their conception are brought out by the various terms used in Mahāyānic works. For instance, when Nirvāṇa is equated with śūnyatā, the implication is that all things which are ordinarily supposed to exist are really non-existent just as the mirage has no substantialtty whatsoever, *e.g.*, the pṛthivī-dhātu is void (śūnya) of real origination, destruction, or existence in reality.[1] When it is equated

1. *Śikṣā.*, p. 246.

wlth Tathatā or Dharmatā, the implication is that all things of this world are essentially of the same nature, void of any name or substratum.[1] It is that which is neither existence nor non-existence.[2] Śūnyatā represents the negative and Tathatā the positive aspects of the Truth. When it is called bhūtakoṭī (true limit), it is implied that on analysis of dharmas, which are false designations, one arrives finally at the Reality, beyond which it is impossible to pass and which alone is truth. Some of the other expressions which are often used as synonyms of Nirvāṇa are avitathatā (not untruth); ananyatathatā (unique); aviparyāsatathatā (irreversible); paramārtha (the highest truth), tattva (the essence); acintya-dhātu (incomprehensible substance), dharmadhātu (totality of things), dharmasthiti (substratum of things); supraśānta (perfectly calm, unruffled by origination or destruction); advaya and advaidhīkāra (non-separable and non-divisible).[3]

The Mahāyānists hold that all beings other than Buddhas are under delusions, the nature of which varies according to their spiritual advancement. An ordinary man is as much under a delusion that he has a son or property as the Hīnayānic saints, the Arhats think that they have attained Nirvāṇa, a state of perfect rest and happiness, and have gone beyond the three worlds. The contention of the Mahāyānists is that the only reality is Nirvāṇa or Dharma-dhātu, everything else being a delusion of the mind. The moment an individual realises that he is the Reality, that Saṃsāra is identical with Nirvāṇa, he becomes perfect, *i.e.*, a Buddha. One must eradicate from his mind the conception not only of his own individuality but also of the substantiality of anything whatsoever perceived or cognized by him. When a being attains a state of mind, in which he cannot distinguish himself from any other thing of the world or from the Absolute, he is said to attain Nirvāṇa in the Mahāyānic sense.

---

1. *Laṅkā.*, p. 226. 2. *Śikṣā.*, p. 263.
3. Cf. *Saṃyutta*, II, pp. 25ff; "Iti kho, bhikkhave, yā tatra *tathatā avitathatā anaññatathatā* idapaccayatā, ayaṃ vuccati. bhikkhave, paṭicca-samuppādo ti. For explanation of the words in italics, see *Vis M.*, p. 518.

CHAPTER VII

Conception of the Truth

An important point of difference between Hīnayāna and Mahāyāna pointed out by the *Saddharma-Puṇḍarīka* is that, according to the former, a being, by comprehending the Āryasatyas including the Pratītyasamutpāda, attains Nirvāṇa, *i.e.*, he passes from saṁsāra to nirvāṇa, from a laukika to lokottara state ; while, according to the latter, a being, by comprehending the fact that there is no difference between saṁsāra and nirvāṇa, that the world has only a relative existence (pratītyasamutpanna) aud that it is unreal but appears real to a deluded mind, realises the true Nirvāṇa, which is nothing but the Śūnyatā or Tathatā, the absolute principle underlying the universe. The conceptions of the Reality being so wide apart, the Hīnayānis and the Mahāyānists look upon everything including the Buddhistic practices from two quite different angles of vision. To the Hīnayānists, the Āryasatyas and the Pratītyasamutpāda are real and hence belong to the domain of the highest truth (*paramattha* and not *sammuti*), while to the Mahāyānists, they are unreal and belong to the domain of convention (*saṁvṛti* or *parikalpita-paratantra*). The Mahāyānists, however, could not do away with the four truths and the formula of the chain of causation, for, they held that beings, deluded as they are, should at the beginning try to comprehend the Pudgala-śūnyatā through them. In convenance with their conception of the Reality. the Mahāyānists said that Buddha had two forms of teaching, conventional and transcendental, and that whatever he said about the Āryasatyas or Pratītya-samutpāda were conventional, his real teaching being Śūnyatā or Tathatā, which could not be imparted by one to another and could be realised only within one's own self. Before we enter into the discussion about his two forms of teaching, let us see what the Āryasatyas and the Pratītyasamutpāda are.

The Āryasatyas

The Āryasatyas, as commonly known, are *dukkha* (misery), *samudaya* (origin of misery), *nirodha* (cessation of misery) and *magga* (means of the cessation of misery). The underlying teaching of these four truths is that they are to be treated as a formulæ for application to everything perceived. That these four truths constitute merely a formula and not a doctrine has been brought out very clearly in many Buddhist texts. In the *Majjhima Nikāya*[1] while giving an exposition of what the right view (sammādiṭṭhij is, according to the Buddhists, Sāriputta takes up, for instance, āhāra (food), dukkha (misery), jarāmaraṇa (old age and death), taṇhā (desire), nāma-rūpa (name and form) and avijjā (ignorance) and applies to each of them the fourfold formula, examining it in this way ; Take up for consideration a material or an immaterial thing. Ascertain its origin. Inquire how it decays. In pursuance of this method Sāriputta defines Sammādiṭṭhi through āhāra thus : One who knows āhāra (food), āhārasamudaya (how food originates), āhāranirodha (how food decays) and āhāranirodhagāminpaṭipadā (the way in which the decay of food happens) possesses Sammādiṭṭhi. The first truth relates to Āhāra which, in the Buddhist philosophy, is of four kinds.[2] The second truth is āhārasamudaya, *i.e*,, āhāra comes into existence on account of taṇhā. The third truth is āhāranirodha, *i.e.*, the ceasing of āhāra when the taṇhā is extinct. The fourth truth is the way in which āhāra ceases ; it happens by the practice of the eightfold path, *viz.*, sammā diṭṭhi, saṅkappa, vācā, *etc.* One who knows correctly these truths gets rid of hatred and attachment, rises above the belief in a self, drives out ignorance, and attains freedom from misery. So, we see that in these four truths there is nothing particularly Buddhism. They are found in the Brahmanical systems of philosphy

---

1. *Majjhima,* I, p. 261. See also *Lal. Vis.*, pp. 349, 416-7 ; *Mtu.*, II, p. 288 ; III, p. 53.
2. *Dīgha,* III, pp. 228, 276 ; *Dhs.* 71-3 ; *Vis. M.*, p. 341.

as well.[1] For instance, the *Yoga-sūtra* of Patañjali (II, 15), says : Yathā cikitsāśāstraṃ caturvyūhaṃ, rogo rogahetur ārogyaṃ bhaiṣajyam iti evam idam api śāstraṃ catur vyūham eva tad yathā saṃsāraḥ saṃsārahetur mokṣo mokṣopāya iti (just as the science of medicine has four sections, dealing with the diagnosis, cause and cure of diseasee, and their remedies, so also this science of spiritual healing has four sections dealing with an examination of the nature of the things of the world, the cause of their origin, their removal, and the factors that bring about the removal)[1]. The *Abhīdharmakośa* also follows up this interpretation by coalescing the four truths into two, viz., cause and effect, saṃsāra (worldly life) and nirvāṇa (cessation), duḥkha and samudaya relate to saṃsāra, while nirodha and mārga to Nirvāṇa. Saṃsāra (worldly life) is the effect while samudaya is its cause ; so also Nirvāṇa (cessation) is the effect while mārga is its cause[2].

This position of the Hīnayānists in regard to the Āryasatyas is logical ; for their cardinal teaching is that a being suffers wrongly life assuming the existence of a self, and thus conceiving himself as a separate entity, standing in some form of relation to every other being or thing of the world, to which again he ascribes an individuality similar to his own. The chief aim of Hīnayāna teaching is to expel from one's mind all ideas of individuality, whether of himself or of any other being or thing of the world, and this can only be effected by an examination of the things of the world under the four aspects mentioned above. Scrutinizing everything in this way, a being gets rid of his wrong assumption and sees things as they really are. This is called sammādiṭṭhi (right view) or vijjā (true knowledge). Once this is reached he can be said to have attained freedom from misery, or Nirvāṇa.

---

1. Prof. Stcherbatsky remarks : "These four topics—the four noble truths as the term has been very inadequately translated and represented as a fundamental principle of Buddhism—contain in reality no doctrine at all." *Con. of N.*, p. 55.

2. *Kośa*, VI. 4 ; see also Sogen, *Sys. of B. Thought*, pp. 69ff : *Sūtrā.*, pp. 137-8 ; it supports the interpretation of the *Kośa*, see *infra*.

The Pratītyasamutpāda

Of the four truths[1], the second and the third comprise the *Pratītyasamutpāda.* The chief object of this formula of causation is to establish that things of this world have only a dependent origination and hence are impermanent and productive of sufferings, and that there is nothing except Nirvāṇa and Ākāśa that does not depend upon cause and condition. This formula of causal law has been utilised by the Hīnayānists to show that all constituted things have a preceding cause and condition as such they are without any substantiality, while it has been used by the Mahāyānists to establish that the world, being relatively existent, is unreal like the objects seen in a dream. The formula explains the fixed, unchangeable, and this-conditioned (*idappccayatā*) nature of things: hence it is a key to the eternal truth. The moment a being realises in his life the truth of this formula he sees the Reality. We find for this reason that the Buddhist texts identify the formula with Buddha and Dhamma.[1] It was this solution of the problem of life and the world that appealed to Sāriputta and proved a fruitful source for Nāgārjuna's speculation.[2]

Many scholars, who have dealt with this formula, have attempted to elicit from it Buddha's theory of the origin of a being and some of them have actually drawn parallels between the links of the formula and the causal series of the Sāṃkhya.[3] It is noteworthy that such attempts were also made in Buddhaghosa's time. Buddhaghosa has, however, pointed out that *avijjā*, the first link of the chain, must not be regarded similar to *pakati* (Prakṛti) of the Pakativādins (Sāṃkhya) because avijjā is neither uncaused (akāraṇam) nor is it the primary cause (mūlakāraṇam) of the world. It owes its origin to āsavas (impurities). The reason adduced by Buddhaghosa for its being made the first link in the chain is that Budha

1. See *ante*.

2. Nāgārjuna devoted his first chapter to the explanation of only this aspect of the law of causation.

3. See Kern, *Manual etc.*, p. 46f. ; for other refs., see Poussin, *Theorie des douze causes*, p. vii, fn. 2.

used 'avijjā' or 'bhavataṇhā' for commencing (sīsabhāvam) his discourses on topics which by their nature are without any beginning or end (vaṭṭakathā or anamatagga)[1]. It is apparent from Buddhaghosa's remark that avijjā needs not necessarily be the first link in the chain of causation but that it is one of the terms found suitable by the author of the formula to begin the chain. It could as well be commenced with bhavataṇhā.[2] In the *Saṃyutta Nikāya*[3], the formula starts with *āhāra* as the first link. Hence, it is apparent that the Pratītyasamutpāda is not meant to be an explanation of the origin of the worldly beings but just a chain of instances to illustrate the law of *idappaccayatā* (this-conditioned nature, *i.e.*, dependent origination) of things. Those scholars, who expected to find in it a key to the origin of the worldly beings, have been disappointed and have condemned it as illogical and incongruous. The author of the formula could not anticipate that his arrangement of the illustrations in a series would give rise to confusion. That the chain was not meant to demonstrate a line of evolution is also apparent from the last two links, *viz.*, jāti and jarāmaraṇa, as the former cannot be the cause of the latter. The underlying idea is that if there be jāti, it is inevitably followed by jarāmaraṇa. The author of the formula wanted us to take up any two links and realise from them the idappaccayatā or the relative nature of worldly things. We may therefore say that the twelve-linked Pratītyasamutpāda like the Āryasatyas is more a general principle than a doctrine peculiar to Buddhism, though undoubtedly, it owes its enunciation to the ancient Buddhist savants. It cannot be stated how far Buddha was responsible for the selection of the links though it was perhaps to his penetrating eyes that the relative existence of all worldly things became apparent for the first time.

As the links of the formula have been explained by Profs.

1. *Vis. M.*, p. 525.

2. *Ibid.*, p. 525: purimā, bhikkhave, koṭi na paññāyati avijjāyā (or bhavataṇhāys), ito pubbe avijjā (or bhavataṇhā) nāhosi atha pacchā sambhavī ti. Evañ c'etaṃ, bhikkhave, vuccati, atha ca pana paññāyati idapaccayā avijjā (or bhavataṇhā). *Cf. Saṃyutta*, II, p. 178; III, p. 149.

3. *Saṃyutta*, II, pp. 101-3, *Mahāniddesa*. I, pp. 25-6.

La Vallée Poussin, Keith, Oldenberg and others, we shall give here only a brief exposition of them[1].

The formula runs as follows[2] : (1) avijjāpaccayā saṅkhārā, (2) saṅkhārāpaccyā viññāṇaṃ, (3) viññāṇap. nāmarūpaṃ[4], (4) nāmarūpap. saḷāyatanaṃ, (5) saḷāyatanap. phasso, (6) phassap. vedanā, (7) vedanāp. taṇhā, (8) taṅhāp. upādānaṃ. (9) upādānap. bhavo, (10) bhavap. jāti, (11 & 12) jātip. jarāmaraṇaṃ.

The first link, avijjā, usually refers to the deluded state of mind which debars a being from taking a true view of worldly things, *e.g.*, mistaking impermanent things as permanent, misery as happiness, a being without a permanent self as possessed of a self and so forth.[5] The second link in the chain is saṅkhārā (impressions or thought-constructions—cetanā) concerning merit (puñña), demerit (apuñña), and qualities that are neither merit nor demerit (aneñja)[6]. This is followed by the third link viññāṇa[7] *i.e.*, perceptions through the six organs of sense. Concomitantly (sahaja) with viññāṇa arise the four composites (khandhas)

---

1. Poussin, *Theorie des douze causes* ; Keith, *B. Phil.*, pp.99ff. ; Oldenberge's *Buddha* (Hoey's transl. 1882) : pp. 223 f ; Gokhale, *Pratitya-samutpādaśāstra des Ullaṅgha*, Bonn, 1930.

2. *Dīgha*, II, pp. 518ff ; La Vallée Poussin, *Thoerie des douze causes*, pp. 69 ff ; *Vis. M.*, 518 ff, quoting *Saṃyutta*, II, pp. 25-7,

3. In the *Saṃyutta* (II, pp. 101-3) avijjā is replaced by āhāra on any such other thing that gives rise to viññāṇa.

4. *Dīgha* (II, p. 56) omits the first two links and begins its formula thus :—Nāmarūpapaccayā viññāṇaṃ, viññāṇapaccayā nāmarūpam, *i.e.* viññṇa and nāma-rūpa are made interdependent. *Śālistambasutra* (p. 82) says that they are sahaja (concomitant).

5. *Śālistambasūtra*, p. 79 : see also *Vis. M.*, p. 526.

6. *Śālistambasūtra*, p. 82 ; to these three, the *Vibhaṅga* (p. 135) and *Visuddhimagga* (p, 530) add three others, *viz.*, kāyasaṅkhāro, vacis. and cittas. The *Śālistambasūtra* explains in another place (p. 79) that rāga, dveṣa and moha in regard to worldly things arising through avidyā are called saṃskāras.

7. *Śālistambasūtra*, p. 82 ; *Vis. M.*, (p. 546) says that puññābhisaṅkhāro produces twenty-one kinds of viññāṇa. apuññābhi° seven, and āneñjābhi° four.

and form a complete being (nāmaiūpa) in the fœtus.[1] With its growth, the nāmarūpa (body) requires the six organs of sense for doing its functions, and these organs in their turn produce six forms of contact (phassa).[2] The nature of the contact produces its corresponding feeling (vedanā) and the feeling in its turn gives rise to desire (taṇhā). Taṇhā leads to upādāna[3] (grasping) of kāma (desire for objects of pleasure), diṭṭhi (wrong views like sassata, asassata, etc.), sīlabbata (religious practices like gosīla and govata) and attavāda (belief in a self). This upādāna, which may also be defined as a strong taṇhā, produces a keen desire in a being for future existance in one of the three worlds, and for this he peforms kamma through words, mind and body. According to his *kamma* he is reborn in one of the various spheres of existence and becomes in due course old and passes away.

Reasons adduced by the Mahāyānists for including the Truth and the Causal Law in their doctrines.

The Mahāyānists highly appreciated the teaching conveyed by the formula of causation but were not interested in the significance of its links as their cardinal tenet was *dharma-śūnyatā* or non-existence of everything worldly. Similarly for the āryasatyas they appreciated the method of analysis of all worldly things as suggested by the satyas but these in their view have existence similar to the objects seen in a dream or a mirage. Thus, if everything be non-existent, the examination of a non-existent thing is absurd ; hence the Mahāyānists should by reasons justify the inclusion of Āryasatyas and the Pratītyasamutpāda in their doctrines. Nāgārjuna and Śāntideva, Asaṅga and Vasubandhu therefore have shown by forcible and illuminating arguments that they were justified in including the Truths and the twelve-linked Law of Causation in their doctrines.

1. In the *Dīgha* (II, p. 63) and *Śālistambasūtra* (p. 82) viññāṇ and nāmaiūpa are shown as resting upon each other, *i.e.*, one cannot remain without the other.

2. Adhivacansamphassa and paṭighasamphassa, *Dīgha*, II, p. 62.

3. *Dīgha*, II, p. 58 ; *Vis. M.*, p. 569.

Nāgārjuna summarises the position of the Hīnayānists

Nāgārjuna has dealt with the Truths incidentally in his examination of Pratyaya, Karmaphala, Ātman,[1] etc., and at length in his treatment of the Āryastyas[2]. He first summarises the arguments of his opponents thus : If everything be non-existent (śūnya), there cannot arise any question about the origin and decay of a thing,—in this case, duḥkha (misery). The five constituents of beings, which come into existence through pre-existent cause and condition, are called duḥkha, because they produce suffering, being subject to change and transformation. That these constituents are a source of suffering realised by the Āryas (*i.e.*, Arhats) only, and not by the common people, for the latter labour under the four misconceptions (viparyāsas)[3] of considering impure things as pure, impermanent as permanent, unhappy as happy, and egoless having ego. The common people are like the sick, to whom sweet things appear bitter. A person who is not yet an arhat (anārya) does not know that the five upādānaskhandhas are a source of suffering. It is for this reason that the Truths (satyas) are called truths for the perfect (āryas) only. If everything be śūnya (non-existent), there cannot be Āryasatya called duḥkha and consequently there can be no samudaya (origin), nirodha (destruction), or mārga (means of destruction of suffering). If the four Āryasatyas do not exist, there cannot exist true knowledge, exertion, or realisation, the four fruits of sanctification or their enjoyer, the Saṅgha, Dharma, or even Buddha. The assertion of śūnyatā (non-existence of everything) goes against the existence of the three ratnas, in fact, of all things, good or bad.

Nāgārjuna's arguments to meet the above charges

Nāgārjuna pities his opponents for their inability to grasp the true sense of śūnyatā, of the object of establishing śūnyatā,

1. *M. Vṛ.*, chs. I, XVIII, XVIII. 2. *Ibid.*, ch. XXV1.

3. *Bodhic.*, p. 375 ! *M. Vṛ.*, pp. 464 and 607 referring to *Netti*, p. 114 and *Index* : *Sikṣā.*, p. 198 ; *Aṅguttarā*, II, p. 52 ; *Patañjala-Yogasūtra*, II, 5 ; *Sarvadarśaua-saṅgraha* (ed. of Mm. Vasudev Abhayankar), p. 361 ; see also, *infra*.

and for their false imagination. The object of teaching śūnyatā, he says, is to bring about a complete cessation of all *prapañca* (*i.e.*, looking upon unity as manifold). The view held by his opponents that mokṣa (emancipation) is attained by the destruction of action (karma) and passion (kleśa) is incorrect. It is a known fact that ordinarily persons are ignorant of the real state of things. They conceive rūpa (form), etc. and allow passion, hatred and delusion to come into existence. From this statement as also from the *Sūtras*, it is evident that saṅkalpa (imagination) is the source of all these, from which it follows that karma and kleśa are only products of imagination and have no real existence. Their origin is due to the *prapañca* (thought-creation), which takes hold of the mind of a worldly being, who from the time immemorial is used to a variety of actions and things such as gain and loss, happiness and misery, action and the actor, known and the knower, and so forth. All these worldly thought-creations cease to exist when a person realises the non-existence of the things which are commonly supposed to have real existence. Just as a person does not form any idea (prapañca) about the 'beauty of a barren woman's daughter' and consequently does not weave a net of fancies (kalpanā) around her so also a Mahāyānist is not troubled with the conception of "I" and "Mine" the roots of a belief in self (satkāyadṛṣṭī), nor is he troubled by any cause for the origin of passions. If a person realises that passions (kleśas) do not originate, he cannot have any idea of good or bad action and consequently of birth, old age, disease and death. Therefore the Yogins (ascetics) established in śūnyatā do not conceive of any real skandha, dhātu, āyatana, etc. and consequently they have no prapañca, vikalpa, satkāyadṛṣṭī, kleśa, karma or mṛtyu. Thus the realisation of śūnyatā brings ubout the complete cessation of all prapañcas, and so it is said that the realisation of śūnyatā is the same as the realisation of Nirvāṇa.[1].

Śūnyatā is neither nāstitva nor abhāvā

Having dealt with the object of the teaching of śūnyatā,

1. *M. Vṛ.*, pp. 350-1.

Nāgārjuna proceeds to an exposition of śūnyatā by stating its essentials (lakṣaṇas), which are as follows[1] :—

(i) It is *aparapratyaya, i.e.*, it cannot be imparted by one to another[2]. One is to realise the Truth within himself (pratyātmavedya), and not to understand it by listening to the instruction of the Āryas (the Perfect), who can speak of the Truth only through superimposition (samāropa).

(ii) It is *śānta, i.e.*, it has the nature of cessation[3], it is undisturbed by origination or destruction.

(iii) It is *prapañcācuiraprpañcitam, i.e.*, it is inexpressible.[4] The first prapañca is taken as a synonym of speech (vāk),[5] *i.e.*, the sense of śūnyatā is not utterable by words.

(iv) It is *nirvikalpa* or unrealisable in concepts. Vikalpa is thought-construction ; so śūnyatā is beyond (lit. devoid of) thought-construction. And lastly.

(v) It is *anānārtha, i.e.*, devoid of different meanings.

Thus, he points out that śūnyatā is not to be taken in the sense of nāstitva (nihilism) or abhāva (absence of something) as wrongly supposed by the Hīnayānists. He continues his exposition of śūnyatā by equating it with the pratītyasamutpāda, saying

yaḥ pratītyasamutpādaḥ śūnyatāṃ taṃ pracakṣmahe,
sā prajñaptir upādāya pratipat saiva madhyamā.

(We say that dependent origination is śūnyatā. It is in that sense that the path is middle.) All phenomenal

1. *M. Vṛ.*, pp. 372-7.

2. Prof. Stcherbastsky (*Con. of Ni.*, p. 41) translates it as "uncognisable from without" but the commentary of Candrakīrti does not seem to warrant the rendering.

3. See *M. Vṛ.*, p. 160 where it is shown why śūññtam is taken in the sense of svabhāva-virahitam. The point is that anything having real existence cannot be subject to the causal law ; so whatever is subject to causal law has no real existence like the seed and the sprout. Hence, both of them can be described as śānta or svabhāva-virahita. Prof. Stcherbatsky (*op. cit.*) uses the word "quiescent" for śānta.

4. Prof. Stcherbatsky (*op. cit.*) translates it as "undifferentiated words."

5. *M. Vṛ.*, p. 373.

things are relatively existent, *e.g.*, sprout and seed, vijñāṇas with reference to cause and condition ; hence, Nāgārjuna says that things, which are only relatively existent, have in reality no origination, and the fact of this non-origination in reality is śūnyatā. So it is asserted by the Teacher in the *Anavataptahradopasaṅkramaṇasūtra*[1] that whatever is said to have come into existence through cause and condition (*i.e.* relatively) is really unborn ; it cannot have real origination ; and whatever is subject to cause and condition is śūnya. The statement made in the *Laṅkāvatāra* and elsewhere that all dharmas are śūnya (non-existent) refers to the non-origination of things in reality. It is in this sense that the connotation of śūnyatā has come into existence. Hence, it is said that śūnyatā, which bears the sign of non-origination in reality, is the middle path. That which is really non-originated can neither be said to exist nor to vanish ; hence, it is neither existent nor non-existent, and as such it is the Middle path, which keeps clear of the two extremes.[2]

We may consider this topic in another way. There is nothing which originates without cause and condition and therefore there is nothing which can be called aśūnya (non-relative). It is said in the *Śataka* and elsewhere that nothing is ever produced without cause and condition, or, in other words, there is nothing eternal. The ignorant only conceives of eternity, etc. in regard to Ākāśa. The wise knows that all things are caused and conditioned, and they never fall into the delusion of either of the two extremes. If it be admitted as is done by some of the Hīnayānists,[3] that things (*i.e.*, the elements that constitute a being) are uncaused and unconditioned, then the four Āryasatyas are contradicted, for how can there be duḥkha, the first truth, if things come into existence without cause and condition (apratītya) ?

1. *M. Vṛ.*. p. 239.
2. Cf. *Bodhic.*, p. 359 :
na san nāsan na snasan na cāpyanuhyātmakam,
catuṣkoṭivinirmuktaṃ tattvaṃ mādhymikā viditaḥ.
3. Referring evidently to the Sarvāstivādins.

Buddha's Teachings were delivered in two ways :

Nāgārjuna, thus establishing that śūnyatā is neither nāstitva nor abhāva but a word signifying the relative existence of things, says that the Hīnayānists, too much engrossed in the studies of texts alone, have misunderstood the sense of śūnyatā and do not understand that the Teacher delivered his teachings in two ways, *viz.*, conventional and real, or empirical and transcendental. So it is said by Nāgārjuna :

dve satye samupāśritya Buddhānāṃ dharmadeśanā,
lokasaṃvṛtisatyaṃ ca satyaṃ ca paramārthataḥ.[1]

(The teachings of Buddhas are based on two kinds of truth : the truth of the world, and the truth in the highest sense).

(*a*) *Saṃvṛti*

Nāgārjuna as well as Śāntideva point out that the words in common usage, *e.g.*, skandha, ātman, loka, etc., being enveloped (sāṃvṛta) on all sides are called conventional. The expression Saṃvṛti has three different senses, which are as follows :—

(1) Saṃvṛti is the same as ignorance on account of its completely enveloping the reality, or, in other words, it is identical with ignorance (avidyā).[2] In elucidation of this, Prajñākaramati, the commentator of the *Bodhicaryāvatāra*, says that ignorance superimposes a form on a non-existent object and thus creates an absolute in the correct view of the reality. In support of his statement he quotes from the *Śālistambasūtra* a stanza, in which it is stated that ignor-

---

1. *M. Vṛ.*, p. 402 ; *Bodhic.*, p. 361. The two kinds of Truth have been dealt with in the *Madhyamakāvatāra* (Chs. V, VI) ; see *Le Muséon*, 1907, N.S., vol. VIII for summary of Ch. V.

2. *Bodhic.*, p. 352 ; Srṃvriyate āvriyate yathābhūtaparijñānaṃ svabhāvāvaraṇād āvṛta(=abhūta)prakāśanāc ca nayeti saṃvṛtiḥ. Avidyā moho viparyāsa iti paryāyāḥ. It is called saṃvṛti because it envelopes the real knowledge and also because it helps to uncover that which is, as a matter of course, enveloped. It is synonymous wlth ignorance, delusion, or misconception. For Paramārtha being the same as Nirvāṇa, see *infra*.

ance (avidyā) is nothing but the non-realisation (apratipatti) of the truth, and faith in falsehood.

(2) Saṃvṛti implies a thing which depends on another for existence, *i.e.*, subject to cause and condition,[1] for a really self-existent thing cannot have origin and decay, or any kind of transformation ; so whatever is caused and conditioned is sāṃvṛta (phenomenal).

(3) Saṃvṛti refers to signs or words current in the world, *i.e.*, accepted by the generality of the people and based on direct perception.[2] Śāntideva desires to point out that rūpa (form), śabda (sound), etc. should not be supposed to be really existing on account of being directly perceived by all in the same way. Their existence is substantiated by proofs, which are valid from the worldly, and not from the transcendental, standpoint. If all that is perceived by the senses be true, then a fool knows the truth, and there is no need of exerting for the acquisition of the truth. In support of his statement, he cites the illustration that the body of a woman, though impure in the highest sense, is regarded as a fact cannot be established merely by experience.

It may be argued that as the expressions like dhātu, āyatana, etc. occur in the scriptures, they are real, and besides had they been non-existent, the Teacher would not have referred to them as momentary, subject to decay, etc. Śāntideva explains this away by saying that the Teacher used them only as artifices to lead men, having minds engrossed in thinking of an object as exlstent, to the conception of śūnyatā, *i.e.*, things as really non-existent. Whatever Buddha said about skandha, dhātu, āyatana or their transitoriness is conventional and not real ; hence the existence of dhātus and āyatanas in reality are not established. If it be held that every object of experience is unreal, how can we account for the experience of kṣaṇikatva (transitoriness) of pudgala by the yogins (ascetics), who have

1. *Bodhic.*, p. 352 ; pratītyasamutpannaṃ vasturūpaṃ saṃvṛtir ucyate.

2. *Ibid.*, pp. 374-5 : pratyakṣyam api rupādi prasiddhyā na pramārthataḥ.

perfected themselves in the meditation of pudgalanairātmya (essencelessness) of constituted things) ? Śāntideva's answer is very simple. He said that even the experiences of yogins are not above saṃvṛti, for saṃvṛti includes everything that falls within the scope of buddhi (intelligence), and the reality lies beyond it. The experience of the yogins that a woman's body is impure contradicts the experience of an ordinary man, who considers it to be pure. Thus it is proved that the scriptural authority does not establish the reality of skandha, dhātu, āyatana, etc.

Two kinds of saṃvṛti-satyas

All that has been said above applies to loka-saṃvṛti only, *i.e.*, truths valid in the world of convention, which are accepted as such by the generality of the people. There is however another kind of the so-called truth, which should be distinguished as Alokasaṃvṛti ; *i.e*,, truths not accepted by the generality of the people. The experiences of a man with diseased eyes or defective organs of sense are peculiar to the man and are not true for all. Such experiences should be called Alokasaṃvṛti (conventional truths but not general).

Śāntideva[1] calls these two kinds of conventional truths Tathya-saṃvṛti and Mithyā-saṃvṛti, and distinguishes them thus : The Tathya-saṃvṛti (phenomenal truth) refers to things which originate out of a cause (kiñcit pratītyajātam) and are perceived in the same way by all persons with unimpaired organs of sense, *e.g.*, the colour blue, etc. The Mithyā-saṃvṛti refers to those things or statements which are accepted only by individuals and not universally, though they may have originated through cause and condition, *i.e.*, they are like things perceived by a person with a defective organ of sense.

(*b*) *Paramārthasatya*

The truth of the Āryas who see things as they really are is quite different from the two so-called truths mentioned

1. *Bodhic.*, p. 353

above. Nāgārjuna says that this truth, Paramārthasatya, is identical with Nirvāṇa.[1] It does not admit of any distinction as subject and object.[1] It is un-originating and undecaying, and as such it is not an object to be grasped by the mind. It is indeterminable by speech and unknowable by knowledge.[2] Hence the highest truth is inexpressible and can be realised only within one's own self.[3] It cannot form the subject-matter or instruction, and hence it cannot be imparted by one to another. Śāntideva explains the truth (tattva or paramārthasatya) as beyond the range of buddhi (intellection or perception) while that which comes within the range of buddhi is conventional (saṃvṛti).[4] According to him, the truth is attainable by giving up all things which act as hindrances to knowledge, *viz.*, impressions (vāsanā), connection (anusandhi) and passion (kleśa) through comprehension of the real nature of things. It is therefore the same as the non-existence of all dharmas and as such it may be taken as a synonym of śūnyatā (essencelessness), tathatā (thatness), bhūtakoṭī (true limit), and dharmadhātu (totality of things). All that is caused and conditional is not really existent, because everything undergoes change with time, while in a really existent thing no change is possible ; neither can the fact of coming and going be attributed to it. Things that are supposed to have existence are like an illusion or an echo, because they arise through cause and condition, and disappear when the cause and condition cease. So, in reality, there can be no origination through cause and condition because real origination does not depend upon and is not subject to something else. All things arise subject to some

1. See *ante*. Saṃvṛti is identified with avidyā and buddhi. See *Bodhic.*, pp. 352, 366, also Stcherbatsky, *op. cit.*, p. 194 n.

2. Cf. *Bodhic.*, p. 366 : Paramārthasatyaṃ sarvavyavahārasamahtihrāntaṃ nirveśaṣaṃ. Asamutpanuam aniruddham. Abhidheyābhidhānajñeyajñānavigatam.

3. *M. Vṛ.*, pp. 364, 493

4. *Bodhic.*, p. 367 : āryāṇām eva svasaṃvidita-svabhāvatayā pratyātmavedyaṃ.

5, *Bodhic.*, p. 354.

preceding causes and conditions; hence they are really non-existent. How then, can an existent thing be expected to arise out of them? Can anybody ascertain whence the illusory things produced by cause come and where they go? In this connection Śāntideva comments elaborately on the famous stanza of Nāgārjuna:

na svato nāpi parato na dvābhyāṃ nāpyahetutaḥ,
utpannā jatu vidyante bhūtāḥ kvacana kecana[1].

(Nowhere and never does a really existent thing originate out of a self or non-self or both self and non-self or without any cause).

The aim of Śāntideva as also of other writers on Mahāyāna is to assert that the real truth (paramārthasatya) is that things of this world have no more existence than the magical figures created by a magician. As these figures and their movements are taken as real by the ordinary people while the magician himself does not concern himself about their reality, so also in this world, the viparyastas *i.e.*, those whose vision is obscured and subject to error run after, or weave their thoughts around, the various phenomenal things, while he who knows the highest reality, does not pay heed to him. In short, the Paramārthasatya is nothing but the realisation of the dream-like things or echo like the nature of Śaṃvṛtisatyas.[2]

If Paramārthasatya be of an inexpressible nature and Saṃvṛtisatya be non-existing like an illusion or echo as urged by Nāgārjuna and Śāntideva, a Hīnayānist may enquire about the necessity of preaching on the topics like skandha, dhātu, āyatana, āryasatyas, pratītyasamutpāda etc., which are conven-

1. *Bodhic.*, p. 357; *M. Vṛ.*, p. 12.

2. *Bodhic.*, pp. 368, 379. The Satyasiddhi school introdueed the two kinds of truth. Vyavahārasatya aud Paramārthasatya into the Buddhist metaphysics. In the *Akṣayamatinirdeśasūtra* these two truths form the principle subject of discussion (Vaidya, *Catuhśatikā*, p. 19). In the Mahāyāna literature there are other expressions bearing the same sense as Paramārtha and Saṃvṛti, e.g., Nītārtha and Neyyārtha, see *M. Vṛ.*, p. 41; V. Sastri, *I.H.Q.*, iv, 2 on Sandhyā-bhāṣā; *M. Vṛ.*, pp. 4[illegible]; *Sūtrā.*, p. 5[illegible].

tionally true and not true in the highest sense (atattva). The reply is

> vyavahāram anāśritya paramārtho na deśyate,
> paramārtham anāgamya nirvāṇaṃ nādhigamyate.[1]

(The highest truth cannot be imparted without having recourse to the conventional truths; and Nirvāṇa cannot be attained without the realisation of the highest truth). In other words, the highest truth cannot be brought home directly to a mind, which normally does not rise above the conventional distinction of subject and object, knower and known ; hence it must be imparted through conventional truths, and unless it is so imparted one cannot be expected to extricate himself from the worldly limitations and arrive at Nirvāṇa. It is for this reason that the Mahāyānists cannot dispense with saṃvṛta topics like dhātu, āyatana, āryasatya and pratītyasamutpāda ; they are like vessels to the seeker of water.

The other reason[2] for which the Mahāyānists cannot dispense with saṃvṛta topics is that the Paramārthasatya cannot be explained to another by signs or predicates, but yet it has to be explained. So the only alternative is to explain it by the negation of saṃvṛta matters. As it is *agocara* (beyond the cognizance of buddhi—intellection), *aviṣaya* (beyond the scope of knowledge), *sarvaprapañcavinirmukta* (beyond the possibility of detailed descriptions), *kalpanāsamatikrānta* (beyond every possible form of imagination, *e.g.*, existence or non-existence, true or untrue, eternal or non-eternal, permanent or impermanent, happy or unhappy, pure or impure, and so forth)[3], the only way to explain it to the people is through common place terms and illustrations. A person with diseased eyes sees a net of hair ; he is corrected by another whose eyes are healthy, the latter negating the afflicted man's statement that there

---

1. *M. Vṛ.*, p. 494 ; *Bodhic.*, p. 365 ; see also p. 372 ; Upāyabhūtaṃ vyavahārasatyam upāyabhūtaṃ paramārthasatyam (also in the *Madhyamakāvatāra*, vi, 10). *Pañca.* (A.S.B. ms.) leaf 56a : Na ca Subhūte saṃskṛtavyatirekena asaṃskṛtaṃ śakyaṃ prajñāpayitum.

2. *Bodhic.*, p. 363.

3. *Ibid.*, pp. 366-7. These terms can be easily multiplied.

(really) is a net of hair. The man with healthy eyes does not indicate by such a negation that he is either denying or affirming something. Similarly, persons with right vision are obstruced by ignorance conceive of the existence of skandha, dhātu, āyatana, etc., which are in reality non-existent phenomenal forms. Buddhas like the persons with healthy eyes know this, and they cannot help saying that there are in reality no skandhs, dhātus, āyantanas, but thereby they neither deny nor affirm their existence. Therefore the highest truth cannot be preached without the help of the conventional truths. So it is said

anakṣaraṣya dharmasya śrutiḥ kā deśanā ca kā,
śruyate deśyate cārthaḥ samāropād anakṣarah[1].

[How can there be hearing and preaching of dharma, which is un-utterable (lit. cannot be articulatend) : it is by the superimposition of ideas on the reality which is inexpressible that the latter can be preached or heard.]

If it be established that all mundane things are really non-existent, there is a probability of the Paramārthasatya (the highest truth) being conceived as nihilism. Nāgārjuna sounds a note of warning against such a conception by saying that śūnyatā should not be identified with the extinction of a thing which existed before. The question of extinction or nihilism does not arise, because the existence of something preceding is not not admitted. Neither should it be regarded as something existing by having recourse to superimpositions. Those, who do not realise the real distinction between these two kinds of truth, fall into the error of either conceiving śūnyatā as the non-existence of saṃskāras (constituents of a being) or assuming the existence of something as the basis of śūnyata. Both are wrong views, and people of limited knowledge misunderstand śūnyatā as the one or the other. The distinction was, in fact, so very subtle that even Buddha hesitated to preach the truth at first.[2]

1. *Bodhic.*, p. 365 ; *M. Vṛ.*, p. 264, xv. 2 ; *cf. Laṅkā.*, p. 194.
2. Buddhaghosa also uses this argument, see *ante*.

The Hīnayānists mistake śūnyatā as abhāva

In concluding his argument, Nāgārjuna says that the Hīnayānists, by attributing the sense of abhāva (absence or non-existence) after assuming the existence of something to śūnyatā, fall into error and fail to understand the standpoint of the Mahāyānists. The Mahāyānic conception of śūnyatā, *i.e.*, that everything is non-existent fits in correctly with all dharmas and all statements ; it is when śūnyatā is seen in this light that one can perceive the reasonableness of the formulæ of Causal Law and the Four Truths, the fruits of sanctification, saṅgha, dharma, Buddha, things worldly and transcendental, deeds right and wrong, a good or bad condition and other conventional matters. Nāgārjuna, having stated his position, attacks the Hīnayānists for their inability to comprehend the correct sense of the Causal Law. He says that just as a rider while riding may forget his horse and revile another for stealing it, so also the Hīnayānists, because of their distracted mind, fail to grasp the truth that śūnyatā is the true sense and the chief chrracteristic of the Causal Law, and attack the Mahāyānists, the Śūnyatāvādins, for misinterpreting it.

The Position of the Hīnayānists with regard to the Truths and the Causal Law is untenable.

Nāgārjuna now proceeds to assail the position of his opponents. He says that those, who admit the reality of unconstituted things, cannot logically support the Āryasatyas and the Pratītyasamutpāda.

It should be remembered that the Hīnayānists apply the Causal Law to constituted things only. Nāgārjuna attempts to make the position of the Hīnayānists untenable by asserting that the Law should be universally applicable, and that there cannot be anything in the world which was excepted by Buddha as beyond its range. He argues that if things exist by themselves, they are not subject to causes and conditions, and such being the case, there is no need to draw distinctions of external and internal, no need of causes and conditions, or the doer and the doing of an action. In short, the Hīnayānic theory contradicts the origin and decay as well as the fruits of sanctification. Hence, the position of the Hīnayānists that things exist by themselves is untenable. It also contradicts the words of Buddha, who said on many occasions: apratītyasamutpanno dharmaḥ kaścin na vidyate (there never exists anything which originated without cause and condition). This statement of Buddha, however, fits in with the definition of śūnyatā as given by the Mahāyānists.

If all things be existent (aśūnya) and if it originates without cause and condition, there cannot be anything impermanent, and consequently there is no duḥkha.

Again, if duḥkha be taken as something existing, then the truths of samudaya and nirodha (origin and decay) of misery, and mārga (the eight-fold path leading to the decay of misery) are meaningless. Nāgārjuna thus pays back the Hīnayānists in their own coin.

Then, with reference to the parijñāṇa (detailed knowledge) of the Hīnayānists, Nāgārjuna shows that it is not logical to maintain that duḥkha, assuming it to be an existent thing, was unknown before, and that it is known subsequently because existent things remain always in the same condition (svabhāvaḥ samavasthitaḥ) and never undergo any change. If an existent thing be not subject to change, it cannot be maintained that duḥkha, which was unknowable at first, was known later on. From this it follows that there is no duḥkha-parijñāna (knowledge of suffering). Consequently, prahāṇa (abandonment), sākṣātkaraṇa (realisation), and bhāvanā (meditation) are meaningless.

As it is unreasonable to claim knowledge of duḥkha, which was formerly by nature unknowable, it is wrong to assume the existence of the fruit of Srotāpatti, which did not exist before but was realised later on; and so with the other fruits of sanctification. The same reasoning—that which was by nature unattainable cannot be attained later on—is applied to show that there can be no one who enjoys these fruits, and consequently no Saṃgha. If there be no Āryasatyas, there cannot be Dharma, and in the absence of Dharma and Saṃgha, there cannot be a Buddha. If it be assumed that Buddha and Bodhi exist by themselves, then one remains without any reference to the other. If Buddhahood be taken as already existing, a person, who by nature is a non-Buddha, can never attain Bodhi, however much he may practise the Bodhisattva duties, because a non-Buddha cannot be expected to change.

Mahāyānic definition of Āryasatyas

Nāgārjuna's point is that if a thing exists by itself then it is absurd to speak of it as created, having a creator, and so forth. Just as nobody speaks of uncovering the sky because the open sky exists by itself, so also nobody should say that a thing, existing by itself, has been made or attained. In fact, the theory of pratītyasamutpanna (one existing with reference to another, *i.e.*, relatively) must be admitted, as otherwise even the expressions of everyday usage such as go, do, cook, read, etc., become meaningless. If the world is supposed to exist by itself, the world would be unoriginating, undecaying and unchangeable as the self-existent is changeless. The world, according to the Aśūnyavādins (*i.e.*, the Realists who do not admit śūnyatā), would have no concern with the Causal Law and be beyond the possibility of discovery. Had the world been so, says the *Pitāputra-samāgama-sūtra*, it would not have been dealt with by Buddha, and the Teacher would have, as the *Hastikakṣyasūtra* says, gone there with all disciples.

Nāgārjuna concludes by saying that he who realises Pratītyasamutpāda can rightly know the four truths and quotes a passage from the *Mañjuśrīparipṛcchā*, dealing with the Mahāyānic view of the four truths. It runs as follows,—he who realises that no dharmas have originated, has known duḥkha ; he who realises the non-existence of all dharmas has suppressed the source (samudaya) of misery ; he who realises that all dharmas are completely extinct (parinirvṛta) has comprehended the truth of nirodha (cessation), and he who realises the means by which the absence of all things is known, he is said to have practised the path (mārga). This has been developed thus in

Dhyāna muṣṭi-sūtra: Unable to comprehend the four truths properly on account of being troubled by the four viparyāsas (misconceptions),[1] sentient beings cannot go beyond the world of transmigration. They conceive ātman (self) and ātmīya (things relating to a self) and thus have karmābhisaṃskāra (actions).[2] Not knowing that all things are completely extinct (parinirvṛta) they imagine the existence of themselves and others, and become engrossed therein to the extent of having affection, infatuation and ultimately delusion. They now perform actions, physically, and mentally and after making some superimpositions of existence on non-existing things, they think that they are subject to affection, infatuation, and delusion. In order to get rid of them, they take initiation into the doctrines of Buddha, observe the precepts and hope to pass beyond the world and attain Nirvāṇa. They imagine that some things are good and some bad; some are to be rejected, some to be realised; that duḥkha is to be known, the samudaya of duḥkha to be given up, the nirodha of duḥkha to be realised, and the mārga to be practised. They also imagine that all constituted things are impermanent and endeavour to pass beyond them. Thus they attain a mental state full of disgust (or contempt) for constituted things, having animitta (absence of sign or cause) as its preceding condition. They think that they have thus known duḥkha, *i.e.*, the transitoriness of constituted things, become terrified by them, and shun their causes. Having imagined something as source (samudaya) of duḥkha, they conceive nirodha of duḥkha and decide to follow the path (mārga) to attain it. They retire to a secluded place with a mind full of disgust and attain quietude (śamatha). Their minds are no longer moved by worldly things and they think that they have done all that is to be done, they are freed from all sufferings and have become arhats. But after death they

1. See *ante*.
2. *Cf Bodhic.* p. 350;
   na san nāsan na sadasan na cāpyanubhayā
   catuṣkoṭivinirmukaṃ
   tu tattvaṃ mādhya-mika-viduḥ

find themselves reborn among the gods and in their minds exist doubts about Buddha and his knowledge. When they die again, they pass to hell because they doubted the existence of the Tathāgata after forming some misconceptions about all dharmas, which are unoriginated. The four truths are therefore to be seen in the light of the *Mañjuśrīsūtra* as pointed out above.

The Prajñāpāramitā on the Āryasatyas

The new point of view from which the Āryasatyas are looked at by Nāgārjuna's school appear in the *Prajñāpāramitās* in connection with the attempt to explain the conception of śūnyatā. The *Pañcaviṃśati-sāhasrikā Prajñāpāramitā* defines the Āryasatyas thus :[1]

What is *duḥkhasatyāvavāda ?* A Bodhisattva while practising the prajñāpāramitā should not consider himself to be attached or unattached (yukta or ayukta) to any one of the five skandhas, or to any organs of sense, or to their āyatanas or to the vijñana produced by the objects, or to any of the organs of sense with their respective objects, or to any of the four truths, twelve links of the chain of causation, eighteen kinds of śūnyatā and so forth. He should not look upon anything as rūpa, vedanā, *etc.*, as connected or unconnected. This is called, according to the *Prajñāpāramitā*, a sermon on the first truth, Duḥkha. The underlying idea is that if a Bodhisattva thinks as connected or unconnected with anything, which, according to the *Prajñāpāramitā*, is non-existent or has only a conventional existence, then the Bodhisattva is subject to duḥkha (suffering) ; even if a Bodhisattva consider himself as having realised the truths or the causal law or śūnyatā, he would be subject to duḥkha, though, according to the Hīnayānists, the Bodhisattva thereby attains sukha or nirvāṇa.

What is *samudayasatyāvavāda ?* A Bodhisattva while practising *prajñāpāramitā* does not consider whether rūpa or any other skandha is subject to origination or destruction (utpādadharmin or nirodhadharmin), or to contamination or

1. *Pañca.*, pp. 43 f.

purification (saṃkleśadharmin or vyāvadānadharmin). He knows that rūpa does not convert (samavasarati) into vedanā, or vedanā into saṃjñā, and so forth ; a dharma, in fact, on account of its nature being unreal (prakṛti-śūnyatā), cannot be converted into another dharma. Neither that which is śūnyatā (non-existence) of rūpa is rūpa, nor does the śūnyatā of rūpa take a rūpa (form); therefore śūnyatā is neither different from, nor identical with, rūpa, and in this way the other skandhas are treated. This is called the sermon on samudaya. The object of this discourse is to establish that the so-called things of the world have really no existence and hence there can be no origination, transformation, or destruction, and so a Bodhisattva should remain unconcerned with the conception of samudaya of things.

What is *nirodhasatyāvavāda ?* A Bodhisattva is to know that śūnyatā has no origin, decay, contamination, purification, decrease, increase, past, present or future. In it, therefore, there can be no rūpa, vedanā *etc.*, no duḥkha, samudaya, *etc.*, not even srotāpanna, sakṛdāgami or Buddha. This is called nirodhasatyāvāvāda. This statement is meant to convey that nirodha is nothing but the realisation of the real nature of śūnyatā.

Arguing in this way, the *Prajñāpāramitā* shows that the truth is śūnyatā, *i.e.*, the non-existence of the so-called things of the world, and this may be called the third truth, nirodha, while duḥkha consists in thinking oneself as related in some way or other to the conventional things, and samudaya in believing that the origination of things does really happen. As the mārga has no place in this interpretation of the āryasatyas, and so, the *Prajñāpāramitā* omits it.

Misconception of the Arhats

Nāgārjuna, as we have seen, establishes by quotations from the Mahāyānic texts that Hīnayānic Arhats labour under misconceptions. Of the four common misconceptions (viparyāsas), they are not free from the fourth, *viz.*, seeing ego in egoless things, thinking non-existence of things as existent.[1]

1. Cf. *Bodhic.*, p. 350.

But this statement of Nāgārjuna or of the Mahāyānic texts with reference to the Hīnayānists has in view the egolessness of things generally (dharmaśūnyatā) and not merely of constituted things with which the Hīnayānists are concerned. Nāgārjuna ends his discourse by asserting that the truth is that all things are like echo, mirage, or images seen in dreams. When one realises this, he has neither love nor hatred for any being and with a mind like the sky, he does not know of any distinctions as Buddha, Dharma, or Saṅgha and does not have doubts regarding anything, Being without doubt and without attachment, he attains parinirvāṇa without upādāna.

Śāntideva[1] also reasons in this way and says that a person's avidyā, the source of delusion, which comes about on account of the attribution of existence (sat) to non-existent things (asat), or ego (ātmā) to egoless things (anātmā), ceases to exist when he realises truly (paramārthataḥ) that things have only a dreamlike or echolike existence. On the cessation of avidyā, the other links of the chain of causation[2] get no opportunity to arise and hence the person obtains Nirodha.

The Mahāyānists thus relegate the four Truths and the Causal Law to the domain of matters conventional and not real, and assert that they are necessary in the doctrines of Mahāyāna inasmuch as they serve as a means for the guidance of living beings, who, as individuals in this world cannot but have their vision distorted or screened by ignorance.[3]

---

1. Cf. *Bodhic.*, pp. 350-1.

2. Śāntideva speaks of the chain of causation as consisting of three parts, *viz.*,

(i) kleśakāṇḍa—avidyā, tṛṣṇā and upādāna ;

(ii) karmakāṇḍa—saṃskāra and bhava ; and

(iii) duḥkhakāṇḍa—all the remaining links of the chain. For such divisions, see also Gokhale, *Pratītyasamutpādasūtra* of Ullaṅgha.

3. The commentator of *Bodhic.* (p. 362), in order to show that the four Āryasatyas are really two, says that duḥkha, samudaya, and mārga should be classified under saṃvṛti, and nirodha under paramārtha.

Yogācāra treatment of the Āryasatyas and the Pratītyasamutpāda

Nāgārjuna and Śāntideva explain the position of the Mādhyamikas with regard to the Four Truths and the Causal Law as shown above.

Asaṅga, Vasubandhu and other writers on the Yogācāra system deal with this topic incidentally. Asaṅga, for instance, refers to the four truths,[1] saying that the first two relate to the origin of the world or the happening of repeated births and the cause thereof, while the second two relate to the disappearance of things and the causes thereof. The first two need suppression while the second two need realisation. In connection with the fourteen ways of practising the smṛtyupasthānas (power of recollection) by Bodhisattvas, it is pointed out that one can enter, and also make others enter into the four truths by means of the smṛtyupasthānas. Other Yogācāra writings, *viz.*, the *Siddhi* and the *Laṅkāvatāra*, do not specifically refer to the four truths but they deal with the doctrines of the Hīnayānists for the sake of comparison and contrast. For instance, they speak of the Hīnayānists as those who maintain the overt sense of Buddha's teachings and not their deeper meaning;[2] being satisfied only with ascertaining the generic characteristics of things but never questioning about their essential unreality.[3] They labour under the misconception

1. *Sūtrā.*, pp. 137-8, 149-1.

2. *Laṅkā.*, p. 14 : yathārutārthābhiniviṣṭā. For a description of the rutārthagrāhī, see *Laṅkā.*, pp. 154f, 160f, 197, 227. *Laṅkā.* (p. 77) states, "sūtrāntaḥ sarvasattvāśayadeśanārthavyabhicāraṇī na sā tattvapratsarvasattvāśaya-deśanartha-vyabhicāraṃ yāvasthānakathā (the discourses are not faithful expositions of the truth because they were preached according to the mental tendencies of beings). For a remark like this, see *M. Vṛ.*, dealt with before; *Sūtrā.*, p. 51; alpaśrutatvaṁ nītārthasūtrāntaśrayaṇāt.

3. *Laṅkā.*, pp. 51, 71, 63 : Yaḥ skandhadhātvāyatana-svasāmānyalakṣaṇaparijñānādhigame deśyamāne romāñcitatanur bhavati. Lakṣaṇaparicayajñāne cāsya buddhiḥ praskandati na pratītyasamutpādāvinirbhāgalakṣaṇaparicaye.

(parikalpanā) of taking the three worlds as real, of postulating distinctions as subject and object, of assuming the existence of skandhas (constituents of beings), dhātus (organs of sense), āyatana (spheres of the organs of sense), citta (mind), hetupratyaya (cause and condition), kriyāyoga (action), utpāda[1] (origin), sthiti (continuance), bhaṅga (dissolution), etc. The *Laṅkāvatāra*,[2] speaking of Pratītyasamutpāda, states that it is by comprehending that things originate through cause and condition that one can get rid of the misconception of taking non-existent things as existent, and of assuming gradual or simultaneous origin of things. Then it explains as usual that the dependent origination happens in two ways, externally and internally, *e.g.*, an earthen pot, butter, sprout, etc., originate through an external cause (hetu)[3] and condition (pratyaya), while ignorance (avidyā), desire (tṛṣṇā), action (karma), etc. originate through an internal cause and condition. The remarks of the Yogācāra writers indicate that the four truths and the causal law of the Hīnayānists belong to the domain of imagination (parikalpanā) and not to that of reality.

The Yogācāras have three truths for two of the Mādhyamikas

It should be remembered that though the Yogācārins are sharply criticised by the Mādhyamikas[4] for their conception of the eighth consciousness called Ālaya-vijñāna (store-consciousness), both these schools of thought agree in holding that all things (dharmas) are non-existent, and are without origin and decay,[5] and that the highest truth is unutterable (anakṣara),[6] is identical with thatness and unchangeableness, possesses the signs of anāyūha and niryūha (non-taking and

1. *Laṅkā.*, pp. 42, 43, 225.
2. *Ibid.*, pp. 82-3, 84, 140.
3. For six kinds of hetu, see *Laṅkā.*, p. 83.
4. *M. Vṛ.*, p. 523.
5. *Triṃśikā*, p. 41 : sarvadharmā niḥsvabhāvā anutpannā aniruddhā iti nirdiśyante.
6. Buddhas are silent (mauna) and never preach a word. *Laṅkā.*, pp. 16, 17, 144, 194.

non-rejecting) and is beyond every possible means of determination[1]. Passages like this can be multiplied from the Yogācāra works to show that their conception of the Reality, apart from Ālayavijñāna, is the same as that of the Mādhyamikas. They also hold with the Mādhyamikas[2] that from time immemorial, the mind has been under the delusion of imputing existence (sat) to non-existent things (asat), and that the Hīnayānists were not able to rid their minds completely of the four viparyāsas (misconceptions)[3] inasmuch as they meditated on Pudgalanimitta (individuality as basis) only and not on sarvadharmanimitta (all things whatsoever as basis) and conceived of Nirvāṇa as something existent[4], full of peace and beyond misery. Their conception is that the highest truth, which they usually call Pariniṣpanna for the Paramārtha of the Mādhyamikas, is the realisation of the fact that all dharmas perceptible to our mind have no more existence than the images seen in a dream or the reflection of the moon in water.

From time immemorial, however, our minds are so deluded that we cannot help perceiving in the images or reflection something existent, or in other words, with our common knowledge we cannot rise above parikalpanā (imaginary existence), the saṃvṛti of the Mādhyamikas and others. The Yogācāras add a rider to the parikalpanā, saying that it depends for origination on something else, and hence it is always paratantra, the pratītyasamutpanna of the Mādhyamikas and others. It is not necessary that the basis of a parikalpanā needs be anything existent or real, *e.g.*, a person may be frightened by an echo. In short, Parikalpita and Paratantra relate to worldly matters only, to the anitya, anātman and duḥkha of the Hīnayānists, while, pariniṣpanna

1. *Laṅkā.*, p. 196 : Tathātvam ananyathātvaṃ tattvam anāyūhaniryūha-lakṣaṇaṃ. sarvaprapañcopaśamaṃ ; p. 73 : śūnyatānutpādādvaya-niḥsvabhāvalakṣaṇaṃ.

2. *M. Vṛ.*, Ch. XXIV quoting Dhyāyitamuṣṭisūtra.

3. *Sūtrā.*, p. 169 : Tatra caturviparyāsānugataṃ pudgalanimittaṃ vibhāvayan yogī śrāvakabodhiṃ pratyekabodhiṃ vā labhate. Sarvadharmanimittaṃ vibhāvayan mahābodhiṃ.

4. *Laṅkā.*, p. 72.

relates to Nirvāṇa, Śānta[1], *i.e.*, where all kleśas and vikalpas cease.

Asaṅga brings out the relation of the three forms of truth thus : The highest truth (paramārtha or pariniṣpanna) is non-duality, which is shown in five ways. Two of these are that it is non-existing under the aspect of Parikalpita and Paratantra and not non-existing under the aspect of Pariniṣpanna. It is not the same, because the Parikalpita and Paratantra are not the same as Pariniṣpanna. It is not different, because the former two are not different from the latter[2]. In another connection Asaṅga says that a Bodhisattva can be truly called a śūnyajña (one who knows the real nature of non-existence) when he understands it under three aspects, *viz.*, first, that the non-existence means the absence of signs which are commonly attributed to an imaginary object (parikalpita), secondly, that the non-existence is the absence of any particular form of existence that one imagines it to be (paratantra), and thirdly, that which is by nature non-existent (pariniṣpanna)[3]. The *Vijñaptimātratāsiddhi*[4] elucidates this point by saying that the nature of non-existence is of three kinds, *viz.*, (i) lakṣaṇa-niḥsvabhāvatā (non-existence of the signs commonly attributed to a thing and hence of the thing itself, *i.e.*, parikalpita), (ii) utpattiniḥsvabhāvatā (non-existence of a thing when considered from the standpoint of its origin, *i.e.*, paratantra) ; and (iii) paramārtha-niḥsvabhāvatā (non-existence of a thing in the highest sense, *i.e.*, pariniṣpanna).

A. *Parikalpita*

Sthiramati, in commenting on the *Siddhi*, says that the first category, Parikalpita, refers to the non-existence of things by their characteristics or signs. A thing cannot be conceived to exist unless it is accompanied by some characteristics, the sign or form is attributed to a feeling. Endless things, which people imagine, not excluding the dharmas attributed to a Buddha,

1. *Sūtrā.*, p. 149 ; cf. *M. Vr.*, Ch. XVIII.
2. *Sūtrā*, p. 22 : na san na casan na tathā na cānyathā, etc.
3. *Ibid.*, pp. 94-5.
4. *Siddhi*, pp. 39-42.

have existence only in one's imagination ; hence they are parikalpita, *i.e.*, have nothing corresponding to them in reality. The *Laṅkāvatara*[1] says that the parikalpita existence is inferred from signs[2] (nimitta) and explains it thus : All dependently originating things are known by their nimitta (signs) and lakṣaṇa (characteristics)[3]. Now, things having nimitta and lakṣaṇa are of two kinds. Things known by nimitta only refer to things generally, internal and external, while things known by nimitta-lakṣaṇa refer to the knowledge of generic characteristics of things both internal and external[4]. Asaṅga[5] distinguishes parikalpita into three kinds : *viz.*, (i) the basis (nimitta or ālambana) of one's thought-constructions, (ii) the unconscious impression (vāsanā) left by them upon one's mind, and (iii) the denominations (arthakhyāti) following the impressions are taken as real.

B. *Paratantra*

The second category, Paratantra, refers to the imaginary existence pointed out above regarded from the aspect of its origin, *i.e.*, all objects or feelings, which have existence only in imagination, and depend for origination on something else (paratantra). Things, as they appear, are not the same as their origin or source ; so it is said that the unreality of things is perceptible when they are viewed from the stand-

---

1. *Laṅka.*, p. 67.

2. Prof. Lévi translates nimitta by "signs of connotation".

3. *Laṅkā.*, pp. 224-6 : five natures of existent things : (i) nāma, (ii) nimitta, (iii) vikalpa, (iv) samyakjñāna and (v) tathatā.

Nāma-saṃjñā, saṃketa. Ignorant persons, deluded by various signs (lakṣaṇa), become attached to things as self or mine, and thus weave a net of thought-constructions around themselves.

Nimitta—the reflection (ābhāsa) of eye-consciousness known as form ; so also the reflections of ear-consciousness, nose-c., tongue-c., body-c., mind-c. known as sound, smell, taste, touch and things are called nimitta.

Nimitta is more or less a sign impressed upon consciousness and lakṣaṇa is definition, or features constituting a definition.

4. *Laṅkā.*, pp. 67, 150, 163.

5. *Sūtrā.*, p. 64.

point of their origin. Though the things, good, bad and indeterminate, or the three worlds (dhātu) or the mind and its various functions have only imaginary existence, they arise, however, from causes and conditions, *i.e.*, they depend for origin on others, and hence they cannot be said to exist really, because a real thing remains always the same and does not depend on cause and condition. The *Laṅkāvatāra* puts it very briefly thus : that which proceeds from a basis is dependently originated or paratantra (yadāśrayālambanāt pravartate tat paratantra). Asaṅga analyses the paratantra in this way ; the mark of being paratantra is the false thought-construction (abhūtaparikalpāt) about the subject (grāhaka) and its object (grājhya).[1]

C. *Parinispanna*

The third category, Pariniṣpanna, refers to the Paramārtha[2] (the highest truth) or Tathatā (Thatness). Like ākāśa (space) it is homogenous (lit. has one taste—ekarasa), pure and changeless. The Pariniṣpanna-svabhāva (absolute reality) is called Paramārtha, because it is the highest aspect in which all dependently originated things are to be looked upon. In this sense, it can be called also dharmatā (the nature of things) or in other words, it is the absolute, immanent in the phenomenal world. The *Siddhi* points out that the pariniṣpanna (the Asolute) is so called because it is absolutely changeless. If it be compared with the Paratantra, it may be said to be that paratantra, which is always and ever completely devoid of the differentiation as subject and object, which are nothing but mere play of imagination, and hence, absolutely non-existing. Thus, it follows that the pariniṣpanna is the same as the parataanta *minus* the parikalpita.[3]

---

1. *Sūtrā.*, p. 65 :
   grāhaka=manas, 5 vijñānas and vikalpa ;
   grāhya=padābhāsa, arthābhāsa and dehābhāsa.
2. For seven different kinds of Paramārtha, see *Laṅkā.*, p. 39.
3. This exposition is based on the *Siddhi*, pp. 39-42. Masuda has utilised the Chinese version of this treatise, for which see his *Der individualistische etc.* pp. 40-43. For general discussion, see La Vallée

Two truths in Hīnayāna

It is clear from the summarised discussions that the Paramārtha of the Mādhyamikas and the Parinispanna of the Yogācārins indicate the Truth as conceived by them. Accepting that the Truth as the only reality, they relegate everything else to the domain of unreality calling them conventional, saṃvṛti or parikalpita, with the reservation that the conventional things appear and disappear subject to causes and conditions, or in other words, they conform to the law of causation, the Pratītya-samutpāda of the Buddhists in general, and the Paratantra of the Yogācāras.

The Hīnayānists utilise these expressions just as much as the Mahāyānists and they also call their Truth the only reality, *Paramattha*, everything else being conventional (*Sammuti*), their truth, in one word, being anattā, non-existence of any substantiality in the so-called things of the world, with the corollary that everything being anattā is impermanent (anicca) and unhappy (dukkha). Buddhaghosa[1] draws the distinction, saying that Buddhas use two kinds of speech, conventional and real. The expressions, satta (being), puggala (person), deva (god), *etc.*, are conventional, while those like anicca (impermanence), dukkha (misery), anattā (essencelessness), khandha (aggregate), dhātu (organs of sense), āyatana (objects of sense), satipaṭṭhāna (practices of self-possession) and sammāppadhāna (right exertion) were used in their true sense. Nāgasena explains that when Buddha said "I shall lead the saṅgha, it is dependent on me,"[2] he used the expression "I" and "me" in the conventional and not in the real sense. Ledi Sadnw[3] explains sammuti-sacca as those statements which are true in popular usage and are opposed to "inconsistency, and untruthfulness in speech" while paramattha-saccas are those which are established by the nature of the things and do not depend on opinion or usage. As

Poussin, *E.R.E.*, *sv.* *Philosophy* (Buddhist); L. D. Barnett, *Path of Light* (Wisdom of the East Series), p. 102; Keith, *B. Phil.*, pp. 235-236; Sogen, *Systems etc.*, pp. 145, 146; Stcherbatsky, *Con. of N.*, p. 33.

1. *Kvu. A.*, pp. 33, 84.
2. *Mil.*, pp. 28, 60.
3. *J.P.T.S.*, 1914, pp. 129 f.

an example, he points out that when it is said "there is a soul," it is conventionally true but ultimately false,[1] for the real ultimate truth is that there is no personal entity." The latter is true in all circumstances and conditions, and does not depend for its validity on usage or popular opinion. The contention of the Hīnayānists is that a name is usually given to constituted things; that name is conventional, *e.g.*, when the wheels, frame, and other parts of a chariot are fitted up in a particular order, all the things taken together go by the name of a chariot. The term 'chariot' therefore depends on convention. If the constituted thing, *e.g.*, the chariot is divided into various parts, it is no longer called a chariot when it is so divided. From this, it follows that the things, at which one ultimately arrives after repeated analysis, are the only real entities. These never undergo changes and bear the same name at all times and places and under all conditions. So, according to the Hīnayānists, all the various ultimate elements, which constitute a being or thing, are real, and when reference is made to them, they may be called ultimate truth or paramattha-sacca; hence the dhātus or āyatanas, satipaṭṭhānas or samma-ppadhānas are expressions used in the ultimate sense.

The *Kośa*[3] explains the two truths in a slightly different manner. It says that the things like a jug and clothes, after they are destroyed, do no longer bear the same name; do also things like water and fire when examined analytically dissolve into some elements and are no longer called water or fire. Hence the things, which on analysis are found to be changing, are given names by convention. Such expressions, which convey ideas temporarily and not permanently, are called Saṃvṛti-satyas. The Paramārthasatyas are those expressions, which convey ideas, which remain unchanged whether the things are

1. *Cf.* Stcherbatsky, *Central Conception of Buddhism*: "Buddhism never denied the existence of a personality, or a soul, in the empirical sense; it only maintained that it was no ultimate reality."

2. See also Prof. Poussin's article in the *J. A.*, 1902, p. 250; *Points of Controversy*, pp. 63 fn., 180.

3. *Kośa*, VI. 4.

dissolved, analysed or not, *e.g.*, rūpa ; one may reduce the rūpa into atoms or withdraw from it taste and other qualities, the idea of the real nature of rūpa persists. In the same way one speaks of feeling (vedanā) ; therefore such expressions are Paramārthasatyas (ultimate truths).

But these ultimate truths of the Hīnayānists, we have seen, are relegated by the Mahāyānists to the domain of convention. Hence, what are real according to the Hīnayānists, namely, the Āryasatyas and the Pratītyasamutpāda, are unreal and matters of convention according to the Mahāyānists.[1]

1. *Cf.* the present writer's Early Monastic Buddhism (1960) Ch. XI.

CHAPTER VIII

Conception of the Absolute

(*Tathatā=Suchness*)

The most authoritative text for the conception of the Absolute is the *Aṣṭasāhasrikā Prajñāpāramitā,* which deals with the diverse aspects of the Absolute and devotes one chapter (XVI) exclusively to the exposition of the conception of Tathatā.

The next authoritative text is Aśvaghoṣa's *Mahāyāna-Śraddhotpāda-sūtra* (=The Awakening of Faith). The Sanskrit original of this text is lost. It was rendered into Chinese by Paramārtha in 554 A. D. and Śikṣānanda in 706 A. D. Mrs. Beatrice Suzuki rendered it from Chinese into English and it happens to be our only source.

Aśvaghoṣa hailed from a Brāhmaṇa family of Eastern India, about 400 years after Buddha's *mahāparinirvāṇa* and was perhaps a contemporary of Emperor Kaṇiṣka. After he retired from worldly life, he refuted many views of the heretical teachers and composed the *Mahālaṅkāra-śāstra.*

Incidentally, it may be mentioned that in Pāli texts as well as in the *Mahāvastu*[1] the term *Tathatā* has been equated to *Tathātvam* or *Tathattam,* meaning sameness ; it has been applied for the deeper aspect of Nibbāna.

Tathatā, the highest Truth or the Reality, according to Aśvaghoṣa, corresponds to the conception of Śūnyatā (=Voidness) of the Mādhyamikas and Vijñaptimātratā (pure consciousness) of the Vijñānavādins (Yogācāras).

The main difference between Tathatā and Śūnyatā or Vijñaptimātratā is that the Tathatā has two aspects, *viz.*, conditioned and unconditioned to be explained hereafter.

Aśvaghoṣa does not deny the reality of the empirical existence of the perceiving egos and the perceived objects but

1. *Mahāvastu,* III, 397. See Also *Dīgha,* I. 175 ; *Saṃyutta,* II. 199 ; Milinda, 255 ; *Visuddhimagga,* 214.

he denies their ontological reality. When Ignorance (*avidyā*) is destroyed by enlightenment, the mind realises its identity with the Absolute, Suchness or the Infinite and apparently thereby vanishes multiplicity of subjects and objects.

Tathatā is the ultimate supreme reality, the Absolute. It is beyond empiricism and phenomenalism.

Tathatā has two aspects : Conditioned and Unconditioned. The conditioned suchness is applicable to the existence of beings subject to birth and death. It does not decrease in common beings nor does it increase in Bodhisattvas, who have perfected themselves in amity (*maitrī*) and compassion (*karuṇā*) as well as in wisdom (*prajñā*).

Tathatā is also known as *Bhūta-tathatā* (perfect knowledge) and *Saṃsāra* (round of rebirths). The former is One Reality and the latter appears as many. The former is the Absolute. It has neither existence nor non-existence nor both nor neither. It is trascendental and transcends the conditioned or relative sphere. It is immanent in the phenomenal sphere. It is the *Dharma-dhātu* (the great comprehensive whole).

Tathatā harmonizes all contradictions, and directs the course of events in the world. It may be equated to *Nirvāṇa*, which is peaceful and blissful. It is also the *Bodhi* (perfect wisdom) and is the sum-total of all roots of meritorious activities (*kuśala-mūlas*). It is in *Bodhi-citta* (Enlightenment-consciousness). It is the Paramārtha-satya (the highest truth). It is also the *Tathāgata-garbha* (the womb of all Tathāgatas) ; in it Tathāgata is conceived, nourished and matured). It is the same as Ālaya-vijñāna, when it is fully purified of habit-energy or impregnation (*vāsanā*) and evil tendencies (dauṣṭhulya).

The conditioned Suchness is manifested in the empirical sphere. It is relative, phenomenal and dualistic of subjects and objects, and is comprehended by a discriminative intellect. It should always be remembered that Suchness, whether conditioned or unconditioned remains unchanged. It is absolute sameness (*samatā*) in all phenomena. It is uncreated and eternal. It can only be comprehended by the highest wisdom (*prajñā-pāramitā*). The conditioned suchness as distinct from the unconditioned suchness is on account of Nescience (*Avidyā*) or Ignorance. From the Absolute under the influence of Ignorance, there is the production of the self as a perceiver of the external world, which exists for him only and is subject to births and deaths, which means misery.

All worldly individuals are not condemned for ever to suffer from non-enlightenment, for Suchness does not remain absolutely apart from empirical existence. The relation between it and Ignorance is that of mutual perfunming or fumigation or impregnation (*vāsanā*).

Ignorance affects Suchness and produces those impressions (*smṛti*), which persist and maintain in Ignorance in beings, creating an eternal world and various modes of individuations. leading to misery.

Suchness also affects ignorance and induces in the mind of the ignorant a disgust for repeated births and deaths and the consequential misery and suffering, and develops in the mind of the ignorant person a strong desire for release from repeated births and deaths.

An illustration may be given to the above-mentioned facts by comparing the calm sea and its waves. The calm sea is the reality while its waves are caused by strong wind of ignorance. The waves do not occur when the wind of ignorance ceases. Similarly Tathatā, i.e., the sea of consciousness can regain the normal calm state if ignorance is counteracted and destroyed. It can be done by removing the cover or obscuration of physical, vocal and mental impurities (*kleśāvaraṇa*) and intellectual blemishes (*jñeyāvaraṇa*).

The Hīnayānic Arhats or Pratyekabuddhas achieve only removal of *kleśas* while the Mahāyānists, i.e., theBuddhas and Bodhisattvas, who have perfected themselves in wisdom (*prajñāpāramitā*) get rid of *jñeyāvaraṇa*.

Conditioned Suchness, as has been stated above, perfumes or impregnates a strong desire (vāsanā) to attain emancipation from sufferings on account of repeated births and deaths. It should be noted that the intellectual development varies from individual to individual., and so also their spiritual development inspite of the efforts of Buddhas and Bodhisattvas, the highest embodiment of Suchness, who on account of their amity (maitrī) and compassion (karuṇā) exert to train them up in their spiritual progress.[1]

Saṃsāra (existence in this world) is an intricate succession of momentary things (kṣaṇika), i.e. Dharmatā, which has not any raison d'étre, i.e., which does not exist by themselves. Just as a monk suffering from opthalmia sees hairs in his alms-bowl, which do not exist, while a healthy monk does not see them. In the same way a saint, who is free from illusion, i. e., free from nescience (avidyā) does not see the dharmas., which constitute the Saṃsāra.

An attempt is now being made to cite passages from the Aṣṭa-sāhasrikā Prajñāpāramitā and a few other texts in support of what has been stated so far. At the outset it should be pointed out that Aśvaghoṣa's conception of Tathatā or the highest truth has two aspects : Conditioned and Unconditioned. The former perfumes or impregnates an ignorant person to seek release from ignorance and consequential repeated births and deaths, while the latter represents the highest truth (paramārtha satya). In the original texts like the Prajñāpāramitā, from which passages are now being cited in support of Tathatā refer only to the Unconditioned.

In texts like the Prajñāpāramitā, beings and objects by causes and conditions are ephemeral, hence non-existent in reality. These are compared to magical figures produced by a magician, echoes, or scences seen in a dream. The real nature of things (bhūta-tathatā) is Tathatā=Tathātvaṃ (thatness) or the Truth (tattvaṃ). The synonyms of Tathatā are Sarva-dharmānupalambhaḥ (all dharmas are inconceivable), Aprati-hata-lakṣaṇā (unobstructed), signless Apratimalakṣaṇā (incomparablity), Ākāśasamatā (similar to the sky).

---

1 The primary source of this chapter is Beatrice Lane Suzuki's English translation of Aśvaghoṣa's Mahāyāna-śraddhotpāda-sūtra and the secondary sources are Prof. A. B. Keith's Buddhist Philosophy and Prof, Jadunath Sinha's History of Indian Philosophy.

A few passages are now being cited in support of what has been stated above :—

Ye Bodhisattvāḥ prajñāpāramitāyaṃ carataḥ sarvadharmā anutpattikā ityadhimuñcanti, na ca tāvadanutpattikā pratilabdhā bhavati. Sarvadharmāḥ śāntā ityadhimuñcanti pratilabdhā bhavanti. Sarvadharmāḥ śāntā ityadhimuñcanti na ca sarvadharmeṣvavinivartanīyā vaśitāprāptim avakrāntā bhavanti. Anenāpi vihāreṇa teṣāṃ Bodhisattvānāṃ te Buddhabhavanto nā mañ ca gotrañ ca balañ ca rūpañ ca parikīrtaya mānarūpā dharmaṃ deśayanti udanaṃ ca udanīyanti. Buddhabhūmsreva teṣaṃ pratikāṅkṣitavyā. Te'pi vyākariṣvante 'nuttarāyaṃ sanyak-saṃbodhan.......adhinancya tathatvāyañ ca dharmaṃ deśayanti

(Trans. Those Bhodhisattvas, who have been perfecting themselves in wisdom and firmly believed that all dharmas are unoriginated, i.e., (quiet, tranquil, i.e., undisturbed by origin and decay) they eschew the stages of Srāvakas and Pratyekabuddhas and seek only to attain the state of Buddha, they will be foretold by Buddhas about their attainment of Samyak Sambuddhahood. After emancipation they take their stand on Suchness and while thus standing they preach the doctrine of omniscience in detail.

Yā ca tathāgata-tathatā,
yā ca sarvadharma-tathatā
Tathata advayādvaidhīkarā
advayā tathatā

(Trans. Suchness of the Tathāgata an d suchness of all dharmas are one and the same and non-duel.

Yā tathāgata-tathatā
nātītā na anāgatā
na pratyutpannā

(Trans. Suchness of Tathāgatas is neither past, nor future nor present, likewise the Suchness is the Suchness of all dharmas.

A few passages are now being cited in support of what has been stated above :—

Ye [illegible] [illegible] sarvadharmā [illegible] [illegible] [illegible] [illegible] [illegible] [illegible] [illegible] [illegible] [illegible] [illegible] [illegible] [illegible] [illegible] [illegible] dharmam [illegible] [illegible] [illegible] [illegible] dharmam [illegible]

(Trans. Those Tathāgatas, who have been perfecting themselves in wisdom and have believed that all dharmas are unoriginated, i.e., quiet, tranquil, pure, undisturbed by origin and decay, they eschew the glories of [illegible] and [illegible], [illegible] not only to attain the [illegible] Buddha, they will be foretold by Buddhas about their attainment of Samyak Sambuddhahood. After contemplation they have been stood on Suchness and while thus standing they preach the doctrine of omniscience in detail.

Yā ca tathāgata-tathatā
[illegible]
[illegible]
[illegible]

(Trans. Suchness of the Tathāgata and Suchness of all dharmas are one and the same and not dual.

Yā tathāgata-tathatā
naiṣā atītā
na pratyutpannā

(Trans. Suchness of Tathāgata is neither past, nor future nor present, likewise the Suchness is the Suchness of all dharmas.

INDEX